PRINCIPLED SENTENCING

This new, third edition of *Principled Sentencing* offers students of law, legal philosophy, criminology and criminal justice a wide-ranging selection of the leading scholarship on contemporary sentencing. The volume offers readers critical readings relating to the key moral, philosophical and policy issues in sentencing today. It contains many new readings on subjects that have recently emerged and which have consequences for sentencing in many jurisdictions. Each chapter consists of a selection of readings, some very recent, some more timeless—but each in its own way important to the field. As before, each chapter begins with an introduction by one of the editors accompanied by a selection of further readings. All the chapters have been substantially revised, as have the editorial introductions.

PRINCIPLED SENTENCING

READINGS ON THEORY AND POLICY

Third Edition

Edited by

Andrew von Hirsch
Andrew Ashworth
and
Julian Roberts

·HART·
PUBLISHING

OXFORD AND PORTLAND, OREGON
2009

Published in North America (US and Canada) by
Hart Publishing
c/o International Specialized Book Services
920 NE 58th Avenue, Suite 300
Portland, OR 97213-3786
USA
Tel: +1 503 287 3093 or toll-free: (1) 800 944 6190
Fax: +1 503 280 8832
E-mail: orders@isbs.com
Website: www.isbs.com

Hart Publishing, 16C Worcester Place, Oxford, OX1 2JW
Telephone: +44 (0)1865 517530 Fax: +44 (0)1865 510710
E-mail: mail@hartpub.co.uk
Website: http://www.hartpub.co.uk

British Library Cataloguing in Publication Data

Data Available

ISBN: 978-1-84113-717-9

Typeset by Forewords, Oxford
Printed and bound in Great Britain by
TJ International Ltd, Padstow, Cornwall

Preface to the Third Edition

That the imposition of sentence is a decision of critical importance can hardly be doubted. It determines how much an offender must suffer for his or her offence, and that suffering may include the deprivation of the individual's liberty. Moreover, when the facts of the offence are undisputed, as is often the case, the nature and quantum of sentence is the primary decision to be made. In most common law jurisdictions courts enjoy wide discretion at sentencing—although this discretion has been circumscribed by guidelines in many countries. In the early 1970s, sentencing theory and practice began at last to receive serious attention from scholars, and the scholarly literature has expanded rapidly ever since.

This Reader continues a series that began in 1981 with the publication of an anthology of readings devoted to sentencing theory and practice.[1] That volume was followed by another collection, 'Principled Sentencing'.[2] The scholarship on sentencing has been accumulating at a remarkable pace in recent decades. Moreover, sentencing guidelines have been developed in a number of jurisdictions, such as England and Wales. Currently, New Zealand is in the process of developing comprehensive sentencing and parole guidelines. Ten years have now past since the second edition of this Reader was published,[3] and for this reason we felt that it was high time for a third edition. In compiling readings and writing the chapter introductions we have almost completely overhauled the previous volume. A number of particularly influential contributions remain, but three-quarters of the readings have been replaced by more recent extracts.

Two new chapters have been added to the volume: 'Sentencing Young Offenders' (Chapter 7) and 'Doing Justice to Difference: Diversity and Sentencing' (Chapter 8). These additions reflect the significant volume of scholarship that has emerged over the past decade on these important topics. Several of the existing chapters have been considerably expanded, for the same reason. Moreover, the introductions to each chapter have been thoroughly rewritten to reflect developments around the world. Readers familiar with the previous edition will notice further changes in the volume's format. Rather than provide a dense page or two of further readings at the end of each chapter, we now provide ten important additional titles for the reader who wishes to pursue the subject in more depth.

We continue in this edition to omit the death penalty as a subject for discussion. A civilised state, we feel, should not employ this atrocious sanction at all, so there should be no occasion for the courts to have to decide whether, when and why it should be imposed as a legal penalty.

As with previous editions, we are indebted to Richard Hart of Hart Publishing for his encouragement and assistance, Melanie Hamill, Rachel Turner and Tom Adams for their help in bringing the manuscript to completion, and Stephen Noguera for research assistance. We are particularly grateful to Lila Kazemian of John Jay College, New York, for contributing to an essay for this volume and to Antony Duff for adapting an essay for inclusion in this volume. Indeed, we are most grateful to all of the authors who agreed to allow extracts of their works to be reproduced in this volume.

AvH
Cambridge

AA
JVR
Oxford
June 2008

Notes

1. Gross, H and von Hirsch, A (eds), (1981) *Sentencing* (New York, Oxford University Press).
2. von Hirsch, A and Ashworth, A (eds), (1992) *Principled Sentencing* (Boston, MA, Northeastern University Press).
3. von Hirsch, A and Ashworth, A (eds), (1998) *Principled Sentencing. Readings on Theory and Policy*, 2nd edn (Oxford, Hart Publishing).

Publisher's Note

The author and publisher gratefully acknowledge the authors and publishers of extracted material which appears in this edition of *Principled Sentencing*, and in particular the following for permission to reprint from the sources indicated.

Ashgate Publishing: C Tata, 'Institutional Consistency: Appeal Court Judgements' in C Tata and N Hutton *Sentencing and Society: International Perspectives* (2002).

Columbia Law Review Association, Inc: R Posner, 'Optimal Sanctions: Any Upper Limits?' from R Posner, *An Economic Theory of Criminal Law* (1985) 85 *Columbia Law Review* 1193.

Manchester University Press: I Brownlee, 'Hanging Judges and Wayward Mechanics: Reply to Michael Tonry' in A Duff, S Marshall, RE Dobash and RP Dobash (eds) *Penal Theory and Practise* (1996).

Oxford University Press: BC Feld, 'The Transformation of the American Juvenile Court' in B C Feld *Bad Kids: Race and the Transformation of the Juvenile Court* (1999).

RS Frase, 'Limiting Retributivism' and M Miller 'Sentencing Information Systems (SIS) Experiments' in M Tonry (ed) *The Future of Imprisonment* (2004).

BA Hudson, 'Justice and Difference' in A Ashworth and M Wasik (eds) *Fundamentals of Sentencing Theory* (1998).

M Tonry, 'Restraining the Use of Custody for Young Offenders: The Canadian Approach' in M Tonry *Malign Neglect—Race, Crime, and Punishment in America* (1995).

Routledge: K Daly, 'The Limits of Restorative Justice', in D Sullivan and L Tifft (eds) *Handbook of Restorative Justice: A Global Perspective* (2006).

Sage Publishing: C Spohn, 'Criticisms of Mandatory Minimums' in C Spohn *How do Judges Decide? The Search for Fairness and Justice in Punishment* (2002).

United Nations: United Nations Standard Minimum Rules for the Administration of Juvenile Justice 'The Beijing Rules'; and United Nations Convention on the Rights of the Child

University of Chicago Press: AN Doob and CM Webster, 'Offenders' Thought Processes'; and 'Studies of the Impact of New Harsh Sentencing Regimes' in M Tonry (ed) *Crime and Justice: A Review of Research*, vol 30 (2003).

FE Zimring 'Rationales for Distinctive Penal Policies for Youth Offenders', from

'Towards a Jurisprudence of Youth Violence' in M Tonry and M Moore (eds) *Youth Violence: Crime and Justice, a Review of Research*, vol 24 (1998).

Willan Publishing: A Bottoms, 'Empirical Research Relevant to Sentencing'; and P Raynor, 'Rehabilitative and Reintegrative Approaches'; in A Bottoms, S Rex and G Robinson (eds) *Frameworks Alternatives to Prison: Options for an Insecure Society* (2004).

RS Frase, 'Sentencing Policy Development under the Minnesota Sentencing Guidelines' in by A Freiberg and K Gelb (eds) *Penal Populism, Sentencing Councils and Sentencing Policy* (2008).

G Johnstone 'Restorative Justice? An Alternative to Punishment or an Alternative Form of Punishment?' in G Johnstone *Restorative Justice: Ideas, Values, Debates* (2001).

M Tonry, 'Abandoning Sentence Discounts for Guilty Pleas' in M Tonry *Punishment and Politics: Evidence and Emulation in the Making of English Crime* (2004).

Yale University Press: FA Allen, *The Decline of the Rehabilitative Ideal: Penal Policy and Social Purpose* (1981)

We also acknowledge the authors and publishers of extracted material which appears in this edition having also previously been published in the first and second editions of this book.

While every care has been taken to establish and acknowledge copyright, and to contact the copyright owners, the publishers apologise for any accidental infringement and would be pleased to come to a suitable agreement with the rightful copyright owners in each case.

Contents

Preface to the Third Edition   v

Publisher's Note   vii

Chapter 1: Rehabilitation   1

1.1   The Decline of the Rehabilitative Ideal   11
      Francis A Allen
1.2   Empirical Research Relevant to Sentencing Frameworks:
      Reform and Rehabilitation   16
      Anthony Bottoms
1.3   Assessing the Research on 'What Works'   19
      Peter Raynor
1.4   Reaffirming Rehabilitation   28
      Francis T Cullen and Karen E Gilbert
1.5   Should Penal Rehabilitationism Be Revived?   33
      Andrew von Hirsch and Lisa Maher

Chapter 2: Deterrence   39

2.1   Studies of the Impact of New Harsh Sentencing Regimes   49
      AN Doob and CM Webster
2.2   Punishment and Deterrence   53
      Jeremy Bentham
2.3   Deterrent Sentencing as a Crime Prevention Strategy   57
      *Andrew von Hirsch, Anthony E Bottoms, Elizabeth Burney and
      Per-Olot Wikström*
2.4   Optimal Sanctions: Any Upper Limits?   64
      Richard Posner
2.5   Offenders' Thought Processes   71
      AN Doob and CM Webster

Chapter 3: Incapacitation   75

3.1   Incapacitation and "Vivid Danger"   83
      AE Bottoms and Roger Brownsword
3.2   Extending Sentences for Dangerousness: Reflections on the
      Bottoms–Brownsword Model   85
      Andrew von Hirsch and Andrew Ashworth

3.3   Incacitation Within Limits   90
      Norval Morris
3.4   Predictive Sentencing and Selective Incapacitation   95
      Andrew von Hirsch and Lila Kazemian

Chapter 4: Desert   102

4.1   The Moral Worth of Retribution   110
      Michael S Moore
4.2   Proportionate Sentences: a Desert Perspective   115
      Andrew von Hirsch
4.3   Punishment, Retribution and Communication   126
      RA Duff
4.4   Limiting Retributivism   135
      Richard S Frase
4.5   Seriousness, Severity and the Living Standard   143
      Andrew von Hirsch
4.6   The Recidivist Premium: For and Against   148
      Julian V Roberts and Andrew von Hirsch

Chapter 5: Restorative Justice   163

5.1   Conflicts as Property   174
      Nils Christie
5.2   Restoration and Retribution   178
      RA Duff
5.3   Reparation and Retribution: Are They Reconcilable?   189
      Lucia Zedner
5.4   Normative Constraints: Principles of Penality   199
      Jim Dignan
5.5   Restorative Justice: An Alternative to Punishment or an Alternative
      Form of Punishment?   206
      Gerry Johnstone
5.6   Specifying Aims and Limits for Restorative Justice:
      A 'Making Amends' Model?   211
      Andrew von Hirsch, Andrew Ashworth and Clifford Shearing
5.7   The Limits of Restorative Justice   218
      Kathleen Daly

Chapter 6: Structuring Sentencing Discretion   229

6.1   Lawlessness in Sentencing   237
      Marvin Frankel
6.2   Techniques for Reducing Sentence Disparity   243
      Andrew Ashworth

6.3   The Swedish Sentencing Law   258
      Andrew von Hirsch and Nils Jareborg
6.4   Sentencing Policy Development under the Minnesota
      Sentencing Guidelines   270
      Richard S Frase
6.5   Institutional Consistency: Appeal Court Judgements   276
      Cyrus Tata
6.6   Criticisms of Mandatory Minimums   279
      Cassia Spohn
6.7   Sentencing Information System (SIS) Experiments   283
      Marc Miller

Chapter 7: Sentencing Young Offenders   294

7.1   United Nations Standard Minimum Rules for the
      Administration of Juvenile Justice ("The Beijing Rules")   307
7.2   United Nations Convention on the Rights of the Child   313
7.3   Rationales for Distinctive Penal Policies for Youth Offenders 316
      Franklin E Zimring
7.4   Reduced Penalties for Juveniles: the Normative Dimension   323
      Andrew von Hirsch
7.5   The Transformation of the American Juvenile Court   331
      Barry C Feld
7.6   Restraining the Use of Custody for Young Offenders: The Canadian
      Approach   338
      Nicholas Bala and Julian V Roberts

Chapter 8: Doing Justice to Difference:
Diversity and Sentencing   342

8.1   Abandoning Sentence Discounts for Guilty Pleas   351
      Michael Tonry
8.2   Individualizing Punishments   354
      Michael Tonry
8.3   Hanging Judges and Wayward Mechanics: Reply to Michael Tonry 359
      Ian Brownlee
8.4   Justice and Difference   366
      Barbara A Hudson

Index   379

1

Rehabilitation

The rehabilitative ideal—that sentences should aim to reform the criminal tendencies of offenders—was a major force for much of the twentieth century, and remains an important penal rationale. The Model Penal Code, an influential piece of draft legislation written by the American Law Institute in the early 1960s, demonstrates the significance of rehabilitative aims at that time: courts were encouraged not to sentence an offender to imprisonment if, among other things, 'the defendant is particularly likely to respond affirmatively to probationary treatment'.[1] Likewise, one of the three justifications for imposing a sentence of imprisonment was public protection on the ground that 'the defendant is in need of correctional treatment that can be provided most effectively by his commitment to an institution'.[2] The 1960s have often been regarded as the heyday of rehabilitationism, but the subsequent history of this 'welfare' approach to penal policy remains subject to different interpretations.

One view is that the rehabilitative ideal was dominant in the 1960s and then suffered a catastrophic decline in the 1970s, partly because of the publicity given to negative research findings, partly because of wider social and economic changes, and partly because of disenchantment about the intellectual basis of rehabilitative approaches:[3] see the discussion by Francis Allen in Selection 1.1. A more nuanced view is that the rehabilitative ideal was important but never dominant—for example, in the Model Penal Code it sat alongside incapacitation and desert as justifications for imprisonment—and that, even though its foundations were much criticised in the 1970s, it has remained part of penal practice and penal theory throughout.[4] Thus, not only in relation to young offenders (see Chapter 7 below) but also as part of probation for adults and parole, rehabilitation remains a significant penal rationale. This is not to deny that other forces interact with it—for example, surveillance and the control of risk are also key elements in probation and parole—but merely to assert its continued relevance. In Canada rehabilitation is one of the statutory purposes of sentencing,[5] as it is in New Zealand.[6] Similarly, in England and Wales one of the five statutory 'purposes of sentencing' is 'the reform and rehabilitation of offenders',[7] and official interest in rehabilitative programmes has been stimulated by the 'what works' movement, which aims to identify and to publicise programmes that are effective in reducing reoffending.

Definition

Rehabilitation bears a number of different meanings—restoration to full health after a major surgical operation, or re-admission to a community after a rejection by that community. In the penal context, it tends to be used to refer, not so much to the goal of reducing an offender's tendency to commit crimes, but more to the means used in order to try to bring about that goal. In this sense, rehabilitation encompasses approaches to fostering law-abiding habits which are intended to work by changing offenders' attitudes and inclinations. Thus the term 'reform', often used as a synonym for rehabilitation, tends to be written more fully as 'reformation of character', thereby indicating the true target of the methods employed. This longstanding approach has been termed the 'correctional model' of rehabilitation,[8] since it is focused on the offender and on changing the causes of the offending behaviour. The term 'treatment' has often been used in this context, perhaps more so in former years than now, as an allusion to a medical model in which the pathological state of the offender is diagnosed and treated by experts.

Despite the prominence of elements of a non-treatment paradigm,[9] there remains a treatment element in rehabilitative techniques, with expert diagnosis and prescription, and some of the strengths and weaknesses of this approach are considered below. Finally, we should recall that rehabilitation is essentially a consequentialist rationale for compulsory social intervention: in its stronger form the claim is that this approach to the prevention of crime and the reduction of reoffending can benefit society in general, whereas in a weaker form the claim would merely be 'that although we cannot be confident in our ability to change offenders for the better, we can at least avoid unnecessary harm resulting from excessive or damaging penalties.'[10]

In continental Europe it is more common to find the term 'resocialisation' used for these approaches, emphasising the aim of (re)integrating the offender into 'the community'. Terms such as resocialisation and reintegration indicate a rather different approach to rehabilitation than that of the correctional model described above. They envisage a more relational process,[11] which involves not only supervision but also some kind of discourse or negotiation with a range of 'stakeholders', including families, members of the wider community and even victims. The purpose of this process would be to facilitate the re-entry, resettlement or reintegration of the offender into the community. This relational approach is to be found in the recent resurgence of criminological interest in desistance[12] and in resettlement,[13] trying to identify the conditions most favourable to an offender's desisting from offending and becoming resettled in the community after conviction, particularly after a custodial sentence. On the relational approach to rehabilitation, then, the emphasis is not so much on responding to the individual's offending behaviour as on dealing with the aftermath of the offence and the sentence so that the offender can be re-established as a law-abiding member of the community.

In some forms, this emphasis on relational processes with stakeholders appears to merge with a restorative response to offending. It does not necessarily take this course, but readers will find discussion of restorative justice in Chapter 5 below.

Theoretical Underpinnings

Since rehabilitation is a form of prevention, it is fundamental that rehabilitative techniques should be supported only if and insofar as they offer effective methods of reducing reoffending. Beyond this prosaic foundation, however, some rehabilitationists argue that the state's duty to strive to promote security and to reduce crime also supports a positive obligation to provide programmes and other treatment opportunities to enable offenders to break free from lawbreaking and to lead better lives, and that it also has an obligation to adopt the most humane and least intrusive forms of compulsory social intervention. Thus Rotman has argued that:

> rehabilitation becomes a right of offenders to certain minimum services from the correctional services. The purpose of such a right is to offer each offender an opportunity to reintegrate into society as a useful human being.[14]

One reason for thus insisting on these state obligations, as Francis Cullen and Karen Gilbert argue in Selection 1.4, is that a majority of those convicted of offences are people who are socially or otherwise disadvantaged, and that it is the state's duty to compensate for this by offering the kind of support to offenders that is to be found in rehabilitative sentences.

Methods

More light can be cast on the definition of rehabilitation by considering some of the methods used. On the correctional model, the rehabilitative ideal is that the nature of the offender's condition (ie the causes of his or her offending) is diagnosed by an expert, and then the appropriate treatment is made available. There is therefore an assumption that the offender's social or psychological problems may play a significant part in the offending, and that is what the rehabilitative technique should tackle. An obvious example of this would be drug or alcohol misuse leading to dependency or at least to crime: some form of drug or alcohol treatment order would then be imposed, in the expectation that success in treating the substance misuse would bring a reduction or cessation of offending. More generally, use may made of psychological techniques such as counselling or cognitive-behavioural programmes, sometimes delivered individually, though more frequently delivered in a group context, sometimes incorporated into a community sentence and sometimes delivered in prison.

The aim of the correctional approach is to change the attitudes and dispositions of offenders: the method is a form of treatment aimed at producing rehabilitation, even though the ultimate objective may be expressed as the reduction of risk or of reoffending, or indeed the protection of the public. The aim of the relational approach to rehabilitation is to reintegrate the offender by tackling not only behaviour but also social and structural disadvantages relevant to him or her, such as accommodation, employment, financial planning and so forth.

Effectiveness

Although there are those who have sought to justify the pursuit of rehabilitation on grounds of humanity towards offenders,[15] the main justification of correctional rehabilitation is that it seeks to achieve crime reduction by treating the *causes* of offending, thereby achieving a more lasting effect than deterrence or incapacitation. The main justification for relational rehabilitation is that it seeks to achieve crime reduction by ensuring the satisfactory reintegration of the offender into the community where he or she must live. On its own terms, therefore, rehabilitation is rightly judged on its results. If the methods employed cannot be shown to produce better results than other penal methods, its central claims are undermined.

There are, however, formidable difficulties in assessing effectiveness. First, there is a definitional question—effectiveness in what terms? The usual answer is that reconviction rates are the best measure, over (say) a period of two years after the end of the sentence. But the incompleteness of reconvictions is well known, not least because in England and Wales only around a quarter of offences reported each year are brought to justice. Moreover, treating a single reconviction as a failure may be unduly pessimistic: significant reductions in the frequency and/or the seriousness of reoffending may properly be regarded as positive outcomes.

Secondly, even accepting all those problems, how should effectiveness be measured? Often the best that can be achieved is to measure the two-year reconviction rate for offenders with similar characteristics (offence, previous convictions, age) given different sentences. The British Home Office accepts the view that only the random allocation of offenders to different sentences or treatments can produce a 'gold standard' of evaluation[16]; however, randomised controlled trials are rare, and it can be strongly argued that reliance on them alone would produce a narrow and unbalanced evaluation.[17] Evaluations with well-matched comparison groups can provide reasonably robust evidence, as the Home Office has recognised,[18] as can other research methods with proper controls. For most evaluations, all the reservations about reliance on previous convictions remain to be negotiated.

With these qualifications, does the evidence show what works for whom, when and why? International interest in 'what works' was generated by two large meta-analyses of research into rehabilitative interventions in the early 1990s, suggesting that well-targeted rehabilitative programmes could have a significant effect on reoffending.[19] The revival of interest was followed by further analyses by James McGuire, emphasising the need to ensure that various implementation requirements were strictly met if the successes claimed for certain rehabilitative programmes were to be replicated.[20] However, the more cautious side of this literature was not reflected in the Halliday Report of 2001 to the British Government, which included the broad claim that the application of 'what works' developments such as cognitive-behavioural programmes could reduce reoffending 'by 5–15 percentage points'.[21] In Selection 1.2 Anthony Bottoms refers to this claim as 'reckless', and explains why it was a travesty of the available evidence. In practice, however, these programmes were 'rolled out' nationally, somewhat in a 'one size fits all' manner, and it is hardly surprising that the results have not borne out the over-optimistic estimates.[22] The result, in Britain, is that the pendulum may swing too far in the other direction, ignoring the successes of small, well-targeted programmes.

As Peter Raynor argues in Selection 1.3, there is an accumulation of evidence about what works and what does not,[23] and there is reason to expect some schemes to work well if properly funded, targeted and implemented. The Home Office seems to accept this more realistic assessment, at least in its research arm.[24] This suggests that, if rehabilitationism is to continue as one of the major penal rationales, its focus will need to be scaled down so as to relate only to those sub-categories of offenders for whom its techniques can reliably be expected to be effective. In that role, it might be no more than an auxiliary penal aim, always linked to one or more of the other aims.

Sentencing Implications

What implications does a rehabilitative rationale have for sentencing? In principle, the correctional model proposes that sentences should be designed, at least in part, to meet the treatment needs of offenders, in terms of both the method and the duration of intervention. In order to impose such sentences, a reliable diagnostic tool is required to assess the needs of the individual offender. In England and Wales a system known as OASys has been developed to fulfil this function.[25] Assuming that an accurate assessment can be carried out, the courts need to have access to treatment programmes suitable for those offenders said to need them. Usually these will be in the form of a community sentence with a particular requirement, such as drug or alcohol treatment, or attendance at a specified programme (eg anger management, enhanced thinking skills). On a rehabilitative model, the duration of the order would be determined chiefly by the length of time said to be required in order to complete the programme.

For some offenders, the view may be taken that they must be sent to prison and their rehabilitation needs must be met in a custodial setting—whether those needs be drug or alcohol treatment, a cognitive-behavioural programme, sex offender treatment or whatever. However, whether the sentence is community-based or custodial, this approach would vest considerable discretion and power in those who administer the programme and assess the progress of those undergoing it. This approach points towards indeterminate sentences, and is rarely adopted as such in contemporary penal systems. Indeterminate sentences are usually available only for incapacitative purposes. Within such sentences, however, the completion of rehabilitative programmes is often relevant to release decisions, as evidence of a reduced need for public protection from the offender.

The extent to which rehabilitation should determine the duration and onerousness of the sentence would also depend on what other sentencing aims are brought to bear, particularly those of proportionality. It is thus possible to ensure that rehabilitative interventions can be accommodated within sentencing approaches that make the seriousness of the criminal offence an important criterion for deciding the severity of sentence. A rehabilitative scheme, then, may be designed in order to try to reconcile interests in 'offender reform' and 'justice'—while at the same time recognising the potential tensions between these objectives.

Objections to Rehabilitative Sentencing

Among the objections to rehabilitative sentencing, we may discuss five possible arguments: that it proceeds on an inaccurate model of human behaviour; that it is unduly controlling; that it privileges discretion over accountability; that it can lead to disproportionate interventions; and that the problems of establishing effectiveness cannot be satisfactorily overcome.

The first objection is that rehabilitative techniques are connected to a particular positivist strain of criminology that assumes individual pathology in lawbreakers and seeks to tackle the reduction of reoffending through interventions focused on the individual's character and propensities. This is too simple a theory of crime causation. At a minimum, there is a need to develop a theory of individual decision-making and action (as Per-Olof Wikström puts it, 'what moves people to commit acts of crime'), and to combine it with a theory that explains the interaction of individual motivation with other conditioning factors.[26] By abstracting the individual from those other influences, rehabilitative techniques can never confront the whole range of causal factors—for example, the family environment, and social conditions such as poor housing, employment and education policy. Furthermore, there seems to be a tendency to promote programmes rather than other, more individualistic forms of rehabilitative intervention. In response, rehabilitationists may proceed by confession and avoidance, accepting the limitations of their techniques but arguing that interventions may have some effect if they help equip individual offenders to withstand the various temptations, pressures and hardships that they may have to confront.

A second objection is that rehabilitationism posits an authoritarian relationship between the state and the offender, leading to a form of paternalism that may be repressive and tends to give little or no recognition to the offender as a moral agent and autonomous subject. In a way this follows from the first objection, since the model of individual pathology assumes a process of diagnosis and treatment that is controlled by the state official (usually, probation officer). It was in opposition to this that Anthony Bottoms and Bill McWilliams developed their non-treatment paradigm for probation, arguing that the offender should be centrally involved in deciding what caused him or her to offend and what response would be desirable, and promoting a principle of voluntarism in treatment.[27] Coerced treatment is not consistent with the ideals of the liberal state, in the sense that it does not respect the individual (offender) as an autonomous citizen (Allen, Selection 1.1). It is unlike the medical model, since a patient can always refuse the treatment prescribed by the doctor, whereas such a response is at odds with the coercive framework of the sentencing system. Rehabilitationists may deny that there is anything authoritarian about the prevailing practices, but the official trend in recent years has been to emphasise the controlling and disciplinary features of the framework of probation and other interventions.

A third objection is that it privileges discretion over accountability. In principle, if treatment is designed to rehabilitate, it should continue for as long as it takes to achieve that objective; and it is the treatment-administering authorities who should decide when the offender's attitude and dispositions have changed sufficiently to justify release from ongoing obligations. In practice, many programmes now have a finite length, and so they do not raise this particular problem. But some forms of treatment have no prescribed length, and they place a considerable amount of discretion in the hands of the treatment agents or the reviewing body. An example of this in the English system is the release of prisoners from the indeterminate sentence of imprisonment for public protection (IPP) and from the sentence of life imprisonment. These sentences allow considerable discretionary power over the length of an offender's incarceration, and the criteria for release relate to risk to the public and therefore have some connection with correctional rehabilitation.

A fourth objection to rehabilitationism is that it may lead to disproportionate restrictions on, or deprivations of, liberty. As Andrew von Hirsch and Lisa Maher argue in Selection 1.5, it is important to ascertain whether a rehabilitative approach leads to the imposition of measures (deprivations, restrictions) that are more onerous and/or less fair than would otherwise be imposed. This can occur in at least three ways. First, if an assessment of an offender indicates a need for a particular type of programme, the effective length of sentence will be determined by the duration of that programme rather than by the seriousness of the offence. This may mean that either the community sentence or the custodial sentence, whichever is imposed, lasts for longer and is therefore disproportionate to the crime committed. Secondly, for the same reasons, the diagnosed need for a particular programme may lead to the imposition of, say, a community sentence when the seriousness of the offence does not properly justify more than a fine. This may lead to an expansion of social control and a drift towards measures that, albeit well intentioned, are unduly onerous. Thirdly, where an indeterminate custodial sentence (such as IPP) is passed and release depends on the decision that the offender has been successfully rehabilitated, this may result in a deprivation of liberty that is disproportionate to the crime committed.

However, these difficulties may be dealt with by adopting sentencing policies which permit rehabilitative interventions, but only within proportionality constraints (see Chapter 4 below).

A fifth objection is that evaluations of the effectiveness of rehabilitative measures are never likely to reach a satisfactory level of reliability. The incompleteness of statistics relating to reoffending is an abiding weakness of almost all attempts to assess efficacy. Insofar as evaluations have been completed, they suggest that the wider implementation of programmes is bound to have less impact than the demonstration projects on which they were based.[28] Moreover, there remain disagreements about the most accurate methods for evaluation: as stated earlier, there has been reference to randomised controlled trials as providing the 'gold standard' of evaluation, but they do not give a rounded assessment of all the impacts of the different techniques. In reality, the vitality of rehabilitationism and of 'what works' may continue to depend as much on the enthusiasm of its practitioners and its promoters as on the results of evaluations.

AA

Notes

1.   American Law Institute, Model Penal Code (Philadelphia, PA, American Law Institute, 1962), s 7.01(2), paras (i) and (j).
2.   *Ibid*, s 7.01(1)(b).
3.   Eg Garland, D, (2001) *The Culture of Control: Crime and Social Order in Contemporary Society* (Oxford, Oxford University Press) ch 3.
4.   Eg Zedner, L, (2002) 'Dangers of Dystopias in Penal Theory' 22 *Oxford Journal of Legal Studies* 341, 344–6; Raynor, P and Vanstone, M, (2002) *Understanding Community Penalties: Probation, Policy and Social Change* (Buckingham, Open University Press).
5.   Canadian Criminal Code, s 718.
6.   Sentencing Act 2002 (NZ), s 7.
7.   Criminal Justice Act 2003, s 142(1)(c).

8. Raynor, P and Robinson, G, (2005) *Rehabilitation, Crime and Justice* (Basingstoke, Macmillan).

9. See the influential article by Bottoms, AE and McWilliams, B, (1979) 'A Non-Treatment Paradigm for Probation Practice' 9 *British Journal of Social Work* 159.

10. Raynor and Robinson, above n 8, 21.

11. Raynor and Robinson, above n 8.

12. On desistance, see, eg Maruna, S, (2001) *Making Good: How Convicts Reform and Build their Lives* (Washington, DC, American Psychological Association); Farrall, S, (2002) *Rethinking What Works with Offenders: Probation, Social Context, and Desistance from Crime* (Cullompton, Willan), and the special issue at (2004) 43 *Howard Journal of Criminal Justice* 357.

13. On resettlement, see, eg the special issue at (2006) 6 *Criminology and Criminal Justice* 7.

14. Rotman, E, (1990) *Beyond Punishment: A New View of Rehabilitation of Criminal Offenders* (New York, Greenwood Press) 6.

15. See Cullen and Gilbert, Selection 1.4.

16. Harper, G and Chitty, C (eds), (2005) *The Impact of Corrections on Re-offending: a Review of 'What Works'*, Home Office Research Study 291 (London, Home Office Research, Development and Statistics Directorate) 80.

17. Hollin, C, (2008) 'Evaluating Offending Behaviour Programmes: Does only Randomization Glister?' 8 *Criminology and Criminal Justice* 89.

18. Harper and Chitty, above n 16, 7.

19. Andrews, DA *et al*, (1990) 'Does Correctional Treatment Work? A Clinically Relevant and Psychologically Informed Meta-Analysis' 28 *Criminology* 369; Lipsey, M, (1992) 'Juvenile Delinquency Treatment: a Meta-Analytic Enquiry into the Variability of Effects' in T Cool *et al*, *Meta-Analysis for Explanation: a Case-book* (New York, Russell Sage Foundation) 83.

20. McGuire, J (ed), (1995), *What Works: Reducing Reoffending* (Chichester, Wiley), McGuire, J, (2002) 'Integrating Findings from Research Reviews' in J McGuire (ed), *Offender Rehabilitation and Treatment: Effective Programmes and Policies to Reduce Re-offending* (Chichester, Wiley).

21. Home Office, (2001) *Making Punishments Work: Report of a review of the sentencing framework for England and Wales* (London, Home Office) para 1.49.

22. Raynor, P, (2007) 'Community Penalties' in M Maguire, R Morgan and R Reiner (eds), *Oxford Handbook of Criminology*, 4th edn (Oxford, Oxford University Press) 1079–80.

23. Three further meta-analyses are those by Lipton, D *et al*, (2002) 'The Effectiveness of Cognitive-behavioural Treatment Methods on Offender Recidivism' in McGuire (ed), *Offender Rehabilitation*, above n 20; Redondo, S *et al*, (2002) 'Crime Treatment in Europe: a Review of Outcome Studies' in McGuire (ed), *ibid*; and Aos, S *et al*, (2006) *Evidence-based Adult Corrections Programs: What Works and What Does Not* (Olympia, WA, Washington State Institute for Public Policy).

24. Harper and Chitty, above n 16.

25. Developed by the National Probation Service and the Prison Service, the Offender Assessment System (OASys) is a standardised process for the assessment of offenders. See further Merrington, S, (2004) 'Assessment Tools in Probation: their development and potential' in R Burnett and C Roberts (eds), *What Works in Probation and Youth Justice* (Cullompton, Willan).

26. Wikström, P-O, (2006) 'Individuals, Settings and Acts of Crime: Situational Mechanisms and the Explanation of Crime' in P-O Wikström and R Sampson (eds), *The Explanation*

of Crime: Context, Mechanisms, and Development (Cambridge, Cambridge University Press).

27. See above n 6.

28. Lipsey, M, (1999) 'Can Rehabilitative Programs Reduce the Recidivism of Juvenile Offenders? An Enquiry into the Effectiveness of Practical Programs' 6 *Virginia Journal of Social Policy and the Law* 611.

Further Reading

Aos, S, Miller, M and Drake, E, (2006) *Evidence-based Adult Corrections Programs: What Works and What Does Not* (Olympia, WA, Washington State Institute for Public Policy).

Cullen, FT and Gendreau, P, (2001) 'From Nothing Works to What Works: Changing Professional Ideology in the 21 Century' 81 *Prison Journal* 313.

Cullen, FT and Gilbert, KE, (1982) *Reaffirming Rehabilitation* (Cincinnati, OH, Anderson Publishing).

McGuire, J (ed), (2002) *Offender Rehabilitation and Treatment: Effective Programmes and Policies to Reduce Re-offending* (Chichester, Wiley).

McNeill, F, (2004) 'Desistance, Rehabilitation and Correctionalism: Developments and Prospects in Scotland' 43 *Howard Journal of Criminal Justice* 420.

Raynor, P and Robinson, G, (2005) *Rehabilitation, Crime and Justice* (Basingstoke, Palgrave Macmillan).

Rotman, E (1990) *Beyond Punishment: A New View of the Rehabilitation of Criminal Offenders* (New York, Greenwood Press).

Ward, T and Maruna, S (2007) *Rehabilitation: Beyond the Risk Paradigm* (London, Routledge).

1.1

The Decline of the Rehabilitative Ideal

FRANCIS A ALLEN

The modern decline of penal rehabilitationism cannot be fully explained by the persuasiveness of the logical cases arrayed against it. Yet the criticisms are important, for in them may be found the assumptions on which contemporary efforts to recast criminal justice are based. Some modern reactions present very little of intellectual interest; they comprise essentially irritated responses to the prevalence of crime and offer only an all-encompassing faith in the efficacy of coercion and repression. Such a characterization, however, is in no way descriptive of the views of many who today oppose the rehabilitative ideal. The latter are troubled by the political implications of penal rehabilitationism and are sensitive to the conflicts built into a system of criminal justice that seeks to express simultaneously the values of human responsibility and the reform of offenders. Accordingly, attention needs to be given to the modern critique of the rehabilitative ideal.

The modern case against the rehabilitative ideal has been in the making at least since the years immediately preceding World War II. It derives from a variety of sources and was largely formulated before political movements in the late 1960s appropriated it for their own purposes. Although these critics share no common fund of assumptions, the modern critique of the rehabilitative ideal appears to rest on three principal propositions. First, the rehabilitative ideal constitutes a threat to the political values of free societies. Second—a distinct but closely related point—the rehabilitative ideal has revealed itself in practice to be peculiarly vulnerable to debasement and the serving of unintended and unexpressed social ends. Third, either because of scientific ignorance or institutional incapacities, a rehabilitative technique is lacking; we do not know how to prevent criminal recidivism by changing the characters and behaviour of offenders.

The liberal political stance and penal rehabilitationism coexist in a continuing state of tension, even though the resulting unease is more acutely sensed in some periods than in others. From the liberal perspective, any system of penal regulation, however oriented, is at best a necessary evil— the necessity stemming from the presence in the community of those who unjustifiably subvert the interests and volition of other persons. The movement from penal incapacitation of offenders to

From FA Allen, *The Decline of the Rehabilitative Ideal: Penal Policy and Social Purpose* (New Haven, CT, Yale University Press, 1981).

their reform, however, introduces a new order of concerns; for efforts to influence by coercive means the very thoughts, feelings, and aspirations of offenders threaten trespass by the state upon areas of dignity and choice posited as immune by the liberal creed. One reason the tension between liberalism and the rehabilitative ideal has not always been seen as critical is that the means often employed in rehabilitative efforts have been such that, if at all successful, they require a considerable voluntary cooperative effort on the part of the subject. When, however, the rehabilitative effort moves from the use of devices like those of traditional psychotherapy to what have been called the extreme therapies—psychosurgery, aversive conditioning, and certain other forms of behavioural modification—the state employs rehabilitative techniques that typically impose feelings and perceptions on the subject that in a meaningful sense are not of his own making, techniques that one observer describes as "manipulating people inside the perimeter of their conscious defenses".[1] The liberal unease with such forms of rehabilitation reflects, not a Luddite rejection of scientific "advance", but rather an awareness that they constitute incursions by the state into areas of human freedom and autonomy believed to lie outside the proper province of state action.

The principles of consent and voluntarism derived from liberal political values suggest certain limitations on the methods that may legitimately be employed in rehabilitative efforts. The widespread disregard of these limitations, both in this country and around the world, constitutes one of the serious modern complaints about penal rehabilitationism.

The political implications of the rehabilitative ideal, however, encompass far more than the kinds of rehabilitative techniques employed. Regardless of the means applied, a range of problems emerge involving control of the discretion of public agencies, and these problems have proved persistent and disturbing. The issues are among the most frequently discussed in the recent legal literature on corrections.

Therapeutic theories of penal treatment have often conceived of crime as symptomatic of an affliction, but the nature of the disease and how it differs from other pathologies are generally obscure. Vagueness in the conception of the disorder is communicated, in turn, to thought about its cure. Much of the political unease engendered by this version of the rehabilitative ideal stems from its central conception. One immediate consequence of a rehabilitative regime is a drastic enlargement of state concerns. The state's interests now embrace not only the offender's conduct but, as Michel Foucault has put it, his "soul"; his motives, his history, his social environment.[2] A traditional restraint on governmental authority is the notion of relevance: the state is limited in its inquiries and actions to that which is pertinent to its legitimate purposes. But when there are no clear limits on what may be relevant to the treatment process and when the goals of treatment have not been clearly defined, the idea of relevance as a regulator of public authority is destroyed or impaired.

The assumption of the benevolent purpose of the rehabilitative regime and the highly subjective and ill-defined notions of how rehabilitation is to be achieved and of what it consists, generate other problems. One of these is the tendency of those engaged in rehabilitative efforts to define as therapy anything that a therapist does. Because such disabilities as loss of liberty and other privileges are defined as therapeutic, the officer's sense of self-restraint may be weakened. One consequence, frequently remarked, is the tendency of rehabilitative regimes to inflict larger deprivations of liberty and volition on its subjects than is sometimes exacted from prisoners in more overtly punitive programmes.

These, then, constitute part of the catalogue of political concerns that have been engendered by the rehabilitative ideal. Whether they or any part of them counsel the total abandonment of penal rehabilitationism or whether it is prudent to persist in rehabilitative efforts if forewarned of their perils, requires further consideration. For the moment, however, it is sufficient to say that the political concerns just discussed take on even greater seriousness when a second broad tendency of the rehabilitative ideal is considered: its tendency in practical application to become debased and to serve other social ends far removed from and sometimes inconsistent with the reform of offenders.

Understanding the phenomena of debasement is advanced if attention is first directed to the ways in which language has been employed by those initiating and administering programmes of penal rehabilitation. What is involved is more than the usual insistence on a technical vocabulary, but rather a marked tendency toward euphemism and obfuscation. What distinguishes the language of rehabilitation is the degree of faith reflected in the efficacy of label changes, the extraordinary gaps between the epithets employed and the commonsense realities that the words are intended to describe, the amorphousness of concepts central to the system of thought. In one place or another solitary confinement has been called "constructive mediation" and a cell for such confinement "the quiet room". Incarceration without treatment of any kind is seen as "milieu therapy" and a detention facility is labelled "Cloud Nine". The catalogue is almost endless. Some of the euphemisms are conscious distortions of reality and are employed sardonically or with deliberate purpose to deceive. The more serious distortions, however, are those that reflect the self-deception of correctional functionaries. The burgeoning of euphemisms and the insecure grasp on reality that their use often reveals, signal a system of thought and action under extreme pressure. They are symptomatic of factors contributing to the debasement of rehabilitative objectives in practical application.

Central among the causes of debasement is the conceptual weakness of the rehabilitative ideal. Vagueness and ambiguity shroud its most basic suppositions. The ambitious scope and complexity of its agenda make these characteristics comprehensible and perhaps inevitable. Ambiguities afflict the very notion of what rehabilitation consists. A consensus on the ends of rehabilitation sufficient to spark movements of penal reform may, however, camouflage wide diversities of orientation that became critical when institutional programmes are attempted.

Equally serious is the vagueness that surrounds the means to effect rehabilitation. Much that is most bizarre in the history of penal rehabilita-tionism stems from scientific ignorance about how changes in the behaviour of offenders are to be achieved. In general, scientific ignorance has not inspired caution in the devotees of the rehabilitative ideal. On the contrary, the very absence of knowledge has encouraged confident assertions and dogmatic claims. One consequence is the creation of expectations that are inevitably disappointed. As programmes fail, euphemisms and pretext burgeon. Among the groups most seriously disenchanted by this cycle are the inmates themselves. A profound obstacle to penal rehabilitation in the contemporary world is the cynicism of the prisoners engendered, at least in part, by such institutional charades.

This leads naturally to the third and final proposition in the critique of the rehabilitative ideal. The proposition is that there is no evidence that an effective rehabilitative technique exists, that we do not know how to prevent criminal recidivism through rehabilitative effort. The statement of the proposition that has received widest attention was that of Robert Martinson. "With few isolated exceptions", he wrote in 1974, "the rehabilitative efforts that have been reported so far have had no appreciable effect on recidivism".[3] One of the most important aspects of the Martinson study may well be that its immediate and widespread impact constitutes a demonstration of public attitudes in the 1970s receptive to the conclusions stated.

In a remarkably short time a new orthodoxy has been established asserting that rehabilitative objectives are largely unattainable and that rehabilitative programmes and research are dubious or misdirected. The new attitudes resemble in their dominance and pervasiveness those of the old orthodoxy, prevailing only a few years ago, that mandated rehabilitative efforts and exuded optimism about rehabilitative capabilities. Those who resist the hegemony of the new orthodoxy have challenged the criteria of success imposed by the critics on rehabilitative programmes and research and have argued that the critics' own studies provide basis for at least moderate optimism about future prospects of rehabilitative attempts.[4] Some have suggested that the methods employed in the modern attack on the rehabilitative ideal are often more polemic and ideological in their nature than scientific.[5] Even though these controversies continue, it is not too soon for certain general observations to be made. Proponents of rehabilitative research have argued with considerable force that to the extent the modern critique of the rehabilitative ideal rests on scientific ignorance of many matters vital to rehabilitative programmes, the indicated response is not the abandonment of those efforts but, rather, the production of new knowledge. Yet the proponents share with the critics a profound dissatisfaction with most past examples of rehabilitative research and practice. They express an awareness of the complexities inherent in such endeavours that was typically lacking in the enthusiasm for penal rehabilitation even in the recent past. A new spirit of caution pervades claims about the rehabilitative potential of correctional programmes; and the era when penal rehabilitationism can be accepted as the dominant mode of crime control seems more remote today than at many times in the past.

What role is likely to be accorded the rehabilitative ideal in the emerging modern synthesis? One point seems clear: whatever functions are assigned to penal rehabilitationism in the remaining years of the twentieth century, they are likely to be peripheral rather than central to the administration of criminal justice. This is true not only because of the new awareness of the limited efficacy of rehabilitative programmes and the other factors making up the modern critique of the rehabilitative ideal, but also because even an effective programme of inmate reform contributes only tangentially to the strategy of public order. In that strategy the deterrence of the great majority of the population from serious criminal activity is always the consideration of first importance, not the rehabilitation or incapacitation of the much smaller number of persons convicted of criminal offences.

Notes

1. Neville, *Ethical and Philosophical Issues of Behavior Control* (Am. Assn. for the Advancement of Science, 27 December 1972) 4.
2. M. Foucault, *Discipline and Punish* (New York: Pantheon Books, 1977), at 19.
3. "What Works? Questions and Answers about Prison Reform", *Pub. Interest* 24, 25 (Spring 1974). See also Martinson, "New Findings, New Views: A Note of Caution Regarding Sentencing Reform", (1979) 7 *Hofstra L. Rev.* 243.
4. See, e.g., Palmer, "Martinson Revisited", 12 *J. Research in Crime and Delin.* 133 (1975). Cf. Martinson, "California Research at the Crossroads", (1976) 22 *Crime and Delin.* 180.
5. Gottfredson, "Treatment Destruction Techniques", 16 *J. Research in Crime and Delin.* 39 (January 1979).

1.2

Empirical Research Relevant to Sentencing Frameworks: Reform and Rehabilitation

ANTHONY BOTTOMS

In its quest for a way to achieve greater crime reduction through use of the sentencing framework, the Halliday Report (Home Office 2001) placed by far its greatest emphasis on what it called 'reform and rehabilitation'. In contrast to deterrence and incapacitation (see later sub-sections), with regard to reform/rehabilitation Halliday thought that 'the position is a bit clearer, and more positive'. Referring to the so-called 'What Works' developments, and the implementation of associated policies, the Report commented that 'although the evidence to support them is as yet incomplete, there is a strong enough case to justify looking for a [sentencing] framework that would be more supportive of the attempts being made to reduce reoffending' (Home Office 2001: para 1.69). In an earlier section of the Report which specifically discussed the 'What Works' developments, the following concluding comment was made:

> A reasonable estimate at this stage is that, if the programmes are developed and applied as intended, to the maximum extent possible, reconviction rates might be reduced by 5-15 percentage points (i.e. from the present level of 56% within two years to (perhaps) 40%). In the face of historically unchanging levels of reoffending, that would be a remarkable success. (Home Office 2001: para 1.49; see also Appendix 6 of the same report)

Sadly, three years later this appears to be a most unfortunate, and indeed in some ways a reckless, claim. It is important to spell out with some precision why this is so.

First, and most obviously, recent research evidence on the success of cognitive-behavioural programmes is substantially less promising than the earlier results on smaller-scale, more exploratory programmes. It is very likely, though not yet certain, that these disappointing results are largely attributable precisely to the scale of the operation – that is, for a variety of reasons it is much easier to achieve

From A Bottoms, 'Empirical Research Relevant to Sentencing Frameworks', in A Bottoms, S Rex and G Robinson (eds), *Alternatives to Prison: Options for an Insecure Society* (Cullompton, Willan, 2004) 61–63.

success with small-scale programmes run by enthusiasts, with tight control over programme integrity, and with well-motivated groups of offenders, than it is when similar programmes are 'rolled out' on a national scale, as has recently been the case in England and Wales.

Second, Halliday's claim was in any case fairly reckless even at the time it was made. The reference, within the paragraph cited above, to *national* reconviction rates appears to suggest that the new 'What Works' programmes might be applied to all offenders in prison and on probation, and that an across-the-board reconviction reduction of up to 15 percentage points could be achieved. The busy policy-maker reading the paragraph was given no hint that, at that date, 'What Works' programmes were actually being applied to only a smallish minority of offenders in prison and on probation. Moreover, it is a cardinal principle of the 'What Works' philosophy that programmes should be carefully targeted, so that they are applied to offenders likely to be suitable for them, and to respond to them, rather than 'across the board' (i.e. 'risk and responsivity': see McGuire and Priestley 1995); and offenders are regularly rejected from programmes for this reason. These simple points should clearly have led to a significantly less ambitious claim than Halliday made.

Third, Halliday's emphasis, within the cited paragraph, is solely on *offending behaviour programmes*, with other possible promising approaches to rehabilitation being left aside in silence. This is extremely unfortunate, since the evidence for the possible success of other approaches is not negligible (see for example Rex 2001, Farrall 2002).

In summary, then, the empirical evidence on reform/rehabilitation is both more promising than Halliday realised (because his attention was virtually confined to offending behaviour programmes), and also less promising than he hypothesised (in relation to programmes). There remains considerable promise in the rehabilitative approach, but whether that promise is sufficient for it to influence the sentencing framework substantially is another question.

Before leaving the topic of reform/rehabilitation, it is worth noting that the naivete of Halliday's optimistic conclusions on this issue carries its own lessons. He is by no means the first person to have been over-impressed by an apparent 'new Utopia' in crime policy; but history teaches that a more sober assessment is normally appropriate when framing policies.

References

Farrall, S. (2002), *Rethinking What Works with Offenders: Probation, Social Context and Desistance from Crime* (Cullompton: Willan).

Home Office (2001), *Making Punishments Work: Report of a Review of the Sentencing Framework for England and Wales* (London: the Home Office), 'the Halliday Report.'

McGuire, J., and Priestley, P. (1995), 'Reviewing "What Works": past, present and future', in J. McGuire (ed), *What Works: Reducing Reoffending* (Chichester: John Wiley).

Rex, S. (2001), 'Beyond cognitive-behaviouralism? Reflections on the effectiveness literature', in A.E. Bottoms, L. Gelsthorpe and S. Rex (eds), *Community Penalties: Changes and Challenges* (Cullompton: Willan).

1.3

Assessing the Research on 'What Works'

PETER RAYNOR

The Contribution of Systematic Research Reviews

Initially the most influential of the meta-analytic reviews were those of Andrews and his colleagues in Canada (Andrews *et al*. 1990) and of Lipsey in the United States, which mainly concerned work with young offenders (Lipsey 1992). Some uses of meta-analysis have been subject to criticisms concerning, for example, the risk of subjective judgement in the coding of studies, the small results base for some conclusions, and possible bias resulting from the greater probability of positive findings being accepted for publication (for these and other problems, see Mair 1994). However, the overall conclusions seem sound, particularly considering the large number of studies with contrary findings that would be needed to overturn them. Similar conclusions have been reached by other substantial and rigorous reviews of the crime reduction literature (including Gaes *et al*. 1999; Sherman *et al*. 1998), and the extreme scepticism still shown by some commentators (for example, Mair 2004) can no longer be regarded as realistic.

In meta-analytic reviews, the impact of methods or approaches on offenders is typically expressed as an 'effect size' which indicates the difference in reconviction rates, or sometimes another measure, between those offenders who have experienced particular methods or services and those who have had some other input, or no input at all, depending on the particular study design. 'Effect sizes' can be expressed in a number of ways, including correlation coefficients, odds ratios, 'binomial effect size display' (BESD) or, in the case of outcomes such as change in test scores, the mean change divided by the standard deviation of the initial scores. However, those of most interest for our current purpose concern the reductions in reconviction which are greater than the reductions which would have been produced either by the customary methods or by doing nothing.

A recent comprehensive overview of 30 meta-analytic reviews published between 1985 and 2001 (McGuire 2002: 13) pointed out that 'the impact of 'treatment' that can be defined in numerous ways is, on average, positive' but 'the mean effect taken

From P Raynor, 'Rehabilitative and Reintegrative Approaches' in A Bottoms, S Rex and G Robinson (eds), *Alternatives to Prison: Options for an Insecure Society* (Cullompton, Willan 2004), excerpted from 199–217.

across a broad spectrum of treatment or intervention types is relatively modest'. McGuire summarises that there is a 9 to 10 per cent reduction in reconviction rates in favour of those receiving 'treatment'. Such differences, although 'modest', have considerable policy implications if they can be achieved consistently in an area accustomed to results showing no difference. When types of intervention are restricted to those considered most likely to be useful, effect sizes tend to rise: for example, a meta-analysis of 68 studies looking at the effectiveness of cognitive-behavioural methods with offenders, published at the same time as McGuire's review and therefore not included in it, shows an average effect size approaching 13 per cent (Lipton *et al.* 2002). Using the BESD convention this is approximately equivalent to the difference between a 44 per cent reconviction rate for a 'treatment' group and a 56 per cent reconviction rate in a comparison group. Another review of effective projects in Europe reported a 21 per cent difference in re-offending, measured in various ways between intervention groups and comparison groups (Redondo *et al.* 2002). Lipsey and Wilson (1998) reported some even larger effect sizes from effective work with young offenders.

Meta-analysis in this field has also been concerned to establish not only whether appropriate work with offenders typically has an impact on future offending but, more ambitiously, to discover what approaches and methods typically produce good results. It is important to recognise that finding an association between particular methods and positive outcomes does not in and of itself demonstrate a causal relationship. Attempts to maximise effects by putting a number of probably effective ingredients together rest at best on a plausible hypothesis which itself requires further evaluation. Nevertheless, throughout the 1990s efforts were made to draw up lists of the characteristics of effective rehabilitative efforts and to use them as a basis for planning services. For example, the Correctional Services Accreditation Panel (CSAP), which approves programmes for implementation with offenders in prisons and within the community in England and Wales, requires applicants to have at least a plausible evidence-based hypothesis and a reasonable plan to test it if they cannot point to positive results already achieved in pilot studies (see Rex *et al.* 2003).

Lists of the characteristics of successful programmes have been produced and updated by a number of commentators, particularly by Andrews and by McGuire, and the latest version points to 18 'principles of effective interventions to reduce recidivism' (McGuire 2002: 24, drawing on Andrews 2001). These can be summarised and in some cases grouped together, hopefully without too much oversimplification, in the following 11 approaches to design and delivery:

- using human service strategies based on 'personality and social learning' theories and on evidence about factors which increase the risk of offending;
- using community-based settings or, if in custody, making services as community-oriented as possible;

- using risk levels and criminogenic needs, assessed by properly validated methods, to inform targeting and allocation to services;
- using multi-modal approaches which match services to learning styles, motivation and aptitude;
- adapting services to difference and diversity, and recognising participants' strengths;
- monitoring continuity of services and care, including relapse prevention;
- giving staff clear guidance on principles and on where they can use discretion;
- monitoring and maintaining programme integrity, i.e. that services are delivered as intended;
- developing staff skills, including the capacity to maintain 'high-quality interpersonal relationships';
- ensuring good knowledgeable management;
- adapting services to local context/client groups and services.

Such lists are, of course, easier to draw up than to embody consistently in service designs. However, it is also striking to see how closely this recent list resembles similar lists drawn up nearly ten years ago (for example, McGuire 1995; Raynor 1996). The message from research has been consistent for some time: the most obvious differences in the new list are a stronger focus on the need for practitioners to use interpersonal skills and exercise some discretion, on the need to take diversity among participants into account, and on the importance of the broader service context in supporting effective intervention.

Interpreting the 'What Works' Research in Practice

At this point it is necessary to record some cautionary notes about how this kind of research is often interpreted. First, it does not offer a guaranteed recipe for success. Lipsey (1999) points to the difference between 'demonstration' and 'practical' interventions. The former are the special pilot projects, which are often the source of the research reviewed, and the latter are the routine implementations that follow organisational decisions to adopt new methods. Better results are more commonly found among the 'demonstration' projects: in Lipsey's study the 196 'practical' programmes reviewed were on average half as effective as the 205 'demonstration' programmes. Even this level of effectiveness depended heavily on a few programmes, as 57 per cent of the 'practical' programmes had no appreciable effect. As Lipsey points out, 'rehabilitative programmes of a practical "real world" sort clearly can be effective; the challenge is to design and implement them so that they are, in fact, effective' (Lipsey 1999: 641). Other researchers have recently drawn attention to the crucial importance of implementation, described as 'the forgotten issue in effective correctional treatment' (Gendreau *et al.* 1999; see also Bernfeld *et al.* 2001). Some studies (for example, Raynor and Vanstone 2001) have pointed to the particular context of some successful interventions, including enthusiastic practitioners, a culture of curiosity about results and a management style which openly debates principles and methods and encourages staff to own them. Not even the most optimistic senior manager would claim these are always present.

Not Only Programmes Work

Another area of concern about interpretation of the 'what works' literature concerns the concept of a 'programme'. Many attempts to implement the lessons of research have taken the form of structured group programmes, and these are certainly well represented among the interventions that have demonstrated some effectiveness. However, this does not mean that only group programmes work, or that all effective service delivery must take the form of group programmes regardless of context and practicalities. One reason researchers have been particularly interested in these is that they lend themselves much better to systematic research than many other ways of working with offenders. It is a commonplace of human service research that it is very difficult to know what practitioners are really doing, so that even if some good outcomes can be documented, it is impossible to know what produced them. This places enormous difficulties in the way of replication and knowledge accumulation. Structured group programmes, with prescribed content and strategies such as videotaping to confirm delivery as intended, offer a solution to this problem by providing an unusual degree of clarity about what is actually being done with whom, and for how long. The attractions of this for researchers are self-evident. But programmes are not the only form of effective intervention, and even within the programme paradigm groups are not the only delivery option. McGuire defines a programme simply as a 'structured sequence of opportunities for learning and change' (McGuire 2002: 27), while the definition used by the Correctional Services Accreditation Panel for England and Wales is 'a systematic, reproducible set of activities in which offenders can participate' (CSAP 2003: 25).

Over-preoccupation with group programmes also runs the risk of sidelining or neglecting the importance of practitioner skills in the case management and supervision process. There is a substantial research literature concerned with effective practice in psychotherapy and social work, some of which would have been familiar to probation officers trained in England and Wales before the separation of probation officer training from social work training in 1997, and should still be covered in the training of probation and criminal justice staff who gain social work qualifications in other jurisdictions. Particular areas of interest here include core facilitative or therapeutic skills, widely researched in the 1960s (Truax and Carkhuff 1967), which include empathy, positive regard or concern, 'genuineness', and a concrete and specific approach to goals, expectations and processes. Similar issues continue to be identified in more recent research, and are brought together by McGuire (2003) in a recent discussion of the need for a 'working alliance' rather than a coercive or confrontational relationship. These are not woolly aspirations but concrete skills that are strongly supported by evidence and can be enhanced by training (for an example from social work education, see Raynor and Vanstone 1984}). There is also a useful body of research on the enhancement of motivation to change (Miller and Rollnick 1992) by using skilled interviewing to increase awareness of a need to change and willingness to do so. Much of the evidence here comes from the field of substance abuse, but there are increasing indications of the relevance of motivational work with offenders (for example, Harper and Hardy 2000).

Other useful components for the development of a 'what works' approach to individual supervision and case management include the practice of 'pro-social modelling', applied to probation practice in Australia by Trotter (1993, 2001) and taken up more recently in a number of British projects (Rex and Matravers 1998). In Trotter's formulation the approach involves both the modelling of prosocial attitudes and behaviour by staff supervising offenders and the acknowledgment and rewarding of such behaviour on the part of offenders themselves. Early research indicated that supervision by officers trained in this approach resulted in lower reconviction rates (Trotter 1993). While official attempts to build on these findings are now beginning in Britain (for example, in the new Enhanced Community Punishment Scheme), other forms of practice which have empirical support are not discussed much, perhaps because they are seen as belonging to the social work tradition rather than the correctional field. These include, for example, 'task-centred casework' (Reid and Epstein 1972), a highly focused approach to identifying problems, reaching agreements about them, sharing responsibility for addressing them and evaluating outcomes. This approach suggests a' number of interesting starting-points for thinking about case management, and has even been evaluated in a probation setting with interesting results (Goldberg *et al.* 1985). However, there has been little sign of any recent attempts to build on these,

In a recent article Dowden and Andrews (2004) report on a meta-analysis of the contribution of certain staff skills to the effectiveness of rehabilitative work with offenders. They define these skills as 'core correctional practices' or CCPs, which can be summarised briefly as effective use of authority; appropriate modelling and reinforcement; the use of a problem-solving approach; and the development of relationships characterised by openness, warmth, empathy, enthusiasm, directiveness and structure. The mean effect sizes of programmes were found to be higher when these were present, and significantly higher when other principles of programme effectiveness were also applied: staff skills and programme design complemented each other, rather than one being a substitute for the other. However, the authors point out that

> Clearly these CCPs were rarely used in the human service programs that were surveyed in this meta-analysis . . . These results suggest that the emphasis placed on developing

and utilizing appropriate staff techniques has been sorely lacking within correctional treatment programmes. (Dowden and Andrews 2004: 209)

Counter-productive Attrition

A third reason for care in drawing practical inferences from the 'what works' research is the problem of those who fail to attend programmes, or who start them but do not complete them. When it is possible to establish what happened to non-completers (which is difficult in some studies), it is not unusual to find that, instead of showing a lower degree of positive programme effects than the completers, they actually show negative effects, faring worse than both the completers and the comparison or control groups. Recent examples of this in British research include the STOP experiment (Raynor and Vanstone 1997) and the evaluation of prison-based cognitive-behavioural programmes (Cann *et al.* 2003). A Canadian example can be found in Robinson (1995). While there may be some selection effects at work here, for example, participants less suitable for the programme or with more problems may be less likely to complete, findings of this kind lead to particular worries about the overall impact of low completion rates. For example, a hypothetical programme which shows offending 10 per cent lower than expected among completers but 10 per cent higher than expected among non-completers will be negative in its overall effect if less than half the participants complete it. It will also be extraordinarily difficult for researchers to determine how far, if at all, any 'programme effect' is present which can be reliably distinguished from a selection effect. Some recent British research reviewed below shows that such an example is not simply fanciful, and this is confirmed by the continuing high rate of attrition reported for current programmes (National Probation Service 2004). However, other recent research suggests that such high attrition is not an inevitable feature of community-based programmes, and that much better completion rates have been achieved in jurisdictions where case management and enforcement are handled differently (see, for example, Miles and Raynor 2004) . . .

Conclusion: Widening the Scope of the Evidence-based Approach

Several aspects of this new context point strongly to the need for a broader approach to evidence-based rehabilitation and reintegration. It needs to be broader in two senses. First, it needs to be concerned with the impact of the whole of an offender's supervision or correctional involvement, not just with 'programmes' as currently understood. There is plenty of evidence, some of which is reviewed above, that proper assessment, preparation, motivation, case-management and reinforcement of learning are essential to support programme effects. Development and evaluation should focus increasingly on this broader concept of human services in rehabilitation, rather than primarily on programmes. Second, the focus needs to expand to consider the operation of the wider criminal justice system within which rehabilitative efforts are located: the impact of the system on the offender, and the capacity of those working with the offender to influence decisions taken about him or her in the system. There is an obvious connection to be made between the attempt to keep an individual offender out of prison and the collective goal of reducing reliance on custodial punishment.

It is now clear that there has been a downward drift in the seriousness of the probation order caseload since, for political reasons, reduction in custodial sentencing ceased to be an avowable aim in 1993 (Morga 2003). Since then there has been a very substantial investment in documenting and evaluating the effects of programmes on offenders, but an almost complete neglect, at least in the adult jurisdiction, of the impact of new developments on sentencing decisions. Until the collapse and reversal of the core elements of the 1991 Criminal Justice Act, it was not unusual for commentators to describe the Probation Service as capable of having a dual impact, both on the behaviour of individual offenders and on the patterns of decision-making in the criminal justice system, including particularly the level of custodial sentencing (Bottoms and McWilliams 1979; Raynor *et al.* 1994). The main instrument available to influence sentencing patterns was the social inquiry report (now known as the pre-sentence report), which was, at its best, demonstrably effective in this role (Gelsthorpe and Raynor 1995). The absence of any discussion of pre-sentence reports in the Carter Report (Carter 2003) and the lack of attention to system impacts in general in recent British 'what works' research are both regrettable; to continue to ignore these issues in the new policy context would be disastrous.

Among the key practice issues to address in the new context will be:

- Consistent assessment of risks and needs (generally recognised as a necessary underpinning for a range of effective practices but regrettably not yet in general use in Britain).
- Appropriate targeting of the right offenders, including strategies to influence sentencers.
- Programme provision to reflect evidence of needs and likely benefit, rather than pressure to recruit offenders into programmes to meet treasury targets. This could well result in fewer people doing programmes.
- Building positive motivation rather than relying on deterrence.
- Maintaining engagement in change efforts.
- Assisting access to relevant resources and services (e;g. advocacy).
- Maintaining and reinforcing learning.
- Facilitating continued pro-social support.

All of these could be encompassed under the heading of effective correctional case management, and they point to a need for systematic research in this area with a focus both on outcomes, for offenders and for the system, and on a qualitative and appreciative approach to understanding how offenders experience it, how they use it and what they believe they learn . . .

References

D.A. Andrews 'Principles of Effective Correctional Programming', in L. Motiuk and R. Serin (eds), *Compendium 2000 on Effective Correctional Programming* (2001), 9.
D.A. Andrews, I. Zinger, R.D. Hoge, J. Bonta, P. Gendreau and F.T. Cullen 'Does Correctional Treatment Work?' 28 *Criminology* 369.
G. Bemfeld, D. Farrington and A. Leschied (eds), *Offender Rehabilitation in Practice* (2001).
A.E. Bottoms and W. McWilliams, 'A Non-Treatment Paradigm for Probation Practice', (1979) 9 *B.J. Social Work* 159.
J. Cann et al., *Understanding What Works,* Home Office Research Study 226 (2003).
P. Carter, *Managing Offenders, Reducing Crime* (2003).
CSAP, *Correctional Services Accreditation Panel: Report 2002-03* (2003).
C. Dowden and D. Andrews, 'The Importance of Staff Practice in Delivering Effective Correctional Treatment: a Meta-Analysis', (2004) 48 *Int. J. of Offender Therapy and Comparative Criminology* 203.
G. Gaes et al., 'Adult Correctional Treatment', in M. Tonry and J. Petersilia (eds), *Crime and Justice: a Review of Research* (1999), 361.
L. Gelsthorpe and P. Raynor, 'Quality and Effectiveness in Probation Officers' Reports to Sentencers', (1995) 35 *B.J. Criminology* 188.
P. Gendreau et al., 'The Forgotten Issue in Effective Correctional Treatment Program Implementation', (1999) 43 *Int. J. of Offender Therapy and Comparative Criminology* 180.
E.M. Goldberg, J. Gibbons and I. Sinclair, *Problems, Tasks and Outcomes* (1985).
R. Harper and S. Hardy, 'An Evaluation of Motivational Interviewing as a Method of Intervention with Clients in a Probation Setting', (2000) 30 *B.J. Social Work* 393.
M. Lipsey, 'Juvenile Delinquency Treatment: a Meta-Analytic Enquiry into the Variability of Effects' in T. Cook, H. Cooper, D.S. Cordray, H. Hartman, L.V. Hedges, R.L. Light, T.A. Louis and F. Mosteller (eds), *Meta-Analysis for Explanation: a Casebook* (1992), 83.
M. Lipsey, 'Can Rehabilitative Programs Reduce the Recidivism of Young Juvenile Offenders' (1999) 6 *Virginia J. Social Policy & Law* 611.
M. Lipsey and D. Wilson, 'Effective Intervention for Serious Juvenile Offenders' in R. Loeber and D. Farrington (eds)., *Serious and Violent Juvenile Offenders: Risk Factors and Successful Interventions* (1998), 83.
D. Lipton et al., 'The Effectiveness of Cognitive-Behavioural Treatment Methods on Offender Recidivism', in J. McGuire (ed), *Offender Rehabilitation and Treatment* (2002), 79.
J. McGuire (ed), *What Works: Reducing Reoffending* (1995).
G. Mair, 'Standing at the Crossroads: What Works in Community Penalties?', paper presented to the National Conference for Probation Committee Members, Scarborough (1994).
G. Mair (ed), *What Matters in Probation* (2004).
J. McGuire, 'Integrating Findings from Research Reviews', in J. McGuire (ed), *Offender Rehabilitation and Treatment* (2002), 3.
J. McGuire, 'Maintaining Change: Converging Legal and Psychological Initiatives in a Therapeutic Jurisprudence Framework', (2003) 4 *Western Criminology Review* 108.
H. Miles and P. Raynor, *Community Sentences in Jersey: Risks, Needs and Rehabilitation* (2004).
W.R. Miller and S. Rollnick (eds), *Motivational Interviewing: Preparing People to Change Addictive Behaviour* (1992).
R. Morgan, 'Foreword,' *Her Majesty's Inspectorate of Probation Annual Report 2002-03* (2003).
National Probation Service, *Accredited Programmes Performance Report 2002-3* (2004).

P. Raynor, 'Evaluating Probation: the Rehabilitation of Effectiveness' in T. May and A. Vass (eds), *Working with Offenders* (1996), 242.

P. Raynor and M. Vanstone, *Straight Thinking on Probation (STOP): the Mid-Glamorgan Experiment* (1997).

P. Raynor and M. Vanstone, 'Straight Thinking on Probation: Evidence-based Practice and the Culture of Curiosity' in G. Bernfeld, D. Farrington and A. Leschied (eds), *Offender Rehabilitation in Practice* (2001).

P. Raynor, D. Smith and M Vanstone., *Effective Probation Practice* (1994).

S. Redondo et al., 'Crime Treatment in Europe: a Review of Outcome Studies', in J. McGuire (ed), *Offender Rehabilitation and Treatment* (2002), 131.

W.J. Reid and L. Epstein, *Task Centred Casework* (1972).

S. Rex and A. Matravers (eds), *Pro-Social Modelling and Legitimacy* (1998).

D. Robinson, *The Impact of Cognitive Skills Training on Post-Release Recidivism among Canadian Federal Offenders* (1995).

L. Sherman et al.. *Preventing Crime: What Works, What Doesn't, What's Promising* (1998).

C. Trotter, *The Supervision of Offenders – What Works?* (1993).

C. Trotter, *Focus on People: Effect Change* (2001).

C. Truax and R. Carkhuff, *Towards Effective Counselling and Psychotherapy* (1967).

1.4

Reaffirming Rehabilitation

FRANCIS T CULLEN AND KAREN E GILBERT

There can be little dispute that the rehabilitative ideal has been conveniently employed as a mask for inequities in the administration of criminal penalties and for brutality behind the walls of our penal institutions. However, the existence of inhumanity and injustice in the arena of crime control does not depend on the vitality of rehabilitation. Indeed, a punitive "just deserts" philosophy would serve the purposes of repressive forces equally well, if not with greater facility. It would thus seem prudent to exercise caution before concluding that the failure of the criminal justice system to sanction effectively and benevolently is intimately linked to the rehabilitative ideal and that the ills of the system will vanish as the influence of rehabilitation diminishes.

This line of reasoning is liberating in the sense that it prompts us to consider that the state's machinery of justice might well have been *more* and not less repressive had history not encouraged the evolution of the rehabilitative ideal. This suggests in turn that preoccupation with the misuses and limitations of treatment programmes has perhaps blinded many current-day liberals to the important benefits that have been or can be derived from popular belief in the notion that offenders should be saved and not simply punished. In this respect, the persistence of a strong rehabilitative ideology can be seen to function as a valuable resource for those seeking to move toward the liberal goal of introducing greater benevolence into the criminal justice system. Alternatively, we can begin to question whether the reform movement sponsored by the left will not be undermined should liberal faith in rehabilitation reach a complete demise. In this context, several major reasons are offered below for why we believe that liberals should reaffirm and not reject the correctional ideology of rehabilitation.

Admittedly, rehabilitation promises a payoff to society in the form of offenders transformed into law-abiding, productive citizens who no longer desire to victimize the public. Yet treatment ideology also conveys the strong message that this utilitarian outcome can only be achieved if society is willing to punish its captives humanely and to compensate offenders for the social disadvantages that have constrained them to undertake a life in crime. In contrast, the three competing

From FT Cullen and KE Gilbert, *Reaffirming Rehabilitation* (Cincinnati, OH, Anderson Publishing, 1982).

justifications of criminal sanctioning—deterrence, incapacitation, and retribution (or just deserts)—contain not even the pretense that the state has an obligation to do good for its charges. The only responsibility of the state is to inflict the pains that accompany the deprivation of liberty or of material resources (e.g., fines); whatever utility such practices engender flows only to society and not to its captives. It is difficult to imagine that reform efforts will be more humanizing if liberals willingly accept the premise that the state has no responsibility to do good, only to inflict pain.

Now it might be objected by liberal critics of rehabilitation that favouring desert as the rationale for criminal sanctioning does not mean adopting an uncaring orientation toward the welfare of offenders. The reform agenda of the justice model not only suggests that punishment be fitted to the crime and not the criminal, but also that those sent to prison be accorded an array of rights that will humanize their existence. The rehabilitative ideal, it is countered, justifies the benevolent treatment of the incarcerated but only as a means to achieving another end—the transformation of the criminal into the conforming. In contrast, the justice perspective argues for humanity as an end in and of itself, something that should not in any way be made to seem conditional on accomplishing the difficult task of changing the deep-seated criminogenic inclinations of offenders. As such, liberals should not rely on state-enforced rehabilitation to somehow lessen the rigours of imprisonment, but instead should campaign to win legal rights for convicts that directly bind the state to provide its captives with decent living conditions.

However, we must stand firm against efforts to promote the position that the justice model with its emphasis on rights should replace the rehabilitative ideal with its emphasis on caring as the major avenue of liberal reform. Support for the principles of just deserts and determinacy has only exacerbated the plight of offenders both before and after their incarceration. But there are additional dangers to undertaking a reform programme that abandons rehabilitation and seeks *exclusively* to broaden prisoner rights. More importantly, the realities of the day furnish little optimism that such a campaign would enjoy success. The promise of the rights perspective is based on the shaky assumption that more benevolence will occur if the relationship of the state to its deviants is fully adversarial and purged of its paternalistic dimensions. Instead of the government being entrusted to reform its charges through care, now offenders will have the comfort of being equipped with a new weapon—"rights"—that will serve them well in their battle against the state for a humane and justly administered correctional system.

The rights perspective is a two-edged sword. While rights ideally bind the state to abide by standards insuring a certain level of due process protection and acceptable penal living conditions, rights also establish the limits of the good that the state can be expected or obligated to provide. A rehabilitative ideology, in contrast, constantly pricks the conscience of the state with its assertion that the useful and moral goal of offender reformation can only be effected in a truly humane environment. Should treatment ideology be stripped away by liberal activists and the ascendancy of the rights model secured, it would thus create a situation in which criminal justice officials would remain largely immune from criticism as long as they "gave inmates their rights"—however few they may be at the time.

Those embracing the conservatives' call for "law and order" place immense faith in the premise that tough rather than humane justice is the answer to society's crime problem. In the political right's view, unlawful acts occur only when individuals have calculated that they are advantageous, and thus the public's victimization will only subside if criminal choices are made more costly. This can be best accomplished by sending more offenders away to prison for more extended and uncomfortable stays.

Liberals have traditionally attacked this logic on the grounds that repressive tactics do not touch upon the real social roots of crime and hence rarely succeed in even marginally reducing criminal involvement. Campaigns to heighten the harshness of existing criminal penalties— already notable for their severity—will only serve to fuel the problem of burgeoning prison populations and result in a further deterioration of penal living standards. The strategy of "getting tough" thus promises to have substantial costs, both in terms of the money wasted on the excessive use of incarceration and in terms of the inhumanity it shamefully introduces.

It is clear that proponents of the justice model share these intense liberal concerns over the appealing but illusory claims of those preaching law and order. However, their opposition to repressive crime control policies encounters difficulties because core assumptions of the justice model converge closely with those found in the paradigm for crime control espoused by conservatives. Both perspectives, for instance, argue that (1) offenders are responsible beings who freely choose to engage in crime; (2) regardless of the social injustices that may have prompted an individual to breach the law, the nature of the crime and not the nature of the circumstances surrounding a crime should regulate the severity of the sanction meted out; and (3) the punishment of offenders is deserved—that is, the state's infliction of pain for pain's sake is a positive good to be encouraged and not a likely evil to be discouraged. Admittedly, those wishing to "do justice" would contend that current sanctions are too harsh and that prison conditions should be made less rigorous. But having already agreed with conservatives that punishing criminals is the fully legitimate purpose of the criminal justice system, they are left with little basis on which to challenge the logic or moral justification of proposals to get tough.

In contrast, the ideology of rehabilitation disputes every facet of the conclusion that the constant escalation of punishment will mitigate the spectre of crime. To say that offenders are in need of rehabilitation is to reject the conservatives' notion that individuals, regardless of their position in the social order—whether black or white, rich or poor—exercise equal freedom in deciding whether to commit a crime. Instead, it is to reason that social and personal circumstances often constrain, if not compel, people to violate the law and unless efforts are made to enable offenders to escape these criminogenic constraints, little relief in the crime rate can be anticipated. Policies that insist on ignoring these realities by assuming a vengeful posture toward offenders promise to succeed only in fostering hardships that will, if anything, deepen the resentment that many inmates find difficult to suppress upon their release back into society.

Existing survey data suggest that rehabilitation persists as a prevailing ideology within the arena of criminal justice. This does not mean that treatment programmes in our prisons are flourishing and remain unthreatened by the pragmatics and punitiveness of our day. But it is to assert that the rehabilitative ideal and the benevolent potential it holds are deeply anchored within our correctional and broader cultural heritage. That is, rehabilitation constitutes an ongoing rationale that is accepted by or "makes sense to" the electorate as well as to criminal justice interest groups and policymakers. Consequently, it provides reformers with a valuable vocabulary with which to justify changes in policy and practice aimed at mitigating the harshness of criminal sanctions—such as the diversion of offenders into the community for "treatment" or the humanization of the prison to develop a more effective "therapeutic environment". Unlike direct appeals for inmate rights to humane and just living conditions that can be quickly dismissed as the mere coddling of the dangerous, liberal reforms undertaken in the name of rehabilitation have the advantage of resonating with accepted ideology and hence of retaining an air of legitimacy.

Liberal critics have supplied ample evidence to confirm their suspicions that state-enforced therapy has too frequently encouraged the unconscionable exploitation of society's captives. However, while the damages permitted by the corruption of the rehabilitative ideal should neither be denied nor casually swept aside, it would be misleading to idealize the "curious" but brutal punishments of "bygone days" and to ignore that reforms undertaken in the name of rehabilitation have been a crucial humanizing influence in the darker regions of the sanctioning process.

We have argued that rehabilitation is an ideology of benevolence that not only has precipitated reform movements that have tempered the harshness of punishments but also, as a persisting rationale for criminal sanctioning, retains the potential to be mobilized to justify future ameliorations of the correctional system. However, we are not insensitive to the abuse inherent in a system that links liberty to self-improvement but furnishes few means to secure this end. Under the practice of enforced therapy, the state ideally institutes comprehensive treatment programmes and in return demands that offenders take advantage of these opportunities and show signs of their willingness to conform. Liberal advocates of the justice model have argued that this link between being cured and being set free is coercive and must be broken. In place of enforced therapy which compels offenders to seek reform on the threat of longer stays behind bars, they assert that rehabilitation must become "voluntary".

We do not mean to imply that liberals should simply become resigned to accept state-enforced therapy as it is currently practiced—however despairing this alternative might seem—because it is the lesser of two evils. While we have argued for the advantages of trumpeting treatment ideology, we believe that it is equally important that liberal reform seeks to reaffirm rehabilitation in ways that negate its more abusive features. In this regard, a crucial flaw of state-enforced therapy is that it is imbalanced: the inmate has the obligation to be reformed in order to win release, but in the absence of sufficient pressure, the state has no real obligation to rehabilitate. It is thus incumbent upon liberals to attack this imbalance by exerting pressure on the state to fulfil more adequately its half of the bargain. This would involve undertaking a persistent campaign to expose the state's failure to meet its responsibilities and to institute policies that obligate correctional officials to supply inmates with the educational, occupational, and psychological services as well as the community programmes it has so long promised to deliver.

In short, we are proposing that liberals discard state-enforced therapy and embrace *state-obligated therapy* as an avenue of criminal justice reform. Since it has been tragically and repeatedly demonstrated that the state cannot be trusted through appeals to its good will to create uniformly meaningful treatment programmes, reforms aimed at obligating the state to rehabilitate must be sensitive to the need to restructure the prevailing interests in the correctional system that have long undermined the provision of treatment services to offenders.

1.5

Should Penal Rehabilitationism Be Revived?

ANDREW VON HIRSCH AND LISA MAHER

Penal rehabilitationism was in eclipse from the early 1970s to the middle of the 1980s. Treatment efforts seemed to offer only limited hope for success. Relying on treatment seemed also to lead to unjust results—for example, to excessive intrusion into offenders' lives in the name of cure.

Recently, however, there have been attempts at revival. Some researchers claim striking new successes in treatment techniques. These successes, Ted Palmer concludes in a 1991 survey of treatment methods, suggest that rehabilitative intervention has gained "increased moral and philosophical legitimacy", and that it is no longer the case that rehabilitation "should be secondary to punishment . . . whether for short- or long-term goals".[1] Some penologists—for example, Francis Cullen and Karen Gilbert—argue that a revival of the penal treatment ethic could help lead to a gentler and more caring penal system (see Selection 1.4 above). Interestingly, such arguments sometimes come from the ideological and political left—which had once been so critical of treatment-based punishments.

Reinstatement of a treatment ethic would raise a number of questions, however. How much more is known about the treatment of offenders now than was a few years ago? How often can treatment give us answers about how severely to sentence convicted offenders? Is treatment really as humane as it is made out to be? How fair is it to base the sentence on an offender's supposed rehabilitative needs? Rehabilitationism went into eclipse some years ago partly because it could not answer these questions satisfactorily. To what extent are better answers available today?

We approach these issues from heterogeneous viewpoints. One of us (von Hirsch) is a philosophical liberal and has long been an advocate of the desert model (see Selection 4.2 below). The other (Maher) has a feminist orientation and is sceptical of a retributive penal ethic. In our present discussion of the new rehabilitationism, we will not be assuming another articulated sentencing philosophy. What we agree on are the questions, not the answers . . .

This is an abbreviated and somewhat revised version of an essay that appeared in (1992) 11(1) *Criminal Justice Ethics* and also in the first edition of this volume.

Questions of Humaneness

Some new advocates of penal rehabilitationism, such as Cullen and Gilbert, stress its humaneness. Reemphasizing treatment, they assert, is humane because it is more caring: it looks to the needs of the offender, rather than seeking merely to punish or prevent (see Selection 1.4 above). Is it true that rehabilitation is concerned chiefly with the offender's own needs? That depends on whether one is speaking of social service or of measures aimed at recidivism prevention.

Social service is benevolent in intent, if not always in actual application: the aim is to help the offender lead a less deprived life. It can sometimes be achieved by fairly modest interventions: the unskilled offender, for example, might be taught skills that make him better able to cope. Providing these services is, we agree, desirable, although it is far from clear to what extent they reduce recidivism. The offender who is taught to read will not necessarily desist from crime as a result.

Treatment programmes, however, seldom aim merely at social service. The objective, instead, is recidivism prevention: protecting *us* against future depredations on the offender's part. To accomplish that crime-preventive aim, the intervention may well have to be more drastic. It will take more to get the drug-abusing robber to stop committing further robberies than to teach him or her a skill. (A review of current research suggests that the best indicator of successful drug treatment outcomes is length of time in treatment.)[2] To describe such strategies as intrinsically humane or caring is misleading: it confuses humanitarian concerns with treatment-as-crime-prevention.

Cullen and Gilbert admit this last point—that rehabilitation is aimed at recidivism prevention. They argue, however, that few people care much about being humane or benevolent to convicted criminals as an end in itself. Rehabilitationism, they argue, offers a more attractive reason—a crime-preventive one—for decent penal policies. There is something circular about this argument. It assumes that rehabilitative punishments *are* capable of reducing crime significantly, or at least that people will believe they are. And it assumes that treatment-oriented punishments are inherently gentle.

Are rehabilitative responses intrinsically less onerous? Not necessarily. Consider offenders convicted of crimes of intermediate or lesser gravity. A proportionate sanction for such offenses should be of no more than moderate severity. What of a rehabilitative response? That would depend on how much intervention, and how long, is required to alter the offender's criminal propensities—and to succeed, the intervention may have to be quite substantial (as in the just-noted case of drug treatments).

A rehabilitative ethic also tends to shift attention from the offender's actual criminal conduct to his or her lifestyle or personal characteristics. For example, the cultural presumption that women are less "rational" often results in their lawbreaking being perceived as symptomatic of social (or biological) pathology. Women found guilty of relatively minor offenses thus are readily subjected to substantial treatment interventions.[3] Concerns about offenders' attitudes may elicit intrusive responses aimed at "correcting" individual ways of thinking and feeling.

Cullen and Gilbert, and some other new rehabilitationists, argue for a return to a treatment model, on grounds that other models (e.g., desert) have led to harsh results. How supportable are such claims? The severity or leniency with which a given sentencing philosophy is implemented will vary with the manner of its implementation and the criminal justice politics of the jurisdiction involved. That legislatively mandated "deserved" penalties were harsh in California seems attributable mostly to the character of criminal justice politics in that state, and to the legislature's having set the specific penalties. A similar philosophy led to different (and less harsh) results in Minnesota and Oregon, where both the form of guidance and the criminal justice politics were different.[4] Similar considerations apply also to rehabilitationism. Were California to return to a rehabilitative ethos, it is far from certain—given California's politics—how "humane" or benevolent the results would be.

Some new rehabilitationists' rejection of other models, such as desert, is based on a socially critical perspective: how the rationale is likely to be implemented in a society characterized by race, class, and gender inequalities. Such a critique, however, cuts both ways: one would need also to consider how rehabilitationism might be implemented in such an unpropitious social setting. It is fallacious to reject desert, for example, because of how "they" might carry it out, and then urge a treatment ethic on the basis of how "we" might implement it—that is, on the assumption of a much more supportive social system and legal culture than exists today. If rehabilitation is kinder, gentler, or better because that is how good people would implement it, then please tell us when and how, in a society such as our own, the good people take over.

While the new rehabilitationists are taking such a critical stance, they might also apply it to the rehabilitative ethic itself. Historically, the treatment ethos supported (as Michel Foucault has pointed out)[5] expansion of official and expert power/ knowledge. If penal rehabilitationism is revived, what checks are there against a further proliferation of these powers?

Questions of Fairness

Criminal punishment, by its nature, condemns. The sanction not only visits deprivation but also conveys that the conduct is wrong and the offender to blame for having committed it. This holds whatever purpose is adopted for deciding sentences. Whether the sentence is based on the seriousness of the offender's crime or on his or her need for treatment, it will still imply something about the impropriety of the behaviour.

The basis for the principle of proportionality of sentence is the criminal sanction's censuring implications. Conduct that is more blameworthy—in the sense of involving greater harm and culpability—is to be punished (and thereby condemned) more severely; conduct that is less reprehensible is to be punished (and hence censured) more mildly (see Selection 4.4 below). Treatment, however, can seldom rely on criteria relating to the blame-worthiness of the conduct; whether the offender is amenable to a particular treatment depends, instead, on his or her social and personal characteristics. This creates the potential problem of fairness: one is using criminal punishment, a blame-conveying response, and yet deciding the intervention on the basis of those personal and social variables that have little to do with how reprehensible the behaviour is.

How serious is this problem? The answer depends, of course, on how much emphasis proportionality receives. A thoroughgoing desert conception would require the severity of the penal response to depend heavily on the degree of reprehensibleness of the conduct—thus limiting the scope for rehabilitative considerations to deciding among responses of comparable severity. Not everyone supports a desert model, and some new rehabilitationists say they reject it. But then, it needs to be explained what role, if any, the degree of blameworthiness of the conduct should play.

One possibility would be to give proportionality a limiting role: the seriousness of the criminal conduct would set upper and lower bounds on the quantum of punishment—within which rehabilitation could be invoked to fix the sentence (see Selection 4.5 below). That kind of solution requires one to specify how much weight its desert elements should have—that is, how narrow or broad the offence-based limits on the sentence should be. Here, one faces the familiar dilemma: the narrower that one sets those limits, the less room there would be for treatment considerations; whereas the wider one sets the limits, the more one needs to worry about seemingly disparate or disproportionate responses.

Another possibility would be to try to dispense with notions of proportionality altogether.[6] Such a strategy, however, would pose its own difficulties. It would, first, have to be explained how it is justifiable to employ punishment—a blaming institution—without regard to the blame-worthiness of the conduct. Or, if one proposes to eliminate the censuring element in punishment, it needs to be explained how this possibly may be accomplished. (The juvenile justice system, for example, long purported to convey no blame, but who was fooled?) Second, the absence of significant proportionality constraints could open the way for abuses of the kind that discredited the old rehabilitation—for example, long-term, open-ended intervention against those deemed to be in special need of treatment. (One thinks of the young car thief who was confined for sixteen years at Patuxent Institution in Maryland, because he refused to talk to the therapists.) One might hope that we are more sophisticated now about the therapeutic value of such interventions—but are such hopes enough without some *principled* restraint upon rehabilitative responses?

Finally, one could be more ambitious and think of replacing the criminal sanction with a wholly different set of measures. Nils Christie has argued that state punishment be supplanted by communitarian responses aimed at resolution of conflicts (see Selection 5.1 below). Some feminist writers have been exploring alternative conceptions of justice. This, however, would involve not just a change in sentencing philosophy, but a completely new set of institutions for responding to what is now termed criminal behaviour. One would have to consider whether, and how, these new institutions could afford protection against excessive, or seemingly unfair, intrusions. Whatever one thinks of such suggestions (and one of us has been sceptical of Christie's),[7] they constitute a different level of argument: one that concerns basic social and institutional change. These writers are not speaking, as the new rehabilitationists are, about retaining the criminal sanction and merely giving sentencing more of a treatment emphasis.

Concluding Thoughts

In offering the foregoing criticisms of the new rehabilitationists, we are not denying that treatment can have a legitimate role in a fair system of sanctions. How large that role should be depends not only on how much is known about treatment but also on what normative assumptions one makes—including those regarding proportionality.[8] Rehabilitation, however, cannot be the primary basis for deciding the sentence, nor can it be the rationale for supporting less harsh sanctions than we have today. If we want sanctions scaled down, as they surely should be, the main and explicitly stated reason for so doing should concern equity and the diminution of suffering.

The most dangerous temptation is to treat the treatment ethic as a kind of edifying fiction,[9] that if we only act as though we cared—and minister treatment to offenders as a sign of our caring—a more humane penal system will emerge. No serious inquiry would be needed, on this view, about the criteria for deciding what constitutes a humane penal system or about how a renewed treatment emphasis could achieve its intended effects or lead to reasonably just outcomes.

Such thinking is a recipe for failure. It is likely to cause the new treatment ethos to be rejected, once its specifics (or lack of them) are subject to critical scrutiny. And it could do no more good than the old, largely hortatory treatment ethic: create a facade of treatment behind which decision-makers act as they choose. Those who wish to revive penal rehabilitationism need to address the hard questions, including the ones we have tried to raise here.

Notes

1. Palmer, "The Effectiveness of Intervention: Recent Trends and Current Issues" (1991) 37 *Crime & Delinq.* 330, 342.
2. Anglin and Hser, "The Treatment of Drug Offenders", in *Drugs and Crime* (J. Wilson and M. Tonry, eds., 1990).

3. See, e.g., Pearson, "Women Defendants in Magistrates' Courts", (1976) 3 *British J. L. & Society* 265; Phillips and De Fleur, "Gender Ascription and the Stereotyping of Deviants", (1982) 20 *Criminology* 431.
4. A. von Hirsch, *Censure and Sanctions* (1993), ch. 10; see also Selection 5.2 below.
5. M. Foucault, *Discipline and Punish* (1977).
6. An attempt to develop an alternative penal theory that dispenses with desert principles is set forth in J. Braithwaite and P. Pettit, *Not Just Deserts* (1990), at 124–5. That theory, however, relies primarily on deterrence and incapacitation rather than treatment. In our view, the theory has manifold difficulties, discussed in von Hirsch and Ashworth, "Not Not Just Deserts: A Critique of Braithwaite and Pettit", (1992) 12 *Oxford J. Legal Studies* 83.
7. von Hirsch, "Review of N. Christie", (1982) 28 *Crime & Delinq.* 315. See also Selection 7.2 below.
8. For a limited suggested role of treatment considerations under a desert model, see Selection 1.6 below. For a somewhat expanded role under a "mixed" model, see N. Morris and M. Tonry, *Between Prison and Probation* (1990), ch. 7; see also Selection 6.5 below.
9. See Rothman, "Decarcerating Prisoners and Patients", (1973) 1 *Civil Liberties Rev.* 8.

2

Deterrence

As a sentencing objective, deterrence has a long history. This explains in part why deterrence is almost always included in statutory statements of the objectives of sentencing.[1] Moreover, the idea that awareness of possible punishment will inhibit offending carries great intuitive appeal. Most people are deterred from violating minor laws out of fear of the penalties that may ensue. Illegal parking is a good example. Drivers cruising around the city in search of a parking spot consider the probability that if they park illegally their vehicle will attract the attention of a traffic warden, as well as the magnitude of any parking fine. Similarly, compliance with income tax laws is affected by taxpayers' estimation of the likelihood that their return will be subject to a careful audit, with the possibility of a fine. Most people file their tax returns on time not out of a collective sense of duty to the state, but because they fear facing a hefty fine for late filing.

Members of the public often extrapolate from their own personal experience, and infer that deterrence—popularly associated with harsher sentences—is a good way of preventing a wide range of criminal conduct. This explains the strong public support for harsher sentencing as a response to rising crime rates.[2] In Selection 2.1, Doob and Webster discuss case studies of jurisdictions in which the introduction of harsher sentencing policies has had very limited effects upon levels of crime. As will be discussed later in this essay, the concept of deterrence, so omnipresent in everyday life, appears far less apparent once we move into the domain of more serious forms of delinquency.

Deterrence, as an aim of sentencing, is one of a number of consequentialist aims which share the goal of preventing crime. Other such objectives include rehabilitation and incapacitation. These aims share the idea that punishment is justified by reference to its crime-preventive consequences and are advanced within a utilitarian framework. According to this framework, the justification for punishment and the measure of punishment are found in a calculation of its utility compared with the attendant disutilities. Utilitarian theory has a range of complex principles which are best exemplified in Jeremy Bentham's ingenious and detailed writings on punishment, excerpts from which appear in Selection 2.2a, b and c.

Thus deterrence and the other consequentialist aims may be subsumed beneath the overall aim of the prevention of crime. This is, in turn, part of a set of social and political objectives for government. Crime prevention is regarded as an aim of the criminal justice system as a whole, including sentencing but also extending to other elements of the justice system, such as pre-trial detention, policing and community-based prevention projects. If we confine ourselves to sentencing, we find that the prevention of crime, as an aim, may be pursued by a number of different methods: rehabilitation, which seeks to alter offenders' attitudes so that they desist from crime (see Chapter 1 above); incapacitation, which seeks to restrain the offender from re-offending for a specified period (see Chapter 3 below); and possibly vindication, which favours the imposition of punishments sufficient to ensure that citizens aggrieved by offences accept the state's response and do not seek to take the law into their own hands.[3] That leaves special deterrence and general deterrence, the subjects of the readings in this chapter.

Special deterrence is aimed at the particular offender before the court; general deterrence seeks to influence the behaviour of other potential offenders in the population. Both objectives employ the mechanism of fear: the threat of punishment (or further punishment in the case of individual deterrence) acts as a deterrent. There are generally three components to deterrence: certainty, severity and celerity. Penalties will deter offenders (or potential offenders), so the theory posits, to the extent that they are relatively certain to be imposed, sufficiently severe as to prove aversive and are imposed sufficiently soon after the offence occurs. Since deterrence is a psychological mechanism, it is the offender's or potential offender's subjective expectations of these dimensions that matter, not the objective values (although the two may be correlated). A penalty may be very severe, and imposed swiftly upon conviction, but if potential offenders consider it to be highly unlikely to be imposed, there may be little deterrent effect. Moreover, while courts have considerable control over the severity of penalties, they have little or no influence over the certainty and celerity dimensions. And research has demonstrated that severity is the least important of the three dimensions in terms of preventing offending, as noted by Andrew von Hirsch and his collaborators in Selection 2.3. This underscores one of the limits of deterrence as a preventive strategy. While criminal penalties may be severe, they are seldom certain and almost never imposed in close temporal proximity to the crime.

The Development of Deterrence Theory

Deterrent theories reached the height of their influence in the first half of the nineteenth century, inspired by Bentham's many writings on penal policy. Doubts about the practicality of those theories and misgivings about the resulting severity of punishments grew in the second half of the century, although in England there were some who continued to advocate a strong policy of special deterrence toward persistent offenders. The growing interest in rehabilitation became evident toward the end of the nineteenth century and in the early twentieth century with the beginnings of probation, the American reformatory schools and the English borstal system.[4] However, deterrent assumptions continued to exert an influence on sentencing, and in the 1960s the Norwegian penologist Johannes Andenaes rekindled the theoretical debate on general deterrence.[5] Despite the accumulation of empirical research casting doubts upon the effectiveness of deterrence as a crime prevention strategy (see below), deterrence perspectives retain some influence on both sides of the Atlantic. Mandatory minimum sentences are often justified by reference to deterrence, and deterrence is still an issue discussed at length in the sentencing literature.[6]

Complexities of Deterrence

A sentencing system based on special deterrence would need to ensure that courts have detailed information on the character, circumstances and previous record of the particular offender, and would then require courts to calculate the sentence necessary to induce the particular offender to comply. Punishments might have to be increased substantially for persistent offenders,[7] even despite adherence to the limiting principle of frugality or parsimony (that the court should always impose the least punitive measure available, since punishment is an evil in itself). And such a system would give no appearance of consistency, since each sentence would be specially calculated so as to influence the specific offender before the court.

In the utilitarian philosophy of Bentham, the special or individual deterrent approach is placed second in order of priority to general deterrence, and relatively little is heard of individual deterrence as a specific aim of sentencing in the modern debate. As appears from Selection 2.2(a), Bentham regarded punishment as an evil because it involves the infliction of 'pain'. It can therefore be justified only if there are beneficial consequences to outweigh it, and these are to be found in the deterrence of persons from committing offences. It is assumed that citizens are rational persons and that a well-constructed sentencing system will in general present them with a sufficient disincentive to crime. A modern version of this, forming part of the economic theory of law, will be found in Selection 2.4, from the writings of Richard Posner.

The essence of the economic theory of criminal behaviour is that a person will commit a crime if the expected net benefit of doing so exceeds the expected net benefit of behaving lawfully. In calculating the expected net benefit of offending, account must be taken not only of the likely punishment but also of the probability of being detected and convicted. Economic theorists are not purely deterrence theorists: their concern is to promote economically efficient penalties, and this optimising approach leads them to take account of the costs of law enforcement as well as the probable costs and benefits from the offender's point of view. It may also lead economic theorists to conclude that, because of the differing impact of deterrence and/or the differing costs of enforcement, certain serious crimes should be punished less severely than certain less serious offences. This is regarded as problematic by some economic theorists, including the British writer David Pyle, who recognises that one consequence is that:

> the criminal justice system might produce strange incentives, inducing individuals to
> switch from less serious to more serious crimes. It may be necessary to structure pun-

ishments so that such an incentive cannot exist. In other words, an element of marginal deterrence should be retained.[8]

How convincingly does Posner deal with this issue in Selection 2.4? Pyle goes on to argue that sentences for attempted crimes should generally be set at the same level as for completed crimes, except in cases where the offender voluntarily abandons the attempt before completion, and that punishments should be escalated for repeat offenders. But there remain general questions about both the theoretical reasoning on which the economic approach to punishment is based and the empirical foundations that are claimed for it.

Normative Objections to Deterrent Sentencing

What are the normative objections to general deterrence as a sentencing policy? A major objection has been that, since its distinctive aim and method is to create fear of punishment in other persons, it may sometimes require the punishment of an innocent person or the excessive punishment of an offender in order to achieve this greater social effect. The calculation may be either (i) 'punish someone now in order to prevent a number of probable future crimes', the sacrifice of an innocent person being regarded as justified by reference to the number of probable future victims who are thereby spared; or (ii) 'punish this offender with exceptional severity in order to prevent a number of probable future crimes', the excessive punishment being likewise regarded as justified by reference to the number of probable future victims who may be spared. In both instances the avoidance of a greater future harm (to victims of probable future offences) is taken to justify the infliction of present harm which the punishment represents.

Deterrence theorists may attempt to avoid the reproach that they accept the punishment of the innocent, by arguing that such practices would not be permitted because they are not 'punishment'. This, however, is unconvincing, because utilitarian theories do not include a principle for the distribution of punishment which restricts it to those properly convicted of an offence. The objection is often expressed by recalling Kant's injunction that a person should be treated as an end in himself, and never only as a means, and it is important to notice the two elements of this formulation. One is that to regard citizens merely as numbers to be aggregated in an overall social calculation is to show no respect for the moral worth and the autonomy of each individual. This, then, is the liberal objection based on respect for individual autonomy and the separateness of persons.[9]

The other element is that citizens should not be used *merely* as a means to an end—the limitation 'merely' draws attention to the fact that punishment is, to some extent, a means to a social end. It is justified insofar as modern societies seem incapable of responding adequately to harmful behaviour without resort to punishment. The point here is that the punishment of any given individual cannot be justified solely by reference to wider social benefits. A theory of punishment should include a link with both the general social justification for the institution of punishment and the principles of distribution which restrict its imposition to properly convicted offenders and which place limits on the amount of punishment.[10]

What of the justification for 'exemplary sentences', imposing an unusually severe sentence on an individual offender for a given type of offence, in the hope of deterring potential imitators? Bentham would consider the justification for such a sentence by reference to its wider social effects—for example, on public respect for the law—but it is by no means certain that he would rule out such sentences, especially in a situation where there is apparent public concern about a particular kind of criminal behaviour. The objection to exemplary sentences is that the quantum of a convicted offender's punishment is influenced by the expected future conduct of other persons, not exclusively determined by his own past behaviour. This objection reaches into the very foundations of deterrence theory, for it raises the question whether punishments should in some way be proportional to offences. It will be seen from Bentham's rules 2 and 3, in Selection 2.2(b), that the gravity of the type of offence is indeed relevant to the amount of punishment which may be justified to restrain it. This, however, does not sustain the claim that utilitarians can treat proportionality as a limiting principle on the amount of punishment. For one thing, Bentham is referring to proportionality between the punishment and probable future offences rather than the particular crime for which this offender is now being sentenced. And, for another thing, each of Bentham's 'rules' is merely one of several factors relevant to the overall utilitarian calculation: the effect of the proportionality principle may be smothered by the influence of one or more of the other rules. Thus, if the general deterrence theorist has reason to anticipate an increase in a particular type of offence, this would seem to justify the imposition of an unusually high sentence on a particular offender as an 'example' to potential offenders and in order to deter them.

How Effective is Deterrence as a Crime Prevention Strategy?

Leaving aside the problems created by 'punishing' the innocent and by 'exemplary' sentences, how effective is general deterrence in achieving its goal of crime prevention? There are various explanations for the difficulties which criminologists have experienced in conducting and interpreting general deterrence research. One is that it is hard to discover how often the threat of legal punishment (rather than any other motivation) turns people away from offending, since its successful operation means that those concerned are not readily discoverable in most instances. Another is that it is hard to find out about 'marginal deterrence', that is, how much extra deterrence is achieved by increasing the severity of sanctions. This is an issue of crucial importance if sentence levels are to be set on deterrence grounds. Moreover, in respect of both these points, a statistical association which appears to establish cause and effect, such as the decrease of an offence rate following an increase in the penalty, may have an entirely different explanation: complex research strategies would need to attempt to eliminate such possibilities.[11]

A related difficulty is that criminological research has not always been designed to separate deterrent effects from the results of other influences such as situational factors. Surveys of the available research have shown that there are relatively few studies which have genuinely identified the existence and extent of general deterrent effects flowing from the legal penalty, and that it would be unsafe to generalise from these specific studies to broad policy prescriptions. Yet this does not mean that general deterrent effects never occur; the difficulty has been in establishing where and why deterrence is strongest. Only the most extreme sanctions are likely to have deterrent effects which are easily detectable. In less extreme situations the main contribution of criminological research has been to point out the pitfalls of simple-looking explanations and expectations of human behaviour.

As noted, the logic of deterrence has a strong intuitive appeal, but a close study of the requirements of general deterrence and of the available empirical evidence suggests that the simple logic cannot be translated easily into social situations. A great deal of research has now accumulated on the effectiveness of deterrence, and one lesson which emerges from this body of work is that there are important limitations on the ability of criminal sentencing to prevent crime. Significant reductions in the aggregate crime rate are unlikely to be achieved by even a very punitive sentencing strategy.[12] Several reasons may be advanced to explain this conclusion.

First, the relative effectiveness of general deterrent strategies may vary from one context to another. Secondly, most offenders do not consider the likelihood of conviction or the severity of punishment when contemplating the commission of an offence. Thirdly, it is wrong to assume that the penalty for an offence is always or often the most powerful influence on people's behaviour. Fourthly, the phenomenon of case attrition means that only a very small percentage of all offenders appear for sentencing. This reality severely limits the ability of the sentencing process to have a great effect on crime rates, whether through deterrence or any other utilitarian objectives. Let us examine these four propositions in order.

The first proposition is that deterrence may only be effective in certain situations.[13] This is not simply a repetition of the point that few studies have detected a significant general deterrent effect. Rather, it is an assertion that the conditions must be favourable if general deterrence is to operate. This refers, moreover, less to the actual or objective conditions in the world than to the conditions as potential offenders believe them to be: deterrence must work through the mind of the actor, and so the reasoning should always be in terms of what potential offenders believe. Thus, the risk of detection for the crime must not be thought so low as to make the threat of the penalty seem too remote and thus readily discounted. The penalty which is meant to constitute the deterrent must be publicised adequately, so that it comes to the attention of potential offenders. That penalty must also be perceived as a deterrent—which may rarely be a problem, but there are some forms of sentence (such as the suspended sentence) which may be intended as a deterrent but regarded by potential offenders as a 'soft option'.

The second proposition is that those who may commit the particular type of offence must be likely to consider the risks rationally: one study of English burglars found that they rarely thought they would be caught for the present offence, that they were not worried about the consequences of being caught (either because the expected sentence was accepted as an 'occupational hazard' or because they refused to think about the consequences at all) and that the rewards of the burglary were rarely known in advance.[14] Offenders can only be deterred if they are aware of the penalties and believe that these penalties will be imposed. A considerable body of literature suggests that only the most experienced recidivists have an accurate idea of the magnitude of penalties, or the probability that these penalties will be imposed. As researchers such as Gary Kleck have recently demonstrated, the results of systematic research show that there is generally no correlation between perceptions of punishment levels and actual levels of punishment.[15] In order for deterrence to succeed, subjective and objective levels of punishment must be strongly related. These findings do not exclude the possibility that others were deterred, although they do shed some light on the thought processes of those for whom deterrence appears not to have worked and therefore suggest limits to its efficacy.

One might expect that for impulsive crimes the likelihood of rational calculation is even lower, while for some organised fraud or drugs offences the likelihood might be high. One study of weapon choice for armed robbery claims to have identified the operation of marginal deterrence, in that higher penalties deter many robbers from carrying firearms.[16] Indeed, most offending reflects spontaneous decisions taken by individuals with little regard for future consequences. In research by Shover, for example, even persistent thieves who might be expected to contemplate the likelihood of future punishment gave little or no thought to the possibility of punishment when they were considering whether and when to offend.[17] In addition, offenders' inclination to consider the legal consequences of their conduct is often impaired by alcohol, drugs or extreme emotional states. Crime is in this sense the opposite of a professional career in which people surrender much of their time and freedom in training towards a distant qualification which will generate large rewards. Thus, general deterrence might be expected to work selectively, and only where the conditions (as perceived by potential offenders) favour it. In Selection 2.5, Doob and Webster summarise and discuss research which explores the question of why offenders do not 'act as the economists say that they should'.

The third proposition amounts to another attack upon, or qualification of, reasoning from 'common experience' or 'common sense'. One of the most frequent fallacies in popular discussions of deterrence is to assume that the nature and magnitude of the probable penalty are the only or necessarily the most powerful influence on a person's behaviour. There is evidence that other indirect consequences of conviction, particularly what the offender's family would think and the probability of losing one's job, exert a more powerful effect. While fear of punishment may play a role in ensuring compliance with the law, for most people the magnitude of a legal penalty is a minor factor in determining, for example, whether they rob a bank, or even steal from a shop. This shows the fragility of assuming that the criminal justice system and its penalty scale will be the most powerful motivating force in people's behaviour (cf Posner in Selection 2.4).

The final point to be made about the effectiveness of deterrence raises a general concern about the ability of the sentencing process to have a significant impact on the overall crime rate. There is a very high attrition rate in the criminal process. Only a small minority of all crimes is reported to the police, and cases drop out of the system after the first report. The consequence is that courts impose a sentence upon only about 2% of all offenders in any given year.[18] This means that, whatever the sentence the court imposes on a specific offender in the hope of deterring him or her, it will affect just a small percentage of the total offender population. Of course, deterrence might still work if the sentences actually imposed are very severe and come to the attention of the wider public, but, as we have noted, few offenders or potential offenders are aware of the severity of sentences imposed.

Deterrent Power of the Criminal Justice System

On one point, however, there is strong empirical evidence of the effectiveness of general deterrence. This is that the absence of any punishment structure (police, courts and sentences) substantially reduces compliance with the law. The police strikes in Melbourne, Australia in 1918 and in Liverpool, England in 1919 show that overall offence rates increase significantly in the absence of such a structure in practice; the imprisonment of the Danish police force in 1944 had similar consequences. Thus, one fundamental justification for the institution of state punishment is that it exerts this overall restraining effect: it deters many offences that would have been committed in the absence of such institution. So an advocate of proportionate sanctions—who seeks fairer principles for the distribution of punishments and the calculation of punishments than general deterrence can offer—may still accept general deterrence as an integral part of the justification for why the institution of legal punishment should exist.[19]

JVR

AA

Notes

1. Thus both general and specific deterrence appear in the statutory statement of purpose of sentencing adults in Canada (s 718(b) of the Criminal Code). They are also in the list of sentencing objectives placed on a statutory footing in England and Wales in 2003 (s 142(1)(b)). However, it is worth noting that when the Canadian Parliament legislated the sentencing objectives of youth courts, deterrence was conspicuous by its absence. This difference reflected recognition by the Canadian Parliament that deterrence was not an effective way of preventing crime by young people. See Corrado, R, Gronsdahl, K, MacAlister, D and Cohen, I, (2006) 'Should Deterrence be a Sentencing Principle under the Youth Criminal Justice Act?' 85 *Canadian Bar Review* 539.
2. See Roberts, JV and Hough, M, (2005) *Understanding Public Attitudes to Criminal Justice* (Maidenhead, Open University Press).
3. On the little-discussed concept of 'vindicative satisfaction', see Bentham, J, (1789) *Introduction to the Principles of Morals and Legislation*, ch 13, para 1; Cross, Sir R, (1980) *The English Sentencing System*, 3rd edn (London, Butterworth) 128–30 and 139–40. See also the discussion of 'Montero's aim' by Walker, N, (1980) *Punishment, Danger, and Stigma* (Oxford, Blackwell) ch 1.
4. For detailed analysis of trends in penal practice and theory in nineteenth century England, see Radzinowicz, L and Hood, R, (1985) *History of English Criminal Law: Volume 5. The Emergence of Penal Policy* (London, Stevens).
5. See, eg 'The General Preventive Effects of Punishment' (1966) 114 *University of Pennsylvania Law Review* 949, and 'The Morality of Deterrence' (1970) 37 *University of Chicago Law Review* 649.
6. Eg Wilson, JQ, (1975) *Thinking about Crime*, 1st edn (New York, Basic Books (2nd edn 1983, New York, Vintage Books); Walker, above n 3; Walker, N, (1996) *Sentencing: Theory, Law and Practice* (2nd ed, London, Butterworth) ch 7.
7. For a nineteenth-century English approach of this kind, see the discussion of Barwick Baker's ideas by Radzinowicz and Hood, above n 4, ch 23.
8. Pyle, DJ, (1995) *Cutting the Costs of Crime: the Economics of Crime and Criminal Justice* (London, Institute of Economic Affairs) 36.
9. See Morris, H, (1968) 'Persons and Punishment' 52 *The Monist* 475.
10. See Hart, HLA, (1968) *Punishment and Responsibility* (Oxford, Oxford University Press) ch 1.
11. For a vivid example, see Appendix 6 to the Report of the Royal Commission on Capital Punishment (1953), excerpted in the first edition of this book at 75–76.
12. The reverse of this proposition further sustains the view that penalty levels have little impact on aggregate crime rates. Research examining punitiveness and crime trends in a number of jurisdictions has demonstrated no relationship between severity of sentencing and crime rates; see, eg Kury, H, Ferdinand, T and Obergfell-Fuchs, J, (2003) 'Does Severe Punishment Mean Less Criminality?' 13 *International Criminal Justice Review* 110; Ouimet, M, (2002) 'Explaining the American and Canadian Crime "Drop" in the 1990s' 44 *Canadian Journal of Criminology* 33.
13. A similar problem besets rehabilitation when promoted as a general sentencing objective. Successful rehabilitation depends on a close fit between the nature of the intervention and the risk and needs of the individual offender. What works for one person may be ineffective or even counter-productive for another; this empirical reality undermines the ability of rehabilitation to simultaneously promote desistance and consistency of sentencing practices.

14. Bennett, T and Wright, R, (1984) *Burglars on Burglary: Prevention and the Offender* (Aldershot, Gower) chs 5 and 6.
15. Kleck, G, (2003) 'Constricted Rationality and the Limits of General Deterrence' in T Blomberg and S Cohen (eds), *Punishment and Social Control* (New York, Aldine de Gruyter).
16. Harding, R, (1990) 'Rational-choice Gun Use in Armed Robbery: The Likely Deterrent Effect on Gun Use of Mandatory Additional Imprisonment' 1 *Criminal Law Forum* 427.
17. See Shover, N, (1996) *Great Pretenders: Pursuits and Careers of Persistent Thieves* (Boulder, CO, Westview Press).
18. See Barclay, G and Tavares, C (eds), (1999) *Information on the Criminal Justice System in England and Wales*, Digest 4 (London, Home Office, Research, Development and Statistics Directorate).
19. See further von Hirsch, A, (1993) *Censure and Sanctions* (Oxford, Clarendon Press) ch 2.

Further Reading

Andenaes, J (1974) Punishment and Deterrence (Ann Arbor, University of Michigan Press).

Doob, AN and Webster, C, (2003) 'Sentence Severity and Crime: Accepting the Null Hypothesis' in M Tonry (ed), *Crime and Justice: A Review of Research* (Chicago, University of Chicago Press).

Gibbs, J, (1975) *Crime, Punishment and Deterrence* (London, Elsevier).

Klepper, S and Nagin, D, (1989) 'The deterrent effect of perceived certainty and severity of punishment revisited' 27 *Criminology* 721.

Nagin, D, (1998) 'Criminal deterrence research at the outset of the twenty-first century' in M Tonry and N Morris (eds), *Crime and Justice: An Annual Review of Research* (Chicago, IL, University of Chicago Press).

Nagin, D and Pogarsky, G, (2001) 'Integrating Celerity, Impulsivity, and Extralegal Sanction Threats into a Model of General Deterrence: Theory and Evidence' 39 *Criminology* 865.

von Hirsch, A, Bottoms, A, Burney, E and Wikstrom, P-O, (1999) *Criminal Deterrence and Sentence Severity* (Oxford, Hart Publishing).

Wikstrom, P-O, (2008) 'Deterrence and Deterrence Experiences: Preventing Crime Through the Threat of Punishment' in S Shoham, O Beck and M Kett (eds), *International Handbook of Penology and Criminal Justice* (London, Taylor & Francis).

Wright, B, Caspi, T, Moffitt, T and Paternoster, R, (2004) 'Does the Perceived Risk of Punishment Deter Criminally Prone Individuals? Rational Choice, Self-control and Crime' 41 *Journal of Research in Crime and Delinquency* 180.

Zimring, F and Hawkins, G, (1973) *Deterrence: The Legal Threat in Crime Control* (Chicago, IL, University of Chicago Press).

2.1

Studies of the Impact of New Harsh Sentencing Regimes

AN DOOB AND CM WEBSTER

Research has examined the effects of harsh sentencing policies. For instance, a study by Wicharaya (1995) assesses changes in sentencing law that took place in forty-five states from 1959 to 1987. Using time-series techniques, Wicharaya examined the impact of these alterations in sentencing structure across jurisdictions, rather than concentrating on a single or a small number of states. These changes generally fall into the category of "get tough on crime" (1995, p. 161), and include such regimes as mandatory or presumptive sentences and mandatory minimum sentences. The premise of most of these reforms was to make prison sentences more certain or longer. Not surprisingly, many were undermined in the court process in various ways. Nevertheless, because they typically came into force as a result of high-profile political processes and appear—at least on the surface—to meet the criteria of increasing the perception that harsh sentences would flow from a conviction for one of the relevant offenses, they can be seen as forming a reasonable basis for expecting deterrence effects. These results show the importance of replication. Indeed, a focus on a single state might have led to a conclusion that would not describe the chaotic nature of the findings. Wicharaya examined data from forty-five states on four violent crimes. His findings are summarized in table 5.

Wicharaya notes that the relationship between sentencing reform and these offenses is mixed. Changes are as likely to be in one direction as the other. One can hardly suggest that the data in table 5 support the notion that increased severity of sentences is associated with a decline in crime. In his own words, "Sentencing reforms have not yet proved to be efficacious anticrime measures" (1995, p. 161).

Wicharaya (1995) subsequently extends this analysis by employing a more elaborate statistical approach to these same data—a "pooled time series" technique—that allows a generalizable conclusion (across states) on the effects of sentencing reforms. The author summarizes these findings as again showing "no crime reduction effects of the reform on any crime type nationwide. Both murder and robbery rates remain unaffected in some states, but increased significantly in the remaining part of the country. Similarly, both rape and aggravated assault rates increased significantly throughout the United States. The evidence of no deterrent

From M Tonry (ed), *Crime and Justice: A Review of Research*, vol 30 (Chicago, IL, University of Chicago Press, 2003).

TABLE 5

Number of States in Which Changes in Their Crime Rates (Following the Introduction of New Sentencing Regimes) Are Consistent/Inconsistent with a
Deterrent Effect of Harsher Sanctions

	No. of States with a Change in the Direction Expected by Deterrence Theory (Decline in Crime)		No. of States with a Change in the Direction Opposite to That Expected by Deterrence Theory (Increase in Crime)		
CrimeType	Significant Decline	Nonsigni-ficant Decline	Significant Increase	Nonsigni-ficant Increase	Total No. of States
Murder	4	14	7	20	45
Rape	4	10	6	25	45
Robbery	4	13	7	21	45
Assault	6	IS	7	17	45

Source: Data adapted from Wicharaya 1995, p. 162, table 7.2.

effects is consistent across all crime types" (1995, pp. 150–51). The author is even
more definitive in his conclusions later in the paper: "Violent crime rates were not
deterred by the new sentencing policies" (1995, p. 164). It should be noted that
another part of this study shows that harsh sentencing regimes were typically not
successfully (or consistently) implemented. A true believer in deterrence could
argue that this study does not constitute a fair test of deterrence. However, to argue
this is to ignore one important fact: deterrence, by definition, is a perceptual theory.
Hence, it is perception that counts. The publicized legal changes did not affect the
crimes upon which the author focused.

Beyond the U.S. reality, mandatory sentences in the form of three-strikes legislation also found their way to Australia in the 1990s (Morgan 2000). Although
mandatory (prison) sentences came under fire in early 2000 when the predictable
types of cases occurred and were publicized (e.g., mandatory imprisonment for a
yo-yo thief, a year in prison for an aboriginal man who stole a towel from a
washing line to use as a blanket, and a prison sentence for a one-legged pensioner
who damaged a hotel fence), the laws in western Australia and the Northern
Territory were written broadly enough to ensure that these kinds of cases would
result in a prison sentence.

The rationales given for mandatory sentencing laws in Australia (as elsewhere)
have varied over time. General deterrence constituted one justification. However,
the evidence as summarized by Morgan (2000) showed that crime rates were

unaffected by mandatory minimums. Notwithstanding the fact that the laws unequivocally increased the likelihood of a prison sentence and received considerable publicity (providing optimal conditions for deterrence effects), there is "compelling evidence" that the laws did not achieve a deterrent effect (Morgan 2000, p. 172). The author notes that governments "have effectively conceded that mandatory sentences have no deterrent effect, and that there is a need for judicial discretion and for the more vigorous use of diversionary schemes and alternative strategies" (2000, p. 182).

Further evidence of a lack of deterrent effects of new harsh sentencing laws comes from a careful analysis by Kovandzic (1999) of the impact of Florida's habitual offender law. While often justified as an effective way of incapacitating high-rate offenders, this type of legislation is also sometimes justified in terms of deterrence. Kovandzic examined the deterrent effects of the additional amount of prison time imposed by the habitual offender law at a county level. His findings— using data from all Florida counties for a seventeen-year period (1981–97)—would not bring cheer to those who think that crime can easily be legislated away. As the author states, "The results suggest that incarcerating [habitual offenders] for extended periods of time has no significant impact on short or long-term crime rates" (1999, p. viii).

Notwithstanding this overall assessment, Kovandzic did find what he describes as "weak empirical support for the [habitual offender] law effectiveness hypothesis in high population counties, but the reasons for the significant results remain ambiguous" (1999, p. 69). In the face of these findings, this author recommends that these significant effects be seen in the context of the existence of other effects in the opposite direction from that which would be expected (1999, pp. 68–69). In addition, there is no theoretical reason to expect effects in one size county but not another. One may add another argument in favor of largely dismissing this particular finding. The problem with large studies such as this one (and others) in which numerous statistical tests are being carried out is that some of them are going to be "significant" simply by chance. Kovandzic concludes that the results of this study should not be used to support the view that there is a deterrent impact of the legislation: "Of the 720 crime [analyses performed], no [measures—habitual offender prison months, or the extra months that habitual offenders received in that county] show consistent effects across crime types, varying model specifications, or samples. The few lags that are significant and negative (48) [more imprisonment, less crime] are not consistent with any theory of deterrent or incapacitative effects and are usually balanced by positive, significant associations (24)" (1999, p. 72).

References

Kovandzic, T (1999) 'Crime Prevention through Selective Incapacitation: An Empirical Assessment of Florida's Habitual Offender Law', PhD Dissertation, School of Criminology and Criminal Justice, Florida State University.

Morgan, N (2000) 'Mandatory Sentences in Australia: Where have we been and where are we going?' 24 *Criminal Law Journal* 164.

Wicharaya, T (1995) *Simple Theory, Hard Reality: The Impact of Sentencing Reforms on Courts, Prisons, and Crime* (Albany, NY, State University of New York Press).

2.2

Punishment and Deterrence

JEREMY BENTHAM

2.2(a) The Aims of Punishment

When any act has been committed which is followed, or threatens to be followed, by such effects as a provident legislator would be anxious to prevent, two wishes naturally and immediately suggest themselves to his mind: first, to obviate the danger of the like mischief in future: secondly, to compensate the mischief that has already been done.

The mischief likely to ensue from acts of the like kind may arise from either of two sources—either the conduct of the party himself who has been the author of the mischief already done, or the conduct of such other persons as may have adequate motives and sufficient opportunities to do the like.

Hence the prevention of offences divides itself into two branches: *particular prevention*, which applies to the delinquent himself; and *general prevention*, which is applicable to all the members of the community without exception.

Pain and pleasure are the great springs of human action. When a man perceives or supposes pain to be the consequence of an act, he is acted upon in such a manner as tends, with a certain force, to withdraw him, as it were, from the commission of that act. If the apparent magnitude of that pain be greater than the apparent magnitude of the pleasure or good he expects to be the consequence of the act, he will be absolutely prevented from performing it. The mischief which would have ensued from the act, if performed, will also by that means be prevented.

With respect to a given individual, the recurrence of an offence may be provided against in three ways:

1. By taking from him the physical power of offending.
2. By taking away the desire of offending.
3. By making him afraid of offending.

In the first case, the individual can no more commit the offence; in the second, he

From 'The Principles of Penal Law', in J Bowring (ed), *The Works of Jeremy Bentham* (1838–43) 396.

no longer desires to commit it; in the third, he may still wish to commit it, but he no longer dares to do it. In the first case, there is a physical incapacity; in the second, a moral reformation; in the third, there is intimidation or terror of the law.

General prevention is effected by the denunciation of punishment, and by its application, which, according to the common expression, *serves for an example*. The punishment suffered by the offender presents to every one an example of what he himself will have to suffer, if he is guilty of the same offence.

General prevention ought to be the chief end of punishment, as it is its real justification. If we could consider an offence which has been committed as an isolated fact, the like of which would never recur, punishment would be useless. It would be only adding one evil to another. But when we consider that an unpunished crime leaves the path of crime open, not only to the same delinquent, but also to all those who may have the same motives and opportunities for entering upon it, we perceive that the punishment inflicted on the individual becomes a source of security to all. That punishment which, considered in itself, appeared base and repugnant to all generous sentiments, is elevated to the first rank of benefits, when it is regarded not as an act of wrath or of vengeance against a guilty or unfortunate individual who has given way to mischievous inclinations, but as an indispensable sacrifice to the common safety.

2.2(b) The Quantum of Punishment

Rule 1. The first object, it has been seen, is to prevent, in as far as it is worth while, all sorts of offences; therefore,

The value of the punishment must not be less in any case than what is sufficient to outweigh that of the profit of the offence.

If it be, the offence (unless some other considerations, independent of the punishment, should intervene and operate efficaciously in the character of tutelary motives) will be sure to be committed notwithstanding: the whole lot of punishment will be thrown away: it will be altogether *inefficacious*.

The above rule has been often objected to, on account of its seeming harshness: but this can only have happened for want of its being properly understood. The strength of the temptation, *ceteris paribus*, is as the profit of the offence: the quantum of the punishment must rise with the profit of the offence: *ceteris paribus*, it must therefore rise with the strength of the temptation. This there is no disputing. True it is that the stronger the temptation, the less conclusive is the indication which the act of delinquency affords of the depravity of the offender's disposition. So far then as the absence of any aggravation, arising from extraor-

From *An Introduction to the Principles of Morals and Legislation* (1789) ch 14.

dinary depravity of disposition, may operate, or at the utmost, so far as the presence of a ground of extenuation, resulting from the innocence or beneficence of the offender's disposition, can operate, the strength of the temptation may operate in abatement of the demand for punishment. But it can never operate so far as to indicate the propriety of making the punishment ineffectual, which it is sure to be when brought below the level of the apparent profit of the offence.

The partial benevolence which should prevail for the reduction of it below this level, would counteract as well those purposes which such a motive would actually have in view, as those more extensive purposes which benevolence ought to have in view: it would be cruelty not only to the public, but to the very persons in whose behalf it pleads: in its effects, I mean, however opposite in its intention. Cruelty to the public, that is cruelty to the innocent, by suffering them, for want of an adequate protection, to lie exposed to the mischief of the offence: cruelty even to the offender himself, by punishing him to no purpose, and without the chance of compassing that beneficial end, by which alone the introduction of the evil of punishment is to be justified.

Rule 2. But whether a given offence shall be prevented in a given degree by a given quantity of punishment, is never any thing better than a chance; for the purchasing of which, whatever punishment is employed, is so much expended in advance. However, for the sake of giving it the better chance of outweighing the profit of the offence,

The greater the mischief of the offence, the greater is the expense, which it may be worth while to be at, in the way of punishment.

Rule 3. The next object is, to induce a man to choose always the least mischievous of two offences; therefore

Where two offences come in competition, the punishment for the greater offence must be sufficient to induce a man to prefer the less.

Rule 4. When a man has resolved upon a particular offence, the next object is, to induce him to do no more mischief than what is necessary for his purpose: therefore

The punishment should be adjusted in such manner to each particular offence, that for every part of the mischief there may be a motive to restrain the offender from giving birth to it.

Rule 5. The last object is, whatever mischief is guarded against, to guard against it at as cheap a rate as possible: therefore

The punishment ought in no case to be more than what is necessary to bring it into conformity with the rules here given.

Rule 6. It is further to be observed, that owing to the different manners and degrees in which persons under different circumstances are affected by the same exciting cause, a punishment which is the same in name will not always either really produce, or even so much as appear to others to produce, in two different persons the same degree of pain: therefore

That the quantity actually inflicted on each individual offender may correspond to the quantity intended for similar offenders in general, the several circumstances influencing sensibility ought always to be taken into account.

Of the above rules of proportion, the four first, we may perceive, serve to mark out the limits on the side of diminution; the limits *below* which a punishment ought not to be *diminished*: the fifth, the limits on the side of increase; the limits *above* which it ought not to be *increased*. The five first are calculated to serve as guides to the legislator: the sixth is calculated, in some measure, indeed, for the same purpose; but principally for guiding the judge in his endeavours to conform, on both sides, to the intentions of the legislator.

2.2(c) Cases Where Punishment is Unjustified

All punishment is mischief: all punishment in itself is evil. Upon the principle of utility, if it ought at all to be admitted, it ought only to be admitted in as far as it promises to exclude some greater evil.

It is plain, therefore, that in the following cases punishment ought not to be inflicted.

1. Where it is *groundless*: where there is no mischief for it to prevent: the act not being mischievous upon the whole.
2. Where it must be *inefficacious*: where it cannot act so as to prevent the mischief.
3. Where it is *unprofitable*, or too *expensive*: where the mischief it would produce would be greater than what it prevented.
4. Where it is *needless*: where the mischief may be prevented, or cease of itself, without it: that is, at a cheaper rate.

From *An Introduction to the Principles of Morals and Legislation* (1789) ch 13.

2.3

Deterrent Sentencing as a Crime Prevention Strategy

ANDREW VON HIRSCH, ANTHONY E BOTTOMS, ELIZABETH BURNEY AND
PER-OLOT WIKSTRÖM

10.1. The Present State of the Research

The present state of deterrence research may be briefly summarized as follows.

(1) Correlations. The research examined in § 6.1(b) reveals negative statistical associations between CERTAINTY of punishment and crime rates. The most comprehensive available studies, Farrington, Langan and Wikström (1994), and Langan and Farrington (1998), generally show significant negative relationships between likelihood of conviction and crime rates—over a ten-year period, for England, the USA and Sweden, and over a fifteen-year period for England and the USA. This comports with the findings of earlier research regarding the possible effects of certainty, noted in § 4. It would be important, however, to see whether such correlations continue to hold up when English data are compared with those of Scotland and of other West European and Commonwealth countries (see § 6.2). It would be helpful also to disaggregate the American figures by state.

The statistical associations between severity of punishment and crime rates are considerably weaker, however. Farrington and his co-authors report that the negative correlations between sentence severities and crime rates during the periods studied generally are not sufficient to achieve statistical significance (see § 6.1(b)). This, again, is consistent with earlier research discussed in § 4. Of the three recent econometric studies we examine (see § 6.3), two use a measure that fails to distinguish certainty from severity, or fails to specify severity adequately. The third, by Levitt, *might* be read as suggesting a substantial negative correlation between one measure of severity (time served in prison) and crime rates. However, this study's figures would seem to square less well with marginal deterrence than with possible incapacitative effects.

(2) Controlling for other influences. An association study needs to examine other

From A von Hirsch, AE Bottoms, E Burney and P-O Wikström, *Criminal Deterrence and Sentencing Severity: An Analysis of Recent Research* (Oxford, Hart Publishing, 1999, for The University of Cambridge Institute of Criminology).

possible influences on crime rates (see § 5.1(f)). There can be no foolproof way of doing this, as it is always possible to overlook a factor that could matter. But it should be possible to control for some of the variables that might plausibly affect crime rates, given currently available criminological theory and research. As we have *some* idea about the various indicia of social decay in poor neighbourhoods that are associated with crime rates, these indicia (or at least, some of them or proxies for them) should be employed as controls. The studies we have examined do not do this sufficiently. When controls are employed at all in the studies, these tend to be jurisdiction-wide variables (such as national or state unemployment statistics) that have little known relationship with variations in crime rates under contemporary social conditions. Only one study—Reilly and Witt—makes use of local unemployment statistics and even its measure may not be sufficiently sensitive to neighbourhood differences (see § 6.3(a)).

(3) Simultaneity. The "simultaneity" problem is a variant of this issue of other influences, the "other influence", in this instance, being crime rates' possible reciprocal effects on certainty variables or punishment levels. One econometric study examined herein addresses this issue by seeking to utilize a punishment variable that is less likely to be influenced by crime rate changes; another, by exploring temporal sequences between penal policy changes and crime rates (see §6.3(b)).

Both approaches show some promise, and might profitably be utilized in future research. Both, however, have limitations. The first approach, exemplified by the Levitt study, tends to restrict the choice of the punishment variables that can be employed—which may also (as noted next) limit the generalizability of the results. The second approach, utilizing time lags, still leaves the task of controlling for possible other influences on the lagged variable. The study adopting that tactic, Marvell and Moody (1994), did not attempt this latter step.

(4) Distinguishing incapacitative effects. Most of the studies we have reviewed in § 6 which address changes in the use or duration of imprisonment do not attempt to distinguish possible incapacitative from deterrent effects. This would be an issue of some importance were strong negative associations between severities of punishment and crime rates to be found present; but this generally has not been the case, as just noted.

The one exception, as just noted, is the study by Levitt, which might be interpreted as providing some evidence concerning incapacitation. But since the study addresses only changes in prison-release policy, and since it does not examine either the risk profiles of those confined or the criteria used for release, any conclusions regarding possible incapacitative effects would be difficult to generalize to other settings.

(5) Perceptions of sanction risk. This is a central issue, not just a technical one. Deterrence concerns fear of punishment and desistance in virtue of that fear—and a

potential offender cannot fear consequences of which he is unaware. Thus even if crime rates were to show a strong negative correlation with (say) changes in likelihood of conviction or severity of sentence in a given jurisdiction, this would not establish any deterrent effect unless there were also evidence that substantial numbers of potential offenders were aware of those changes (see § 5.1(j)).

The most serious deficiency of current deterrence research—as Nagin (1998) also points out—is the absence of systematic inquiry into how much people know about changes in the certainty or severity of punishment. None of the recent studies we have reviewed seeks to obtain or make use of evidence of perceptions of sanction risk. The perceptual studies we discuss (§ 7) consider only the link between perceptions of sanction risk and actual (or hypothetical) decisions to offend; what such studies do not, however, address is the issue of which we are speaking here—the link between changes in certainty or severity of punishment and potential offenders' awareness of the existence or extent of such changes.

A recent study by Hough and Roberts (1998) based on the British Crime Survey shows that members of the public tend systematically to be in error about sanction risks, in the direction of substantially underestimating the severity of sanctions actually imposed. (For example, the public's median estimate was that 35 per cent of convicted muggers go to prison, whereas the approximate actual rate of imprisonment is 70 per cent; for rape, similarly, the public's estimate of the rate of imprisonment averaged at 50 per cent, whereas in fact 97 per cent of convicted adult male rapists were imprisoned in 1995). To the extent these misconceptions are shared by those tempted to offend, changes in sentencing policy will fail to achieve their deterrent objectives. It is true that when such changes are introduced, newly-sentenced offenders may experience their effects; and that information may be communicated through their social networks. But it is not known how widely, or how quickly, such information spreads. Since general deterrence is addressed to potential offenders, and not necessarily only convicted offenders and their immediate peers, this issue of dissemination is a critical, and unexplored, area of study.

(6) Perceptual and contextual deterrence. The survey-based perceptual deterrence studies reviewed in § 7.1 suggest, for at least some classes of potential offenders, that their perceptions of the risks of being apprehended and punished (when they are aware of those risks) can affect their choice of whether to offend. This confirms our everyday understanding that known penal threats can have a deterrent effect. However, the perceptual studies with the least methodological problems—the scenario-based ones—are mostly concerned with informal sanctions and, to the extent they address formal criminal-law responses at all, deal with such "certainty" variables as perceived probability of prosecution. Thus they do not shed much light on the main question we are addressing, of the marginal deterrent effects of altering the *severity* of criminal penalties.

Studies of offender decision-making, reviewed in § 7.2, provide only tentative—but nevertheless interesting—evidence. Research on decision-making by persistent burglars suggests that the most active offenders seem to be influenced, in the manner in which they commit offences, by perceived risk of detection; but that they appear to be less readily amenable to deterrence with regard to decisions about whether or not to offend. For less active potential offenders, experimental studies on domestic violence suggest that deterrability depends in important measure on social context—particularly, the degree of potential offenders' conventional social bonds and stakes in conformity. The studies do not, however, consider severity effects.

10.2. How Much Evidence for Marginal Deterrence?

Notwithstanding its limitations as just noted, the current research *does* tell us something about general deterrent effects. Let us try to summarize what we think the studies teach us.

(1) The existence of deterrence. When the 1978 US Panel wrote its report, the existence of deterrent effects achieved through criminal punishment was still in some doubt (see § 4.2). The more recent research— particularly, the scenario-based perceptual studies (discussed in § 7.1) and the various quasi-experimental studies (eg of drink driving, see § 4.3)—largely dispel those doubts. The studies plainly suggest that when potential offenders are made aware of substantial risks of being punished, many of them are induced to desist. We share Nagin's (1998) view that criminal punishment has by now been shown capable of having deterrent effects.

(2) Marginal deterrence—certainty effects. Marginal deterrence is a harder question: it deals not with whether the threat of punishment can deter (yes, it can), but with how much *extra* deterrence is achieved by increasing the certainty or severity of punishment. Current understanding of marginal deterrent effects is still limited, for the various reasons just noted (§ 10.1)—and especially, in view of the paucity of research on the crucial issue of potential offenders' knowledge of sanction risks.

There is, however, a notable difference between certainty and severity effects. The current research, confirming earlier correlational and quasi-experimental studies, indicates that there are consistent and significant negative correlations between likelihood of conviction and crime rates (see § 6.1(b)). While the further steps we mention would be needed to confirm that these correlations are actually attributable to deterrence, such a pattern is at least consistent with an hypothesis of marginal deterrence with respect to certainty of punishment. What needs to be explored, among other things, is *how* certainty of punishment might best be enhanced. Here the considerable literature on policing and its possible effects on crime might be of some assistance.

(3) Marginal deterrence—severity effects. The evidence concerning severity effects is less impressive. Present association research, mirroring earlier studies, fails—as just noted to disclose significant and consistent negative associations between severity levels (such as likelihood or duration of imprisonment) and crime rates (see, particularly, the Farrington studies discussed in§6.1(b)).

The USA has had severer sentences than England in the last decade and a half, and US crime rates have generally been falling or steady while England's (at least, until recently) have been rising. But a closer analysis of the trends, as just noted, generally does not show substantial negative correlations between sentence levels and crime rates. Such figures thus give scant support to recent claims that America's tougher penalties have shown demonstrably greater success in deterring crime.

These conclusions, however, need some qualification. Even the Farrington studies (§ 6.1(b)) point to modest negative correlations between some severity variables and crime rates, albeit ones that seldom achieve statistical significance. In the Levitt study, the possibility that changes in duration of confinement affected marginal deterrence cannot be excluded altogether. Considerations of rational choice also suggest that the degree of onerousness of potential penalties should matter—at least, for potential offenders who are sufficiently aware of those penalties, who believe they face a significant probability of being apprehended, and who have the requisite subjective utilities. If severity does matter, however, then the problem of possible countervailing effects due to reduced differential disincentives among crimes, discussed in § 9, also needs to be considered.

Where knowledge clearly is lacking, however, concerns the critical question of *how much* extra punishment. The existing studies clearly do not provide a valid basis of inference regarding the extent to which penalties would need to be increased in order to achieve a substantial reduction in crime rates. Small increases in punishment levels may matter little, in terms of potential offenders' subjective utilities. Large increases *might* have some impact, but whether and to what extent they actually do so depend on little-understood questions of potential offenders' thresholds (see §§ 3(e) and 7.2 above). Large increases could also flatten the sentencing gradient, and thus raise the question of possible counterproductive effects with respect to the most serious offences, discussed in § 9.

What might account for severity's uncertain and seemingly limited effects? Any confident answer would call for evidence that is not yet available, but we might speculate that some of the following factors might be at work:

(1) Information about changes in certainty of punishment seems easier for potential offenders to obtain than information about changes in severity. If the police step up their presence or activity in a neighbourhood, or if tempting target areas are visibly being surveyed by closed-circuit TV cameras, this will suggest even to the casual observer, that the risks of being caught have increased. The severity of criminal sentences which courts actually impose is a less visible phenomenon for many potential offenders.

(2) Additions to severity of punishment are contingent future events. Before higher sentence levels can apply to an offender, he must be caught and convicted; if the sentence increase involves a longer prison term, the extra time in confinement lies still further in the future. There is a general tendency to discount contingent future costs—and to the extent that potential offenders are more oriented to immediate satisfactions, this tendency is heightened (see § 7.2).

(3) Threshold effects may also produce diminishing deterrent returns. As penalties rise, they may already have crossed the thresholds of the more deterrable potential offenders, leaving a residue of those increasingly less likely to be affected by increased threats.

These last observations need to be qualified, to a degree. Future contingent costs may be discounted less, if their magnitude is sufficiently great *and* their likelihood of being incurred increases. Severe sentencing policies thus might possibly have an impact if coupled with much higher probabilities of conviction. But this may have limited relevance to public policy, given the apparent difficulties of making large increases in the latter probabilities.

10.3. Deterrence and Crime Policy

It is not our remit to offer specific policy recommendations. But it may be worth mentioning certain dimensions along which deterrence policies might be considered, namely (i) the policies' costs, (ii) the likelihood under current knowledge of substantial deterrent benefits and the possibility of counterproductive effects, (iii) possible tensions with proportionality concerns, and (iv) possible alternative preventive strategies. These considerations may seem familiar enough (indeed, anodyne); but their application might help provide some degree of guidance. Let us consider their bearing on the question of whether, in England, large overall increases in penalty levels would be advisable for the sake of enhanced deterrence:

(1) *The known (or likely) financial and social costs of the proposed policy.* Large severity increases, especially when applied to commonplace middle-level offences such as burglary, would involve large financial costs, raising questions of competing priorities. Also a matter of potential concern is the social effects of holding in custody significant proportions of young males in socially excluded groups, a phenomenon which the USA is already experiencing.

(2) *The likelihood under current knowledge of deterrent benefits, and the possibility of counterproductive effects.* The research we have reviewed provides no definitive answers to whether and to what extent substantial increases in the use and duration of custody could enhance marginal deterrence. However, recent studies' findings—particularly, of the absence of strong and consistent negative statistical correlations between severity and crime rates—do diminish the plausibility of

expecting large deterrent benefits (see §§ 6 and 10.2). Against any possible bene-fits, there also should be weighed the possible counterproductive effects relating to reduced differential disincentives against the most serious crimes of violence (see § 9). Also to be considered, is the destigmatization of punishment that may occur, if severe sanctions are very widely employed (see § 3 (f)).

(3) *Possible tensions with norms of proportionality.* Because the graver forms of vio-lent crime appear to be much more serious than burglary and other property offences, a more steeply graded sentencing scale would seem to accord better with proportionality and "just deserts" than a flattened one (see von Hirsch, 1993, chapters 2, 4). A policy of substantial sentence increases—to the extent it leads to a flattening of the sentencing gradient— would thus stand in tension with fairness concerns. Similarly problematic would be the singling out of particular types of crime for enhanced punishment for deterrent ends, as mandatory minimum sen-tences do—as that would disturb the rank ordering of penalties (*ibid.*, page 18; von Hirsch, 1986, chapters 4–7). Were the evidence regarding the deterrence potential of such increases strongly favourable, that would raise familiar ethical dilemmas about whether preventing more crime (especially, middle-level prop-erty crime such as birglary) is "worth" such a sacrifice of proportionality.

2.4

Optimal Sanctions: Any Upper Limits?

RICHARD POSNER

[Posner's theory is based on the assumption that criminals in general behave as "national calculators" or, to be more precise, that a sentencing strategy which is based on this assumption will have the greatest preventive power. On this view, which is developed further in the sentencing context and more generally in Posner's *Economic Analysis of Law,* 2nd edn. (1977), ch. 7, and *passim*), crimes are committed because the expected benefits outweigh the expected costs; or, at least, significantly fewer crimes would be committed if the expected costs were known to exceed the expected benefits. In these calculations, benefits include any economic gain from the offence and other non-economic satisfactions (e.g., in crimes of passion or revenge); and costs include not only the expected punishment but also the opportunity costs of the criminal's time, expenses necessary to commit the crime, etc. These last points are important in Posner's theory because they suggest other possibilities of controlling crime apart from increasing punishments on convicted offenders (e.g., increasing the cost or scarcity of guns, or redistributing wealth). The extract below, however, concentrates on the potential of the criminal sanction for controlling crime—eds.]

We have seen that the main thing the criminal law punishes is the pure coercive transfer, or, as it might better be described in a case of tax evasion or price-fixing, the pure involuntary transfer, of wealth or utility. In discussing what criminal penalties are optimal to deter such transfers, I shall assume that most potential criminals are sufficiently rational to be deterrable—an assumption that has the support of an extensive literature.

We saw earlier that the sanction for a pure coercive transfer should be designed so that the criminal is made worse off by his act, but now a series of qualifications must be introduced. First, some criminal acts actually are wealth-maximizing. Suppose I lose my way in the woods and, as an alternative to starving, enter an unoccupied cabin and "steal" some food. Should the punishment be death, on the theory that the crime saved my life, and therefore no lesser penalty would deter? Of course not. The problem is that while the law of theft generally punishes takings in settings of low transaction costs, in this example the costs of transacting with the

From R Posner, 'An Economic Theory of Criminal Law' (1985) 85 *Columbia Law Review* 1193.

absent owner of the cabin are prohibitive. One approach is to define theft so as to exclude such examples; the criminal law has a defense of necessity that probably would succeed in this example. But defenses make the law more complicated, and an alternative that sometimes will be superior is to employ a somewhat overinclusive definition of the crime but set the expected punishment cost at a level that will not deter the occasional crime that is value-maximizing.

There is a related but more important reason for putting a ceiling on criminal punishments such that not all crimes are deterred. If there is a risk either of accidental violation of the criminal law or of legal error, an expected penalty will induce innocent people to forgo socially desirable activities at the borderline of criminal activity. The effect is magnified if people are risk averse and penalties are severe. If for example, the penalty for carelessly injuring someone in an automobile accident were death, people would drive too slowly, or not at all, to avoid an accidental violation or an erroneous conviction.

1. "Afflictive" Punishment

The foregoing analysis shows that there is a place in the criminal justice system, and a big one, for imprisonment; and perhaps for other non-monetary criminal sanctions as well. Since the cost of murder to the victim approaches infinity, even very heavy fines will not provide sufficient deterrence of murder, and even life imprisonment may not impose costs on the murderer equal to those of the victim. It might seem, however, that the important thing is not that the punishment for murder equal the cost to the victim but that it be high enough to make the murder not pay—and surely imprisoning the murderer for the rest of his life or, if he is wealthy, confiscating his wealth would cost him more than the murder could possibly have gained him. But this analysis implicitly treats the probability of apprehension and conviction as one. If it is less than one, as of course it is, then the murderer will not be comparing the gain from the crime with the loss if he is caught and sentenced; he will be comparing it with the disutility of the sentence discounted by the probability that it will actually be imposed. Suppose, for example, that the loss to the murder victim is one hundred million dollars, the probability of punishing the murderer is .5, and the murderer's total wealth is one million dollars and will be confiscated upon conviction Then his expected punishment cost when he is deciding whether to commit the crime is only $500,000—much less than his total wealth.

This analysis suggests incidentally that the much heavier punishment of crimes of violence than seemingly more serious white-collar crimes is not, as so often thought, an example of class bias. Once it is recognized that most people would demand astronomical sums to assume a substantial risk of death, it becomes apparent that even very large financial crimes are less serious than most crimes of violence. The same people who would accept quite modest sums to run very small risks of death would demand extremely large sums to run the substantial risks that many crimes of violence create, even when death does not ensue. This point holds even if the white-collar crime (say, violating a pollution regulation) creates a safety hazard, provided that the probability that the hazard will result in the death of any given person is low. Even if it were a virtual certainty that some people would die as a result of the crime, the aggregate disutility of many small risks of death may be much smaller than a single large risk of death to a particular person. This is the nonlinear relationship between utility and risk of death that I have stressed.[1]

By the same token the argument sketched above for capital punishment is not conclusive. Because the penalty is so severe, and irreversible, the cost of mistaken imposition is very high; therefore greater resources are invested in the litigation of a capital case. Indeed, if I am right in suggesting that the cost of death inflicted with a high probability (a reasonable description of capital punishment) is not just a linear extrapolation from less severe injuries, it is not surprising that the resources invested in the litigation of a capital case may, as one observes, greatly exceed those invested in litigation in cases where the maximum punishment is life imprisonment, even if there is no possibility of parole. The additional resources expended on the litigation of capital cases may not be justified if the added deterrent effect of capital punishment over long prison terms is small. But there is scientific evidence to support the layman's intuition that it is great.[2]

Capital punishment is also supported by considerations of marginal deterrence, which require as big a spread as possible between the punishments for the least and most serious crimes. If the maximum punishment for murder is life imprisonment, we may not want to make armed robbery also punishable by life imprisonment, for then armed robbers would have no additional incentive not to murder their victims. But arguments based on marginal deterrence for a differentiated penalty structure are inconclusive, particularly when the greater offence is a complement of the lesser one, as is often the case with murder. Moreover, the argument does not lead inexorably to the conclusion that capital punishment should be the punishment for simple murder. For if it is, then we have the problem of marginally deterring the multiple murderer. Maybe capital punishment should be reserved for him, so that murderers have a disincentive to kill witnesses to the murder, though again the number of such complementary murders may be less if the initial murder is punished severely.

An important application of this principle is to prison murders. A prisoner who is serving a life sentence for murder and is not likely to be paroled has no disincentive not to kill in prison, unless prison murder is punishable by death. Considerations of complementarity might argue for making out-of-prison murders capital also, since reducing the number of murders and the fraction of murderers in prison would reduce the occasions for prison murder. What makes little sense is to have capital punishment for neither out-of-prison nor prison murders, so that the latter becomes close to a free good. This is the present situation in federal law. Notice that varying the probability of apprehension and conviction cannot preserve marginal deterrence in this situation. The probability of apprehension and conviction in the prison murder case is close to one; the problem is that for the murderer already fated to spend the rest of his life in prison, there is no incremental punishment from being convicted of murder again.

Of course there is no realistic method of preserving marginal deterrence for every crime, although medieval law tried. It is a reasonable conjecture (if no more than that) that because more medieval than modern people believed in an afterlife, because life was more brutal and painful, and because life expectancy was short, capital punishment was not so serious a punishment in those days as it is today. Furthermore, because society was poor, severe punishments were badly needed and law enforcement was inefficient, so that devoting much greater resources to catching criminals would not have been feasible or productive. In an effort to make capital punishment a more costly punishment to the criminal, especially gruesome methods of execution (for example, drawing and quartering)[3] were prescribed for especially heinous crimes, such as treason. Boiling in oil, considered more horrible than hanging or beheading, was used to punish murder by poisoning; since poisoners were especially difficult to apprehend in those times, a heavier punishment than that prescribed for ordinary murderers was (economically) indicated.

The hanging of horse thieves in the nineteenth-century American West is another example of a penalty whose great severity reflects the low probability of punishment more than the high social cost of the crime. But the most famous example is the punishment of all serious (and some not so serious) crimes by death in pre-nineteenth-century England,[4] when there was no organized police force and the probability of punishment was therefore very low for most crimes.[5]

Death is not the only modern form of "afflictive" punishment. Flogging is still used by many parents and, in attenuated form, in some schools. The economic objection to punishing by inflicting physical pain is not that it is disgusting or that people have different thresholds of pain that make it difficult to calibrate the severity of the punishment—imprisonment and death are subject to the same problem. The objection is that it may be a poor method of inflicting severe but not lethal punishment. Just to inflict a momentary excruciating pain with no aftereffects might be a trivial deterrent, especially for people who had never experienced such pain; while to inflict a level of pain that would be the equivalent of five years in prison would require measures so drastic that they might endanger the life, or destroy the physical or mental health, of the offender. For slight punishments, fines will do. Incidentally, I do not mean, by omission, to disparage non-economic objections to "afflictive punishment". But this is an article about economics.

The infliction of physical pain is not the only way in which the severity of punishment can be varied other than by varying the length of imprisonment. Size of prison cell, temperature, and quality of food could also be used as "amenity variables". It may seem very attractive from a cost-effectiveness standpoint to reduce the length of imprisonment but compensate by reducing the quality of the food served the prisoners; the costs of imprisonment to the state, but not to the prisoners, would be reduced. The problem is that this would make information about sanctions very costly, because there would be so many dimensions to evaluate. Time has the attractive characteristic of being one-dimensional, and differs from pain in that it has more variability. But as a matter of fact, society does vary the amenities of prison life for different criminals. Minimum security prisons are more comfortable than intermediate security prisons, and the latter are more comfortable than maximum security prisons. Assignments to these different tiers are related to the gravity of the crime, and in the direction one would predict.

2. Imprisonment

If society must continue to rely heavily on imprisonment as a criminal sanction, there is an argument—subject to caveats that should be familiar to the reader by now, based on risk aversion, overinclusion, avoidance and error costs, and (less clearly) marginal deterrence—for combining heavy prison terms for convicted criminals with low probabilities of apprehension and conviction. Consider the choice between combining a .1 probability of apprehension and conviction with a 10-year prison term and a .2 probability of apprehension and conviction with a five-year term. Under the second approach twice as many individuals are imprisoned but for only half as long, so the total costs of imprisonment to the government will be the same under the two approaches. But the costs of police, court officials, and the like will probably be lower under the first approach. The probability of apprehension and conviction, and hence the number of prosecutions, is only half as great. Although more resources will be devoted to a trial where the possible punishment is greater, these resources will be incurred in fewer trials because fewer people will be punished, and even if the total litigation resources are no lower, police and prosecution costs will clearly be much lower. And notice that this variant of our earlier model of high fines and trivial probabilities of apprehension and conviction corrects the most serious problem with that model—that is, solvency.

But isn't a system under which probabilities of punishment are low "unfair", because it creates ex post inequality among offenders? Many go scot-free; others serve longer prison sentences than they would if more offenders were caught. However, to object to this result is like saying that all lotteries are unfair because, ex post, they create wealth differences among the players. In an equally significant sense both the criminal justice system that creates low probabilities of apprehension and conviction and the lottery are fair so long as the ex ante costs and benefits are equalized among the participants. Nor is it correct that while real lotteries are voluntary the criminal justice "lottery" is not. The criminal justice system is voluntary: you keep out of it by not committing crimes. Maybe, though, such a system of punishment is not sustainable in practice, because judges and jurors underestimate the benefits of what would seem, viewed in isolation, savagely cruel sentences. The prisoner who is to receive the sentence will be there in the dock, in person; the victims of the crimes for which he has not been prosecuted (because the fraction of crimes prosecuted is very low) will not be present—they will be statistics. I hesitate, though, to call this an economic argument; it could be stated in economic terms by reference to costs of information, but more analysis would be needed before this could be regarded as anything better than relabelling.

There is, however, another and more clearly economic problem with combining very long prison sentences with very low probabilities of apprehension and conviction. A prison term is lengthened, of course, by adding time on to the end of it. If the criminal has a significant discount rate, the added years may not create a substantial added disutility. At a discount rate of 10 per cent, a 10-year prison term imposes a disutility only 6.1 times the disutility of a one-year sentence, and a 20-year sentence increases this figure to only 8.5 times; the corresponding figures for a five per cent discount rate are 7.7 and 12.5 times.

Discount rates may seem out of place in a discussion of non-monetary utilities and disutilities, though imprisonment has a monetary dimension, because a prisoner will have a lower income in prison than on the outside. But the reason that interest (discount) rates are positive even when there is no risk of default and the expected rate of inflation is zero is that people prefer present to future consumption and so must be paid to defer consumption. A criminal, too, will value his future consumption, which imprisonment will reduce, less than his present consumption.

The discounting problem could be ameliorated by preventive detention, whereby the defendant in effect begins to serve his sentence before he is convicted, or sometimes before his appeal rights are exhausted. The pros and cons of preventive detention involve issues of criminal procedure that would carry us beyond the scope of this article, and here I merely note that the argument for preventive detention is stronger the graver the defendant's crime (and hence the longer the optimal length of imprisonment), regardless of whether the defendant is likely to commit a crime if he is released on bail pending trial.

The major lesson to be drawn from this is that criminal sanctions are costly. A tort sanction is close to a costless transfer payment. A criminal sanction, even when it takes the form of a fine, and patently when it takes the form of imprisonment or death, is not. And yet it appears to be the optimal method of deterring most pure coercive transfers—which are therefore the central concern of the criminal law.

Notes

1. This point is overlooked in "radical" critiques of criminal law. See, e.g., S. Box, *Power, Crime, and Mystification* (1983), 9.
2. See, e.g., D. Pyle, *The Economics of Crime and Law Enforcement* (London, 1983); Ehrlich, "The Deterrent Effect of Capital Punishment: A Question of Life and Death", (1975) 65 *Am. Econ. Rev.* 397; Ehrlich and Gibbons, "On the Measurement of the Deterrent Effect of Capital Punishment and the Theory of Deterrence", (1977) 6 *J. Legal Stud.* 35; Layson, "Homicide and Deterrence: A Re-examination of the U.S.

Time-Series Evidence" (August 1984) (unpublished manuscript on file at the offices of the *Columbia Law Review*). The evidence has not gone unchallenged, of course. See D. Pyle, above, ch. 4, for discussion and references.

3. This punishment was still "on the books" in eighteenth-century England. For the grisly details, see W. Blackstone, *Commentaries* 92.

4. See, e.g., Langbein, "Shaping the Eighteenth-Century Criminal Trial: A View from the Ryder Sources", (1983) 50 *U. Chi. L Rev.* 1, 36–49.

5. Many capital sentences, however, were commuted to banishment to the colonies.

2.5

Offenders' Thought Processes

AN DOOB AND CM WEBSTER

The reduction of crime through general deterrence is based on a perceptual theory: the behavior of a person is hypothesized to be related to the severity of sentences because he or she knows—or perceives—the sanctions to have a certain level of magnitude. Within this context, it is worthwhile to examine several studies in which offenders or potential offenders are asked about the importance of penalties. This approach is particularly relevant to consider after looking at the impact of sentencing law changes such as the three-strikes legislation. Indeed, the findings from this research naturally raise the intriguing question of why offenders do not understand (or do not accept or care) that they will be punished harshly. Asked differently, why it is that offenders do not appear to act as the economists say they should (i.e., calculating utility functions before deciding whether to commit an offense).

Like scenario-based research, these studies of offenders' post hoc explanations of their own thought processes need to be interpreted cautiously. In everyday life, we are often not particularly good at identifying the importance or relevance of factors that affect our behavior. Furthermore, the samples of those caught may not be representative of offenders, generally, or of potential offenders. Nevertheless, they are worth examining, in part because they may tell us something about offenders' thought processes in deciding whether or how to carry out an offense.

In a study of eighty largely middle-class former sellers of cocaine, Waldorf and Murphy (1995) were able to identify only two people for whom fear of rearrest or imprisonment had been one of the influences in their decision to stop selling cocaine. This is interesting for a number of reasons. It is not what we would have anticipated. On the contrary, one would have expected, at least, that the normal job stresses they experienced due to concerns about apprehension would have been a major factor in a decision to look for another profession. However, the subjects of this study were not impetuous street sellers of drugs. Rather, they were, for the most part, relatively well-educated, middle-aged men who were making a living or supplementing their income by selling cocaine, often to other middle-class people. That only two of the eighty appeared to have been stopped in part because of criminal justice concerns is notable. Concerns about customers, informants, and so

From M Tonry (ed), *Crime and Justice: A Review of Research*, vol 30 (Chicago, IL, University of Chicago Press, 2003).

on were more important than police investigations (let alone court decisions). "More than half reported that they felt no criminal justice pressures at all to stop sales. Of those who reported pressures there were near equal percentages of direct [e.g., police investigations] and indirect pressures. The most frequently mentioned indirect pressure to stop was an arrest of a member of a supply network" (1995, p. 31). The severity of the punishment that they might receive from the criminal justice system was not important in their decision to abandon the trade.

Similar findings were reported in a study of ordinary repetitive offenders by Tunnell (1996). This author interviewed sixty prisoners who had been in prison twice or more and at least once for armed robbery or burglary. Respondents were asked to describe their most recent crime, the context in which they made the decision to commit it, and their method of assessing the risk and rewards of committing the crime. The respondents were blunt in reporting that neither they nor other thieves whom they knew considered legal consequences when planning crimes. Thoughts about getting caught were put out of their minds. As one burglar responded to the question of whether "the crime or thinking about getting caught for the crime" came first, "The crime comes first because it's enough to worry about doing the actual crime itself without worrying about what's going to happen if you get caught" (1996, p. 43). Fifty-two of the sixty prisoners reported that they did not think that they would be caught and, as a result, punishment size was unimportant. Thirty-two of the same sixty inmates apparently did not know what the punishment would likely be. Most (fifty-one of the sixty) believed that they would not be arrested. Even with regard to those who had stopped offending at one point in their lives, the reasons reported were other than threats of punishment.

There was some evidence of short-term individual deterrence. In particular, some of those who had previously been threatened with being declared habitual criminals expressed concern about this possibility in the future. However, predicting the future is more risky than describing the past. Just as one would not want to put much faith in the view of a murderer that capital punishment would have deterred him, one would not want to build criminal justice policy on the views or predictions of repeat property offenders regarding what they would do in the future. Further, these findings should be interpreted, as the author points out, in the context of the sample: imprisoned offenders. While this study sheds some light on the decision-making processes of those who were caught, it does not necessarily inform us of the factors that may affect other groups of people.

Despite these limitations to the generalizability of the findings, it is interesting that the lack of thought given by offenders to criminal justice consequences is replicated by Benaquisto (1997) in an interview study of 152 inmates in three Canadian penitentiaries. Focusing on the 122 inmates whose own description of their offenses was corroborated by information in their prison files, she asked inmates to talk about the circumstances that led to their arrest. The goal was to try to understand whether the inmate had "anything in mind about whether they would be punished." As Benaquisto notes, "it was relatively rare for an inmate to offer a "crime story' without referring to the potential risk of being caught or punished. A dominant theme in most such stories is why the deed was done in spite of the consequences, or why and how deterrence failed" (1997, p. 11).

Only 13 percent of her sample "explicitly spoke of their actions in terms of costs and benefits" (1997, pp. 17–18). These individuals tended, it seemed, to be accomplished "professional" offenders (e.g., high-level drug dealers with a great deal of experience) who felt that they could beat the system. In contrast, the largest group of offenders—the noncalculators—simply did not think about the possible consequences. More precisely, it is not that they calculated incorrectly. Rather, they did not calculate consequences at all. As Benaquisto affirms, "crime that results in incarceration is, much more often than not, action taken without any attention, much less reasoned attention to the possible incarceration as a consequence" (1997, pp. 31–32). Not surprisingly, her conclusion is pessimistic: "the vast majority of those already engaging in criminal activities, activities of the most serious nature (and who have, for the most part, experienced punishments prior to the one they are currently experiencing) are very bad candidates for an enhanced deterrence model" (1997, p. 31). Perhaps the only optimism resides with the small minority of federal prisoners whose consideration of utility functions of offending reassures economists that they are not alone in believing in deterrence.

Benaquisto's general conclusion is consistent with that drawn by von Hirsch et al. (1999). In discussing a study of active and persistent burglars (who were interviewed in the community rather than in prison), they note that most of the burglars "consciously refused to dwell on the possibility of getting caught" (1999, p. 36). Apprehension risk affected "*how* they committed the burglary . . . to a much greater extent than *whether* they offended" (1999, p. 36). As von Hirsch et al. (1999) point out, improving marginal deterrence would require that such people—currently inclined to offend—be persuaded not to offend because of the enhanced penalty. This practice is unlikely if the possible penalty is not part of their decision-making process.

One situation in which one might expect people to calculate utility functions of offending is a crime that people commit with calculators in their hands: tax evasion. In a Canadian survey carried out in 1990 (Varma and Doob 1998), 18.4 percent of respondents indicated that they had evaded tax. By interviewing both offenders and nonoffenders, this study has the advantage of being able to compare their views of punishment. The sample of offenders (tax evaders) involved, almost exclusively, those who had not been apprehended. Not surprisingly, those who thought that tax evaders (by way of either undeclared cash income, undeclared small business income, or falsified business deductions) would be likely to be caught were less likely to report that they had evaded tax in the previous three years than were those who thought that tax evaders would not be caught. As in other areas of crime, the perceived likelihood of apprehension for a crime is negatively related to involvement in the crime and consistent with deterrence theory.

To test the effect of severity, people were also asked what they thought the penalty would be for evading tax on one of three different amounts ($500, $5,000, and $100,000). Predictably, people thought that the sanction would increase with the size of the tax evasion. However, what is important is that the relationship between expected penalty and reported tax evasion was opposite to what would be predicted by deterrence theory. For example, 27 percent of those who thought that jail would be the likely penalty for evading $5,000 in tax had evaded tax in the previous three years. In contrast, the tax evasion rate for those who thought that a fine would be the result was 16 percent. Said differently, tax evaders do not appear to be controlled by the expected size of the criminal justice penalty.

References

Benaquisto, L (1997) 'The Non-calculating Criminal: Inattention to Consequences in Decisions to Commit Crime', unpublished paper, Department of Sociology, McGill University.

Tunnell, K. (1996) 'Choosing Crime: Close Your Eyes and Take Your Chances' in B Hancock and P Sharp (eds), *Criminal Justice in America: Theory, Practice, and Policy* (Englewood Cliffs, NJ, Prentice Hall).

Varma, K and Doob, AN (1998) 'Deterring Economic Crimes: the Case of Tax Evasion' 40 *Canadian Journal of Criminology* 165.

von Hirsch, A, Bottoms, A, Burney, E and Wikstrom, P-O (1999) *Criminal Deterrence and Sentence Severity: An Analysis of Recent Research* (Oxford, Hart Publishing).

Waldorf, D and Murphy, S (1995) 'Perceived Risks and Criminal Justice Pressures on Middle Class Cocaine Sellers' 25 *Journal of Drug Issues* 11.

3

Incapacitation

Incapacitation is the idea of simple restraint: rendering the convicted offender incapable, for a period of time, of offending again. Whereas rehabilitation involves changing the person's habits or attitudes so that he or she becomes less criminally inclined, incapacitation presupposes no such change. Instead, obstacles are interposed which impede the person from carrying out whatever criminal inclinations he or she may have. Usually, the obstacle is the walls of a prison, but other incapacitative techniques are possible—such as exile or house arrest, or, on a more limited scale, disqualification from driving.

Incapacitation has usually been sought through predicting the offender's likelihood of reoffending. Those deemed more likely to reoffend are to be restrained, for example, by the imposition of a term of imprisonment, or of a prison term of longer duration than they otherwise would receive.

Who, then, is likely to reoffend? Prediction research in criminology has been undertaken for than 60 years, beginning with SB Warner's statistical studies of recidivism among Massachusetts parolees in the 1920s and the Gluecks's prediction studies among juvenile delinquents in the 1930s. The basic research technique has been straightforward enough. Various facts about convicted criminals are recorded: previous arrests and convictions, social and employment history, drug use, and so forth; and those factors that are statistically most strongly associated with recidivism are identified. A prediction instrument based on such factors is then constructed and tested. The studies suggest that a limited capacity to predict does exist. Certain facts about offenders—principally, their previous criminal histories, drug habits and histories of unemployment—are (albeit only to a modest extent) indicative of increased likelihood of recidivism.[1]

Incapacitation has also been an important (although less visible) element in the traditional rehabilitative penal ethic. Sentencing judges and correctional officials were supposed to gauge not only offenders' treatment needs but also their likelihood of reoffending. 'Curable' offenders were to be treated (in the community, if possible), but those judged to be bad risks were to be restrained. The traditional view had its appeal precisely because it thus offered both therapy and restraint. One did not have to assume that all criminals really were treatable, merely that some of them might be. Therapy could be tried on the potentially responsive, but always with a fail-safe: the offender who seemed unsuitable for treatment could be separated from the community.

This would assume that we can make an accurate assessment of 'curable' versus 'incurable' offenders—which is not easy to assess.

Illustrative of this dual approach—treatment in the community for seemingly treatable offenders, restraint for the bad risks—is an American scheme of the early 1970s: the National Council on Crime and Delinquency's proposed Model Sentencing Act.[2] This scheme makes much of treatment: offenders, it asserts, 'shall be dealt with in accordance with their potential for rehabilitation, considering their individual characteristics, circumstances, and needs'. In their commentary, the Act's drafters also emphasise a preference for community sanctions and for reduced reliance on imprisonment. Nevertheless, the scope for predictive confinement is great. The proposed statute provides that, whereas non-dangerous offenders are to be dealt with by non-custodial sentences, 'dangerous offenders shall be identified [and] segregated . . . for long terms as needed'.[3] (During that custody, they are also to be 'correctively treated'.) Terms of up to five years are authorised for such individuals, with still longer maximum terms—of up to 30 years—authorised for those deemed to be especially dangerous.[4]

This scheme prompts a number of questions. Under its provisions, the seriousness of the defendant's crime of conviction would not matter at all: a defendant convicted of *any* crime could be confined for up to five years if deemed a bad risk. (It is only for extended terms of up to 30 years that the Act requires the current crime to be one involving violence.) Does this virtual disregard of the gravity of the current crime pose questions of fairness—particularly of proportionality? The drafters of the Act, in their comments, say not—because concern over the gravity of the current offence would fail to take the actor's personality, and hence his possible dangerousness, into account. Is this a sufficient reply? Another question is the degree of discretion the Act would allow. For sentences up to five years, the judge would have unfettered leeway to decide whether and how long to imprison any defendant.[5] Is such broad leeway consistent with the idea of government by law? Finally, how reliable are such predictions? Under the Act, the judge would ordinarily need to consult only his or her own sense of how likely the defendant is to reoffend—except that for the longer terms, he would be required to obtain a diagnostic report. But how trustworthy is a judge's (or even a diagnostician's) assessment of dangerousness?

Beginning in the 1970s, some penologists began raising doubts about predictive sentencing. In one discussion, Andrew von Hirsch[6] points to the tendency of forecasts of criminality to over-predict. Although statistical forecasting methods can identify groups of offenders having higher than average probabilities of recidivism, these methods show a disturbing incidence of 'false positives'. Many of those classified as potential recidivists will, in fact, not be found to offend again. The rate of false positives is particularly high when forecasting serious criminality—for example, violence. The majority of those designated as dangerous turn out, when the predictions are followed up, to be persons who do not commit the predicted acts of violence when allowed to remain at large.

This tendency to over-predict is not easily remediable because it results from the comparative rarity of the conduct to be forecasted. Serious crimes, such as acts of violence, are infrequent events. When the conduct to be predicted occurs infrequently in the sample—and when the prediction method relies (as it must) on rough correlations between criminals' observed characteristics and their subsequent unlawful behaviour—the actual violators can be identified only if a large number of false positives are also included. It is like trying to shoot at a small, distant target with a blunderbuss: one can strike the target only if much of the discharge hits outside it.

False positives raise questions about the justice of predictive sentencing. Ostensibly, the offender classified as dangerous is confined to prevent him or her from infringing the rights of others. But to the extent that the classification is mistaken, the offender would not have committed the infringement. The person's liberty is lost merely because some people like him or her will offend again, and we cannot specify which of them will actually do so.

It should be noted, however, that the false positives argument is only a conditional challenge to predictive sentencing: it questions not the propriety per se of confining a convicted offender to prevent injury to others in future, but only the propriety of doing so erroneously. Concern about false positives might thus conceivably diminish if it became possible to predict future offending more accurately. Yet, as von Hirsch points out in a subsequent commentary (from the mid-1980s),[7] these more accurate predictions might have to rely even more on information concerning the defendant's social and personal history—which would have still less to do with the degree of blameworthiness of his criminal choices. False positives, he concludes, may not be the central issue. Extending a person's punishment beyond his or her deserved term raises problems of proportionality (see Chapter 4 below), and would do so even if the predictions were quite accurate.

The question of dangerousness became the focus of debate in Great Britain, after the publication of the so-called Floud Report in 1981.[8] The report concedes the recalcitrance of the false positives problem: in predictions of dangerousness, at least half of those classified as risks will mistakenly be so classified. With such a high incidence of error, how can sentencing on the basis of dangerousness be justified? The Report concludes that the protective sentence—defined as a term of confinement exceeding the deserved term for the past crime—should be limited to cases where the predicted harm from the offender is severe.

The Floud Report drew a number of replies—addressing the question of whether, and, if so, why, the supposedly dangerous offender may be held beyond his or her deserved term. One defence of the Report's conclusions was put forward by the British criminologist Nigel Walker.[9] In the interest of liberty, he argues, unconvicted persons should be presumed to be harmless, and thus need not fear losing their freedom on grounds of their supposed dangerousness. Any resulting risk to potential victims must be borne by those victims themselves. Once someone acts on his dangerous inclinations and is convicted of seriously harming others, however, he forfeits this presumption of harmlessness, so that he now may be held longer on grounds of the risk he presents to others. How persuasive is this argument? Punishing the offender as he deserves does involve depriving him of some of his rights; but should dangerousness result in a greater forfeiture of his rights? And how is the forfeiture argument anything more than a restatement in other words of the conclusion which Walker wishes to draw, that dangerous offenders may be held longer?

A more critical response to the Floud Report is set forth in Selection 3.1, by Anthony Bottoms and Roger Brownsword. These authors reject the forfeiture thesis, and hold that being punished no more than one deserves is a requirement of fairness. Extending the sentence longer, then, sacrifices equity and the defendant's rights, and that sacrifice needs to be acknowledged. Rights, however, are only prima facie claims; and these may sometimes have to be overridden when the countervailing concerns are of sufficient urgency. Such urgency is present when an individual constitutes a 'vivid danger' of seriously injuring others. Because a sacrifice of fairness is involved, however, a longer-than-deserved sentence should be invoked only when there is a substantial and immediate likelihood of serious injury occurring. Is any response to this argument possible? Is the 'vivid danger' situation really one involving conflicting rights—or is it a conflict between the defendant's right not to be held longer than he deserves and the public interest in crime prevention?

A recent discussion by Andrew von Hirsch and Andrew Ashworth revisits Bottoms' and Brownsword's thesis (Selection 3.2). The 'vivid danger' situation, they argue, is not a situation of conflicting rights. When considering rights violations, they note, it is important to bear in mind the question of agent responsibility: against whom the right is held, and who would primarily be responsible were the victim's entitlement to personal safety violated. When the state infringes the rights of a person, that is a wrong for which it is directly responsible; the state thus bears the moral onus for treating the offender unfairly if it imposes a disproportionate sentence. However, when he is given a proportionate sentence and subsequently decides to commit an offence, that is a wrong for which the offender, not the state, bears primary responsibility. The state has the duty to take reasonable steps to prevent such crimes, but that is subject to ethical constraints on how it may carry out its crime-prevention role; and unfair treatment of convicted offenders would violate such constraints.

Extending the sentence of a dangerous offender, on these authors' view, constitutes a prima facie infringement of the important fairness-constraint of proportionality. Perhaps such a constraint may be still be derogated from in the interests of public safety when the threatened harmful consequences are of extraordinary gravity. We thus might insist on observing proportionality requirements ordinarily, but allow substantially longer sentences for cases involving a substantial risk of grave injury. Where this is done, however, the derogation from justice involved must be recognised explicitly; and extensions of sentence should only be invoked very sparingly indeed, where exceptional danger is involved.

A different kind of defence of predictive sentencing is provided by Norval Morris in Selection 3.3. Morris sees notions of desert as offering no more than broad limits on permissible punishment. (His view of desert is re-stated and defended by Frase in Selection 4.4.) His point here is simply that prediction is justified within such bounds. If a fair reflection of the blameworthiness of a given offence consists of a term of imprisonment somewhere between x and y months, then a non-dangerous offender may legitimately receive a sentence closer to the lower bound, x, and the high-risk offender may legitimately receive one closer to the upper bound, y. Of course, this view is only as strong as its major premise, that desert offers only broad limits; and would require a theory about how those limits are to be identified.

If one accepts Morris's premise, the further question arises about whether—within his purported desert limits—there should be *any* requirement regarding the accuracy of the prediction. Could one offender get near the lower limit, x, and another near the upper limit, y, merely on the basis of a decision-maker's perception that the latter person is more dangerous? Here, Morris adopts a fairly stringent criterion of what an adequate prediction should be: it needs to be supported statistically, and those statistics must show the person has a significantly higher likelihood of offending than other offenders of comparable crimes and criminal record. How drastically would this requirement restrict the use of prediction? How could the requirement be implemented?

In the early 1980s, a number of studies, based mainly on interviews with incarcerated offenders, suggested that offence patterns are highly skewed, even among those individuals who reoffend after being convicted. While some recidivists reoffended only occasionally, others appeared to go on to frequent and serious reoffending. If incapacitative techniques could be targeted at the latter group—the frequent, serious recidivists—might not these techniques offer hope for reducing overall rates of crime?

It was during this period that Peter Greenwood, a RAND Corporation researcher, published a report on a prediction technique which he termed 'selective incapacitation'.[10] The technique, derived from interviews with confined offenders, made use of a few simple indicia of dangerousness, concerned mainly with offenders' criminal, unemployment and drug-use histories. It was designed to identify 'high-rate' predators—those who would commit violent offences (such as robbery) frequently. Because so many robberies are committed by a small group of active robbers, he argued, identifying and isolating these persons could considerably reduce the aggregate incidence of such crimes. Greenwood devised a method of projecting the resulting crime reduction effect. He estimated that imposing substantially longer prison terms for the high-rate offenders could reduce the robbery rate by as much as 15–20%, without any significant increase in prison populations.

At its initial appearance, Greenwood's report generated considerable interest among criminologists and policy-makers. His technique was cited with approval by an American criminologist and political scientist, James Q Wilson, in a widely read

1983 book.[11] In addition to citing Greenwood's estimates that the technique could reduce crime rates substantially, Wilson turns to the possible moral objections to selective incapacitation and dismisses them. Selective incapacitation is not unfair or undeserved, he asserts, because desert sets merely very broad outer limits on permissible punishments. Reliance on status factors such as employment is no serious problem, because such factors are used by the criminal justice system in other contexts. The possible inaccuracies of the prediction technique should be no bar to use, because the technique is superior to the informal predictive judgements that judges and prosecutors make today. How convincing are these arguments?

Later in the 1980s, however, selective incapacitation came to be viewed with more scepticism in criminological circles. Some of the objections concerned the empirical soundness of the prediction technique. It was pointed out that Greenwood's factors could no longer identify the high-rate offenders if the courts had to rely upon official data, rather than offenders' self-reports of their own criminal activities. The projections of large crime-reduction effects were also questioned. Those projections relied on doubtful extrapolations from the criminal activity of those offenders who had been incarcerated to the activity of offenders generally. The projections also appeared to make unrealistic estimates of the anticipated length of offenders' residual criminal careers. In 1986, a research panel of the National Academy of Sciences examined these issues and concluded that selective incapacitation, at least as of the time the panel was writing, would have only a quite modest crime-reduction potential.[12]

In the National Academy's report, the problem of residual criminal careers was cited as being of particular concern. In his calculations, Greenwood had assumed that the high-frequency serious offender would, were he permitted to remain at large, continue to offend with the same frequency as he did when apprehended. Actually, rates of offending tend to decline with age even among active offenders. An offender's declining offence rate would mean, however, a diminishing incapacitative payoff from incarcerating him. The National Academy thus emphasised the importance of conducting further research into criminal careers.

The final selection in this chapter, Selection 3.4, by Lila Kazemian and Andrew von Hirsch, summarises this debate over the effectiveness of selective incapacitation. It also examines recent research in which residual criminal careers were examined more closely. This research—including analyses undertaken in the mid-2000s by Kazemian and David Farrington[13]—indicates that it is possible to estimate residual career trajectories. These projections confirm, however, a tendency to diminished criminal activity over time, and hence a reduced incapacitative yield of selective-incapacitation strategies.

Selection 3.4 also addresses the ethical issues raised by selective incapacitation. The problem with the strategy consists chiefly in its conflict with the requirements of proportionality. Selective incapacitation relies upon factors (early criminal history, drug use, and so forth) that have little bearing on the blameworthiness of the criminal conduct for which the offender stands convicted. The strategy can have significant crime prevention effects even by its own proponents' reckoning, moreover, only if the differences in sentence length among those convicted of comparable offences are large: prison sentences visited on 'high-risk' felons must be much longer than those visited on lower-risk felons convicted of similar offences. To sustain such large disparities, however, proportionality must either be disregarded entirely or be treated as only a marginal constraint.[14] Responding to such an argument remains a significant challenge for selective-incapacitation strategies.

AvH

Notes

1. For a fuller description of these prediction techniques and their methodology and results, see Gottfredson, DM, (1967) 'Assessment and Prediction Methods in Crime and Delinquency' in President's National Commission for Law Enforcement and Administration of Justice, *Task Force Report: Juvenile Delinquency and Youth Crime* (Washington, DC, US Government Printing Office).
2. The Act was prepared by an advisory council of judges, sponsored by the National Council on Crime and Delinquency. The Act is model legislation only. This is the Second edition, published in 1972. The first edition appeared in 1963.
3. See s 1 of the draft Act.
4. The 5-year limit is set out in s 9 of the Act, and the 30-year limit for dangerous offenders in s 5.
5. Even for the longer terms authorised in the Act for especially dangerous offenders, wide discretion remains: the judge merely 'may' impose such extended terms.
6. von Hirsch, A, (1976) *Doing Justice: The Choice of Punishments: Report for the Study of Incarceration* (New York, Hill & Wang) ch 3.
7. von Hirsch, A, (1985) *Past or Future Crimes: Deservedness and Dangerousness in the Sentencing of Criminals* (New Brunswick, NJ, Rutgers University Press) 176–8.
8. Floud, J and Young, W, (1981) *Dangerousness and Criminal Justice* (London, Heinemann).
9. Walker, N, (1996) 'Ethical and Other Problems' in N Walker (ed), *Dangerous People* (London, Blackstone) 7.
10. Greenwood, PW, (1982) *Selective Incapacitation* (Santa Monica, CA, RAND Corporation).
11. Wilson, JQ, (1983) *Thinking about Crime*, 2d edn, New York, Basic Books) ch 8.
12. The report is set out in National Academy of Sciences, Panel of Research on Criminal Careers, 'Report' in A Blumstein, J Cohen, J Roth and C Visher (eds), (1986) *Criminal Careers and 'Career Criminals'* (Washington, DC, National Academy Press). For analysis of this report, see von Hirsch, A, (1988) 'Selective Incapacitation Re-examined' 7(1) *Criminal Justice Ethics* 19.
13. Kazemian, L and Farrington, DP, (2006) 'Exploring Residual Career Length and Residual Number of Offenses for two Generations of Repeat Offenders' 43 *Journal of Research in Crime and Delinquency* 89.
14. For fuller discussion, see von Hirsch, above n 7, chs 12 and 15.

Further Reading

Blumstein, A, Cohen, J and Nagin, D (eds), (1978) *Deterrence and Incapacitation: Estimating the Effects of Criminal Sanctions on Crime Rates* (Washington, DC, National Academy of Sciences).

Blumstein, A, Cohen, J, Roth, J and Visher, C (eds), (1986) *Criminal Careers and 'Career Criminals'* (Washington, DC, National Academy of Sciences).

Floud, J and Young, W, (1981) *Dangerousness and Criminal Justice* (London, Heinemann).

Gottfredson, GM, (1967) 'Assessment and Prediction Methods in Crime and Delinquency' in President's Commission for Law Enforcement and Administration of Justice, *Task Force Report: Juvenile Delinquency and Youth Crime*, (Washington, DC, US Government Printing Office).

Greenwood, PW and Abrahamse, A, (1982) *Selective Incapacitation* (Santa Monica, CA, RAND Corporation).

Kazemian, L and Farrington, DP, (2006) 'Exploring Residual Career Length and Residual Number of Offences for Two Generations of Repeat Offenders' 43 *Journal of Research in Crime and Delinquency* 89.

Morris, N and Miller, M, (1985) 'Predictions of Dangerousness' in M Tonry and N Morris (eds), *Crime and Justice: An Annual Review of Research*, vol 6 (Chicago, IL, University of Chicago Press).

Zimring, FE and Hawkins, J, (1995) *Incapacitation: Penal Confinement and the Restraint of Crime* (New York, Oxford University Press).

von Hirsch, A and Ashworth, A, (2005) *Proportionate Sentencing: Exploring the Principles* (Oxford, Oxford University Press) ch 4.

3.1

Incapacitation and "Vivid Danger"

AE BOTTOMS AND ROGER BROWNSWORD

We have taken a position in the dangerousness debate which has owed a great deal to Ronald Dworkin's (1977) seminal work on rights theory (see Bottoms and Brownsword, 1982). The ingredients of our position are these. We start by assuming that the State has the duty to treat its members with equal concern and respect; and the members have the correlative right against the State. Dworkin (1977, pp. 272–3) expresses the idea thus: "I presume that we all accept the following postulates of political morality. Government must treat those whom it governs with concern, that is, as human beings who are capable of suffering and frustration, and with respect, that is, as human beings who are capable of forming and acting on intelligent conceptions of how their lives should be lived. Government must not only treat people with concern and respect, but with equal concern and respect".

We would wish to argue that the right to equal concern and respect is axiomatic regardless of popular acceptance of the idea, but this apart we would adopt Dworkin's statement without qualification. The force of a right is that it shuts out appeals to expediency, or convenience, or public interest. A right can only be defeated by a competing right.

If A's exercise of his rights interferes with B's exercise of his rights, then we have a situation of competing rights. Suppose that A wishes to speak on some issue in a public place (we assume that A is exercising his right to freedom of expression) but that A's speech will precipitate large-scale public disorder which will result in B's subjection to physical aggression (we assume that B has the right not to be assaulted). Here we have a case of competing rights. It is, of course, no easy matter to decide which right should prevail. However, if the State limited A's right in the interests of safeguarding B's right then at least the *form* of the justification would be sound. A right can only be limited for the sake of a more pressing right. Thus, our response to the various riddles thrown up by the dangerousness debate would have two stages: (i) to determine whether or not any rights are at stake; and (ii) to resolve any problems presented by competing rights. We can start by rehearsing the approach that we would take towards protective sentences.

The question of protective sentencing seems to us quite clearly to involve rights.

From AE Bottoms and R Brownsword, "The Dangerousness Debate After the Floud Report' (1982) 22 *British Journal of Criminology* 12.9, with some textual changes.

An offender has a right to release at the end of normal term; equally we believe that citizens have, *inter alia*, the right not to be physically assaulted and the right to pursue an intelligent conception of the good life. So, we have a problem of competing rights. We suggest, following a rather under-developed remark by Dworkin (1977, p. 11), that a "vivid danger" test should be employed. The idea is that the offender's right to release should not be violated by imposing a protective sentence unless his release posed a vivid danger to other rights-holders. Therefore we set up a test with the following components: (i) *seriousness* (what type and degree of injury is in contemplation?); (ii) *temporality,* which breaks down into *frequency* (over a given period, how many injurious acts are expected?) and *immediacy* (how soon is the next injurious act?); and (iii) *certainty* (how sure are we that this person will act as predicted?) Within the vivid danger test the certainty component is absolutely crucial. For a protective sentence will certainly violate an offender's right to release, and will probably do so for a very long time; thus we need a pretty powerful reason for acting in this fashion. It simply will not do to say that there is an outside chance that some other person's rights will be infringed by the offender should he be released. So long as we are less certain about the offender violating somebody else's rights than we are about violating the offender's rights, then we have to tread extremely carefully in violating the latter's rights. Given the present state of the predictive art in relation to dangerousness sentences (a false positive rate of up to 66 per cent) we conclude that protective sentences would only *very exceptionally* be justified, the justification laying in the anticipated depth of the offender's violation of the rights of others (discounted by the degree of uncertainty) outweighing the depth of the known violation of the offender's rights.

References

Bottoms, A. E. and Brownsword, R. (1982), "Dangerousness and Rights", in J. Hinton (ed.), *Dangerousness: Problems of Assessment and Prediction* (London: Allen and Unwin).
Dworkin, R. (1977), *Taking Rights Seriously* (London: Duckworth).

3.2

Extending Sentences for Dangerousness: Reflections on the Bottoms–Brownsword Model

ANDREW VON HIRSCH AND ANDREW ASHWORTH

In this Selection we shall consider whether, in a criminal sentencing system emphasising proportionality of sentence, there should be exceptional authority to extend the sentence for especially dangerous offenders beyond the terms commensurate with their offences. For this purpose, we shall examine a model (hereafter the 'B-B model') that has been proposed by Anthony Bottoms and Roger Brownsword (see Selection 3.1).

These authors assume, as we do, that desert principles ordinarily should govern sentencing decisions; and that extending sentences for dangerous offenders could constitute only a narrowly drawn exception to this general rule of proportionate sanctions.[1] According to the B-B model, it would only be those convicted offenders presenting a 'vivid danger' to others who should be given a period of confinement in excess of what they deserve in virtue of the gravity of their offences.[2] We examine Bottoms and Brownsword's account because these authors offer normative arguments for their proposals that are important to consider.

To provide a justification for their proposed scheme, Bottoms and Brownsword invoke Ronald Dworkin's model of rights.[3] Dworkin maintains that rights (and for present purposes, fairness constraints should be treated as rights) constitute claims against the general welfare: the right should be respected, that is, even if disregarding it would provide greater net social benefits. An example of such a fairness constraint is the requirement of proof beyond reasonable doubt in criminal trials. This is designed to avoid the injustice of convicting innocent people—and hence should apply even if a lower standard-of-proof were to provide greater aggregate crime-preventive yields, by making it easier to convict actually guilty (and possibly still criminally inclined) persons. The principle of proportionality likewise is a fairness requirement; as such, it should be observed even at some possible sacrifice of crime-preventive effectiveness[4].

Fairness claims, on Dworkin's analysis, are prima facie claims: they may be overridden in exceptional cases, when the countervailing concerns are of sufficient urgency.[5] He suggests two such overriding grounds. One ground is where a competing right is involved (eg when an individual's right to privacy collides with

This Selection is published here for the first time.

other persons' entitlement as citizens to have access to official information). The other overriding ground is where the loss of social utility in maintaining the fairness constraint would be of extraordinary dimensions: when, in Dworkin's words,

> the cost to society would not simply be incremental, but would be of a degree beyond the [social] cost paid to grant the original right, a degree great enough to justify whatever assault on dignity or equality might be involved.[6]

Of Dworkin's two possible grounds for departing from fairness requirements, Bottoms and Brownsword opt for the first (that of conflict of rights) as the purported basis for their model. The defendant's entitlement to a proportionate sentence is defeated, they assert, by the potential victim's competing 'right' not to be seriously injured by the exceptionally dangerous offender.[7] But is this correct? Granted, the prospective victim has a right vis-à-vis the prospective attacker that the latter not infringe his personal security. But would it be proper to transform that claim into a victim's 'right' against the state: namely, that the state provide potential victims with a rights-based guarantee of protection from criminal harm that is capable of overriding other persons' entitlement to be treated unfairly when the state punishes them? We think not.

It is crucial, here, to bear in mind the question of agent responsibility: against whom is a right held, and who would directly and primarily be responsible were the victim's entitlement to personal safety infringed?[8] When the state must infringe one person's rights in order to protect the rights of another person, that is the true situation of the conflict-of-rights of which Dworkin is speaking. But when what is being compared is an action by the state (in the present instance, imposing a disproportionate sentence) and an action by a private individual (that individual's injuring another person), this is not a situation involving conflict of rights.

When the state infringes the rights of a person, that is a wrong for which it is directly responsible. The state thus would bear the moral onus for treating a convicted offender unfairly if it imposes a disproportionately long sentence. If, however, the offender is given a proportionate sentence—and he decides to commit an offence after expiration of his normal, proportionate term—the wrong thus perpetrated is one for which the offender (and not the state) bears primary moral responsibility. Granted, the state has the duty to take reasonable steps to prevent crime. But that duty is subject to ethical constraints on how the state may carry out this crime-prevention role, and unfair treatment of convicted offenders would violate such constraints.

To view the state's law-enforcement duties as 'rights' which victims hold against the state—which may then be 'balanced' against the offender's moral entitlement not to be treated unfairly—would reduce the entire analysis into a form of cost–benefit reckoning. An offender's entitlement to fair treatment then could readily be 'trumped' by crime-prevention concerns, because these now could be redenominated as purported 'rights' of potential victims. It could be argued, for example, that the proof-beyond-reasonable-doubt standard in criminal trails be diluted—because this might promote a victim's 'right' not to be victimised by actually guilty individuals who could be acquitted under the higher standard and might go out to commit further crimes. It ought not be permissible to dilute important requirements of fairness so easily.

Might there be an alternative basis for the B-B model? Let us consider, for this purpose, Dworkin's second ground for derogation. This permits a requirement of fairness to be overridden when harmful consequences of extraordinary gravity would otherwise occur. This is not an issue of conflict of rights. It addresses, rather, situations where abiding by a fairness constraint (here, proportionality of sentence) might involve evil consequences of such exceptional magnitude. We might, arguably, insist on observing proportionality requirements ordinarily, while allowing a longer-than-proportionate sentence for cases potentially involving exceptionally grave injury. When this is done, however, the derogation from justice involved would also need to be recognised explicitly.

What difference would this shift of rationale make? Invoking Dworkin's second argument would create a considerably higher threshold, before derogations from proportionality would become permissible. One would no longer have a rights-based reason for derogation. Instead, one would have to recognise that imposing a more-severe-than-deserved sentence would be an infringement of fairness requirements that could no longer be supported on grounds of defending ulterior rights. It would then have to be shown that extraordinary losses of social utility are at stake—a burden that is not easily met.

Having such a higher threshold would, we think, be a positive advantage. It would help ensure that the exception be invoked only narrowly. Bottoms and Brownsword wish to avoid wide invocation, which is why they impose their strict standard for 'vivid danger'.[9] But it is at least arguable that on Dworkin's first ('conflict-of-rights') ground derogations could be invoked rather extensively—namely, whenever crime-prevention interests become sufficient in aggregate to 'outweigh' offenders' interests in being punished proportionately. However, on Dworkin's second ground, with its higher threshold for deviating from fairness requirements, the case for longer-than-proportionate sentences would become more difficult to sustain.

This alternative rationale, however, generates its own problems. Dworkin's second ground applies most readily to situations where there is a derogation from rights done in order to avert catastrophic consequences on a large scale. An example would be the quarantine of persons infected with a deadly pandemic disease. Quarantined persons do not deserve to lose their liberty, for it is not their fault that they are disease carriers. They are deprived of their freedom in order to protect against widespread and deadly infection. The reason for allowing quarantine is that the prevention of mass mortality is deemed paramount to concerns about justice.

Such an approach, based on Dworkin's second ground for derogation, seems plausible in the case of quarantine because of several features. The potential harm is of extraordinary magnitude, not only in the seriousness of the possible consequences in the individual case, but also in the pervasiveness of the harm: pandemic diseases such as typhoid cause widespread suffering and death. The risk is immediate: members of the public will begin to be infected unless prompt steps are taken to isolate the carriers of the disease. Quarantine also does not involve blaming: the confined disease-carrier is not treated as though he were a wrongdoer.

These special features are no longer present in the case of extending sentences of dangerous offenders. The risk is long-postponed and contingent: it would materialise only much later, after the offender's deserved term of sentence for his current offence has expired and if he still remains dangerous. However, it would be difficult, if not impossible, to make empirically supportable predictions for behaviour so remote in the future.[10] Such a measure has strongly condemnatory connotations, moreover: by having to serve a substantially extended prison sentence on account of his supposed future dangerousness, he is being implicitly visited with more censure. Whereas we do not treat the quarantined disease-carrier as being reprehensible, we would be treating the offender who is given a lengthy sentence extension as substantially more blameworthy than someone who has committed similarly serious crimes but is not deemed dangerous.[11] In sum, Bottoms and Brownsword's extended-sentence scheme might possibly be analysed as an application of Dworkin's second ground for derogation; but there remain significant difficulties with such an extension of his theory.

Notes

1. For general discussions of the issue of limited deviations from proportionality under a desert-based sentencing model, see Robinson, P, (1987) 'Hybrid Principles for the Distribution of Criminal Sanctions' 82 *Northwestern Law Review* 19; von Hirsch, A, (1993) *Censure and Sanctions* (Oxford, Oxford University Press) ch 6.
2. Bottoms, AE and Brownsword, R, (1977) 'Dangerousness and Rights' in JW Hinton (ed), *Dangerousness: Problems of Assessment and Prediction* (London, Allen & Unwin) 17–21.
3. Dworkin, R, (1977) *Taking Rights Seriously* (London, Duckworth) ch 7.
4. See more fully, von Hirsch, A and Ashworth, A, (2005) *Proportionate Sentencing: Exploring the Principles* (Oxford, Oxford University Press) ch 9 and especially 140–1.
5. *Ibid*, 200.
6. *Ibid*.
7. Bottoms and Brownsword, above n 2, 16.
8. See more fully on this question of agency, Williams, B, (1973) 'A Critique of Utilitarianism' in JJL Smart and B Williams, *Utilitarianism: For and Against* (Cambridge, Cambridge University Press).
9. Bottoms and Brownsword, above n 2, 17.
10. See more fully, von Hirsch and Ashworth, above n 4, 58–59.
11. A conceivable alternative could be that of treating the period of preventive confinement after the completion of the served sentence as something other than punishment. Paragraph 66 of the German Penal Code takes this approach: a convicted offender who is deemed dangerous may, after completion of the sentence for his offence, receive

'Sicherungsverwahrung': a period of confinement in a special institution, which is not supposed to be part of his sentence, but rather a kind of 'civil' restraint. This approach, however, would involve the drawback of losing the basis for an important limiting principle. Paul Robinson, above n 1, has suggested that more-than-proportionate sentences should be subjected to the outer constraint that the extra quantum of punishment should not be 'intolerably unjust'. If the extra preventive term were deemed part of the punishment, it would be possible to provide a rationale for Robinson's suggested limit: the additional penal censure conveyed by the extra incarceration must not become wholly out of keeping with the blameworthiness of the offence; see von Hirsch, above n 1, 50. But if the extra time is deemed to be 'civil' and not punishment at all, then it will be more difficult to provide any kind of principled limit.

3.3

Incapacitation Within Limits

NORVAL MORRIS

In the criminal law, if not in international relations, the pre-emptive strike has great attraction; to capture the criminal before the crime is surely an alluring idea. In a variety of ways, implicit and expressed, that idea has been pursued for centuries and is being more vigorously pursued today— and, of course, it is also at the foundation of the civil commitment of those mentally ill or retarded persons who are thought likely to be a danger to themselves or others.

My purpose here, as I have tried to define it, is not at all to attack the idea of the pre-emptive strike. I think one could easily attack it—it is far from invulnerable—but my effort is different, and is clearly more difficult. I will try to enunciate those principles under which such pre-emptive strikes would be jurisprudentially acceptable.

To discuss the definition and application of concepts of dangerousness in the criminal law, and in the law relating to mental health, may give the impression that I favour the widespread application of this concept. I certainly do not. My submission is different. It is that a jurisprudence that pretends to exclude such concepts is self-deceptive; they will frequently figure prominently in decision-making, whether or not they are spelled out in jurisprudence. One can pretend to ignore such predictions, but it will be a pretense. My view is that it is better to recognize the reality of such predictions and try to put them into their proper jurisprudential place, difficult though that may be.

But that is not the only reason for pursuing this topic of reliance on predictions of dangerousness. There is a larger justification. Suppose our present weak predictive capacity proves to be the best we can do for decades, which I think quite likely. Suppose for a high risk of a crime of violence the best we can do at present is to predict one in three, in the sense that to be sure of preventing one crime we would have to lock up three people. My submission is, and it is a difficult one, that it is still ethically appropriate and socially desirable to take such predictions into account in many police, prosecutorial, judicial, correctional, and legislative decisions.

From N Morris, "On "Dangerousness" in the Judicial Process' (1982) 39 *Record of the Association of the Bar of the City of New York* 102 with some textual changes. The original lecture was the Thirty-eighth Annual Cardozo Lecture of the Association of the Bar of the City of New York.

A statement of a prediction of dangerousness is a statement of a present condition, not the prediction of a particular result. The belief that it is the prediction of a result is an error that is constantly made and leads many astray. An analogy to a dangerous object rather than to a dangerous person may help clarify my point.

I remember the drab postwar days in London. The bombing had stopped but the scars of war were pervasive. And on occasion the risks of war returned in their earlier force. An unexploded bomb would be found and would have to be moved and rendered safe. Death and severe injuries were very rare; the base expectancy rate was very low; there were large numbers of "false positives" for every "true positive"—bombs that didn't go off, as distinguished from those that did. The area would be cleared; the bomb disposal crew would begin their delicate work and in all but a few instances manage it successfully. When the talk resumed that night in the neighbouring pub, would anyone say the bomb was not dangerous because it did not go off? Would anyone say that because it proved to be a "false positive" it was not dangerous? Of course not; that is not how words are used when the focus is on dangerous things as distinct from dangerous people. Yet the similarities of risk and analysis are great. Why the difference of usage? In part, I think, because we tend to think of dangerous people as those who intend harm—yet that view conceals the psychological reality. In sum, that the person predicted as dangerous does no future injury does not mean that the classification was erroneous.

False Positives and the Conviction of the Innocent

I want to defend three submissions, which are:

1. Punishment should not be imposed, nor the term of punishment extended, by virtue of a prediction of dangerousness, beyond that which would be justified as a deserved punishment independently of that prediction.
2. Provided the previous limitation is respected, predictions of dangerousness may properly influence sentencing decisions (and other decisions under the criminal law).
3. The base expectancy rate for the criminal predicted as dangerous must be shown by reliable evidence to be substantially higher than the base expectancy rate for another criminal, with a closely similar criminal record and convicted of a closely similar crime, but not so predicted as unusually dangerous, before any distinction based on his higher dangerousness may be relied on to intensify or extend his punishment.

These three submissions form an effort to state a jurisprudence of predictions of dangerousness for punishment purposes that would achieve both individual justice and better community protection. It would seem futile to deny the relevance and propriety of such predictions to a wide range of discretions exercised under the aegis of the criminal law, and in particular to decisions whether to imprison and for how long. Yet, if moral issues are to be taken seriously, the fact of approved use is not compelling and the morality of applying predictions based on group behaviour to predict the likely behaviour of the individual requires justification.

Thought has been led astray here, by equating the assumption of power (or of extra power) over the individual on a basis of a prediction of dangerousness to reluctance to risk convicting the innocent. The model of the criminal trial has confused analysis.

If it is true that it is better that nine guilty men be acquitted rather than one innocent man be convicted, why does not a similar though more compelling equation apply to the prediction of dangerousness—so that it is better that two men who would not in fact injure or threaten others (two false positives) should be released rather than one who would (one true positive) be detained? If one to nine is unacceptable in one case, how can two to one be acceptable in the other?

This line of reasoning, though it has persuaded many commentators and some judges, seems to me deeply flawed. The equation with the proof of guilt misses the point. Let us assume a properly convicted criminal, criminal X, with a one-in-three base expectancy rate of violence (as we have defined it), and another criminal, criminal Y, also properly convicted of the identical offence, but who has a very much lower base expectancy rate—same record, same offence. Unlike X, Y was not a school dropout; he has a job to which he may return and a supportive family who will take him back if he is not imprisoned, or after this release from prison. May criminal X be sent to prison while criminal Y is not? Or may criminal X be sent to prison for a longer term than criminal Y, despite the same record and the same gravity of offence, the longer sentence being justified by the utilitarian advantages of selective incapacitation? My answer to both questions is in the affirmative; he may. But since this appears to be the advocacy of locking up two "innocent" men to prevent crime by a third, I must offer a brief defence of my view.

The central idea that moves me in defining the foregoing submissions and the conclusion about criminal X is recognition of the imprecision of our moral callipers. In no exact sense can one say of punishment: "That was a just punishment". All I have ever been able to say about the justice of a particular sentence on a convicted criminal, and all I have ever thought people sensibly said was: "As we know our community and its values, that does not seem to be an unjust punishment". Retributive sentiments properly limit but do not define a just punishment.

The injustice of a punishment, assuming proper proof of guilt, is thus defined in part deontologically, in limited retributivist terms and not solely in utilitarian terms. The upper and lower limits of "deserved" punishment set the range in which utilitarian values, including values of mercy and human understanding, may properly fix the punishment to be imposed. There is always a range of a "not unjust" punishment, measured in relation to the gravity of an offence and the offender's criminal record.

The philosophy of punishment I am offering is that of a limiting retributivist, and I suggest that punishments, and a just scale of punishment, should always allow for discretion to be exercised, under proper legislative guidance, by the judicial officer of the state.

The key to the argument I am advancing is my third submission—that the base expectancy rate for the criminal predicted as dangerous must be shown by reliable evidence to be substantially higher than the base expectancy rate for another criminal, with a closely similar criminal record and convicted of a closely similar crime, but not so predicted as unusually dangerous, before any distinction based on his higher danger-ousness may be relied on to intensify or extend his punishment. This may seem a pallid and toothless proposition, but if accepted it would have a dramatically restrictive effect onto the acceptability of predictions of dangerousness in the criminal law. Rightly or wrongly, prior record and severity of the last offence are seen in all legal systems as defining the retributive range of punishment. Once criminal record and severity of the last offence are included, the definition of groups with higher base expectancy rates than those with similar crimes and similar criminal records becomes very much more difficult of proof.

Let me test this submission in relation to my criminals X and Y and show you one real defect in what I am offering.

Criminals X and Y had identical criminal records and had committed identical crimes, but Y was not a school dropout, Y had a job to which he could return if not sent to prison, and Y had a supportive family who would take him back if allowed to do so, while the unfortunate X was a school dropout, was unemployed, and lacked a supportive family. And let us suppose that past studies reveal that criminals with X's criminal record and with his environmental circumstances have a base expectancy rate of 1 in 10 of being involved in a crime of personal violence. While no such calculations have been made for criminals like Y, it is quite clear that they have a much lower base expectancy rate of future violent criminality. I suggest that X should be held longer than Y based on these predictions.

In fairness I must note that I have lured myself onto some very unpleasant terrain, for the reality in the USA at this time will be that my apparently aseptic principles will grossly favour the wealthy to the detriment of the poor, and will be used to justify even more imprisonment of blacks and other underclass minorities than at present obtains—as will the whole "selective incapacitation" process. Put curtly, without knowing more about our hypothetical criminals, we already confidently guess the pigmentation of X and Y. As a matter of statistical likelihood, Y is white and X is black.

I do not take lightly this line of criticism of the thesis I have offered here. I do not enjoy advancing principles which if accepted would have those effects. So let me offer one or two comments by way of explanation—not really apology—for my thesis. The sad fact is that in our society predictors of violence are not racially neutral. How could they be racially neutral, when at this moment one of every twenty black males in their twenties is either in prison or in jail? And that really underestimates the difference between blacks and whites in prisons and jails, since when black youths move into the middle class their crime rates are just the same as those of white youths. It is the black underclass, left behind, which has these enormously high rates of imprisonment and jailing and very much higher rates of violence. Predicting violence in the inner-city slum is grossly easier than predicting it in the dormitory suburb. And what else is characteristic of the inner-city ghetto? Much else that distinguishes our criminal X from our criminal Y—school absenteeism, unemployment, functional illiteracy, generations on welfare, no supportive families. Blackness and a higher base expectancy rate of violence overlap. And that is the problem of all these pre-emptive sentencing processes.

What, then, is the conclusion properly to be drawn from these sad realities? Some would say: "Don't base decisions in the criminal justice system at all on predictions of dangerousness; they are racially skewed, and we already lock up too many members of our minorities". I sympathize with the reason, but reject the conclusion. The criminal justice system cannot rectify racial inequalities and social injustices; it will do well if it does not exacerbate them. It is proper that predictions of violence should figure in many decisions in applying the criminal law, and if they are applied within principles that I am seeking to tease out, that is all that can be expected. My submissions may be in error, but if they are, then anyone seeking to apply predictions should offer alternative predictions. We cannot properly close our eyes to the different threats that criminal X and criminal Y pose to the community. But it is of first importance that we base our decisions about their respective dangerousness on validated knowledge and not on prejudice, particularly racial prejudice, and hence that we insist on the most careful validation of such stereotypes of dangerousness; my submissions are an effort to define what is required to achieve such validation. We must insist, if predictions are to be used, that they be reliable.

To conclude. As is so often the case with issues of justice, procedural and evidentiary issues become of central importance. Let me put the point curtly and again. Clinical predictions of dangerousness unsupported by actuarial studies should never be relied on. Clinical judgments firmly grounded on well-established base expectancy rates are a precondition, rarely fulfilled, to the just invocation of prediction of dangerousness as a ground for intensifying punishment.

I must admit that, if my submissions are accepted, I doubt the availability of sufficient knowledge to meet the necessary preconditions of just sentencing based on express predictions of violence. Further, that gap in our knowledge should make us sceptical about our present widespread reliance on implicit and intuitive predictions of dangerousness in exercising discretion—in situations where we do not declare that usage as we do in the situations I have been discussing.

3.4

Predictive Sentencing and Selective Incapacitation

ANDREW VON HIRSCH AND LILA KAZEMIAN

Prediction research in criminology has, by and large, focused on characteristics of offenders: various facts about criminals are recorded: their age, previous arrests and convictions, social history, and so forth. It is then statistically determined which of these factors are most strongly associated with subsequent offending.[1] The result is a 'selective' prediction strategy: among those convicted of a given type of offence, some will be identified as bad risks and others will not.

Traditional prediction methods

Traditional statistical prediction techniques pursued this selective approach. Generally, they found that certain facts about an offender—principally, previous criminal history, drug habits and history of unemployment—were to a modest extent indicative of increased likelihood of recidivism.[2]

These techniques did not, however, distinguish between serious and trivial recidivism. Both the offender who subsequently committed a single minor offence and the individual who committed many serious new crimes were lumped together as recidivists. Moreover, the techniques offered no promise of reduced crime rates, as they did not attempt to estimate aggregate crime-prevention effects. Locking up the potential recidivist thus assured only that he or she would be restrained; since other criminals remained at large, it did not necessarily diminish the overall risk of victimisation. These limitations eventually reduced penologists' interest in traditional prediction techniques.

'Selective Incapacitation'

Surveys of imprisoned offenders conducted in the US in the early 1980s found that a small number of such persons admitted responsibility for a disproportionate number of serious offences. If that minority of dangerous offenders could be identified

This Selection is published here for the first time.

and segregated, perhaps this would reduce crime rates after all. These surveys thus generated a renewed interest in prediction research.

The most notable product was a RAND Corporation study by Peter W Greenwood (Greenwood and Abrahamse, 1982). He named his prediction strategy 'selective incapacitation'. His idea was to target high-rate, serious offenders—those likely to commit frequent acts of robbery or other violent crimes in future. For that purpose, he took a group of incarcerated robbers, asked them how frequently they had committed such crimes and then identified the characteristics of those reporting the highest robbery rates. From this, he fashioned a seven-factor predictive index, which identified the high-rate offenders on the basis of their early criminal records and histories of drug use and unemployment.[3]

Greenwood also devised a novel method of projecting the aggregate crime reduction impact of this technique. On the basis of offender self-reports, he estimated the average annual rate of offending of those robbers who were identified as high risks by his prediction index. He then calculated the number of robberies that would be prevented by incarcerating such individuals for given periods. By increasing the prison terms for the high-risk robbers while reducing the terms for the others, he concluded, it would become possible to reduce the robbery rate by as much as 15–20% without causing prison populations to rise.

Queries about Effectiveness

While Greenwood's study initially attracted much interest, certain difficulties became apparent. One difficulty was making the predictions hold up when official data of the kind that sentencing courts have available are relied upon. The objective of selective incapacitation is to target the potential high-rate serious offenders and distinguish them from recidivists who reoffend less frequently or gravely. To make this distinction, the RAND studies, including Greenwood's, relied upon offender self-reports. A sentencing court, however, is seldom in the position to rely upon defendants' willingness to supply the necessary information about their criminal past histories. The court will need to rely instead on officially recorded information about offenders' adult and juvenile records, and such records make the distinction poorly. When Greenwood's data were reanalysed to see how well the potential high-risk serious offenders could be identified from the information available in court records, the results were disappointing. The officially recorded facts—arrests, convictions and meagre information about offenders' personal histories—did not permit the potential high-rate robbers to be distinguished from (say) the potential car thieves. The factors in the self-report study that had proved the most useful—such as early and extensive youthful violence and multiple drug use—were not reflected in court records.[4] To make the predictions work, the courts would have to obtain and rely on information in school and social-service files—with all the problems of practicability and due process that would involve.

Questions became apparent, also, in the projections of preventive impact. Greenwood based his crime reduction estimates on the self-reported activities of only incarcerated robbers, then extrapolated those estimates to robbers generally. Incarcerated robbers, however, are scarcely a representative group: they tend to offend more frequently than robbers generally in the community. (It is like trying to learn about the smoking habits of smokers generally by studying the self-reported smoking activities of admissions to a lung cancer ward.) When this extrapolation is eliminated, the projected crime reduction impact is reduced by about half.[5] Other problems with the projections also became apparent. Greenwood assumed, for example, that his high-rate robbers would continue offending for a long time. When shorter (and perhaps more realistic) residual criminal careers are assumed instead, the estimated preventive effect shrinks. The accuracy of the forecasts were also somewhat disappointing: comparing predicted and actual offending rates, Greenwood and Abrahamse's analysis[6] showed that only about half of the respondents were categorized accurately by the predictive scale.

These doubts were confirmed by a report of the National Academy of Sciences' panel on criminal careers that appeared two years after the Greenwood study.[7] The panel included several noted advocates of predictively based sentencing, and the report endorsed the idea of predictive strategies (within certain limits) so long as these could be shown to be effective. Nevertheless, the panel's conclusions on the crime-preventive effects of selective incapacitation were rather sceptical. After recalculating Greenwood's results and scaling its initial preventive estimates down considerably, the panel noted that even those revised estimates would shrink further were the scale drawn from a broader and potentially more heterogeneous population than persons in confinement and were to utilise officially recorded rather than self-reported information; and that even those projected effects would virtually disappear if the estimated length of the residual criminal career were scaled down.

Prospects for Improving Predictive Techniques

Could these difficulties be overcome? Greenwood's research was only a beginning, and future selective incapacitation studies might conceivably do better. The obstacles are considerable, however. If the aim is to distinguish potential high-rate, serious offenders from lesser potential criminals, this remains difficult to achieve using the scant official records courts have at their disposal. Records of early offending might become somewhat more accessible with a change in the law concerning the confidentiality of juvenile records—but such records notoriously suffer from incompleteness and inaccuracy. Social histories, such as drug use and employment, will be even more difficult to ascertain accurately.

Estimation of the impact of selective incapacitation on crime rates involves difficult problems of sampling. Analyses of convicted or incarcerated offenders' criminal activities suffer from the difficulty mentioned already: it is not clear to what extent these persons' activities are representative of the activity of offenders in the community. Samples drawn from the general population are free from such bias, but may contain too small a number of active offenders.

The most troublesome issue, however, remains that of estimating the length of offenders' criminal careers. The serious offenders who are the targets of selective incapacitation policies ordinarily would be imprisoned in any event; the main policy issue is the length of their confinement. The strategy is to impose longer terms on the supposed high-risk offenders, but that assumes they will continue their criminal activities for an extended time. Little prevention is achieved if the bad risks who are confined are those whose active careers will terminate fairly soon. This means that selective incapacitation, to succeed, needs not merely to pick out high-risk offenders during periods of high-rate offending, but also those who are likely to go on offending. But how much do we know about forecasting residual careers?

A number of recent criminal-career studies have attempted to make estimates of the duration and intensity of offenders' residual criminal careers.[8] These studies confirm that residual career length and frequency of offending decline at a fairly steady pace with age.[9] Moreover, offenders' scores on risk-assessment indices—when based mainly on information included in official records—were significantly but only modestly associated with the extent of their remaining criminal careers. These results highlight the difficulties associated with predictions based on information included in official records (ie information that is most often available to decision-makers in the criminal justice system). These findings also suggest that incapacitative benefits will decline significantly during the remainder of a predictively based sentence—thus limiting the crime-preventive payoff of selective incapacitation strategies.[10]

Even with improved predictive efficacy, there would be no assurance as to how much confining the higher-risk offenders will prevent offences from taking place. With group crimes and network offences, for example, the offender may be replaced easily by other actors. Moreover, it also needs to be borne in mind that individuals who are admitted into prisons must eventually be released. Sampson and Laub's theory of cumulative disadvantage, for example, emphasizes the '*indirect* role of incarceration in generating future crime', which may occur through severance of bonds to conventional social institutions.[11]

Proportionality Problems

Selective prediction strategies—whether the traditional sort or methods such as Greenwood's—must confront an important ethical question: their apparent conflict with the requirements of proportionality. The conflict stems from the character of the factors relied upon to predict. Those predictive factors tend to have little bearing on the degree of reprehensibleness of the offender's criminal choices.

Proportionality requires that penalties be based chiefly on the gravity of the crime for which the offender currently stands convicted. The offender's previous criminal record, if considered at all, should have a secondary role and the offender's social status is largely immaterial to the penalty he or she deserves.

With selective prediction, the emphasis necessarily shifts away from the seriousness of the current offence. In fact, Kazemian and Farrington found that offence type was not a significant predictor of residual career length or residual number of offences.[12] Since the aim is to select the higher-risk individuals from among those convicted of a specific type of crime, the character of the current crime cannot have much weight. Traditional prediction indices largely ignored the gravity of the current offence and concentrated on the offender's earlier criminal and social histories. 'Selective incapacitation' techniques have a similar emphasis: of Greenwood's seven predictive factors, three do not measure criminal activity of a significant nature at all, but instead measure the offender's personal drug consumption and lack of stable employment. Of the four other factors, only two measure the offender's recent criminal record; and none measure the heinousness (eg the degree of violence) of the offender's current offence.

When aggregate preventive effects are taken into account, the proportionality problems become more worrisome still. Selective incapacitation techniques, by their own proponent's reckoning, could promise significant crime reduction effects only by infringing proportionality requirements to a very substantial degree. Greenwood's projection of a significant reduction in the robbery rate was made on the assumption that robbers who score badly on his prediction index would receive about eight years' imprisonment, whereas better-scoring robbers would receive only one year in jail.[13] This means a great difference in severity—of about 800%—in the punishment of offenders convicted of the same type of offence; and one that can scarcely begin to be accounted for by distinctions in the seriousness of the offender's criminal conduct. When this punishment differential is narrowed—when high-risk robbers receive only modestly longer terms than robbers deemed lower risks—the crime reduction payoff shrinks to slender proportions, even by Greenwood's estimation methods.[14]

Conclusions

Where does this leave us? A limited capacity to forecast risk has long existed: persons with criminal records, drug habits and no jobs tend to recidivate at a higher rate than other offenders, as researchers have known for decades. However, the limitations in that forecasting capacity must be recognised—for selective incapacitation as well as more traditional forecasting techniques. Identifying high-risk, serious offenders will be impeded by the quality of information available (or likely to become available) to sentencing courts. The potential impact of selective incapacitation on crime rates is far below proponents' initial estimates, and is likely to be modest. Considerations of proportionality limit the inequalities in sentence that may fairly be visited for the sake of restraining high-risk offenders; and limiting these permissible inequalities will, in turn, further restrict the technique's impact on crime. In order for this sentencing model to be effective, some important empirical and ethical caveats associated with selective incapacitation policies must be addressed.

Notes

1. For a description of prediction techniques, see Gottfredson, DM, (1967) 'Assessment and Prediction Methods in Crime and Delinquency' in President's National Commission for Law Enforcement and Criminal Justice, *Task Force Report: Juvenile Delinquency and Youth Crime* (Washington, DC).
2. *Ibid.*
3. Greenwood's seven predictive factors are: (1) prior convictions of instant offence type; (2) incarceration of more than half the preceding two years; (3) conviction before the age of 16; (4) time served in a state juvenile facility; (5) drug use during the preceding two years; (6) drug use as a juvenile; (7) employment for less than 50% of the preceding two years. He defines 'high-risk' offenders as those for whom at least four of these factors are present.
4. Chaiken M. and Chaiken J. (1985) 'Offender Types and Public Policy', *Crime and Delinquency*, 30, 195.
5. von Hirsch, A, (1986) *Past or Future Crimes* (New Brunswick, NJ) ch 10. For the method of estimation, see von Hirsch, A and Gottfredson, DM, (1983–4) 'Selective Incapacitation: Some Queries on Research Design and Equity', 12 *New York University Review of Law and Social Change* 11.
6. Greenwood, PW and Abrahamse, A, (1982) *Selective Incapacitation* (Santa Monica, CA Rand Corporation).
7. The panel's report is set forth in Blumstein, A, Cohen, J, Roth, J and Visher, C (eds), (1986) *Criminal Careers and 'Career Criminals'* (Washington, DC), vol 1, 1–209. For an examination of the report, see von Hirsch, A, (1988) 'Selective Incapacitation Re-examined' 7 *Criminal Justice Ethics* 19.
8. Kazemian, L and Farrington, DP, (2006) 'Exploring Residual Career Length and Residual Number of Offences for Two Generations of Repeat Offenders' 43 *Journal of Research in Crime and Delinquency* 898; Kazemian, L *et al*, (2007) 'Patterns of Residual Criminal Careers Among a Sample of Adjudicated French-Canadian Males' 49 *Canadian Journal of Criminology and Criminal Justice* 307.
9. Kazemian and Farrington, above n 8.
10. However, consistent with the results reported in Blumstein, A, Cohen, J and Hsieh, P, (1982) *The Duration of Adult Criminal Careers: Final Report to the National Institute of Justice* (Pittsburgh, PA, Carnegie-Mellon University), Kazemian and colleagues (above n 8) showed that individuals who remained active in crime in their early thirties were likely to persist offending for a non-trivial number of years. Therefore, whilst incapacitation effects may generally decline with age, there may be greater incapacitation effects among certain groups of high-rate 'persisters'. However, confining these individuals

could yield such effects only if a sufficient number of them were present among the defendants being sentenced, or if there were fewer such individuals but their continuing rate of criminal activities was very high..

11. Sampson, RJ and Laub, JH, (1997) 'A Life-Course Theory of Cumulative Disadvantage and the Stability of Delinquency' in TP Thornberry (ed), *Developmental Theories of Crime and Delinquency: Advances in Criminological Theory* (New Brunswick, NJ, Transaction) vol 7, 133–61.

12. Kazemian and Farrington, above n 8.

13. Greenwood did not publish these proposed durations in his report, but they are estimated in the reanalysis of his data done for the National Academy of Sciences' panel. See Blumstein *et al*, above n 7, 131–2.

14. For his estimates, see Greenwood and Abrahamse, above n 6, 78–9.

4

Desert

Retributivist theories of punishment have a long history which includes the writings of Kant and Hegel, but their revival in modern times can be traced to various philosophical writings in the 1960s and early 1970s.[1] This increased philosophical interest percolated through into penal theory later in the 1970s—most notably, in the espousal of 'just deserts' in the report of the Committee for the Study of Incarceration, *Doing Justice*.[2] Since then, this desert-oriented approach has had significant prominence in writings on sentencing theory, and continuing (though sometimes disputed) influence on the sentencing policies of several jurisdictions, illustrated by its adoption in several US sentencing guideline systems (such as Minnesota and Oregon), in the Finnish law of 1976 and the Swedish sentencing law of 1988, in recently proposed sentencing reforms in New Zealand and, to a lesser extent, in the English sentencing-reform statutes of 1991 and 2003.[3]

For present purposes, a desert theorist will be regarded as someone who claims that the quantum of punishment for crimes should, on grounds of justice, be proportionate to their relative seriousness. In terms of the three main issues in the justification of punishment—Why punish? Whom to punish? and How much to punish?—desert theorists will agree in principle about the second and third.

In response to the first question—Why punish?—there appear to be at least three different approaches among modern desert theorists. One approach, advanced in Selection 4.1 by Michael Moore, is essentially that those who commit crimes deserve to be punished for the same reason that those who commit civil wrongs deserve to be made to pay damages: there is a fundamental intuitive connection between crime and punishment, of the same order as the promissory theory of contract or the corrective theory of tort liability. Wrongdoers deserve to suffer.[4] Punishment as a practice or institution needs no further justification than this. A second approach, adopted by writers such as Finnis[5] and Davis,[6] is the 'unfair advantage' theory: that the offender gains an unfair advantage over law-abiding citizens by committing the offence, and that the purpose of sentencing is to remove or cancel out that unfair advantage and thus restore the social equilibrium. The third approach, elaborated in the writings of von Hirsch (see Selection 4.2), regards desert as an integral part of everyday judgments of praise and blame, which is institutionalised in state punishment to express disapprobation of the conduct and its perpetrators.[7] This is the censuring function of punishment, to which the concept of proportionality is crucial.

The other element of von Hirsch's justification is preventive: the institution of legal punishment provides a disincentive against engaging in certain conduct.

Without the regular official punishment of crimes, 'it seems likely that victimising conduct would become so prevalent as to make life nasty and brutish, indeed'.[8] For von Hirsch, therefore, the notion of deserved censure is necessary but not sufficient as a justification: an element of hard treatment is necessary for the prevention of crime.[9] Critics of desert theory have argued that 'a judgment that D has behaved wrongly does not involve or justify the further judgment that [he or she] should be punished'.[10] Those who adopt von Hirsch's view would agree, since general prevention forms part of their justification. But those who follow Moore's view would disagree, as Selection 4.1 shows.

Recognition of the need for hard treatment as part of the censuring response to criminal offences raises the question of the state's role in punishment. No definitive answer to this question can be given without a view on the legitimacy of state authority, or of a particular state's authority. However, insofar as a degree of legitimacy is assumed, it may be argued that the state (through its judiciary) is well placed to provide authoritative censure of offenders for their crimes, and that this facilitates the rule of law by the exercise of what John Gardner terms the 'displacement function'—justifying an official state response in order to displace the unjustifiable retaliatory or vigilante action that might otherwise ensue.[11]

An interesting variant of modern desert theory is developed by RA Duff in Selection 4.3. He agrees with von Hirsch that punishment's main justifying role is to convey censure of criminal conduct. However, he thinks this account supports not only punishment's symbolic role of conveying disapproval of the offender's conduct, but also its 'hard treatment' aspect of imposing deprivations on the offender. Punishment, he suggests, should be seen as a kind of secular penance, aiming not only at focusing the offender's attention on the wrongfulness of his conduct, but also at providing (through the suffering it inflicts) a vehicle through which the offender can reach a penitent understanding of his wrong. As such, the sanction is both backward-looking (to the wrongfulness of the conduct) and forward-looking (as repentance should involve efforts to desist in future). Seeing punishment as having this penitential function, he argues, need not involve an undue focus on the offender's spiritual condition, more suitable to a monastic institution than to a state in a free society. The scope of the criminal law can still be restricted to harmful conduct, and the concern about the actor's moral condition to culpability as expressed in such conduct. But does this suffice to distinguish Duff's secular penances from other (eg monastic) ones? A penance involves not only confronting the actor with his wrongdoing, but also making him suffer as a way of allowing him to expiate his guilt. How can this latter function be justified, as a role appropriate to a secular state in a free society?[12]

In answer to the second question—Whom to punish?—desert theorists agree that only those who have been proved to have committed an offence ought to be punished. This marks an important difference from some versions of deterrence theory, as noted in the introduction to Chapter 2 above.[13] Limiting punishment to convicted offenders is a necessary condition of just sentencing: as HLA Hart argued in his principle of 'retribution in distribution', it is morally wrong to inflict 'punishment' on a person who has not been convicted of an offence.[14] This is a more convincing position than the definitional approach of saying that the imposition of suffering on a non-offender cannot qualify as punishment. Further, a desert-orientated theory can provide better support for the fairness requirements of the substantive law. Thus the basic culpability requirement—that punishable conduct must be accompanied with the requisite criminal intent—can be derived from the principle that criminal law not only does but should involve blame, and that blaming is not appropriate where a person acts without fault.

The third question—How much to punish?—leads to the main distinguishing feature of desert theory in sentencing. Desert theorists' answer to this third question is the principle of proportionality: sentences should be proportionate in their severity to the seriousness of the criminal conduct. The proportionality principle's contours, and its difference from the deterrent and rehabilitative rationales, are set out in Selection 4.2, by Andrew von Hirsch. Within the general principle of proportionality, the major requirement is ordinal proportionality, which concerns how serious the punishment for a certain crime is compared to that for similar criminal acts, and compared to that for other crimes of a more or less serious nature. Thus, once the penal sanction has been established as a condemnatory institution to respond to criminal acts, its sentences ought to reflect the relative reprehensibleness of those acts. Proportionality requires crimes to be ranked according to their relative seriousness, as determined by the harm done or risked by the offence and by the degree of culpability of the offender.

Other writers have accepted only parts of desert theory's answer to the question, How much to punish? Following the lead of Norval Morris, Richard Frase in Selection 4.4 argues that we can be much more confident of judgements of *dis*proportionality than of the so-called requirements of proportionality. Desert should therefore be recognised only as a limiting principle: so long as the punishment is 'not undeserved' and is therefore within the outer limits of permissible punishment, decisions may be taken within those limits to try to advance various other purposes which seem appropriate in particular cases. One difficulty with this approach would be that persons committing equally reprehensible criminal conduct could receive quite unequal sentences. If punishment embodies blame as a central characteristic, surely it would be unfair to visit such divergent severities (and implicitly, unequal blame) on offenders who commit comparably blameworthy transgressions. How might limiting retributivists reply to such an argument?

To establish a principled basis for desert theory is no more than the first step in fashioning a coherent theory of sentencing. Several of the elements of desert theory stand in need of further exploration, both in their own right and in relation to the theory itself. First, by what criteria can it be assessed that a penalty scale is appropriately anchored—that is, how should its overall degree of punitiveness be decided? The magnitude of a penalty scale seems to derive from tradition and from the habit of associating offences of a certain gravity with penalties of a certain severity. However, there are reasons militating in favour of keeping overall punitiveness at moderate levels. One reason, advocated by Norval Morris and Michael Tonry and discussed by Frase in Selection 4.4, is the principle of penal parsimony—that the state should act with moderation in inflicting deprivations on its citizens, and should never inflict greater pain than is absolutely necessary in any particular case.[15]

Another reason, internal to desert theory itself, derives from the notion of penal censure. The criminal sanction should serve primarily to support citizens' moral inhibitions for desisting from crime; to perform this function of normative communication the law's threats should not be so harsh as to 'drown out' that moral appeal, a consideration that tells in favour of penal parsimony.[16] One difference between these two approaches to parsimony is that the former, emphasising individualised parsimony, is likely to lead to the imposition of sentences of different severity on similarly situated offenders, whereas the latter, arguing for system-wide parsimony, would preserve proportionality of sentencing and public valuations of blameworthiness. The fact that the latter approach derives from the foundations of desert theory itself is overlooked by those who argue that desert naturally leads to more severe sanctions.[17]

Secondly, by what criteria can it be assessed whether or not a sentencing system achieves ordinal proportionality? How can we determine whether robberies of a given kind should be regarded as more or less serious than certain forms of burglary or of rape? Many would maintain that these are largely uncontroversial matters: not only do most members of most societies rank most offences in a similar order of relative gravity, but also those states which have recently introduced sentencing guidelines have not found this to be a contentious part of the enterprise. Critics would assault this cosy, consensus view from various angles. First, there is no agreement on some matters such as the determinants of culpability (eg should intoxication ever mitigate?) and the relevance of the presence or absence of actual resulting harm (eg in attempted crimes). Secondly, the writings of desert theorists have focused on 'conventional' crimes, and it is unclear whether and in what way so-called 'white collar' crimes can be accommodated, especially when committed in relation to public funds. Thirdly, and more generally, the quantification of harms is both a complex and a changing enterprise. Recent years have seen changes, for example, in the assessment of such conduct as domestic violence, drinking and driving, and use of hard drugs.

How can desert theory prescribe criteria for offence seriousness in such changing social contexts? One response to this challenge, based on a study by Andrew von Hirsch and Nils Jareborg,[18] is sketched in Selection 4.5: it seeks to develop a framework for rating crimes according to their effect on persons' 'living standard'. The seriousness of a criminal offence depends on its degree of harmfulness (or potential harmfulness) and on the degree of culpability of the perpetrator. With harm, the problem has been to compare the injuriousness of criminal acts that invade different interests—to compare takings of property with, say, invasions of privacy. Here, a broad notion of quality of life may be helpful: invasions of different interests can be compared according to the degree to which they ordinarily affect a person's 'living standard' in the sense constituted by the stand-ardised means and resources (both economic and non-economic) for living a good life. Such an analysis can also applied, the Selection suggests, to rating the degree of onerousness of criminal penalties.

This living-standard approach is necessarily at a high level of generality. It may need to be supplemented by a more culturally specific examination of the values implicit in existing offence ratings, although even in pluralist societies there are probably some shared values which are relevant to crime seriousness. It may also need to be adapted to take account of the many crimes which do not have individual victims: there is a need to develop the theory so as to comprehend not only crimes against the state (such as espionage or perjury) but also offences which affect public welfare (such as pollution). Once it is accepted that ordinal propor-tionality is a requirement of fairness, the importance of pursuing this inquiry into how it is structured is beyond doubt.[19]

Thirdly, the effect of previous convictions on sentence remains an unsettled issue among desert theorists. Some argue that each offence should be treated in isolation, without prior record having any effect on sentence. On this view, any increases in sentence on account of prior record stem from aims of social protection (especially incapacitation) that are inconsistent with a desert rationale.[20] Two different views are presented in Selection 4.6. In Selection 4.6a Julian V Roberts argues in favour of an 'enhanced culpability' thesis that would regard prior convictions as having a bearing on the culpability of the offender and therefore on the appropriate sentence. Roberts accepts that proportionality to the seriousness of the offence should remain the strongest determinant of sentence, but maintains that desert theorists should place greater emphasis on previous convictions. In Selection 4.6(b) Andrew von Hirsch argues that a first offender ought to receive a reduced sentence because this recognises human beings as fallible and shows respect for their capacity to respond to censure. Such discount should diminish with the second and third convictions, and eventually be lost ('progressive loss of mitigation').[21] Several more detailed questions remain—about the significance of such matters as the similarity or dissimilarity of the previous offences, their relative seriousness, their frequency, and their recency or staleness[22]—but the two essays in Selection 4.6 serve to rekindle the debate about the principles upon which desert theory should respond to previous convictions.

Fourthly, considerable interest has been shown in hybrid sentencing schemes which combine desert theory with aspects of other approaches to punishment. The best known are schemes based on limiting retributivism, which, as elaborated by Richard Frase in Selection 4.4, use desert principles to set the upper limit on the punishment ordinarily permissible for a given offence, but then invoke the parsimony principle and other relevant rationales for setting the actual penalty up to that limit. That raises the question, however, of how the relevance and appropriateness of other rationales should be determined. If it is a matter of the degree of risk the offender poses, the scheme would be close to that sketched by Norval Morris in Selection 3.5 above. If deterrence is the rationale, how does that overcome the difficulties raised in Chapter 2 above? If rehabilitation is the chosen rationale, how does that overcome the difficulties raise in Chapter 1 above? What about factors such as the offender's efforts to remedy the damage done, his efforts to return to a law-abiding existence or the impact of the penalty on the offender's family? These are matters going beyond the gravity of the offence, but nevertheless they seem to be justice-related in a broad sense.[23] How could such considerations be defined more fully?

The strengths of desert theory may be recognised in its basis in everyday conceptions of crime and punishment, in its close links with modern liberal political theory, in its insistence that state power be subject to limitations, in its model of individuals as autonomous, choosing beings, and in its protagonists' insistence that sentencing systems should have coherent aims and predictable sentences. In this introduction we have raised questions about how it deals with four particular challenges—that of limiting retributivism, that of severity versus penal parsimony, the problems of assessing ordinal proportionality, and the relevance and impact of previous convictions. Among other challenges are those of diversity and discrimination: desert theory would seem ordinarily to rule out considerations of race, culture, family circumstances and employment in determining the severity of sentence, as discussed in Chapter 8 below, but there are arguments in favour of making allowances in mitigation for certain social groups.[24]

AA

Notes

1. Eg Armstrong, KG, (1961) 'The Retributivist Hits Back' 70 *Mind* 471; McCloskey, HG, (1965) 'A Non-utilitarian Approach to Punishment' 8 *Inquiry* 249; Kleinig, J, (1973) *Punishment and Desert* (The Hague, Martinus Nijhoff).
2. Committee for the Study of Incarceration, (1976) *Doing Justice* (New York, Hill & Wang).
3. For a brief survey, see von Hirsch, A and Ashworth, A, (2005) *Proportionate Sentencing: Exploring the Principles* (Oxford, Oxford University Press) ch 1; see also the discussion of the Minnesota and Oregon guidelines in Selection 6.2 and the Swedish statute in Selection 6.3 below. For an analysis of the English statutes, see Ashworth, A, (2005) *Sentencing and Criminal Justice*, 4th edn (Cambridge, Cambridge University Press) ch 3.
4. Cf Ryberg, J, (2004) *The Ethics of Proportionate Punishment: A Critical Investigation* (Dordrecht, Kluwer Academic Publishers) 15.
5. Finnis, JM, (1980) *Natural Law and Natural Rights* (Oxford, Clarendon Press) 263–4.

6. Davis, M, (1983) 'How to Make the Punishment Fit the Crime' 93 *Ethics* 726. For critical assessment of forms of 'unfair advantage' theory, see Ryberg, above n 4, 36–42.

7. For fuller discussion, see von Hirsch and Ashworth, above n 3, ch 2.

8. von Hirsch, A, (1985) *Past or Future Crimes: Deservedness or Dangerousness in the Sentencing of Criminals* (New Brunswick, NJ, Rutgers University Press) 55; for further discussion of the censuring and preventive functions of punishment, see von Hirsch and Ashworth, above n 3, ch 2.

9. Selection 4.4 above; von Hirsch and Ashworth, above n 3, 21–7.

10. Lacey, N, (1988) *State Punishment* (London, Routledge) 21.

11. Gardner, J, (1998) 'Crime—in Proportion and in Perspective' in A Ashworth and M Wasik (eds), *Fundamentals of Sentencing Theory: Essays in Honour of Andrew von Hirsch* (Oxford, Clarendon Press); cf von Hirsch and Ashworth, above n 3, 27–31.

12. For more on this question, see von Hirsch, A, (1993) *Censure and Sanctions* (Oxford, Clarendon Press) 72–7.

13. For detailed discussion and critique, see Christopher, RL, (2002) 'Deterring Retributivism: the Injustice of "Just" Punishment' 96 *Northwestern University Law Review* 843.

14. Hart, HLA, (2008) *Punishment and Responsibility: Essays in the Philosophy of Law*, 2nd edn (Oxford, Oxford University Press) ch 1; see also the Introduction by J Gardner at xxiii–xxxi.

15. See further Morris, N, (1976) *Punishment, Desert and Rehabilitation* (Washington, DC, US Government Printing Office); Morris, N and Tonry, M, (1990) *Between Prison and Probation: Intermediate Punishments in a Rational Sentencing System* (New York, Oxford University Press).

16. This argument is developed in von Hirsch and Ashworth, above n 3, 21–7. See also von Hirsch, above n 12, 38–46, where two limiting concepts are developed in the discussion of anchoring the penalty scale. One is that of 'cardinal proportionality', which sets broad outer limits on the potential severity of the scale (*ibid*, 36–8); the other is the argument (referred to in the text) concerning not 'drowning out' the censure's moral appeal (*ibid*, 38–46). This latter argument furnishes grounds for scaling punishments downward within the broad limits set by cardinal proportionality.

17. Compare Whitman, JQ, (2003) 'A Plea against Retributivism' 7 *Buffalo Criminal Law Review* 85, and Rubin, E, (2003) 'Just Say No to Retribution' 7 *Buffalo Criminal Law Review* 17, with von Hirsch and Ashworth, above n 3, ch 6.

18. von Hirsch, A and Jareborg, N, (1991) 'Gauging Criminal Harm: A Living-standards Analysis' 11 *Oxford Journal of Legal Studies* 1.

19. See the discussion by Ryberg, above n 4, ch 2.

20. See Fletcher, G, (1978) *Rethinking Criminal Law* (Boston, MA, Little, Brown & Company) 460–6; Bagaric, M, (2001) *Punishment and Sentencing: a Rational Approach* (London, Cavendish) ch 10.

21. See also Wasik, M and von Hirsch, A, (1994) 'Section 29 Revised: Previous Convictions in Sentencing' 24 *Criminal Law Review* 409; von Hirsch and Ashworth, above n 3, 148–55.

22. See further Wasik, M, (1987) 'Guidance, Guidelines and Criminal Record' in K Pease and M Wasik (eds), *Sentencing Reform—Guidance or Guidelines?* (Manchester, Manchester University Press).

23. See also the discussion of this issue in von Hirsch and Ashworth, above n 3, app 1; and from a different perspective, Norrie, A, (1991) *Law, Ideology and Punishment: Retrieval*

and Critique of the Liberal Ideal of Criminal Justice (Dordrecht, Kluwer Academic Publishers) ch IX.

24. See Selection 8.4 below, by Barbara Hudson, and also Hudson, B, (1995) 'Beyond Proportionate Punishment: Difficult Cases and the 1991 Criminal Justice Act' 22 *Crime, Law and Social Change* 59; but cf von Hirsch and Ashworth, above n 3, ch 5.

Further Reading

Ashworth, A and Wasik, M (eds), (1998) *Fundamentals of Sentencing Theory: Essays in Honour of Andrew von Hirsch* (Oxford, Clarendon Press).

Duff, RA, (2001) *Punishment, Communication and Community* (Oxford, Oxford University Press).

Christopher, RL, (2002) 'Deterring Retributivism: the Injustice of 'Just' Punishment' 96 *Northwestern University Law Review* 843.

Kleinig, J, (1973) *Punishment and Desert* (The Hague, Martinus Nijhoff).

Lippke, RL, (2007) *Rethinking Imprisonment* (Oxford, Oxford University Press) Chs 1 and 2.

Morris, N and Tonry, M, (1990) *Between Prison and Probation: Intermediate Punishments in a Rational Sentencing System* (New York, Oxford, Oxford University Press).

Roberts, JV, (2008) *Punishing Persistent Offenders: Exploring Community and Offender Perspectives* (Oxford, Oxford University Press).

Ryberg, J, (2005) *The Ethics of Proportionate Punishment* (Dordrecht, Kluwer Academic Publishers).

von Hirsch, A, (1993) *Censure and Sanctions* (Oxford, Clarendon Press).

von Hirsch, A and Ashworth, A, (2005) *Proportionate Sentencing: Exploring the Principles* (Oxford, Oxford University Press).

4.1

The Moral Worth of Retribution

MICHAEL S MOORE

Retributivism is a very straightforward theory of punishment: we are justified in punishing because and only because offenders deserve it. Moral culpability (desert) is in such a view both a sufficient as well as a necessary condition of liability to punitive sanctions. Such justification gives society more than merely a right to punish culpable offenders. It does this, making it not unfair to punish them, but retributivism justifies more than this. For a retributivist, the moral culpability of an offender also gives society the *duty to* punish. Retributivism, in other words, is truly a theory of justice such that, if it is true, we have an obligation to set up institutions so that retribution is achieved.

Retributivism, so construed, joins corrective justice theories of torts, natural right theories of property, and promissory theories of contract as deontological alternatives to utilitarian justifications; in each case, the institutions of punishment, tort compensation, property, and contract are justified by the rightness or fairness of the institution in question, not by the good consequences such institutions may generate. Further, for each of these theories, moral desert plays the crucial justificatory role. Tort sanctions are justified whenever the plaintiff does not deserve to suffer the harm uncompensated and the defendant by his or her conduct has created an unjust situation that merits corrective action; property rights are justified whenever one party, by his or her labour, first possession, or intrinsic ownership of his or her own body, has come by such actions or status morally to deserve such entitlements; and contractual liability is justified by the fairness of imposing it on one who deserves it (because of his or her voluntary undertaking, but subsequent and unexcused breach).

Once the deontological nature of retributivism is fully appreciated, it is often concluded that such a view cannot be justified. You either believe punishment to be inherently right, or you do not, and that is all there is to be said about it. As Hugo Bedau (1978) once put it:

From MS Moore, "The Moral Worth of Retribution" in F Schoeman (ed), *Responsibility, Character, and the Emotions: New Essays in Moral Psychology* (Cambridge, Cambridge University Press, 1987).

"Either he [the retributivist] appeals to something else—some good end—that is accomplished by the practice of punishment, in which case he is open to the criticism that he has a nonretributivist, consequentialist justification for the practice of punishment. Or his justification does not appeal to something else, in which case it is open to the criticism that it is circular and futile".

Such a restricted view of the justifications open to a retributivist leads theorists in one of two directions: Either they hang on to retributivism, urging that it is to be justified "logically" (i.e., non-morally) as inherent in the ideas of punishment (Quinton, 1954) or of law (Fingarette, 1977); or they give up retributivism as an inherently unjustifiable view (Benn and Peters, 1959). In either case, retributivism is unfairly treated, since the first alternative trivializes it and the second eliminates it.

Bedau's dilemma is surely overstated. Retributivism is no worse off in the modes of its possible justification than any other deontological theory. In the first place, one might become (like Bedau himself, apparently) a kind of "reluctant retributivist". A reluctant retributivist is someone who is somewhat repelled by retributivism but who nonetheless believes: (1) that there should be punishment; (2) that the only theories of punishment possible are utilitarian, rehabilitative, retributive, or some mixture of these; and (3) that there are decisive objections to utilitarian and rehabilitative theories of punishment, as well as to any mixed theory that uses either of these views in any combination. Such a person becomes, however reluctantly, a retributivist by default.

In the second place, positive arguments can be given for retributivism that do not appeal to some good consequences of punishing. It simply is not true that "appeals to authority apart, we can justify rules and institutions only by showing that they yield advantages" or that "to justify is to provide reasons in terms of something else accepted as valuable" (Benn and Peters, 1959, 175-6). Coherence theories of justification in ethics allow two non-consequentialist possibilities here:

1. We might justify a principle such as retributivism by showing how it follows from some yet more general principle of justice that we think to be true.
2. Alternatively, we can justify a moral principle by showing that it best accounts for those of our more particular judgments that we also believe to be true.

In a perfectly coherent moral system, the retributive principle would be justified in both these ways, by being part of the best theory of our moral sentiments, considered as a whole.

The first of these deontological argument strategies is made familiar to us by arguments such as that of Herbert Morris (1976), who urges that retributivism follows from some general ideas about reciprocal advantage in social relations. Without assessing the merits of these proposals one way or another, I wish to pursue the other strategy. I examine the more particular judgments that seem to be best accounted for in terms of a principle of punishment for just deserts.

These more particular judgements are quite familiar. I suspect that almost everyone at least has a tendency—one that he may correct as soon as he detects it himself, but at least a tendency—to judge culpable wrongdoers as deserving of punishment.

Most people react to [atrocious crimes] with an intuitive judgment that punishment (at least of some kind and to some degree) is warranted. Many will quickly add, however, that what accounts for their intuitive judgment is the need for deterrence, or the need to incapacitate such a dangerous person, or the need to reform the person. My own view is that these addenda are just "bad reasons for what we believe on instinct anyway", to paraphrase Bradley's general view of justi-fication in ethics.

To see whether this is so, construct a thought experiment of the kind Kant origi-nated. Imagine that [atrocious] crimes are being done, but that there is no utilitarian or rehabilitative reason to punish. The murderer has truly found Christ, for example, so that he or she does not need to be reformed; he or she is not dangerous for the same reason; and the crime can go undetected so that general deterrence does not demand punishment (alternatively, we can pretend to punish and pay the person the money the punishment would have cost us to keep his or her mouth shut, which will also serve the ends of general deterrence). In such a situation, should the criminal still be punished? My hypothesis is that most of us still feel some inclination, no matter how tentative, to punish.

The puzzle I put about particular retributive judgments is this: Why are these particular judgments so suspect—"primitive", "barbarous", "a throwback"—when other judgments in terms of moral desert are accorded places of honour in widely accepted moral arguments? Very generally, there seem to me to be several explana-tions (and supposed justifications) for this discriminatory treatment of retributive judgments about deserved punishment.

1. First and foremost there is the popularly accepted belief that punishment for its own sake does no good. "By punishing the offender you cannot undo the crime", might be the slogan for this point of view. I mention this view only to put it aside, for it is but a reiteration of the consequentialist idea that only further good consequences achieved by punishment could possibly justify the practice. Unnoticed by those who hold this position is that they abandon such consequentialism when it comes to other areas of morals. It is a sufficient justification not to scapegoat innocent individuals, that they do not deserve to be punished; the injustice of punishing those who did not deserve it seems to stand perfectly well by itself as a justification of our practices, without need for further good consequences we might achieve. Why do we not similarly say that the injustice of the guilty going unpun-ished can equally stand by itself as a justification for punishment, without need of a showing of further good consequences? It simply is not the case that justification always requires the showing of further good consequences.

Those who oppose retributivism often protest at this point that punishment is a clear harm to the one punished, and the intentional causing of this harm requires some good thereby achieved to justify it; whereas *not* punishing the innocent is not a harm and thus does not stand in need of justification by good consequences. Yet this response simply begs the question against retributivism. Retributivism purports to be a theory of justice, and as such claims that punishing the guilty achieves something good— namely, justice—and that therefore reference to any other good consequences is simply beside the point. One cannot defeat the central retributivist claim—that justice is achieved by punishing the guilty—simply by assuming that it is false.

The question-begging character of this response can be seen by imaging a like response in areas of tort, property, or contract law. Forcing another to pay tort or contract damages, or to forgo use and possession of some thing, is a clear harm that corrective justice theories of tort, promissory theories of contract, or natural right theories of property are willing to impose on defendants. Suppose no one gains anything of economic significance by certain classes of such impositions—as, for example, in cases where the plaintiff has died without heirs after his cause of action accrued. "It does no good to force the defendant to pay", interposed as an objection to corrective justice theories of tort, promissory theories of contract, or natural right theories of property simply denies what these theories assert: that something good *is* achieved by imposing liability in such cases— namely, that justice is done.

This "harm requires justification" objection thus leaves untouched the question of whether the rendering of justice cannot in all such cases be the good that justifies the harm all such theories impose on defendants. I accordingly put aside this initial objection to retributivism, relying as it does either on an unjustifiable discrimination between retributivism and other deontological theories, or upon a blunderbuss assault on deontological theories as such.

2. A second and very popular suspicion about retributive judgments is that they presuppose an indefensible objectivism about morals. Sometimes this objection is put metaphysically: There is no such thing as desert or culpability (Mackie, 1982). More often the point is put as a more cautious epistemological modesty: "Even if there is such a thing as desert, we can never know who is deserving". For religious people, this last variation usually contrasts us to God, who alone can know what people truly deserve. We might call this the "don't play God" objection.

A striking feature of the "don't play God" objection is how inconsistently it is applied. Let us revert to our use of desert as a limiting condition on punishment: We certainly seem confident both that it is true and that we can know that it is true, that we should not punish the morally innocent because they do not deserve it. Neither metaphysical scepticism nor epistemological modesty gets in our way when we use lack of moral desert as a reason not to punish. Why should it be different when we use the presence of desert as a reason to punish? If we can know when someone does *not* deserve punishment, mustn't we know when someone *does* deserve punishment? Consider the illogic in the following passages from Karl Menninger (1968):

> "It does not advance a solution to use the word *justice*. It is a subjective emotional word . . . The concept is so vague, so distorted in its applications, so hypocritical, and

usually so irrelevant that it offers no help in the solution of the crime problem which it exists to combat but results in its exact opposite—injustice, injustice to everybody" (10–11).

Apparently Dr. Karl knows injustice when he sees it, even if justice is a useless concept.

Analogously, consider our reliance on moral desert when we allocate initial property entitlements. We think that the person who works hard to produce a novel deserves the right to determine when and under what conditions the novel will be copied for others to read. The novelist's labour gives him or her the moral right. How can we know this—how can it be true—if desert can be judged only by those with godlike omniscience, or worse, does not even exist? Such scepticism about just deserts would throw out a great deal that we will not throw out. To me, this shows that no one really believes that moral desert does not exist or that we could not know it if it did. Something else makes us suspect our retributive judgments than supposed moral scepticism or epistemological modesty.

References

Bedau, H. (1978), "Retribution and the Theory of Punishment", 75 *Journal of Philosophy* 601.

Benn, S. I., and R.S. Peters (19659), *Social Principles and the Democratic State* (London: Allen and Unwin).

Fingarette, H. (1977), "Punishment and Suffering", 50 *Proceedings of American Philosophical Association* 499.

Mackie, J (1982), "Morality and the Retributive Emotions", 1 *Criminal Justice Ethics* 3.

Menninger, K (1968), *The Crime of Punishment* (New York: Viking Press).

Moore, M. S. (1982), "Moral Reality", *Wisconsin Law Review* 1061.

Morris, H. (1976), *On Guilt and Innocence* (Berkeley and Los Angeles: University of California Press).

Quinton, A. M. (1954), "On Punishment", 14 *Analysis*.

4.2

Proportionate Sentences: a Desert Perspective

ANDREW VON HIRSCH

Criminologists' interest in desert dates from the mid-1970s, with the publication of a number of works arguing that this notion should be seen as the central requirement of justice in sentencing. Once broached, the idea of desert quickly became influential. A number of American states' sentencing-guidelines systems (most notable, those of Minnesota and Oregon) have explicitly relied on it; some European sentencing-reform efforts (particularly those of Finland, Sweden and, somewhat less systematically, England) have done likewise, although these latter schemes make use of statutory statements of guiding principle, rather than specific, numerical guidelines.[1]

The groundwork for this revival of interest in desert was laid already in the post-Second World War literature of analytical moral philosophy. These writings supplied a principled critique of purely instrumental ways thinking about social and penal issues, suggesting how such reckonings were capable of sacrificing individual rights to serve majority interests. The philosophical literature also began exploring the conception of desert, suggesting how it constitutes an integral part of everyday moral judgements.[2]

The movement toward a proportionality-based sentencing theory began, perhaps, in 1971 with the publication of the Quaker-sponsored American Friends Service Committee report, *Struggle for Justice* (1971). The report recommended moderate, proportionate punishments, and opposed deciding sentence severity on predictive or rehabilitative grounds. The Friends Committee report did not rely explicitly on the idea of desert as the basis for its proposals; that was left to subsequent writings, including the Australian philosopher John Kleinig's *Punishment and Desert* (1973), my own *Doing Justice* (1976), and the British philosopher RA Duff's *Trials and Punishments* (1986). A number of influential British and Scandinavian penologists have also contributed to this literature, including AE Bottoms, Andrew Ashworth, Martin Wasik and Nils Jareborg.[3] The present essay is designed to summarise recent writing in this area, including subsequent work of Duff's and mine (von Hirsch, 1993; Duff, 2001; von Hirsch and Ashworth, 2005).

Desert theories for sentencing have had the attraction that they purport to be about *just* outcomes: the emphasis is on what the offender should fairly receive for

Originally published in the previous (first) edition of this book as Selection 4.4.

his crime, rather than how his punishment might affect his future behaviour or that of others. It also seems capable of providing more guidance: the sentencer, instead of having to address elusive empirical questions of the crime-preventative effect of the sentence, can address matters more within his or her ken, concerning the seriousness of the criminal offence—how harmful the conduct typically is, how culpable the offender was in committing it (see Selection 4.5 below).

Censure and Penal Desert

There have been a variety of retributive or desert-based accounts of punishment, ranging from intuitionist theories (see Selection 4.1 above), to talionic notions of requiting evil for evil, to conceptions that see punishment as taking away the 'unjust advantage' over others which the offender obtains by choosing to offend (see Finnis, 1980, 263–4).[4] The desert-based conception examined in this essay, how-ever, relies on a different account: one emphasizing the communicative features of punishment.

The criminal sanction conveys censure: punishing consists of imposing a depri-vation on someone, because he purportedly has committed a wrong, under circumstances and in a manner that conveys disapprobation of him for his wrong. Treating the offender as a wrongdoer, Richard Wasserstrom (1980) has pointed out, is central to the idea of punishment. The difference between a tax and a fine, for example, does not rest in the material deprivation imposed—which is money in both cases. It consists, rather, in the fact that with a fine, money is taken in a manner that conveys disapproval or censure; whereas with a tax, no disapproval is implied.

A sanction that treats the conduct as wrong—that is, not a 'neutral' sanction—has two important moral functions that are not reducible to crime prevention. One is to recognise the importance of the rights that have been infringed. The censure in punishment conveys to victims and potential victims the acknowledgement that they are wronged by criminal conduct, that rights to which they properly are entitled have been infringed. The other (and perhaps still more important) role of censure is that of addressing the offender as a moral agent, by appealing to his or her sense of right and wrong. This is not just a crime-prevention strategy, however, for otherwise there would be no point in censuring actors who are repentant already (since they need no blame to make them regret their actions and to try to desist in future) or who seemingly are incorrigible (since they will not change despite the censure). Any human actor, this communicative perspective suggests, should be treated as a moral agent, having the capacity (unless clearly incompetent) of evaluating others' assessment of their conduct. A response to criminal wrongdoing that conveys blame gives the individual the opportunity to respond in ways that are typically those of an agent capable of moral deliberation: to recognise the wrongfulness of action; feel remorse; to make efforts to desist in future—or try to give reasons why the conduct was not actually wrong. What a purely 'neutral' sanction not embodying blame would deny, even if no less effective in preventing crime, is precisely this recognition of the person's status as a moral agent. A neutral sanction would treat offenders and potential offenders much as beasts in a circus—as beings which must be restrained, intimidated, or conditioned into submission because they are incapable of understanding that predatory conduct is wrong (von Hirsch, 1993; and, more fully, von Hirsch and Ashworth, 2005, ch 2).

Relying on this idea of censure helps remove some of the seeming mysteriousness of penal desert judgements: censure or blaming involves everyday moral judgements used in a wide variety of social contexts, of which punishment is just one. This account also helps address another objection traditionally raised against retributive penal theories, namely, their seeming harshness—their apparent insistence on an eye for an eye. Once the paying back of evil for evil is not seen as the underlying idea, penal desert does not demand visitation of suffering equal to the harm done. What is called for instead is punishments that are *proportionate* to the seriousness of the criminal conduct. Proportionate punishments—even if not involving harm-for-harm equivalence—would suffice to convey blame for various crimes according to their degree of reprehensibleness. Indeed, several advocates of the desert perspective (including myself) have advocated substantial reductions of penalty levels (see, eg Singer, 1979; Duff, 1986; von Hirsch, 1993, ch 2; Ashworth, 2005, ch 9; Jareborg, 1995).

Can the institution of punishment be explained purely in terms of censure? Punishment does convey blame, but does so in a special way—through visitation of deprivation ('hard treatment') on the offender. That deprivation is, of course, the vehicle through which the blame is expressed. But why use this vehicle, rather than simply expressing blame in symbolic fashion? Some adherents of the communicative view of desert, most notably RA Duff, hold that the hard-treatment component of the penal sanction can itself be explained in desert terms: Duff treats the deprivation involved in punishment as providing a kind of secular penance (see Selection 4.3).[5] I have my doubts, however. The reason for having the institution of punishment (that is, for expressing disapproval through hard treatment, instead of merely censuring) seems to have to do with keeping predatory behaviour within tolerable limits. Had the criminal sanction no usefulness in preventing crime, there should be no need to visit material deprivation on those who offend. True, we might still wish to devise another way of issuing authoritative judgements of blaming, for such predatory behaviour as occurs. But those judgements, in the interest of keeping state-inflicted suffering to a minimum, would no longer be linked to purposive infliction of suffering (von Hirsch, 1993, 14; von Hirsch and Ashworth, 2005, ch 2).

If the criminal sanction thus serves to prevent crime as well as censure, how is this consistent with treating offenders and potential offenders as moral agents? The hard-treatment in punishment, in my view, serves as a prudential reason for obedience to those insufficiently motivated by the penal censure's moral appeal. But this should *supplement* rather than replace the normative reasons for desisting from crime conveyed by penal censure—that is, it provides an *additional* reason for compliance to those who are capable of recognising the law's moral demands, but who are also tempted to disobey them. The law thus addresses *ourselves*, not a distinct 'criminal' class of those considered incapable of grasping moral appeals. And it addresses us neither as perfectly moral agents (we are not like angels) nor as beasts which only can be coerced through threats, but, rather, as moral but fallible agents who need some prudential supplement to help us resist criminal temptation (see von Hirsch and Ashworth, 2005, ch 2; see also Narayan, 1993). However, this account (as will be discussed further below) calls for moderation in the overall severity in punishment levels. The harsher the penalty system is, the less plausible it becomes to see it as embodying chiefly a moral appeal rather than a system of bare threats.

The Rationale for Proportionality

In a minimal sense, proportionality always had a role in sentencing policy: penalties that were grossly excessive in relation to the gravity of the offence were perceived as unfair. Statutory maximum sentences reflected that understanding, and it also had a constitutional dimension: some jurisdictions have adopted a constitutional bar against grossly excessive punishments.[6] This, however, gave the notion of proportionality only the outer, constraining role of barring draconian sanctions for lesser offences. Short of these (rather high) maximum limits, proportionality had small weight in theories about how sanctions should be determined, with consequentialist concerns (about rehabilitation, incapacitation and deterrence) counting chiefly instead.

What is distinctive about contemporary desert theory is that it moves notions of proportionality from this merely peripheral to a central role in deciding sanctions. The primary basis for deciding quanta of punishments, under this theory, is the principle of proportionality or 'commensurate deserts', requiring the severity of the penalty to be proportionate to the gravity of the defendant's criminal conduct. The criterion for deciding the quantum of punishment is thus retrospective rather than consequentialist: the seriousness of the offence for which the defendant stands convicted.

What is the basis for this principle? The censure account, just discussed, provides the explanation. If punishment embodies blame, then how much one punishes will convey how much the conduct is condemned. If crime X is punished more severely than crime Y, this connotes the greater disapprobation of crime X. Punishments, consequently, should be allocated consistently with their blaming implications. When penalties are arrayed in severity according to the gravity of offences, the disapprobation thereby conveyed will reflect the degree of reprehensibleness of the conduct. When punishments are arrayed otherwise, this is not merely inefficient (who knows, it might sometimes work), it is also unfair; offenders are being visited with more or less censure than the comparative blameworthiness of their conduct would warrant (von Hirsch, 1993, ch 2; von Hirsch and Ashworth, 2005, ch 9).

Equity is sacrificed when the proportionality principle is disregarded, even when this is done for the sake of crime prevention. Suppose that offenders A and B commit and are convicted of criminal conduct of approximately the same degree of seriousness. Suppose B is deemed more likely to reoffend, and therefore is given a longer sentence. Notwithstanding the possible preventative utility of that sentence, the objection remains that B, through his more severe punishment, is being treated as more to blame than A, though their conduct had the same degree of blameworthiness.

A possible objection (see Dolinko, 1992) to this argument might run as follows: if the component of 'hard treatment' in the criminal sanction serves a crime-preventative as well as a purely censuring function (as argued earlier in this essay), then why cannot one allocate the relative severities of punishment in part on preventative grounds rather than purely on the basis of offence seriousness? The reply is that punishment's deprivations and its reprobative connotations are inextricably intermixed: it is the threatened penal deprivation that expresses the degree of censure. If the deprivations visited on a given type of crime are increased, even for preventative reasons, this (necessarily) increases the severity of the punishment. But changing the severity, relative to other penalties, alters the implicit censure—which would not be justified if the seriousness of the conduct is itself unchanged (von Hirsch, 1993, 16–17; von Hirsch and Ashworth, 2005, ch 9).

Desert as 'Determining' or 'Limiting'?

If the principle of proportionality is so important, is it a 'determining' or merely a 'limiting' principle? While our sense of justice tells us that criminals should be punished as they deserve, there do not seem to be definite quanta of severity associated with our desert-judgements. Armed robbers have committed a serious offence, deserving of substantial punishment, but it is not apparent whether that should consist of two years' confinement, three years, or some shorter or longer period.

One response to this problem has been Norval Morris's: to say that desert is merely a limiting principle (see Selection 4.4 below by Richard Frase, elaborating on Morris's views). It tells us, he asserts, not how much robbers deserve, but only some broad limits beyond which their punishments would be *un*deserved. Within such limits, the sentence can be decided on other (for example, predictive) grounds. This view, however, would mean that persons who commit similar crimes could receive quite different amounts of punishment. If punishment embodies blame as a central characteristic, it becomes morally problematic to visit such different degrees of severity, and hence of implicit blame, on comparably blameworthy transgressions.

A conceivable opposite response, but scarcely a plausible one, would be the heroic intuitionist stance: that if we only ponder hard enough we will perceive deserved quanta of punishments: that robbers ordinarily deserve so-and-so many months or years of confinement, and so forth. Our intuitions, however, fail to provide such answers.

The way out of this apparent dilemma is to recognise the crucial difference between the comparative ranking of punishments on one hand, and the overall magnitude and anchoring of the penalty scale on the other. With respect to comparative rankings, *ordinal* proportionality provides considerable guidance: persons convicted of similar crimes should receive punishments of comparable severity (save in special aggravating or mitigating circumstances altering the harm or culpability of the conduct in the particular circumstances); and persons convicted of crimes of differing gravity should suffer punishments correspondingly graded in onerousness. These ordinal-proportionality requirements are no mere limits, and they are infringed when equally reprehensible conduct is punished markedly unequally in the manner that Frase, following Morris, suggests (von Hirsch, 1986, ch 4; von Hirsch and Ashworth, 2005, ch 9).

Desert provides less constraint, however, on the penalty scale's overall dimensions and anchoring points. This is because the censure expressed through penal deprivations is, to a considerable degree, a convention. When a penalty scale reflects the comparative gravity of crimes, making pro rata decreases or increases in the prescribed sanctions constitutes a change in that convention.

This distinction helps resolve the dilemma just mentioned. The leeway which desert allows in fixing the scale's overall degree of onerousness explains why we cannot perceive a single right or fitting penalty for a crime. Whether X months, Y months or somewhere in between is the appropriate penalty for robbery depends on how the scale has been anchored and what punishments are prescribed for other crimes. Once those anchoring points are decided, however, the more restrictive requirements of ordinal proportionality apply. This explains why it would be inappropriate to give short prison terms to some robbers and long ones to other robbers on the basis of (say) predictive factors not reflecting the degree of seriousness of the criminal conduct.

Does this purported solution still leave the anchoring of the scale too wide open? Could it not permit a very severe penalty scale, as long it is not so harsh as to impose drastic penalties on manifestly trivial crimes? My suggested answer to this question has been that high overall severity levels are inconsistent with the moral functions of penal censure. Through punishments' censuring features, the criminal sanction offers a normative reason for desisting to human beings seen as moral agents: that doing certain acts is wrong and hence should be refrained from. Punishments' material deprivations can then be viewed (as noted earlier) as providing a supplemental disincentive—as providing humans (given human fallibility and the temptations of offending) an additional prudential reason for complying with the law. The higher penalty levels rise, however, the less the normative reasons for desisting supplied by penal censure will count and the more the system becomes in effect a bare system of threats (in Hegel's apt words, a stick that might be raised to a dog). Very high penalty levels thus would 'drown out' the moral message embodied in penal censure. To the extent this argument is accepted, it points towards keeping penalties at moderate levels (von Hirsch, 1993, ch 5).[7]

Inclusion of Crime-control Aims?

Desert theory sets priorities among sentencing aims: it assumes that a just system accords greater importance to proportionately ordered sanctions than to the pursuit of other objectives—say, incapacitating those deemed higher risks. This understandably evokes discomfort: why cannot one seek proportionality and pursue other desired ends, whether they be treatment, incapacitation or something else?

To an extent, a desert model permits consideration of other aims: namely, to the degree this is consistent with the proportionate ordering of penalties. Thus, when there is a choice between two non-custodial sanctions of approximately equivalent severity (say, a unit-fine of so many days' earnings and intensive probation for a specified duration), proportionality constraints are not offended when one of these is chosen over the other on (say) treatment grounds. Desert theorists thus have come forward with schemes for scaling intermediate, non-custodial penalties; these sanctions would be ranked in severity according to the gravity of the crime, but penalties of roughly equivalent onerousness could be substituted for one another when treatment or feasibility concerns so indicate (see Wasik and von Hirsch, 1988). Nevertheless, a pure desert model remains a somewhat constraining one: ulterior aims may be relied upon only where these do not substantially alter the comparative severity of penalties. Giving substantial extra prison time to persons deemed high risks would thus breach the model's requirements. Why not, then, relax the model's constraints to allow greater scope to such other aspirations?

A possibility—sometimes referred to as a 'modified' desert model— would be to relax the constraints to a limited degree. Proportionality would ordinarily determine comparative punishment levels, but deviations would be permitted in case of the gravest risks of crime (see Robinson, 1987; von Hirsch, 1993: 48–53). Here, the idea is that avoiding extraordinary harms is so important a goal as to warrant some sacrifice of fairness. This position differs from ordinary penal consequentialism, however, in that departures from desert requirements could be invoked only exceptionally, to deal with threats of an extraordinary nature (see Selection 3.3 above). Alternatively, deviations could more regularly be permitted, but these would be restricted ones: say, a deviation of no more than 10 or 15% from the deserved sentence. While departures from proportionality involve a sacrifice of equity, the extent of that sacrifice depends on the degree of the deviation from desert constraints. Limited deviations, it might be argued, would permit the pursuit of ulterior objectives without 'too much' unfairness (von Hirsch, 1993: 54–56; von Hirsch and Ashworth, 2005: appendix 2).

These mixed approaches still make desert the primary determinant for the ordering of penalties, but give some extra scope for ulterior purposes. Even such schemes remain constraining, however: especially dangerous offenders might be given substantial extra prison time, but not the ordinary potential recidivist; some extra leeway might be granted to suit a non-custodial penalty to the offender's apparent treatment needs, but not a great deal.

Could still more scope be given to non-desert considerations? In a hybrid rationale, either desert will predominate or something else will. If—in the ordinary case—the seriousness of the crime is the penalty's primary determinant, the system remains desert-dominated. If other (say, crime-preventive) aims are given the greater emphasis, however, that creates a system dominated by those aims. That will reintroduce the familiar problems of consequentialist sentencing schemes—for example, those relating to equity among offenders – and those of insufficient systematic knowledge of preventive effects (see Chapters 1–3 above).

In assessing these alternatives, it needs to be borne in mind that even a 'purely' desert-based sentencing scale is likely to have collateral crime-prevention benefits—in such deterrence as its penalties achieve, and in the possible incapacitative effects of the prison sentences it prescribes for serious crimes. Departing from proportionality for the sake of crime prevention, then, will call not just for a showing that preventive effects might be achieved (for a desert-based system may achieve these too); instead, it would call for a showing that departures are likely to yield *enhanced* preventative effects—which is no easy matter to establish. And here one is likely to confront a fairness/effectiveness trade-off: because crime rates tend to be rather insensitive to small variations in punishment, modest departures from proportionality are likely to have relatively little impact; large departures might possibly work better, but these precisely are the ones that are most troublesome on moral grounds (see Selection 3.4 above).

Other Issues: Severity and Social Deprivation

Must desert lead to harsh penalties? As the theory emerged and became influential at a time when penalty levels rose in many jurisdictions, some critics have argued that the theory must in part be responsible for such increases (Braithwaite and Pettit, 1990: 15–16; Garland, 2001: 9). However, desert theory itself does not require a severe sentencing policy— indeed, as noted earlier, it permits (indeed, arguably points toward) considerable penalty reductions. Moreover, the sentence-reform schemes which rely explicitly on notions of desert tend not to be severe ones: the Minnesota and Oregon sentencing guidelines, for example, call for relatively modest penalties by American standards; European desert-orientated sentencing standards, such as those of Finland and Sweden, are likewise associated with penal moderation (von Hirsch and Ashworth, 2005: ch 6). Measures which most clearly call for tougher sanctions tend to utilise criteria inconsistent with proportionality: mandatory sentences, for example, select particular offence categories for harsh treatment, without regard to the gravity of the offence involved, or the penalties imposed for other offences (*idem*).

Another issue is that concerning just punishment and social deprivation (see Murphy, 1973). Many offenders live in grim social environments that restrict their opportunities for living tolerable and law-abiding lives. Should such persons be punished differently? The penal law is a poor instrument for rectifying social ills: it is social policy, rather than criminal policy, that is the appropriate instrument for addressing problems of social deprivation. But the question remains disturbing, nevertheless. If social policy fails to alleviate poverty and deprivation, how should the deprived offender be sentenced?

It has been pointed out that desert theory at least does not *add* to the punishment imposed on deprived persons—whereas penal consequentialism would do so, to the extent that social deprivation is a sign (say) of greater dangerousness (von Hirsch, 1976, ch 17). But the questions remain whether such persons should have their penalties *reduced*, in view of the obstacles they face in leading law-abiding lives. And if they are to be reduced, puzzling questions remain concerning the grounds for reduction: whether on the basis of diminished culpability (see Hudson, 1998), or for compassion-related reasons (as Andrew Ashworth and I have recently suggested).[8] Granting such mitigation would also create a host of practical and political difficulties—so that the perplexity remains.

Notes

1. For an analysis of the Oregon and Minnesota Guidelines, see von Hirsch *et al* (1987), ch 5 and von Hirsch (1995); for the Swedish sentencing scheme, see Jareborg (1995); for the English system after the Criminal Justice Act 1991, see Ashworth (2005). Proportionality-based systems of sentencing guidance are now being developed in New Zealand, and have been proposed for South Africa (South African Law Commission, 2000).
2. For a critique of utilitarianism, see Williams (1973); for earlier philosophical writings on the idea of desert, see Armstrong (1961) and Morris (1968).
3. See Suggestions for Further Reading, this chapter, for references.
4. For a critique of the 'unjust advantage' theory, see von Hirsch (1986), 57–9; Duff (1986), ch 8.
5. In Duff's view, the hard treatment in punishment should serve to bring the criminal to understand, and repent of, his wrongdoing—and also to provide a vehicle which will enable him to work through and express his penitent understanding.
6. The US Supreme Court formerly held that grossly excessive punishments violated the Constitutional ban on cruel and unusual punishments (see *Weems v US* [(1910) 217 US 349]), but the Court later overruled that doctrine (see *Rummel v Estelle* (1980) 445 US

263). The German Constitutional Court has adopted doctrines barring gross disproportionality of sentence in relation to the seriousness of the crime. For fuller discussion of this question of excessive punishments, see van Zyl Smit and Ashworth (2004).

7.   There exists a conceptually separate further reason for keeping penalty levels low—namely, the idea of 'parsimony'—of keeping state-inflicted suffering to a minimum; see von Hirsch and Ashworth (2005), 142.

8.   For a fuller recent discussion of such compassion-based grounds, see von Hirsch and Ashworth (2005), ch 5.

References

American Friends Service Committee, (1971) *Struggle for Justice* (New York: Hill & Wang).

Armstrong, KG, (1961) 'The Retributivist Hits Back' 70 *Mind* 471.

Ashworth, A, (2005) *Sentencing and Criminal Justice*, 4th edn (Cambridge, Cambridge University Press).

Braithwaite, J, and Pettit, P, (1990) *Not Just Deserts* (Oxford, Oxford University Press).

Dolinko, D, (1992) 'Three Mistakes of Retributivism' 39 *UCLA Law Review* 1623.

Duff, RA, (1986) *Trials and Punishments* (Cambridge: Cambridge University Press).

—— (2001) *Punishment, Communication and Community* (Oxford, Oxford University Press).

Finnis, J, (1980) *Natural Law and Natural Rights* (Oxford, Oxford University Press)

Garland, D, (2001) *The Culture of Control: Crime and Social Order in Contemporary Society* (Oxford, Oxford University Press).

Hudson, B, (1998) 'Doing Justice to Difference' in A Ashworth and M Wasik (eds), *Fundamentals of Sentencing Theory: Essays in Honour of Andrew von Hirsch* (Oxford, Oxford University Press) ch 9.

Jareborg, N, (1995) 'The Swedish Sentencing Reform', in: C.M.V. Clarkson and R. Morgan (eds), *The Politics of Sentencing Reform* (Oxford, Oxford University Press).

Kleinig, J, (1973) *Punishment and Desert* (The Hague, Martinus Nijhoff).

Morris, H, (1968) 'Persons and Punishment' 52 *The Monist* 475.

Murphy, JG, (1973) 'Marxism and Retribution' 2 *Philosophy and Public Affairs* 217.

Narayan, U, (1993) 'Adequate Responses and Preventive Benefits' 13 *Oxford Journal of Legal Studies* 166.

Robinson, P, (1987) 'Hybrid Principles for the Distribution of Criminal Sanctions' 82 *Northwestern Law Review* 19.

Singer, R, (1979) *Just Deserts* (Cambridge, MA, Ballinger Publishing Co).

South Africa Law Commission (2000) *Report: Sentencing—a New Sentencing Framework* (Pretoria, Law Commission).

von Hirsch, A, (1995) 'Proportionality and Parsimony in American Sentencing Guidelines' in CMV Clarkson and R Morgan (eds) *The Politics of Sentencing Reform* (Oxford, Oxford University Press).

von Hirsch, A, (1993) *Censure and Sanctions* (Oxford, Oxford University Press).

von Hirsch, A, (1986) *Past or Future Crimes* (Manchester, Manchester University Press).

von Hirsch, A, (1976) *Doing Justice* (New York, Hill & Wang).

von Hirsch, A and Ashworth, A, (2005) *Proportionate Sentencing: Exploring the Principles* (Oxford, Oxford University Press).

von Hirsch, A, Knapp, K and Tonry, M, (1987) *The Sentencing Commission and Its Guidelines* (Boston, MA, Northeastern University Press).

van Zyl Smit, D and Ashworth, A, (2004) 'Disproportionate Sentences as Human Rights Violations' 67 *Modern Law Review* 541.

Wasik, M and von Hirsch, A, (1988) 'Non-Custodial Penalties and the Principles of Desert', *Criminal Law Review* 555.

Wasserstrom, R, (1980) 'Punishment' in R Wasserstrom, *Philosophy and Social Issues: Five Studies* (Notre Dame, IN, University of Notre Dame Press).

Williams, B, (1973) 'A Critique of Utilitarianism' in JSC Smart and B Williams, *Utilitarianism: For and Against* (Cambridge, Cambridge University Press).

4.3

Punishment, Retribution and Communication

RA DUFF

1. Punishment as Retributivist Communication

The retributivist revival that was such a striking feature of Anglo-American penal theory in the latter part of the twentieth century claimed to do justice, in a way that neither consequentialist theories nor those 'mixed' theories that allowed only a purely negative or limiting role to the idea of retribution could, to the rights and moral standing both of the innocent and of the guilty: a system of criminal punishment should not only refrain from punishing the (known) innocent, or punishing the relatively innocent by punishing the guilty more harshly than they deserve; it should treat the guilty with the respect due to them as responsible agents, by punishing them in accordance with their deserts.

The central challenge for any retributivist is to explain this notion of penal desert. We are told that 'the guilty deserve to suffer' and that the proper function of punishment is to impose that deserved suffering on them: but just what is it that they deserve to suffer, and why? What is this alleged justificatory relationship between crime and punishment: what is it about crime that makes punishment—the official infliction of something intended to be burdensome—an appropriate (if not the only appropriate) response? Different versions of retributivism offer a range of different answers to these questions: insofar as such answers fail to explain or to persuade, we are driven either to some version of consequentialism that finds the justifying aim of punishment in its beneficial effects (even if our pursuit of those effects is constrained by the non-consequentialist demands of a negative retributivism), or to the abolitionist claim that criminal punishment cannot be justified, since it involves the systematic, deliberate and therefore unjustifiable delivery of pain to those who break the law.

I will not rehearse here the various versions of retributivism that have found favour (and attracted criticism) in recent years; I want instead to focus on one version that still seems to me the most promising. This version begins with the thought that we should focus not merely on the effects of punishment (as consequentialists do) or on its material impact on the interests of the offender (as many retributivists do), but on its meaning—particularly on its meaning as

This Selection is published here for the first time.

conveying censure or condemnation of the crime both to the offender and to a wider audience that includes the victim (if there is one) and the community at large.

A communicative conception of punishment can, first, help to explain *what* the guilty deserve to suffer. They do not deserve simply 'to suffer'—as if any kind of suffering would do. They deserve to suffer the pain of being censured by their fellow citizens; and whatever else might be mysterious in the idea of penal desert, it is not mysterious that wrongdoing deserves censure; and censure is supposed to be painful. They also deserve to suffer the pain of remorse: for if I have done wrong, it is appropriate that I should feel remorse for it; and remorse is necessarily painful. Since punishment, on this conception, aims to communicate censure to wrongdoers, and since censure aims to induce remorse in the person censured, we can say that punishment aims to impose on (or induce in) offenders the suffering they deserve —the kind of suffering that constitutes an appropriate response to their wrongdoing.

Secondly, if we ask why it is a proper task for the state to impose or induce such deserved suffering, the answer is that this is a matter of justice. In a legitimate system of criminal law, crimes are public wrongs—wrongs that violate the political community's core values, and that therefore properly concern the whole polity. They therefore require a public response—an authoritative public condemnation of the wrong and censure of the wrongdoer. We owe this to the victim, since to fail to condemn the wrong is to fail to take it, or her, seriously. We owe it to the polity whose values were violated, since to be committed to those values and to that polity is to be prepared, inter alia, to respond critically to such attacks on them. We also owe it to the wrongdoer, since to take him seriously as a moral agent is to be prepared, inter alia, to respond critically to his wrongdoings.

Thirdly, as a communicative enterprise that takes offenders seriously as moral agents, punishment respects their moral standing: we are not just coercing or manipulating them for the sake of some consequential benefit, or oppressing them out of our vengeful hatred; we are addressing them as responsible moral agents, in terms appropriate to the wrongs they have committed.

However, any communicative account of punishment faces an obvious question about the medium of communication. Censure can be communicated verbally—in the offender's conviction, in a speech by the judge, through other kinds of public denunciation. It could be communicated through purely symbolic punishments, which are painful or burdensome only insofar as the person punished responds to their censorious meaning. But our own systems of criminal law go well beyond such verbal condemnations or purely symbolic punishments, to impose 'hard treatment' sanctions which are burdensome independently of their censorious meaning (Feinberg, 1970). We deprive offenders of their liberty by imprisoning them, of their money by fining them, of their time by requiring them to undertake community service: such penalties involve penal hard treatment, since offenders who are deaf to their censorious message will still find them, and are still meant to find them, burdensome.

Such hard treatment sanctions *can* communicate the censure that offenders deserve; but why should we choose this medium of communication, rather than one that involves no such hard treatment? Why should we not just impose purely verbal censures, or purely symbolic punishments? In the following section, I discuss two answers to this question.

2. Penal Communication and Hard Treatment

There are two ways of trying to justify using hard treatment as the medium of communication from within an approach that posits the communication of censure as the primary justifying rationale of criminal punishment.

First, we could accept that the aim of communicating censure, as a species of retribution that the offender deserves, cannot by itself justify this choice of medium: to justify choosing hard treatment, rather than mere words or purely symbolic punishments, as our medium, we must bring a consequentialist concern for efficient crime prevention back into the picture. We know that merely verbal denunciations and purely symbolic punishments would leave many potential offenders unmoved: the prospect of such sanctions would not dissuade them from crime, since they are not open to that kind of purely moral persuasion. If we do nothing more to dissuade such people from crime, the results will be disastrous, both for the victims of the crimes they will commit and for the community whose peace and security is thus destroyed. For the sake of those victims and the community, we should therefore communicate the censure that wrongdoers deserve through a medium—penal hard treatment—which will also provide an additional prudential deterrent for those who are not moved by the law's moral appeal; the law must speak to those who are deaf to its moral voice in a language of self-interest and threats that they will understand and by which—we can hope—they might be persuaded (see von Hirsch, 1993; for criticism, see Duff, 2001: ch 3.3).

This approach gives us a new kind of 'mixed' theory of punishment. It is 'mixed' in that it appeals both to retributivist and to consequentialist considerations for the justification of a system of criminal punishment. However, the previous kind of mixed theory offered by Hart and others gave consequentialist considerations the primary role, as providing punishment's positive justification or 'general justifying aim'; retributivist considerations figured as side-constraints on our pursuit of that aim (Hart, 2008). On this new kind of account, by contrast, retribution—the communication of deserved censure—is central to the general justifying aim. It is indeed now the primary aim: we fall back on prudential deterrence only in order to dissuade those who remain deaf to the moral voice of censure. Such an account can therefore claim to meet the Hegelian objection that a deterrent system of punishment treats those threatened with punishment like dogs rather than as responsible moral agents (Hegel, 1942, 246; von Hirsch, 1993: 11), for the law initially addresses its citizens as moral agents, demanding (as censure demands) that they refrain from criminal wrongdoing because it is *wrong*doing; the prudential deterrents that its hard treatment offers those who are not sufficiently moved by that moral appeal constitute supplements to rather than replacements of the message of rational moral communication.

This account gives up on the ambition of treating actual and potential offenders purely as moral agents who can be addressed in the language of moral censure; it accepts that we also need an element of prudential deterrence if the criminal law is to provide the protection that a political community must offer its citizens. Perhaps that is the best we can do; perhaps, indeed, we should recognise that such a system is morally appropriate for beings like ourselves, who are neither purely moral angels nor wholly amoral beasts, but morally fallible human beings. But perhaps there is an alternative—another way of justifying the choice of hard treatment as the medium of communication, according to which we should communicate censure by hard treatment (of appropriate kinds), rather than purely verbally or symbolically, because that will serve the aims of the communicative enterprise itself more adequately.

This answer depends on a rather richer account of the aims of the communicative process than is suggested by talking simply of the communication of censure: an account according to which punishment ought to be a two-way process of communication between community and offender (and victim). Hard treatment, it suggests, is crucial to both aspects of this mutually communicative enterprise (see Duff, 2001).

First, in communicating censure from the community to the offender, the aim should not be merely to ensure that he hears the censure, but to persuade him to attend to it, in the hope that he will be persuaded by it to repent his crime (and thus also to see the need to reform his future conduct). But merely verbal or symbolic punishments are likely to be inadequate, since they are all too easily ignored or forgotten: it is a depressingly familiar human characteristic that we find it hard to give our wrongdoings the attention they need and too easy to distract ourselves from thinking about them. One function of hard treatment punishment, then, is to make it harder for the offender to ignore the message that punishment communicates: it is a way of helping to keep his attention focused on his wrongdoing and its implications, with a view to inducing and strengthening a properly repentant understanding of what he has done.

Secondly, something also needs to be communicated from the offender to the community and to the victim (when there is a victim). He has committed a wrong against the victim, and against the whole community, and he must 'make up' for that wrong by making reparation to them. In the context of the criminal law, what matters is not reparation for whatever harm he may have caused (that is a matter of civil rather than of criminal law), but moral reparation for the wrong that he has done. Central to such moral reparation is apology. If I recognise that I have wronged you, I must also recognise that I owe you an apology: that is how I can try to repair the wrong. Apology expresses my repentant recognition of the wrong I did: it owns the wrong as mine but disowns it as something I now repudiate; it implies a commitment to avoid doing wrong in future; and it expresses my desire to seek forgiveness from and reconciliation with the person I wronged.

A verbal apology is often sufficient reparation: nothing more is, or should be, expected. Sometimes, however, when the wrong is more serious, or when victim and wrongdoer do not stand in the kind of relationship in which words can carry sufficient moral weight, words are not enough, since words can be too cheap and too easy: if the apology is to address the wrong adequately, if it is to show the victim that the wrong is taken seriously, and if it is to focus the wrongdoer's attention on the wrong as it should be focused, it must take a more than merely verbal form. That 'more than merely verbal form' will involve something burdensome that the wrongdoer undertakes—some task that he undertakes for the benefit of the victim or the wider community, some penitential suffering that he undergoes, perhaps some burdensome programme aimed at dealing with the roots of his wrongdoing. The key point to note here is that it must be burdensome to him if it is to serve its apologetic purpose: something that was not burdensome, something that cost no more than mere words, would be no more adequate an apology than mere words; and if I am to give material form to my repentant recognition of the burden of guilt that I now carry, that form must itself be something burdensome.

(This is one of many contexts in which we might need to express ourselves in material rather than merely verbal form: consider, for instance, the ways in which we might express gratitude for a great benefit done to us not just by words of thanks, but by offering a reward or gift to our benefactor; or the ways in which we give material form to grief through the rituals and ceremonies of mourning.)

The second communicative aspect of punishment, then, is the communication of apology from the offender to those whom she wronged—the direct victim and the wider community: the penal hard treatment gives material form, and thus greater moral force, to that apology. Of course, we know that many offenders who undergo punishment are not genuinely apologetic; in undergoing their punishment they are not expressing a genuinely repentant recognition of the wrong they have done. Criminal punishment is thus on this account a species of required apology: the offender is required to go through the motions of apology, even if she does not mean it.

It might now be objected that such required apologies lack real value, and that to require people to apologise is inconsistent with a due respect for their autonomy as responsible moral agents. But we can still see value even in required apologies whose sincerity is unknown or doubtful: for they make clear to the offender what she ought to do (apologise sincerely), and to the victim that the community recognises and takes seriously the wrong he has suffered. As to respect for autonomy, what punishment requires of the offender is not actual repentance, but that she undergo the ritual of apology and moral reparation: this respects her autonomy in that it is still up to her to make, or refuse to make, that apology a genuine one. It is still an exercise in rational communication rather than in improper coercion or manipulation, since it still constitutes an attempt to persuade her to recognise and to repent what she has done, an attempt which must leave her free to remain unpersuaded. By requiring her to undergo the burdensome sanction that would constitute appropriate reparation for the wrong that she did, we hope that she will come to recognise the need for that reparation herself, and make it her own: but we still leave it to her to be persuaded or to remain unpersuaded.

Criminal punishment, on this account, can be seen as a species of secular penance: it is a burden that the wrongdoer is required to accept or undertake, in order both to induce, deepen and confirm his own repentant recognition of the wrong he has done and to communicate to his victim and to his fellow citizens his repentantly apologetic desire to make reparation to them and to reconcile himself with them.

It is worth emphasising that whilst this account is retributivist in that it justifies criminal punishment as an intrinsically appropriate, deserved response to a past crime, it also posits a forward-looking purpose for punishment. For communicative punishments, as here portrayed, aim to persuade offenders to repent their crimes and to begin to reform themselves, to make moral reparation for the wrongs they have done, and to reconcile them with their victims and their fellow citizens: these are all goods that punishment aims to achieve. This account thus offers a 'third way' between retributivism and consequentialism: a way that does justice both to the retributivist thought that punishment must be focused on and justified by a past crime and to the consequentialist concern that punishment must aim to achieve some good. This is not to say, however, that I am offering yet another 'mixed' theory that combines retributivist with consequentialist aims: for the connection between punishment and these further aims is on this account not, as it is on a consequentialist account, purely contingent and instrumental.

First, what makes punishment an appropriate method of pursuing those ends (repentance, self-reform, reparation and reconciliation) is not that it is likely to be instrumentally efficient in achieving them, but that it is intrinsically appropriate to them: this is the proper way to try to achieve those ends if we are to show offenders (as well as victims) the respect and concern due to them, since only in this way do we address them as responsible moral agents in terms appropriate to the wrongs that they have committed and must now repair.

Secondly, even if we have good reason to be empirically sure that our attempt to persuade an offender to repentance will fail, we must still make the attempt (whereas a consequentialist interested only in instrumental efficacy would see no reason to make it), for not to make it would be to give up on the offender as a moral agent—as someone within the reach of remorse—which is something we should never do.

Clearly, much more needs to be said to explain and defend this account. However, I will end by sketching some implications that this account has for sentencing, which should also make its character and its merits clearer.

3. Communicative Sentencing

What kinds of sentencing principle and policy would flow from a communicative, penitential conception of punishment? I will note here just three central points—about proportionality, about different modes of punishment and about negotiated sentences.

First, a principle of proportionality is integral to this account—as to any communicative theory (see von Hirsch, 1993: ch 2). For if punishment communicates censure, the severity of the punishment imposed will determine the seriousness of the censure that is communicated: a harsher punishment communicates a harsher censure. If punishment is to address offenders honestly (as it must if it is to address them as responsible agents), its severity must be at least relatively proportionate to the seriousness of the offence for which it is imposed: offences of roughly equal seriousness should receive punishments of roughly equal severity, and more serious offences should be punished more severely. Some communicative theorists argue that proportionality should be the primary consideration in sentencing: the primary task of the sentencer is to identify the, or a, proportionate punishment (see von Hirsch, 1993). My account, by contrast, does not give proportionality so dominant a role. What matters is to find a sentence that will be communicatively adequate to the offence and the offender. This will be possible only if sentencers have some substantial discretion as to the kind of sentence they impose: sentences must not be disproportionate to the seriousness of the crime, but, within the limits set by this looser demand for negative proportionality, sentencers need not try to find *the* proportionate kind or severity of sentence (compare Frase, Selection 4.4 below).

Secondly, this account requires us to attend not just to the general meaning of punishment as a mode of censure, but to the distinctive meanings of different modes of punishment—to ask what kinds of punishment should be available to sentencers, and which are appropriate to what kinds of crime. What does imprisonment or a fine, Community Service Order or probation order say to the offender and others about the offender and her offence? This is a dimension of punishment that has not received enough theoretical attention. Once we attend to it, we will see further reason to reduce our reliance on imprisonment (since the message of imprisonment is complete exclusion from normal community, it can be appropriate only for the most serious crimes); to reduce the use of fines, which are the most widely used form of non-custodial sentence in Britain but which, if too widely used, could be read as implying that money can 'pay for' most crimes (see Young, 1994); and to increase the use both of probation (since it provides a structure within which direct communication can be maintained between the probation officer and the offender) and of various kinds of Community Service Order (which can constitute a vivid way of making reparation to the community).

Thirdly, in our existing systems of law, sentences are typically determined and imposed by the court, perhaps in the light of reports or recommendations from probation officers, social workers or others with some relevant expertise. Some believe that the victim should also be allowed a say in sentencing. It is generally taken for granted, however, that the offender has no active role to play here: he is the passive recipient of whatever sentence the court decides to impose. On a thoroughly communicative account, by contrast, the paradigm of sentencing is precisely a negotiation—a discussion between offender, victim (if there is a victim who is willing) and the wider community (represented by, for example, a probation officer) about the nature and implications of the crime, and about what would count as an appropriate kind of moral reparation—that is, punishment—for it. This is suggested by the very idea of punishment as a communicative enterprise: if our aim is to bring the offender to a clearer moral understanding of the crime and its implications, and to accept the need to make apologetic reparation, such a sentencing discussion has an obviously useful role to play in that exercise. The negotiation will of course be subject to constraints, to ensure that the punishment is not disproportionate to the crime or in other ways inappropriate, and its outcome will need to be approved by the court; but if we are to communicate with the offender as a responsible agent, we should try to involve him in the sentencing discussion (compare Cavadino and Dignan, 1998). This idea has something in common with the kinds of mediation scheme favoured by advocates of 'restorative justice' (see further Chapter 5 below), but there are two crucial differences: first, that it is predicated on an authoritative condemnation of the offence as a wrong; and secondly, that its aim is to determine an appropriate punishment (see Duff, 2003).

One final point should be emphasised. Although I have argued that criminal punishment can, in principle, be adequately justified as an exercise in moral communication, that is not to justify our existing penal practices. Indeed, an important role for normative penal theory is to offer a critical standard against which we can assess existing institutions and practices. Such an assessment must attend both to the operations of the criminal justice system itself and to the social and political conditions on which its legitimacy depends, and I have no doubt that it will show our existing penal institutions to fall well short of being justified (see further Duff, 2001: ch 5); the task then is to work out how we can reform not only those institutions, but also our political and social structures, so that criminal punishment can be justified.

References

Cavadino, M, and Dignan, J, (1998) 'Reparation, Retribution and Rights' in A von Hirsch and A Ashworth (eds), *Principled Sentencing*, 2nd edn (Oxford, Hart Publishing).

Duff, RA, (2001) *Punishment, Communication, and Community* (New York, Oxford University Press).

—— (2003) 'Restoration and Retribution' in A von Hirsch *et al* (eds), *Restorative Justice and Criminal Justice: Competing or Reconcilable Paradigms?* (Oxford, Hart Publishing) 43–59.

Feinberg, J, (1970) 'The Expressive Function of Punishment' in J Feinberg, *Doing and Deserving* (Princeton, NJ, Princeton University Press) 95–118.

Hart, HLA, (2008) *Punishment and Responsibility* (Oxford, Oxford University Press, 2nd edn; first published 1968).

Hegel, GWF, (1942) *The Philosophy of Right* (trans TM Knox) (Oxford, Oxford University Press; first published 1821).

Von Hirsch, A, (1993), *Censure and Sanctions* (Oxford, Oxford University Press).

Young, P, (1994) 'Putting a Price on Harm: The Fine as a Punishment' in RA Duff *et al* (eds), *Penal Theory and Practice* (Manchester, Manchester University Press) 185–96.

4.4

Limiting Retributivism

RICHARD S FRASE

The Emergence of Morris's Limiting Retributive Theory

The first comprehensive statement of Morris's LR theory was presented in his 1974 book. *The Future of Imprisonment*, and was further developed in later lectures and writings. Morris's upper limits of desert are strict and explicit: "No sanction should be imposed greater than that which is 'deserved' for the last crime, or series of crimes" being sentenced (Morris 1974, pp. 60, 73–77). However, Morris strongly emphasized that courts are not obligated to impose the maximum that the offender deserves (ibid., p. 75). In later writings, Morris extended the concept of maximum desert to include the defendant's prior record of convictions (Morris 1982, pp. 151–152, 162–163, 184–186; 1992, p. 145).

In Morris's view, "desert also sometimes dictates the minimum sanction a community will tolerate" (Morris 1974, p. 78), thus, the sentence must not "depreciate the seriousness" of the current offense (ibid., p. 60). This language was taken from the Model Penal Code. Although Morris often refers to this as a retributive concept, he also saw it as consistent with a norm-reinforcement theory: such minimum severity limits are needed because "[t]he criminal law has general behavioral standard-setting functions; it acts as a moral teacher" (Morris 1974, p. 78). However, Morris has consistently opposed mandatory-minimum statutes.

Within the upper and lower limits of desert, Morris envisioned a range of "not undeserved" penalties. In some writings he characterizes these ranges as "overlapping and quite broad" (Morris 1982, p. 151). He also explicitly differentiated his own views from other desert-based theories by distinguishing between purposes of punishment which are "defining," those which are "limiting," and those which are only "guiding" principles (Morris 1977a, pp. 140–142; 1982, pp. 182–187). Morris suggested that deterrent purposes could precisely define the proper punishment, but only if we knew much more than we now do about the deterrent effects of punishment. As for desert, however, he argued that this concept is inherently too imprecise (and perhaps also too lacking in political and philosophical consensus, Morris and Tonry 1990, pp. 86–89) to precisely define

From RS Frase, 'Limiting Retributivism' in M Tonry (ed), *The Future of Imprisonment* (New York, Oxford University Press, 2004) 85–111.

the sentence; it can only establish rough outer limits, an allowable sentencing range, beyond which penalties would be widely seen as clearly undeserved (i.e., either excessively severe or excessively lenient) (Morris 1977a, pp. 158–159; 1982, pp. 198–199; Morris and Tonry 1990, pp. 104–105). Within those broad ranges of desert, other punishment goals, acting as "guiding principles," will interact to "fine-tune" the sentence. A guiding principle is "a general value which should be respected unless other values sufficiently strongly justify its rejection in any given case" (Morris 1977a, p. 142).

What, then, are Morris's "guiding principles" and what precise role does each play? Morris was an early critic of the rehabilitative ideal. In later writings he argued that post-prison risk cannot reliably be predicted based on in-prison behavior; that coerced in-prison treatment programs waste resources on unamenable subjects, while encouraging feigned cooperation which may actually preclude genuine reform; and that such coercive treatment would be morally wrong even if it were effective (Morris and Hawkins 1970, ch. 5; Morris 1974, pp. 12–27; 1977a, p. 139; Morris and Hawkins 1977, ch. 6). Thus, Morris concluded that rehabilitation is not a reason either to impose or to extend a prison sentence, and that all in-prison treatment programs must be voluntary and not linked to the timing of release. However, Morris strongly advocates community-based treatment and apparently does not object to requiring a person on probation or parole to participate in an appropriate community-based treatment program closely related to the conviction offense (Morris and Hawkins 1970, pp. 112–113, 118–124; Morris 1974, pp. 34, 42–43; Morris and Tonry 1990, pp. 186–203, 206–212).

Morris's views on the goal of incapacitation were similarly in conflict with the traditional theory and practices of indeterminate sentencing—he opposed basing prison commitment, duration, and release decisions on individualized assessments of the defendant's degree of "dangerousness" (Morris 1974, pp. 62–73; 1977b, pp. 276–277). Again, Morris argued that we lack the ability to accurately predict future behavior and are very likely to err on the side of massive overprediction and overincarceration. However, he would permit parole release decisions to be based on actuarial predictions of parole success, for various offender categories (Morris 1977a, p. 148), as well as predictions based on the defendant's past behavior (Morris 1974, p. 34). In later writings, Morris—always the realist—recognized that individualized predictions of dangerousness will be made, whether they are formally permitted or not (Morris 1992, p. 139). He therefore sought to define the narrow conditions under which such predictions might be a fair and effective basis for prison commitment and duration decisions. In particular, he argued that sentencing severity may be increased (up to the retributive maximum) if "reliable actuarial data" indicates that the defendant's risk of assaultive behavior is "substantially" higher than that of other offenders with very similar prior record and current offense (Morris 1982, pp. 166–172; 1992, pp. 138–147; see also Morris and Miller 1985 and Miller and Morris 1986). However, Morris felt that these conditions would rarely be met.

Morris would also allow increased severity (up to the retributive maximum) for recidivists, when "other less restrictive sanctions have been frequently or recently applied to this offender" (Morris 1974, pp. 60, 79–80). He seemed to base such increases on retributive grounds (Morris 1974, pp. 79–80), but they can also be justified on a theory of special deterrence or incapacitation of high-risk defendants. Although Morris rejected most individual assessments of risk, he approved of parole release decisions based on actuarial predictions—"[t]he best predictor of future criminality is past criminality" (Morris 1982, pp. 162–163). He would also permit sentencing severity to be increased (up to the retributive maximum) if such an increase "is necessary to achieve socially justified [general] deterrent purposes, and the punishment of this offender is an appropriate vehicle to this end" (Morris 1974, pp. 60, 79).

In Morris's view, the goal of equality in punishment is important "but it is by no means a categorical imperative . . . the principle of equality—that like cases should be treated alike—is . . . only a guiding principle which will enjoin equality of punishment unless there are other substantial utilitarian reasons to the contrary" (Morris 1982, pp. 160, 198; see also Morris 1977a, pp. 137, 142). Morris acknowledges "the long tradition of justice as equality" (Morris 1982, p. 204) and also recognizes that equality is an especially important value in the American context (Morris 1982, p. 180). Nevertheless, he argues that, within the range of "not undeserved" penalties, punishment can be unequal—and even, in some sense, "unfair"—and yet still be "just" (Morris 1977a, pp. 151–163; 1982, pp. 187–192). He noted that numerous traditional law enforcement and sentencing practices (e.g., giving leniency to defendants who turn state's evidence; pardon and amnesty; granting of early parole release to avoid prison overcrowding) are inconsistent with a very restrictive requirement of equality. In light of such substantial (and, perhaps, inevitable) system-wide inequality, the sentencing process cannot, and should not, attempt to observe strict equality constraints (Morris 1982, pp. 206–208). This conclusion also follows from his strong belief in the concept of parsimony (discussed later on), which "overcomes the principle of equality" (Morris 1982, p. 191; 1977a, p. 154).

Parsimony is one of Morris's most important guiding principles—"[t]he least restrictive (punitive) sanction necessary to achieve defined social purposes should be imposed" (Morris 1974, p. 59). Morris found direct support for this principle in the ABA's Sentencing Standards, the Model Penal Code, and Eighth Amendment principles (see the section on "LR Concepts Recognized by Other Writers and in Model Codes and Standards"), as well as in mental health and juvenile justice dispositional standards (Morris 1974, pp. 60–62). For Morris, the principle of parsimony "is both utilitarian and humanitarian" (Morris 1974, p. 61). Parsimony in the use of custodial sentences also permits the preservation of the defendant's social ties (Morris 1974, pp. 8, 75) and the avoidance of needless suffering and expense (Morris 1977a, p. 154). In any event, Morris argued, the ability to grant case-level mitigation of punishment, without strict desert or equality constraints, is a necessary and inevitable feature of our chronically overloaded and underfunded criminal justice system (Morris 1977a, pp 156–158; 1982, p. 190).

To summarize, Morris believed that judges should use the lower end of the range of deserved punishments as a starting point and should increase that penalty only to the extent that one or more of his other guiding factors requires increased severity. Thus, the specific sentence would be determined by whichever factor required the greatest severity. Of course, the guiding principles of equality and parsimony will often be in conflict. But if the presumption in favor of the least severe sentence is a *strong* one, and if judges thus usually sentence near the bottom of the "not-undeserved" range, then sentences will tend to be fairly uniform among offenders whose cases fall in the same range. Morris probably did expect that sentences would cluster near the bottom of the desert range—if only for lack of sufficient utilitarian justification for raising them higher; he has often argued that criminal laws and punishments have very little effect on crime rates (Morris 1977b, pp. 267–269; 1993, P. 309) . . .

The Need for a More Precise Formulation of the LR Model

As a survey of LR theories and systems in practice shows, LR can mean, and has meant, very different things. Indeed, several formulations of this concept can be found even in Morris's own writings. His earlier work suggested very broad, overlapping ranges of "not undeserved" punishment, perhaps not much more confining than the broad statutory ranges provided in most indeterminate sentencing codes of the time. In later writings, Morris's desert ranges seemed to become narrower. He approved of state sentencing guidelines reforms under which the range of presumptively deserved punishment for many offenses is much narrower than typical statutory ranges. He also proposed using interchangeable punishments, and exchange rates between different sanction types, to maintain rough equivalency of sanction severity for equally culpable offenders while allowing sanctions to be tailored to the particular needs of the offender (Morris and Tonry 1990). Morris probably still intended to allow a wider range of sanction severity than pure desert theorists would allow, but how much wider?

The flexibility of the LR concept is part of its strength—it can be accepted and adopted in a wide range of legal, social, and political contexts. But LR must, itself, be kept within some limits or it ceases to have any real meaning or utility. Much of the criticism of Morris's theory is based on his earlier, wider range version. Such critics may have sometimes unfairly characterized Morris's theory and ignored its evolution over time, but one can legitimately object that his theory seems to contain no principles that prevent adherents from adopting an extremely loose version or a very strict one. Without further specification, LR could conceivably include anything between a traditional indeterminate sentencing scheme and the strictest form of determinate sentencing.

State guidelines such as those in Minnesota provide a useful model for a more delimited formulation of LR. Such guidelines narrow the available sentencing range for most cases, thus substantially constraining case-level discretion, while still leaving considerable room for individualization and the parsimonious application of utilitarian sentencing goals. The departure option provides further flexibility, subject to the outer limits of sentence type and severity specified by statute. This structure seeks to reconcile the universal conflict between the values of uniformity (equality, proportionality, predictability) and the advantages of flexibility (efficiency, parsimony, case-specific justice, and crime-control measures). Within a narrow range, comparable to the Minnesota presumptive-prison cell ranges, judges have almost complete discretion, and flexibility is given priority. Within a broader severity range, up to the statutory maximum and down to the statutory minimum, if any, flexibility is tempered by uniformity goals—judges have limited discretion to sentence in this broader range provided they state reasons, based on desert and subject to appellate review. Judges may not, in any case, exceed the absolute outer limits of authorized sentences for the conviction offense, specified by statute; here, uniformity values are preferred.

Critics of Morris have questioned not only how broad his desert ranges are, but also how the particular sentence ranges—or, in the example discussed earlier, the presumptive guidelines cell ranges and outer statutory limits—would be chosen and justified (von Hirsch 1992, p. 90). Morris has implied that this is ultimately a political decision, which could be made in a variety of ways, including public or judicial surveys, and legislative or sentencing commission deliberation and consensus-building (Morris and Tonry 1990, p. 85). It would also seem that the legislature or commission could look to the methods that pure desert theorists have proposed for generating ordinal ranking and spacing, and use these same methods to produce one series of proportioned upper limits (Tonry 1994, p. 80), tied to appropriate desert-based categories of conviction offense and prior record, and a second series of proportioned lower limits (at least for those offenses deemed serious enough to require minimum desert standards).

As for the question, how are the precise sentences within these ranges (the grid cell and the wider, departure zone) determined, Morris's parsimony principle provides considerable guidance: judges should start at the bottom of the range and increase severity only to the extent needed to meet all appropriate utilitarian and case-specific desert needs . . .

A Desert Model with Interchangeable Sanction Types

Some desert theorists have argued that LR is not needed in order to reconcile utilitarian and just deserts values, and preserve substantial case-level sentencing discretion. Sentencing severity can be precisely scaled to desert by means of sanction equivalency scales and interchangeable sanctions. This would allow equally culpable offenders to receive very different forms of punishment that are deemed to have equivalent punitive bite but which can be tailored to the particular crime control, restorative justice, or other needs of the particular case (Robinson 1987; von Hirsch, Wasik, and Greene 1989; von Hirsch 1992). These theorists argue that a looser, Morris-style LR approach fails to give sufficient weight to the values of uniformity and proportionality. Paul Robinson has also argued that punishment severity must be directly proportional to desert in order to effectively control crime. The direct crime-control effects of criminal punishments are minimal, given low detection and conviction rates, but punishments based on community perceptions of desert can control crime both by reinforcing specific social norms violated by the offender's actions and by maintaining public respect and support for criminal laws generally (Robinson and Darley 1997; see also Hart 1968, p. 25). Robinson argues that this is especially true in modern heterogeneous and secular societies such as the United States, where many criminal prohibitions are morally neutral mala prohibita.

There is much truth to Robinson's arguments, but they do not prove that sanction severity must be precisely scaled to desert. What is the evidence that the public's views on desert scaling are so exacting? Given the widespread adoption of various forms of LR sentencing, a more likely assumption is that the public accepts mitigating deviations from desert, provided they are not too large and are based on good reasons—including conserving scarce resources and not making offenders worse than they were before. (Conversely, the public is probably least willing to accept deviations from desert when the latter result from clearly illegitimate reasons such as favoritism or corruption.)

It is also probably true that people obey the law more readily if they view the law as procedurally and substantively fair (Tyler 1990). However, the earlier review of LR concepts suggests that some aspects of perceived fairness are more important than others. Punishment of the innocent, conviction by unfair procedures, and excessive punishment probably undermine legitimacy and respect for the law much more than failures to punish enough. Everyone knows that the law cannot punish all violators. Most people are also familiar with the use of probation and parole, and thus know that many offenders receive conditional remission of their just deserts. The informed public understands the normative premise underlying the requirement of proof beyond a reasonable doubt—that protection of the innocent is more important than conviction of the guilty.

In other words, the public is well accustomed to and seems to accept the essential features of the LR model—unfair conviction and excessive punishment are greater evils than underconviction and underpunishment (or, in Morris's terms, imposition of less than the maximum "not undeserved" penalty). Barring specific research data about the public's tolerance for various types of deviation from desert, the best evidence is the continued existence, in every jurisdiction in every Western nation, of sentencing systems that reject strong proportionality constraints; the majority of systems still use an indeterminate model, and even the most desert-based regimes such as Minnesota's have adopted LR. As Michael Tonry (1994) has argued, there may be substantial support for a "weak form" of proportionality, similar to LR, but very little support for a strong version.

There is also much truth to the argument that the relative severity with which different criminal acts are punished is an important "communication," influencing public views about the wrongness of conduct and reinforcing moral values and inhibitions. But the public knows that sentences imposed on individual offenders must reflect practical as well as theoretical concerns. Moreover, the modified-LR model proposed here provides considerable norm reinforcement by means of the ordinal scaling embedded in statutory sentence maxima, in the presumptive guidelines ranges, and in the prison and jail sentences imposed by courts—even if many of those sentences are initially stayed.

There is also serious doubt whether consensus can be reached on precise exchange rates for all types of sanctions; indeed, desert theorists have conceded this (von Hirsch, Wasik, and Greene 1989, p. 603). In addition, strong punitive equivalency requirements raise many of the previously noted problems associated with minimum severity requirements for probation conditions (lack of enforceability, complexity, etc.).

In any case, such precise scaling of sanction severity to desert has never been achieved in practice and probably never will be. One fundamental practical barrier to any proposal to closely link every offender's punishment to his deserts is the pervasive need to reward guilty pleas and other forms of defendant cooperation. All modern adjudication and sentencing schemes depend to a great extent on such cooperation. Before and at trial, defendants must be promised leniency to induce and reward guilty pleas, jury trial waivers, testimony against other defendants, and so forth. At sentencing, the court must initially give defendants less than they deserve (or less than the maximum "not-undeserved" penalty)—not only to reward the defendant's cooperation up to that point, but also to induce further cooperation (in obtaining and holding employment, supporting dependents, making restitution, accepting treatment and supervision, etc.) and to leave room for subsequent tightening of sanctions (e.g., by revocation of probation) if the defendant fails to cooperate. Desert theorists recognize this need for "backup sanctions" (von Hirsch 1992, n. 12; von Hirsch, Wasik, and Greene 1989, pp. 609–610), but have not explained how it can be reconciled with a pure desert model. Although some forms of cooperation might be seen as reducing the defendant's "deserts" (at least under a broad definition of that term), many forms do not; society often needs and must reward cooperation whether or not mitigation is deserved. Thus, in practice, modern systems of law enforcement and punishment always function according to an LR model. In the real world of law enforcement and sentencing, a pure, "defining" retributive model is unworkable . . .

References

Hart, H.L.A. (1968), *Punishment and Responsibility* (Oxford: Oxford University Press).
Morris, N. (1974), *The Future of Imprisonment* (Chicago: University of Chicago Press).
—— (1977a), 'Punishment, Desert and Rehabilitation', in *Equal Justice under the Law* (Washington D.C.: US Government Printing Office), pp. 137–167.
—— (1977b), Towards Principled Sentencing', *Maryland Law Review,* 37: 267–285.
—— (1982), *Madness and the Criminal Law* (Chicago: University of Chicago Press).
—— and Hawkins, G. (1970), *The Honest Politician's Guide to Crime Control* (Chicago: University of Chicago Press).
—— and Hawkins, G. (1977), *Letter to the President on Crime Control* (Chicago: University of Chicago Press).
—— and Tonry, M. (1990), *Between Prison and Probation: Intermediate Punishments in a Rational Sentencing System* (New York: Oxford University Press).
Robinson, P. (1987), 'Hybrid Principles for the Distribution of Criminal Sanctions', *Northwestern University Law Review,* 82: 19–42.
—— and Darley, J. (1997), 'The Utility of Desert', *Northwestern University Law Review,* 91: 453–499.
Tonry, M. (1994), 'Proportionality, Parsimony, and mterchangeability of Punishments', in R.A. Duff et al (eds). *Penal Theory and Penal Practice* (Manchester: University of Manchester Press).
Tyler, T. (1990), *Why People Obey the Law* (New Haven: Yale U.P.).
Von Hirsch, A. (1992), 'Proportionality in the Philosophy of Punishment', in *Crime and Justice: a Review of Research,* vol. 16, ed. M. Tonry (Chicago: University of Chicago Press).
——, Wasik, M., and Greene, J. (1989), 'Punishments in the Community and Principles of Desert', *Rutgers Law Journal,* 20: 595–618.

4.5

Seriousness, Severity and the Living Standard

ANDREW VON HIRSCH

The principle of proportionality requires the severity of penalties to be determined by reference to the seriousness of crimes. This means that we need a way of gauging the two predicates crime seriousness and punishment severity. Suppose someone proposes that crime X be visited by punishment Y. To tell whether this is a proportionate sanction, one needs to be able to judge how grave X is compared to other crimes, and how onerous Y is compared to other sanctions.

Judging Crimes' Seriousness

Ordinary people, various opinion surveys have suggested, seem capable of reaching a degree of agreement on the comparative seriousness of crimes.[1] And rule-making bodies that have tried to rank crimes in gravity have not run into insuperable practical difficulties. Several American state sentencing commissions (those of Minnesota, Washington State and Oregon), for example, were able to rank the seriousness of offences for use in their numerical guidelines (see, eg von Hirsch *et al*, 1987: ch 5). While the grading task proved time-consuming, it did not generate much dissension within the commissions.

Less satisfactory, however, has been the state of the theory. What criteria should be used for gauging crimes' gravity? The gravity of a crime depends upon the degree of harmfulness of the conduct and the extent of the actor's culpability. Culpability can be gauged with the aid of clues from substantive criminal law. The substantive law already distinguishes intentional conduct from reckless and from criminally negligent behaviour. It should be possible in principle to develop, for sentencing doctrine, more refined distinctions concerning the degree of purposefulness, indifference to consequences, or carelessness in criminal conduct. The doctrines of excuse in the substantive criminal law could also be drawn upon to develop theories of partial excuse—for example, of partial duress and diminished capacity.

The harm dimension of seriousness is more puzzling, however, as the substantive law fails to provide much assistance: it does not formally distinguish degrees of

Originally published in the first edition of this book as Selection 4.6.

harm. How, then, can one compare the harmfulness of acts that invade different interests: say, compare crime X that invades property interests with crime Y that chiefly affects privacy?

To answer that question, I suggest, victimizing harms might be ranked in gravity according to how much they typically would reduce a person's standard of living (see, more fully, von Hirsch and Jareborg, 1991). That term is used here in the broad sense suggested by Amartya Sen (1987), which reflects both economic and non-economic interests.

The living standard is one of a family of related notions, including well-being, that refer to the quality of persons' lives. Well-being, however, can be highly personalised: my well-being depends on my particular focal aims, and to the person who wants to devote his life to contemplation and prayer, material comfort and ordinary social amenities may matter little. However, the living standard, in Sen's sense, does not focus on actual life quality or goal achievement, but on the means or capabilities for achieving a certain quality of life. Some of these means are material (shelter and financial resources), but others are not (eg privacy). It is also standardised, referring to the means and capabilities that would ordinarily promote a good life. Someone has a good standard of living if he has the health, resources and other means that people ordinarily can use to live well.

Using the living standard as a way of gauging harms has a number of advantages. First, it seems to fit the way we usually judge harms. Why is mayhem more harmful than burglary? It is because the overall quality of the person's life has been more adversely affected. Secondly, the living-standard idea permits drawing from a rich array of experience—including experience outside of the criminal law. We can ask how the harm in an arson compares with that in an accidental fire. Finally, a living-standard analysis would allow for cultural variation. Different social living arrangements can affect the consequences of criminal acts, and normative differences among cultures can affect the impact of those consequences on the quality of persons' lives. The harmfulness of burglary, for example, depends on the degree to which the home is ordinarily the focal point for people's private existences, and on the degree to which privacy is valued. A living-standard analysis thus could, in another culture, lead to a different rating for burglary—if the home has a different social role and if a different valuation is given to privacy.

Our suggested analysis begins with parcelling out the various kinds of interests that offences typically involve. After the interests involved in a given type of offence are identified, their importance is judged by assessing their significance for the living standard.[2]

Most victimising offences involve one or more of the following interest-dimensions: (i) physical integrity; (ii) material support and amenity; (iii) freedom from humiliation; and (iv) privacy. A simple residential burglary, for example, chiefly involves material amenity and privacy. The material loss would consist of what is stolen, plus the inconvenience and expense of repairs; the privacy loss consists of the intrusion of a stranger into the person's living space. To rate the harmfulness of the conduct, the living-standard criterion should be applied to each dimension, successively. In the case of the burglary, the analysis would thus begin with its material amenity dimension. Here, the impact on the living standard would ordinarily be rather small: not much is taken in the typical burglary, so that the person's material well-being would not be much affected. Next, the privacy dimension would be considered. Given the importance of privacy to a good existence, the extent to which an intrusion into the home affects privacy could well make this rating somewhat higher. The attraction of this mode of analysis is that each dimension involved—physical integrity, material support, privacy, or whatever—can ultimately be assessed in terms of a common criterion: that of impact on the living standard. This means that, in the burglary, one can compare the living-standard impact of the material loss (rather minor) with that of the privacy intrusion (arguably, somewhat greater). One could also compare a burglary with another victimising offence involving different interests: say, an assault, where physical integrity and freedom from humiliation are primarily involved.

To aid in this analysis, the living standard itself can be graded. One might use three living-standard levels: (i) subsistence; (ii) minimal well-being; and (iii) 'adequate' well-being. The first, subsistence, refers to survival, but with maintenance of no more than elementary human capacities to function—in other words, barely getting by. The remaining levels refer to various degrees of life quality above that of mere subsistence. The function of the gradations is to provide a rough measure of the extent to which a typical criminal act intrudes upon the living standard. To take an obvious example, aggravated assault threatens subsistence, and thus is substantially more harmful than a theft that still leaves the person with an 'adequate' level of comfort and dignity.

This analysis is to be used chiefly in gauging the standard harm involved in various categories or subcategories of offence. The point is to assess the injuriousness of typical instances of (say) residential burglary, or residential burglary of a certain kind (one might, say, distinguish simple burglary from ransacking), rather than gauge the injury done to an individual when her apartment was broken into and her favourite vase was stolen. The living standard relates, as we have noted, to the standardised means or capabilities for a good life—not to the life quality of particular persons. Deviations from such standardised assessments should be made only in certain circumstances, where the differences from the ordinary case are fairly apparent. While assessments of harm are thus to be standardised to a degree, culpability judgements need not be. A desert-based sentencing system may—indeed, should—afford room for pleas of reduced personal culpability on a variety of grounds such as, for example, that of provocation (see Narayan and von Hirsch, 1996).

This harm analysis is no formula for providing ready answers, because the impact of a crime on the living standard is itself very much a matter of factual and normative judgement. However, it may still be helpful as a guide to thinking about rating harms.

Gauging Punishments' Severity

Grading sanctions presupposes an ability to judge their comparative severity. While prison sanctions can be compared by their duration, the onerousness of non-custodial sanctions depends on their intensity as well. Three days of community service may be tougher than three days of probation but not as tough as three days of home detention.

A number of studies have attempted to measure sanction severity through opinion surveys. A selected group of respondents is shown a list of penalties of various sorts, and asked to rate their severity on a numerical rating scale. The surveys tend to show a degree of consensus.[3] These ratings, however, do not attempt to elucidate what is meant by severity; to elicit respondents' reasons for their rankings; or to assess the plausibility of those reasons. It is necessary to consider what *should* be the basis of comparing penalties—ie to develop a theory of severity.

A possible account of severity would be that it depends upon how disagreeable the sanction typically is experienced as being. On this view, surveys would be the best way to assess penalties: they should simply ask people how unpleasant they think various penalties would be. Unpleasantness or discomfort, arguably, is ultimately subjective: a matter of how deprivations typically are experienced. If penalty Y is generally perceived to be more unpleasant than penalty Z, this simply makes it so.

This approach, however, strikes me as being misconceived. What makes punishments more or less onerous is not any identifiable sensation; rather, it is the degree to which those sanctions interfere with people's interests. The unpleasantness of intensive probation supervision, for example, depends not on its 'feeling bad' in some immediate sense, but on its interfering with such important interests as being in charge of one's own life or moving about as one chooses.

It would thus seem preferable to apply an interests analysis comparable to the one just suggested for gauging crime seriousness. The more important the interests intruded upon by a penalty are, on this theory, the severer the penalty should be considered to be. Penalties could be ranked according to the degree to which they typically affect the punished person's freedom of movement, earning ability and so forth. The importance of those interests could then be gauged according to how they typically impinge on a person's 'living standard'—in the sense of that term sketched earlier in this Selection. Such an interests analysis seems to fit the way we often discuss punishment's severity. When asked to explain why long-term imprisonment is a severe sanction, for example, one is tempted to answer in terms of how its deprivations typically impinge on the quality of someone's life.[4]

Adopting an interest-analysis approach means that the assessment of severity is not made dependent on the preferences of particular individuals. The living standard, as noted earlier, refers to the means and capabilities that ordinarily assist persons in achieving a good life. If a given interest is important in this sense to a good existence, it would warrant a high rating—notwithstanding that some persons choose to go without it. Imprisonment qualifies as a severe penalty because the interests in freedom of movement and privacy it takes away are normally so vital to a decent existence—despite the fact that a few defendants might happen to be claustrophobics. This helps answer an objection that Nigel Walker has raised to desert theory: namely, that one never can grade the onerousness of penalties because people's subjective perceptions of painfulness vary so much (see Walker 1992).

Notes

1. For citations, see Ashworth (2005), 104–106.
2. For a fuller description of this method of analysis, see von Hirsch and Jareborg (1991); see also von Hirsch and Ashworth (2005: app 3). The analysis is designed to apply to crimes that typically involve identifiable victims, as burglary and robbery do. For the possibility of carrying this technique over to crimes that risk injury to unidentified persons, or which affect 'collective' interests, see von Hirsch and Ashworth, *ibid*, 32–5.
3. For citations to these studies, see Wasik and von Hirsch (1988: 563 n 20).
4. To apply the living-standard idea to penalties, there would have to be modifications in the analysis. When evaluating harms, the main interests are (as noted above) those of physical integrity, material amenity and so forth. For punishments, other interests also need to be taken into account: for example, the interest in freedom of movement that is affected by incarceration, home detention and intensive probation supervision.

References

Ashworth, A, (2005) *Sentencing and Criminal Justice*, 4th edn. (Cambridge, Cambridge University Press).

Narayan, U and von Hirsch, A, (1996) 'Three Concepts of Provocation' 15 *Criminal Justice Ethics* 15.

Sen, A, (1987) *The Standard of Living* (Cambridge, Cambridge University Press).

von Hirsch, A, (1993) *Censure and Sanctions* (Oxford, Oxford University Press).

von Hirsch, A and Ashworth, A, (2005) *Proportionate Sentencing: Exploring the Principles* (Oxford, Oxford University Press).

von Hirsch, A and Jareborg, N, (1991) 'Gauging Criminal Harm: A Living-Standard Analysis', *Oxford Journal of Legal Studies*, 11, 1.

von Hirsch, A., Knapp, K. and Tonry, M, (1987) *The Sentencing Commission and Its Guidelines* (Boston, MA, Northeastern University Press).

Walker, N, (1992) 'Modern Retributivism' in H Gross and R Harrison (eds), *Jurisprudence: Cambridge Essays* (Oxford, Oxford University Press).

Wasik, M and von Hirsch, A, (1988) 'Punishments in the Community and the Principles of Desert' 35 *Criminal Law Review* 555.

4.6

The Recidivist Premium: For and Against

4.6(a) Revisiting the Recidivist Sentencing Premium

JULIAN V ROBERTS

With respect to the use of prior convictions, retributive theorists fall into one of two camps. One group—the 'Exclusionary' school—excludes prior convictions entirely: sentence severity should be determined only by the seriousness of the offence and the offender's level of culpability (Fletcher, 1978; Bagaric, 2001). Previous convictions do not, according to this account, affect either dimension of a proportional sanction. The consequence of this policy is that all offenders are, and remain over successive sentencing decisions, first offenders. The alternative retributive school of thought assigns a very limited role to an offender's previous convictions. According to this perspective—encapsulated in the Progressive Loss of Mitigation (PLM) doctrine—first offenders should receive a discounted sentence. The mitigation is repeatedly offered, although at lower levels, until the offender has accumulated approximately five convictions (see Selection 4.6(b) below). Once the mitigation accorded these offenders is exhausted, criminal record should play no further role at sentencing (see Wasik and von Hirsch, 1994).

The first offender mitigation derived from the PLM is offered out of recognition that anyone may lapse once into offending. The principle therefore represents state tolerance for human frailty (see Wasik and von Hirsch, 1994; von Hirsch and Ashworth, 2005); it does not reflect a view that first offenders are less culpable or that repeat offenders more culpable. Despite being consigned to the scrapheap of history by retributive theorists, however, there continues to be interest in the argument that prior convictions are relevant to determining an offender's level of culpability. Indeed, recently there has been a recent resurgence of interest in the relationship between culpability and criminal record (eg MacPherson, 2002; Lee, 2009; Roberts, 2008).

This article attempts to explain the abiding appeal of a policy of imposing harsher sentences on repeat offenders by drawing upon a culpability-based justification for the imposition of harsher sentences upon recidivists. The proposed model further assumes that previous convictions influence ascriptions of blame-

Adapted from: JV Roberts, 'Punishing Persistence: Explaining the Enduring Appeal of the Recidivist Sentencing Premium' (2008) 48 *British Journal of Criminology* 468.

worthiness. The model finds support in popular conceptions of sentencing. Public opinion is relevant—but not determinative—in this context because any communicative sentencing scheme—such as a retributive account—must attract community support. A sentencing system that censures conduct that the public feel does not require condemnation or, alternatively, a system that fails to censure actions and actors considered blameworthy will ultimately lose all credibility. As it happens, the lack of public sympathy for a sentencing model that uses previous convictions only to allow mitigation for first offenders is shared by other parties with a stake in the sentencing process (see Roberts, 2008, p. 94).

I advocate a model which contains a number of elements: (i) first offenders should receive a significantly more lenient sentence than second-time offenders; (ii) the difference between first and second-time offenders should be much greater than between other categories of offender[1] (eg third and fourth-time offenders); (iii) sentence severity should increase with each *relevant* previous conviction; (iv) offenders should have ample scope to rebut the assumption of enhanced blameworthiness; and (v) the recidivist premium should be constrained so that it does not eclipse the primary consideration at sentencing, the seriousness of the offence. In practical terms, this means that a recidivist range of sentence length would exist, with the first-time offender receiving the shortest sentence.

Some Problems with the Principle of the Progressive Loss of Mitigation

The justification for treating first offenders more leniently under the PLM is the concept of tolerance for a lapse. We all make mistakes, sometimes even quite serious ones. This tolerance seems to be an appropriate justification for stepping down the penalty for a first offender. But it must be qualified, and clearly circumscribed. Tolerance is a virtue in individuals and societies alike, but it does not follow from this fact that tolerance is intrinsic to a retributive sentencing framework. The tolerance model also transfers to the state the justification for the leniency. Under a tolerance model we say to the novice offender: 'You deserve X, but because we are tolerant, you will get X minus 50%'. Under the PLM model this becomes X minus 40% for the second offender and so on until the fifth or sixth-time offender gets all of X.

According to most sentencing theories, offenders may be arrayed on a dimension. For consequentialists hoping to prevent crime, offenders are seen to fall along a dimension of risk to reoffend. The offender with 10 priors, all related, is much further along the risk scale than a novice offender and this justifies (for the utilitarian) the higher penalty. Culpability accounts place novice and repeat offenders at different points along a culpability dimension: first offenders are deemed less culpable, recidivists more culpable. Whether one accepts these dimensions or not, they are plain for all to see. Yet the progressive loss of mitigation model fails to explain why the third-time offender should be treated with leniency, but less leniency than the second-time offender. How are we to describe the quality that the second-time offender possesses to a greater degree than the third-time offender? There appears no answer to this question because the justification is located not with the offender but with the state that offers the iteratively (but declining) mitigation. We tolerate the fifth-time offender slightly less than the fourth-time offender, the fourth-time offender slightly less than the third-time offender and so on. The dimension then is tolerance, societal tolerance for criminal wrongdoing. But how does this link to retributive sentencing?

Justifying Leniency for the First Offender

Most first offenders are entitled to a more lenient sentence than that imposed on a recidivist convicted of a similar crime. There is no single ground for this position, but several that have been advanced over the years.

First, the novice may reasonably point to a lifetime of compliance with the law. This reduces the extent to which we blame him for this anomalous lapse into offending. In much the same way we are more lenient with offenders who violate their probation conditions just before the term of probation is about to expire rather than shortly after it has been imposed.

Secondly, the novice offender may claim that he was, until charge, prosecution and conviction, less aware of the truly criminal nature of his conduct, or perhaps of the consequences—for himself or others—of violating the law. He may argue that until hearing testimony in court, including and especially victim impact evidence, that he failed to fully appreciate the harm inflicted upon his victim. Someone who is convicted for the first time of defrauding the elderly may not (or may argue that he did not) fully appreciate the vulnerability of this particular population of victims.

Thirdly, Youngjae Lee (2008) has recently proposed another ground for considering repeat offenders to be more blameworthy than first timers. He makes the argument that, having been convicted and sentenced, an offender should take steps to address the causes of his non-compliance. The absence of any such steps represents an example of culpable omission and enhances his blameworthiness for any subsequent offending.[2]

Fourthly, we may well wish as a society to exercise some tolerance for a lapse resulting in a criminal conviction. But the degree of tolerance is likely to vary considerably according to the seriousness of the crime. The magnitude of the reduction between first and repeat offenders must be tied to the gravity of the offence. The degree of tolerance that we can extend to an offender is an inverse function of the seriousness of the conduct. Put another way, our tolerance should reflect the extent to which the behaviour being (partially) tolerated violates societal norms. Behaviour which constitutes a relatively minor transgression—shoplifting for example—can be, should be and in practice is tolerated over more than one repetition. The same cannot be said for assault causing bodily harm. The first offender may still argue that he 'lost it' on one particular occasion, that he was unaware of the full gravity of his conduct and so forth. But there would appear to be little justification for responding with leniency to repetition of this offence, or indeed of defrauding octogenarians of their life savings. The consequence of this is that the lapse justification should only extend to offences of low seriousness.

The progressive loss of mitigation model simply asks too much of society. Consider the first two grounds for first offender leniency cited above ('That's not me! Look at my law-abiding past' and 'I really didn't realise the old folks would be so upset!'). How much credibility can the offender's appeal for leniency have on these grounds when he repeatedly re-appears for sentencing? As for the lapse model as framed in terms of multiple discounts, we may well ask how many lapses we are willing to accept from an individual. How tolerant of recidivist crime must we be as a society?[3] The lapse model is relevant, but surely only for less serious offences,[4] and maps better on to a simple dichotomy: first offenders and repeat offenders. I shall discuss below arguments why there should also be variations in severity within the category of repeat offenders.

Tolerance in Everyday Life

This raises the question of the link between the tolerance expressed in everyday life and the tolerance institutionalised in criminal sentencing. Should the criminal law display greater tolerance, perhaps because criminal sanctions are more severe than those we inflict in response to quotidian delinquency? Consider the transgressions of everyday life—rudeness in public meetings, boorishness on the bus to work—these behaviours we can and do tolerate repeatedly, although even here there are limits. For the more serious forms of misconduct which are proscribed by the criminal law there should surely be less, not more, tolerance. Why should I display more tolerance—in the sense of repetitive discounts—for someone who assaults another person than the co-worker who is rude to me during a public seminar?

Where does this all leave us? Several propositions emerge from the analysis: (i) first offenders should receive a significantly less severe sentence than repeat offenders; (ii) there are several justifications for this distinction, including societal tolerance for a lapse; (iii) none of these justifications, including societal tolerance, may be invoked by an offender convicted of a medium to high serious crime, such as assault causing bodily harm. These propositions pertain to the first offender; at this point I turn to the question of whether a recidivism premium is appropriate between recidivists with varying criminal histories.

The Enhanced Culpability Model

Enhanced Culpability in Practice

Before further considering the normative argument relating to culpability, it is worth noting the strong association between culpability and criminal history found in most jurisdictions (see Roberts, 2008). In addition, many statutory sentencing provisions, sentencing reform proposals, as well as sentencing guidelines assume that previous convictions enhance the offender's level of culpability for the current offence. The drafters of sentencing laws and guidance in a wide range of jurisdictions consider repeat offenders to be more culpable—in stark contrast to the views of retributive theorists. Can such a diverse collection of individuals and agencies have all misinterpreted the concept of criminal culpability? The divergence between the practice of sentencing schemes around the world and the position of retributive theories can be explained by reference to the factors considered when determining the culpability of the offender. Retributivist theories subscribe to a much more circumscribed analysis which excludes factors such as criminal history which are important to criminal justice practitioners and the public.

Previous Convictions and other Aggravating Circumstances

Evidence of planning and premeditation carries important consequences for the offender. When premeditation constitutes an element of the offence it results in a much higher penalty than that which is imposed on people convicted of spontaneous crime. Premeditation is also an important aggravating circumstance at sentencing (Ashworth, 2005). But exactly why are offenders held to be more culpable or blameworthy simply because they planned the offence? This circumstance is external to the crime: the harm caused by an assault or a burglary does not change because the offender carefully planned the act. If premeditation is relevant to a retributive sentencing analysis it must relate to the other branch of proportionality, namely an offender's level of culpability.

Case law in many jurisdictions supports the position that offenders who plan their crimes are in some way more blameworthy, although the justification for this practice is far from clear and reflects the underdeveloped nature of theories of aggravation. Two avenues—one normative and the other psychological—need to be pursued to understand why the existence of premeditation usually aggravates the sentence that should be imposed. However, it is worth noting the nature of public attitudes towards premeditation as a sentencing factor.

Public Reaction to Premeditation as an Aggravating Factor at Sentencing

Empirical research on public attitudes to sentencing clearly demonstrates that people react more punitively towards offenders when there is evidence of premeditation. Research conducted for the Home Office Sentencing Review demonstrates the importance of premeditation to public conceptions of sentencing. When asked to identify important sentencing factors, the three factors that attracted the highest level of support were the existence of previous convictions, the offender's likelihood of reoffending and 'whether the offence was planned' (Home Office, 2001). Why do the public regard premeditation as an important aggravating circumstance? The research evidence suggests that increased attributions of responsibility have the effect of enhancing ascriptions of blame and hence the severity of assigned punishments. Evidence of premeditation will lead observers to infer that the offender was more responsible for the offence than if the crime had been committed spontaneously. The same argument can be made for previous convictions. As the offender continues to reoffend, particularly if the offences form a pattern, people are more inclined to attribute the crime to the individual (rather than the individual) and this justifies a higher ascription of culpability and consequently the imposition of a more severe penalty (eg Carroll and Payne, 1977).

This analysis only takes us part of the way towards justifying a premeditation-based sentencing premium. Ascriptions of responsibility may become almost exclusively focused on the offender to the total exclusion of environmental forces, but this still does not tell us why this kind of conduct—premeditated crime or crime committed by recidivists– is more morally reprehensible and more worthy of condemnation than spontaneous offending. Premeditation generates higher levels of blame for two reasons. First, an offender who plans an offence, particularly one with serious or fatal consequences, is assuming a total disregard for the law; he is effectively placing himself outside the community by his actions. This circumstance alone makes his actions more reprehensible and renders him more blameworthy.

The second reason takes us back to the 'lapse' theory to account for the progressive loss of mitigation. The lapse theory proposes that the criminal law should recognise human frailty to the extent that people can forget (or choose to ignore) their obligations to comply with the law. However, planning to commit a crime implies a level of moral turpitude which exceeds normal expectations. Everyday conceptions of acceptable conduct include some sense of a behavioural norm; the further that conduct departs from the expected norm, the greater the degree of censure that is visited on the offender. Judgements of moral wrongfulness are affected by the degree to which the conduct flouts consensual values. Premeditated crime constitutes an exceptional degree of impunity with respect to the community values enshrined in the criminal law.

Link between Premeditation and Previous Convictions

An offender's previous convictions may be seen in a similar light. The existence of a number of prior convictions changes our evaluation of the mental state of the offender at the time of the commission of the crime. He or she approaches the fresh offence having been charged, convicted and sentenced, possibly on many occasions.

Awareness of this previous legal censure should recall the individual to respect the law; the offender who reoffends is therefore similar to the offender who plans the offence. Both are worthy of a greater degree of moral reprobation to reflect their enhanced level of culpability. The conduct of the premeditated offender and the repeat offender both represent a more marked departure from acceptable conduct.

This explanation does not require the assumptions about the psychology or motivation of offenders that are necessary for the 'defiance' justification for the recidivist sentencing premium. The seriousness of the offender's prior record provides a reflection of the degree to which the offender is considered reprehensible. This perspective therefore makes distinctions between repeat offenders with variable records, and not simply a binary distinction between first offenders and recidivists. The binary approach would be associated with a justification that was founded on simple awareness of having been censured. Under this model, having once been censured for offending, all repeat offenders would be considered equally culpable.

Circumstances associated with the offender's state of mind prior to the offence are therefore relevant to ascriptions of blameworthiness and subsequently sentence severity. This suggests a relatively broad conception of relevance. Further support for a more expansive conception of blameworthiness may be found by examining the offender's conduct after the commission of the offence.

Conduct of the Offender Following Conviction: The Apologetic, Remorseful Offender

Consider the post-offence period and in particular the offender's reaction to his own criminal conduct. Remorse is a sentencing factor that is considered extra-legal from a retributive perspective; it cannot alter the seriousness of the offence or the offender's responsibility for the offence. But this is surely a short-sighted approach to punishment; one that is inconsistent with some of the fundamental social values that the sentencing process should promote. Despite the problematic nature of this variable from the perspective of retributive theories, the sentencing process has long taken the offender's conduct after the offence into account.

Imagine an offender who, having committed a serious assault, immediately afterwards appreciates the wrongfulness of his conduct. He accepts responsibility for the offence, expresses remorse for his unlawful actions and condemns the assault. These steps are of benefit to the victim, the criminal justice system, the community at large and, indeed, the offender as well. These actions may be taken as evidence of 'good character' by some judges, who may then impose a mitigated punishment to reflect this evaluation. This conceptualisation is inappropriate; the consequence of rewarding good conduct would be that the taciturn offender with little or nothing to say at sentencing is penalised more severely as a result of inappropriate inferences about his character based upon his reticence. But the actions of the offender after the commission of the offence can be seen within a more circumscribed framework; they speak to the actor's relation to the act for which he is being punished. The remorseful offender is concerned with achieving some (partial) rectification of his wrongdoing—he is taking a step away from his offending and thereby reducing the extent to which he is considered blameworthy.

Public Reaction to Remorseful Offenders

An examination of public reaction to offenders who are remorseful exposes the same gap between a retributive model of sentencing and community sentiment that exists with respect to previous convictions. Empirical research has repeatedly demonstrated that the remorse has an important influence over public attitudes to sentencing as well as actual sentencing decisions: the expression of remorse decreases the severity of recommended sentences for even the most serious crimes such as rape (eg Kleinke *et al*, 1992). Sentencers and the general public respond to remorseful offenders with leniency because they make a more global assessment of the seriousness of the case, and this approach incorporates factors generally considered extraneous by retributive sentencing theories.

This more expansive analysis of culpability is thus retrospective and prospective in nature. The offender's conduct before and after the offence provides a context in which to judge not the seriousness of the crime (which is unaffected by antecedent offences or the offender's post-conviction conduct) but the extent to which the offender should be considered blameworthy. Premeditation, previous convictions, and remorse are all relevant to culpability and therefore to retributive sentencing. However, since under a retributive sentencing rationale proportionality is the primordial guiding principle, and since blameworthiness or culpability considerations are secondary to crime seriousness, neither the previous misconduct nor the post-offence conduct should fully eclipse the seriousness of the crime as a determinant of sentence severity. But neither should these considerations be ignored.

Does the Enhanced Culpability Model Constitute Punishing Character?

It is now time to revisit the strongest retributive argument against a recidivist sentencing premium, namely that it constitutes punishment of an offender's character, rather than his conduct. According to this view, the recidivist is regarded as having a bad character and suffers accordingly, although his current criminal conduct may be no more harmful or worthy of condemnation than crimes committed by first offenders. This carries clear dangers for a retributive account of sentencing. Singer (1979: 70) states that

> the argument of character clearly raises the specter of bringing into the sentencing process all of that soft data upon which sentencing judges have relied for the last hundred

years—the defendant's religion, his past unemployment, his relations with his spouse, his childhood history, whether he loves animals, and so forth.

This response constitutes a *reductio ad absurdum*.

The apologetic defendant is not simply making a character-based claim by saying 'go easy on me your Honour, I'm not such a bad sort after all'; she is taking a stand in a public forum against her own offending. The expression of remorse is an offence-related communication. Remorse speaks to the relational nature of sentencing. The offender has effectively signalled her intention to rejoin the community against which she offended and this is recognised by members of the public, who subsequently impose less severe punishments. In this way the expression of remorse may be distinguished from less plausible pleas for mitigation that are also character based—such as having a good war record, or a history of volunteering for the community. Some sentencers may be tempted to judge the offender on elements of his past that reflect upon his current character. However, if the sentencing process articulates the way in which previous convictions—and only convictions—enhance sentence severity, then the problem of punishing character does not arise.

Two Objections: Threat to Proportionality and Effect on Prison Population

If ascriptions of blameworthiness incorporate consideration of offender culpability, and if an evaluation of culpability includes the offender's previous convictions and his post-offence conduct, does this approach threaten proportional sentencing? It might, if the offender's level of culpability carried the same weight at sentencing as the seriousness of the crime. Proportional sentencing requires a clear relationship between the severity of sentence imposed,the seriousness of the crime and the level of culpability. Little has been written about the relationship between crime serious- ness and offender culpability, but a sentencing system concerned with condemning acts rather than actors must ensure that culpability considerations do not exceed, or even match, the seriousness of the offence as a determinant of sentence severity. Consequentialists will continue to escalate the severity of sentence to reflect the offender's risk level, or apparent insensitivity to prudential disincentives. Under the model proposed here, the impact of the offender's previous convictions should not swamp proportionality considerations. The mechanics of achieving this are beyond the scope of this essay to delineate. However, a sentencing guidelines authority would simply ensure that the increased severity was capped at some point.[5]

A second objection to increasing the severity of penalties to reflect an offender's previous convictions is that it will result in more admissions to custody, and for longer periods of time. To this objection the answer must surely be that a rising prison population should be addressed by lowering the overall severity of the system, or through other means such as an across the board increased use of community penalties. If a recidivist premium is a sound sentencing policy, it should not be discarded in order to achieve some other goal, however laudable.

To conclude, although previous convictions are excluded from a consideration of the seriousness of the offence, they should enter the sentencing equation through the determination of the offender's level of culpability. It is patently unreasonable to ignore a characteristic such as previous offending that practitioners, victims, offenders and the community regard as highly relevant to the determination of sentence. The best solution to this stand-off between theory and practice involves recognising the relevance of previous convictions to offender blameworthiness (and consequently sentence severity), and then constraining their influence on the determination of sentence.

Notes

1. The use of custody in particular should be influenced by this distinction; custody should be avoided wherever possible for all offenders, but most particularly for first offenders.
2. To this I would add that the reasons for reoffending may lie outside the offender's control. If an offender is not responsible for the circumstances which gave rise to his offending (even though he is still criminally responsible for the conduct), then there is no ground for attributing greater blame. As I have discussed, at sentencing an offender should be encouraged to place before the court evidence to rebut any ascription of heightened culpability based upon his or her previous convictions.
3. Individual victims might have particular difficulty accepting that the state should exercise tolerance towards offenders in this repetitive manner.
4. In practice, offenders convicted of rape or other serious crimes do not receive a mitigated punishment.
5. Represented graphically on a figure which mapped sentence severity by the number of previous convictions, this model would consist of a curve rising rapidly at first then far more slowly thereafter—very different from the cumulative sentencing curve which involves a straight line from the lower left corner to the upper right one.

References

Ashworth, A, (2005) *Sentencing and Criminal Justice*, 4th edn (Cambridge, Cambridge University Press).

Bagaric, M, (2001) *Punishment and Sentencing: A Rational Approach* (Sydney, Cavendish Publishing).

Carroll, J and Payne, J, (1977) 'Judgements about Crime and the Criminal' in B Sales (ed), *Perspectives in Law and Psychology*, vol 1(New York, Plenum Press).

Fletcher, G, (1978) *Rethinking Criminal Law* (Boston, MA, Little, Brown & Company).

Home Office (2001) *Making Punishment Work: Sentencing Review for England and Wales* (London, Home Office).

Kleinke, C, Wallis, R and Stalder, K, (1992) 'Evaluation of Rapist as a Function of Expressed Intent and Remorse' 132 *Journal of Social Psychology* 525.

Lee, Y, (2009) 'Recidivism as Omission: A Relational Account' 87 *Texas Law Review* (forthcoming).

MacPherson, D, (2002) 'The Relevance of Prior Record in the Criminal Law: A Response to the Theory of Professor von Hirsch' 28 *Queen's Law Journal* 177.

Roberts, JV, (2008) *Punishing Persistent Offenders. Community and Offender Perspectives* (Oxford, Oxford University Press).

Singer, R, (1979) *Just Deserts: Sentencing Based on Equality and Desert* (Cambridge, MA, Ballinger).

von Hirsch, A and Ashworth, A, (2005) *Proportionate Sentencing. Exploring the Principles* (Oxford, Oxford University Press).

Wasik, M and von Hirsch, A, (1994) 'Section 29 Revised: Previous Convictions in Sentencing' 24 *Criminal Law Review* 409.

4.6(b) The Discount Approach: Progressive Loss of Mitigation

ANDREW VON HIRSCH

I wish, here, to defend the discount approach to previous convictions.[1] This perspective holds that a reduction in penalty should be provided for first offenders, and for those who have had up to a certain number of previous convictions. However, after the offender has been before the courts on a number of occasions, a 'ceiling' is reached—representing the full deserved measure of punishment for the offence—and all such mitigation is used up. Further repetitions—at least as far as desert is concerned—should be dealt with by the imposition of the full measure of penalty at the level of the 'ceiling' for the offence. The sentencer should not, however, be able to continue to increase sentence after each subsequent repetition. To practice such 'cumulative sentencing' would give undue weight to persistence rather than crime seriousness, and thus sacrifice proportionality.

Tolerance and the 'Lapse'

Why adopt such a discount theory? The reasons can be summarised as follows.[2] Our everyday moral judgements include the notion of the *lapse*. A transgression (even a fairly serious one) should be judged less stringently when it occurs against a background of prior compliance. The idea is that the inhibitions of even an ordinarily well-behaved person can fail in a moment of weakness or wilfulness. Such a temporary breakdown of self-control is a kind of human frailty for which some understanding should be shown. In sentencing, the relevant lapse is an infringement of the criminal law rather than a commonplace moral failure, but the logic of the

This Selection is published here for the first time.

discount remains similar: that of dealing with such lapses more tolerantly. A reason for doing so is respect for the process by which persons can attend to, and respond to, censure for their conduct. The offender, after being confronted with censure or blame, is capable (as a reasoning human being deemed capable of ethical judgements) of reflecting on the wrongfulness of what he has done, and of making an extra effort to show greater self-restraint. The aim, in granting the discount, is to show respect for this capacity—and thereby give the offender 'another chance'. With repetitions, however, the discount should diminish, and eventually disappear. The repeated offence can less and less plausibly be described as a mere lapse; and repeated reoffending after confrontation with penal censure suggests a failure to make that extra effort at self-restraint which was the basis for granting the discount.

How the Criminal Law's Particular Features Affect the 'Lapse' Argument

The account sketched above draws upon everyday moral norms concerning the role of previous wrongdoing. In everyday life, however, discounts for previous misconduct may, in some contexts, be rather restricted: a first misdeed might count as a 'lapse', but perhaps not a second or third. Is there anything about the criminal law that that might warrants more generous standard?

The generosity or stringency of norms concerning about previous offending may depend on the type of enterprise involved. Of particular relevance here may be: (i) how demanding the general behavioural standards for the activity are; (ii) the degree of voluntariness of participation in the activity, and the ease of exit from it; and (iii) the potential severity of sanctions for misconduct. On these dimensions, the criminal law may differ substantially from more informal contexts—and these differences may affect how previous misconduct should be treated.

Consider, first, a non-criminal form of regulation: a university's disciplinary standards. Because of the importance of scholarship to a university's existence, rules concerning plagiarism might well be quite strict. Perhaps a first-offender discount might be allowed for lesser instances of this kind of misconduct, but further repetitions should, arguably, result in expulsion of the offending faculty member. Thus not much scope for 'lapses' would be allowed. Why so? The three factors mentioned above might suggest an explanation. Thus: (i) a university should hold its academic members to high standards of scholarship and scholarly ethics; (ii) participation in the university's academic enterprise is voluntary, so that those who do not wish to abide by such norms of scholarship would still be free to choose some other, less demanding activity. Moreover, expulsion—the ultimate sanction the university can invoke—still leaves the individual free to pursue other forms of work; and (iii) the sanctions the university can levy are of a limited nature. No loss of liberty or deprivation of property may be levied as a sanction

The criminal law's norms concerning previous offending should allow more leeway for lapses, because the nature of its enterprise is quite different—including differences in the above-mentioned respects: (i) the criminal law's standards of appropriate behaviour should be less rigorous. The criminal law serves to establish minimum norms of interaction among citizens. Its mission also includes that of regulating the behaviour of the least fortunate, least well disciplined of society's members; (ii) the duty to abide by the criminal law's norms of conduct is not voluntary. Everyone must comply. No person facing punishment can resign (as the plagiarising academic can), short of emigration or suicide; and (iii) the criminal law's sanctions are potentially very burdensome, and include deprivation of property and liberty. If we wish to impose those severe penalties parsimoniously, this will call for a liberal norm for prior offending.

Two particular features of criminal recidivists (or many of them) militate in favour of a discount norm that provides significant leeway in the norms governing repetition of the offence. First, the criminal law must also apply to those persons with the least self-discipline and with the weakest social inducements to compliance. These individuals are persons who will have the greatest difficulty in complying, and will benefit particularly from a slowly diminishing discount regarding previous offences. Secondly, a significant number of criminal recidivists come to desist after a certain time. Criminal activity tends to diminish with age, and only a minority of active offenders remain involved in criminal activity for a protracted period (see Selection 3.4). The discount rule thus should give offenders a number of opportunities to respond to penal censure and its moral appeal, before being faced with the full measure of the penalty.

An Illustration: Sweden's Treatment of Recidivist Offending

How might such a discount scheme work out in practice? Sweden's approach to punishing recidivists provides an illustration.[3] Under that country's sentencing reform statute, which took effect in 1989, the principle of proportionality is the governing sentencing principle, so that the seriousness of the offence of conviction is the primary determinant of penalties' severity. Serious offenders thus receive custodial sentences, even if not previously convicted; and lesser offenders are given non-custodial sanctions, even if recidivists. Where there are previous convictions, there would be modest adjustments in these sanctions.

In the middle range of crime seriousness, however, the previous record plays a quite significant role, which comports well, I think, with the 'discount' model just described. Upon the first and several subsequent convictions, the offender receives a non-custodial sanction. Imprisonment is imposed only as a last resort, after the offender has accumulated a substantial number of previous convictions—perhaps as many as four or so.

Among such offenders, however, there would be a differentiation in the response depending on the record. Initially, the offender would ordinarily receive a 'unit fine'—that is, a fine equivalent to a specified number of days' earnings, with that number depending on the seriousness of the offence. Next, there would be a somewhat more restrictive non-custodial response: namely, a term of probation involving supervision of the offender in the community. After that, there would be a modest further step-up: a stint of community service as a penalty. Only if the offender continues to offend will he face a term of imprisonment, albeit for a relatively brief term.

This illustration from Sweden suggests that a 'discount' model can be quite feasible in practice. It also suggests the model's further attraction: that of helping to limit reliance on imprisonment. Notwithstanding several incidents of reoffending, the offender will continue to receive non-custodial sanctions, albeit of increasing stringency. It is only with relatively frequent reoffending that the 'ceiling' is finally reached, and the offender suffers a term of imprisonment—albeit still of modest duration.

The 'Recidivist Premium' and its Problems

In Selection 4.6(a) above, Julian V Roberts urges the adoption instead of a recidivist premium for reoffending. With each new offence, the offender would receive a sentence increase, subject to certain proportionality limits. Reoffending, he argues, is mark of increased blameworthiness for reasons similar to why premeditation does: it suggests the presence of a more culpable state of mind. Having been convicted before gives, or should give, the actor increased awareness of the wrongfulness of his behaviour when he contemplates doing it again.

This purported analogy to premeditation, however, does not seem quite convincing. Premeditation is a culpable state of mind: the offender's planning the offence suggests that he really means to do the harm. There is, however, no culpable state of mind necessarily associated with reoffending. Indeed, a mark of much recidivism (especially repeat minor offending) is impulsiveness and lack of reflection. The repeat shoplifter, for example, may simply see the item and grab it without much thought of any kind. It is not easy to identify any typical indicia that underlie the heterogeneous motivations for repeat reoffending.

The recidivist premium also has the apparent drawback of supporting increased penalties. In its pure form, this theory contemplates no penalty reduction for a first offence.[4] The offender, on the first occasion, would get the deserved measure of punishment. Subsequent repetitions would call for further increases, on grounds of enhanced culpability. Is this a desirable result? Could such an approach be reconciled with a scheme such as Sweden's?

In his account, Professor Roberts asserts that the first offender should get a penalty reduction, nevertheless. But how might such a reduction be explained, other than by resort to a discount theory of the kind he rejects? And if a first-offender discount is combined with a repeat-offender premium, could that not produce a puzzling discontinuity in the penalty scale?

A further problem of the recidivist-premium theory is that of establishing limits on penalty increases. If repetition enhances offender culpability, why should further repetitions not enhance culpability still further? The recidivist premium would appear to contain no principle, as the discount theory does, for barring further sentence-level changes after a specified number of acts of reoffending. Professor Roberts's response to this objection is to assert that his conception—since it is a species of desert theory—still accords proportionality the primary role in deciding sentence. Thus a limit on sentence increases would eventually have to be reached in order to preserve that role. But where this limit can be located, after how many repetitions, remains far from clear. The foregoing questions about the premium theory may well have cogent answers, which further discussion will help elicit.

Notes

1. Von Hirsch, A, (1981) 'Desert and Previous Convictions in Sentencing' 65 *Minnesota Law Review* 591; von Hirsch, A and Ashworth, A, (2005) *Proportionate Sentencing: Exploring the Principles* (Oxford, Oxford University Press) 151.
2. *Ibid.*
3. Jareborg, N, (1995) 'The Swedish Sentencing Reform' in CMV Clarkson and R Morgan (eds), *The Politics of Sentencing Reform* (Oxford, Oxford University Press).
4. Roberts, JV, (2008) 'Punishing Persistence: Explaining the Enduring Appeal of the Recidivist Sentencing Premium' 48 *British Journal of Criminology* 468.

5

Restorative Justice

Of all the areas covered by this volume of readings, restorative justice has recently attracted the most attention from scholars. Indeed, there has been a proliferation of programmes and programme evaluations throughout the western world in recent years. In addition, restorative initiatives have been proposed or implemented at the level of international justice as well as what may be termed 'transitional justice'. Selecting readings to reflect the diversity and volume of publications is therefore a daunting task.

The end of the twentieth century witnessed a resurgence of restorative and victim-centred theories of criminal justice. In earlier times, victims played a major role in criminal justice. In the tenth century, many offenders had to pay financial compensation in the form of a *bot* to the victim and a *wite* to the victim's lord. In the twelfth and thirteenth centuries, the king began to assert control over criminal justice, and took over payments by the offender, subsequently replacing them with other forms of sentence.[2] While victims continued to play a primary role in the prosecution of suspected offenders until the nineteenth century, the victim's involvement in what came to be 'sentencing' faded away. Recent years have seen the re-emergence of concern for victims, among political policy-makers, criminal-justice practitioners and criminal-justice theorists. Approaches with somewhat different origins and emphases may be found: restorative theories are not necessarily victim-centred, and victim-centred approaches are not necessarily restorative. There is a wide variety of theories and practical approaches, and this Chapter will necessarily be selective. The first step will be to give brief descriptions of two principal paradigms.

Two Restorative Justice Paradigms: Providing Compensation and Reducing Conflict

One approach would be termed *compensatory* in the UK and *restitutive* in the US; its main component is to assure proper financial recompense to the victim of the crime. This recognises the right of a victim of crime to be compensated by the offender and the duty of the offender to make compensation. However, it does raise questions about who may properly be regarded as victim(s) of a crime. Some restorative writers recognise that criminal offences have a double aspect, impinging on the rights of a victim and constituting some kind of wider harm to society. Insofar as this is correct, it would then be necessary to ensure that the restorative approach applies not only to the direct or primary victim but also to this wider or secondary victim. It will be noticed that restorative theories with this kind of focus may not be presented as theories of punishment: their principal aim is restitution or compensation, although punishment may be a side effect, especially in a mixed system, where compensation is added to another sentence in a fairly conventional criminal justice setting.[3] The reading by Lucia Zedner (Selection 5.3) discusses this paradigm.

Another paradigm is that of *conflict resolution*. A crime is regarded here as constituting a conflict and the proper response is to attempt its resolution. This approach typically relies on mediation and other forms of dispute resolution, not upon a judicial system as conceived in modern western states. Once again, there is the question of who the parties to the conflict are. In particular, does the wider community or the state have a stake, or is it merely the offender and the immediate victim? Insofar as the community is recognised as having an interest, this could shape the form of dispute resolution, and might help ensure that it is not simply a private affair. It will be noticed, again, that such perspectives are not theories of punishment as such: instead, they advance justifications for responding to crimes in a different, socially integrative way. The reading from Nils Christie (Selection 5.1) draws upon this paradigm. In the same vein, Daniel Van Ness has referred to the purpose of criminal justice as 'the restoration into safe communities of victims and offenders who have resolved their conflicts'.[4]

In addition to these two models, two further tendencies in the restorative justice discussion should be noted. One is the argument that victims, so long neglected by the criminal justice system, should be given a voice in proceedings. Sometimes this goes no further than allowing the victim to submit a 'victim impact statement' at sentencing, detailing the effects of the crime on her or his life. In some jurisdictions the approach is taken further, and a victim is empowered to express an opinion on what sentence would be appropriate in the case. The implications of this kind of approach will be examined below. What is apparent at this stage is that this perspective does not belong, necessarily, to either a restorative or a punitive system of criminal justice. It suggests that the victim's preferences ought to be relevant in sentencing, but it may not specify where those preferences should lead. They may well vary from victim to victim: some may be punitive, others non-punitive and still others restorative in their preferences.

The Foundations of Restorative Theories

The re-emergence of restorative theories focuses attention on certain fundamental issues in criminal justice. Both the compensatory paradigm and the conflict-resolution paradigm raise deeper questions about the interests relevant to criminal justice, about the place of crime prevention and about wider community involvement in the administration of criminal justice. Each of these questions will now be discussed briefly.

First, what interests are relevant in a criminal case? It is one thing to argue that the interests of victims have been neglected in many criminal justice systems for much of the twentieth century; it is quite another to specify what interests of victims, or of other persons, ought to be recognised. It has become implicit in much modern Anglo-American legal doctrine that a criminal offence is a matter of concern to the state. The victim's legal interest is an interest in compensation, and the victim also has welfare interests in proper support, information, etc. Christie (Selection 5.1) argues that what has happened over the centuries is that the state has 'stolen' the conflict from the victim (and from society). He claims that the victim's right to a central role in the proceedings should be restored. The implication is that the victim has a right to negotiate (or to be involved in the negotiation of) the resolution of the conflict, with any attendant compensation or penalties. It may be objected that many crimes do not involve a 'conflict', in the sense that there may be no disputed claims and no prospect of future dealings between the parties. However, Christie adopts the 'conflict' model, and he goes on to recognise that the victim's interest is not the only one: he mentions the wider community's interest, too. This suggests that each crime is a wrong against the direct victim and against the community, and that each therefore has some consequential right to participation in the criminal justice process.

This readiness of modern restorative theorists to recognise the wider community's interests in crime should not, however, deflect attention from the question of the nature of the victim's interest. It is evident that one key element in a modern state's role is that the state takes over the responsibility for government and law, and that it does so in order to ensure efficiency and consistency, and also to displace vigilantism and to prevent people from 'taking the law into their own hands'. According to this view, the state should control adjudication and sentencing, but in so doing it ought not to deprive victims of their right to compensation. It may be true that one of the driving forces behind modern restorativism is dissatisfaction with the 'conventional' punishment paradigm, as developed in many criminal justice systems. But the question remains whether it is problematic for the state to have an important role at all or whether the difficulties lie in the manner in which that role has developed. How convincing are Christie's arguments that 'conflicts' should be taken back from the state and returned to the victim and her or his community? If individual D commits an assault upon another person V, is the latter likely to perceive the event as a conflict between parties or as a wrong? In Selection 5.2, RA Duff discusses this issue when he distinguishes between wrongs that are criminal rather than simply tortious in nature.

Similar questions are raised when we turn to the compensatory paradigm. Whether it is a fully compensatory paradigm, in which the whole purpose of criminal justice is to ensure that victim and community are compensated for the crime,[5] or merely a process of grafting such an approach on to a 'conventional' criminal justice system, a range of difficult issues arise. If it is recognised that the victim has a right to compensation and also that fines may properly be levied as penalties, which should be accorded priority, in cases where both cannot be satisfied? Would the answer be different in a punitive system, where the state's role is to ensure the punishment of offenders, and in a reparative system, in which reparation to the community is considered important? These questions raise issues about the theoretical foundations of the interests in a criminal case, although, as Lucia Zedner shows in Selection 5.3, there are also prudential considerations in favour of greater attention to victim compensation.

The principal basis for Christie's advocacy of the conflict-resolving approach is that it can be designed so as to involve the wider community in the administration of criminal justice. This is partly because Christie is mistrustful of lawyers' intense involvement in more traditional criminal justice systems, and partly because he believes that there are great potential advantages for increased social cohesion when ordinary people, including victims and offenders, are drawn into the resolution of criminal cases. These arguments resonate with the views of other restorative justice advocates who deplore the state's dominance of criminal justice on the ground that it produces 'alienation'. Insofar as crimes take place in, and have an impact upon, the community, and almost all offenders will continue to live in or will soon return to that community, there are sound pragmatic reasons for greater community involvement in criminal justice. How strong is this argument, however, when attention is turned to the question of what counts, for these purposes, as 'the community'? How local or national is the community to which reference is made, and can we be sure that dispositions which are labeled 'community sentences' are consistent with the idea of 'community' which inspire many restorative theories?[6]

Restorative and Criminal Justice

Part of the appeal of restorative approaches to resolving criminal incidents arises from dissatisfaction with the current criminal justice system. It is argued that some of the shortcomings of current practice—such as a degree of alienation of the crime victim—may be overcome by a model of justice which pays more attention to the needs of crime victims. At the same time, restorative justice programmes and processes may still be able to express some normative censure of culpable conduct. Jim Dignan takes this position in Selection 5.4.

Some restorative justice theorists adopt what might be termed a purely restorative approach in which punishment plays no role, or which is unconcerned with a retributive principle such as proportionality. According to this view, the imposition of any type of sanction, or adherence to proportionality, may well impede efforts at restoration. The parties should be left relatively free to negotiate an outcome that brings benefits to the two parties in conflict. There would appear to be no retributive considerations under this model. However, a number of writers have argued that there is more common ground between restorative and retributive justice. In Selection 5.2, RA Duff argues that we should seek restoration through retribution because the offender has committed a wrong. Gerry Johnstone pursues the relationship between restorative and criminal justice in Selection 5.5. Another recent discussion, by von Hirsch, Ashworth and Shearing, suggests, similarly, that a restorative disposition could be conceptualised as a negotiated response to an offence, involving (i) an implicit or explicit acknowledgement of fault by the offender to his victim and (ii) an apologetic stance on his part, ordinarily conveyed through having him undertake a reparative task (see Reading 5.6).[7] Finally, in Selection 5.7 Kathleen Daly explores some of the limits of restorative justice.

Some Concerns about Restorative Justice

We return now to the two conceptions of restorative justice sketched earlier, and note some difficulties that may flow from those approaches.

Compensation and Punishment

Confusion often arises between the two distinct concepts of compensation and punishment, and the implications that each of them has. Compensation is a form of financial restoration to the status quo, so far as is possible. In principle, the greater the harm suffered, the greater the compensation due. Punishment is a form of censure, and should be influenced not only by the gravity of the harm done (or threatened) but also by the culpability of the offender. Thus, in two extreme cases, an attempted murder (eg by shooting) which did not actually cause harm would justify severe punishment but low compensation, whereas a death caused by gross negligence might justify a lower punishment but higher compensation. In restorative schemes, what comparative emphasis should be given to these two aims?

Community Restoration

The notion 'community restoration' remains rather unclear. By what metric is it to be decided how much damage has been done to the community and how it needs to be restored? In sketching answers to this question, some writers (such as Van Ness[8]) come close to embracing a desert-based scale, taking account of harm and culpability. It is by no means clear what other metric could be used. There is also the question of what types of measure can be regarded as restorative. Monetary fines would be a clear example, but there are limitations on offenders' ability to pay and on the length of time for which it is fair to exact financial penalties. Lucia Zedner (Selection 5.3) argues that community service orders can readily be conceptualised as a form of community restoration.

Organisations as Victims or Offenders

Restorative theories must deal with the fact that many offences do not involve individual victims or offenders. These may be offences by companies (such as pollution, health and safety violations, and consumer offences), offences against companies (typically theft and deception) or against the government (such as damage to government property and tax evasion), or even 'victimless' crimes (such as drug offences and other crimes of possession). There is no reason in principle why companies should not play their part in a restorative justice system, but one would need to guard against inequalities of power in any negotiations with individual offenders. As for government, it would be possible to designate certain officials as representatives of the state for the purposes of restorative justice, but that raises various questions about the policies they should follow in any negotiations. Some family group conferences are adapted to deal with crimes not involving directly identifiable individual victims, such as drinking-and-driving.

Victims in the service of offenders?

Restorative theories based on the conflict-resolution paradigm depend on the willingness of victims to become involved, and some are unwilling. There should be no question of compelling victims to become involved, especially since the risk of secondary victimisation through the criminal process is a known phenomenon. Nonetheless, conflict-resolution theorists must decide what approach to take if the victim is unwilling to participate. To allow the victim effectively to veto a restorative approach might severely handicap restorative programmes, unless most victims show a willingness to participate. And even then, what should be done in those cases where a victim wants no involvement?

Victim Services or Procedural Rights for Victims?

Those who favour a punishment paradigm for the sentencing process might draw a distinction between a victim's right to services and a victim's procedural rights in the criminal process. As argued earlier, victims may fairly expect support when victimised, respect from the police and lawyers during questioning, accurate information about the progress of the case, separate waiting areas and active support at courts, and so forth. There is also a strong argument that the state should assure compensation to the victims of crime, at least in the broad category of violent crimes.[9] But giving victims the right to be consulted in decisions to prosecute, on the acceptance of a plea of guilty or on matters of sentence, is far more difficult to justify. Victim-centred approaches to criminal justice often seem to assume, without much argument, that victims have some such entitlement to be consulted at sentence. This may draw on Christie's notion that the conflict somehow 'belongs', in part at least, to the victim. It also threatens to lead to a system in which decisions depend on whether the particular victim is forgiving or vengeful. Many jurisdictions now permit a victim to submit a 'victim impact statement' at sentencing. This describes the effect of the crime on the victim and/or the victim's family. Even where such statements do not include any suggestions on sentence, there are difficulties of principle and practice that must not be overlooked.[10]

Restorative Justice in Practice

Although the focus of this book is upon sentencing principles, it is appropriate to devote some attention to the practicalities of restorative justice, if only because they differ from those in 'conventional' criminal justice systems. Few criminal justice systems have embraced a fully compensatory approach. More commonly, a compensatory approach is grafted onto a 'conventional' criminal justice system, giving rise to some of the questions of priority discussed by Zedner (Selection 5.3). The conflict-resolution model has given rise to a range of different initiatives, of which two are outlined here—namely mediation and family group conferences. The tendency thus far has been to use such approaches chiefly (but not exclusively) for minor crimes or when dealing with young offenders.

Mediation

Many mediation schemes in England and Wales focus on non-serious crimes, and many of these deal solely or chiefly with young offenders. The format differs from scheme to scheme: some mediation schemes are used as a means of diversion from prosecution, others as alternatives after conviction and before sentence, with further variations. A mediator, often a member of the Probation Service, will bring together the offender and the victim (provided they are both willing), allowing each of them to make a statement, with a view to trying to bring about some kind of agreement on what should be done (such as an apology, repairing of damage, etc). In cases where the offender is prosecuted, taking account of the outcome is usually a matter for the court's discretion. Some English schemes have been more ambitious, with the Leeds Mediation and Reparation Project aiming at more substantial offences and the Northamptonshire Adult Reparation Scheme aiming at adult offenders, the latter with modest successes in terms of participation and satisfaction of victims. Somewhat similar, and of longer standing in North America, are the various forms of Victim Offender Reconciliation Programs, although these may take place after the offender has been sentenced rather than before. Their chief objective is to bring about some understanding between the victim and the offender.[11]

Family Group Conferences (FGC) and Sentencing Circles

Conferences were introduced in New Zealand in 1985, and are now the principal means of dealing with young offenders under the Children, Young Persons and their

Families Act 1989 (NZ). Although diversion from court processes is one of their functions, they differ from mediation schemes in that there are other people present. Thus an FGC would include a representative of the police, the youth justice coordinator, the young offender and family, and the victim and family. The procedure provides, among other things, for the victim to give his or her view of the offence. The conference should move towards the formulation of an agreed plan, response or outcome. If none can be agreed, the case will be returned to the court—although this does not necessarily mean that the court will impose a punitive, as distinct from a reparative, sentence. Of course, FGCs do not satisfy all victims, but there is evidence of considerable satisfaction, [12] and they have now been introduced in some Australian jurisdictions and in some localities in Britain. Braithwaite has expressed enthusiasm about the prospect of achieving what he refers to as 'reintegrative shaming' through this kind of procedure.[13]

Sentencing circles share many of the characteristics of conferences. They are generally found in Aboriginal communities or in societies with a significant Aboriginal minority, such as Canada or Australia. Circles require the consent of the victim. The participants—including family and friends of both the victim and the offender, as well as important members of the community, such as elders form a circle—are allowed to speak. Legal professionals may be present but play no more active role than any other participant. At the conclusion of the hearing, a course of action is devised to which all give their consent. In Canada, this 'disposition' is considered by a judge, who will then formally impose the sanction or substitute another.[14]

Research on Restorative Justice

A great deal of research has been conducted into the nature and effects of restorative justice policies and programmes.[15] Many research projects have used designs in which participants have been randomly assigned to either a restorative or a criminal justice process. The results to date have been encouraging. In one of the most recent systematic reviews of the literature, Sherman and Strang reviewed research involving 36 comparisons between restorative and criminal justice. The principal forms of restorative justice consisted of face-to-face meetings of all affected parties, including the offender, the victim and the family and friends of both, and court-ordered financial restitution. Thus they conform to the compensation and conflict reduction models alluded to earlier in this essay. Sherman and Strang reported positive findings in a number of areas. First, victims appeared to benefit from the conferences in which they participate. Secondly, larger numbers of offences were brought to justice when restorative justice initiatives were offered to arrestees prior to the laying of a charge. Finally, although the magnitudes of the effects varied depending upon the kinds of participants, reductions in repeat offending were observed for both violent and property offenders.[16]

Conclusions

Restorative theories of criminal justice have a long history and a powerful contemporary presence. Many of those who oppose the repressive tendencies in recent penal policy are bound to be interested in restorative approaches, if only as less punitive alternatives. Some writers, such as Nils Christie, would go further and argue for a fuller commitment to restorative justice. Others advocate a middle ground, one which might invoke both retributive and restorative elements. The evolving research into the effects of restorative justice interventions suggests that restorative justice can promote victim satisfaction and subsequent desistance by offenders, and result in substantial cost savings for the state.

JVR

Notes

1. This introduction draws heavily upon the material in this chapter in the previous edition that was written by Andrew Ashworth.
2. For discussions of the history, see Schafer, S, (1960) *Restitution to Victims of Crime* (London, Stevens/Chicago, IL, Quadrangle Books); Wright, M, (1996) *Justice for Victims and Offenders: a Restorative Response to Crime*, 2nd edn (Winchester, Waterside Press).
3. See Walgrave, L, (1995) 'Restorative Justice for Juveniles: Just a Technique or a Fully Fledged Alternative?' 34 *Howard Journal of Crime and Justice* 228, 234.
4. Van Ness, D, (1993) 'New Wine and Old Wineskins: Four Challenges of Restorative Justice' 4 *Criminal Law Forum* 251.
5. See, eg del Vecchio, G, 'The Struggle against Crime', discussed by Ashworth, A, (1986) 'Punishment and Compensation: Offenders, Victims and the State' 6 *Oxford Journal of Legal Studies* 86, 92–4.
6. For an analysis of variations in the use of the term 'community' in contemporary criminal justice, see Lacey, N and Zedner, L, (1995) 'Discourses of Community in Criminal Justice' 22 *Journal of Law and Society* 301.
7. von Hirsch, A, Shearing, C and Ashworth, A, (2003) 'Specifying Aims and Limits for Restorative Justice: A 'Making Amends' Model?' in A von Hirsch *et al* (eds), *Restorative Justice and Criminal Justice: Competing or Reconcilable Paradigms?* (Oxford, Hart Publishing).
8. Van Ness, above n 4; see the critique by Ashworth, A, (1993) 'Some Doubts about Restorative Justice' 4 *Criminal Law Forum* 277; and the reply by Van Ness, D, (1993) 4 *Criminal Law Forum* 301.
9. European Convention on Compensation for the Victims of Crimes of Violence (1984).
10. See Ashworth, A, (1993) 'Victim Impact Statements and Sentencing' *Criminal Law Review* 498; Sanders, A *et al*, (2001) 'Victim Impact Statements: Don't Work, Can't Work' *Criminal Law Review* 447; for a discussion of the benefits of victim impact statements at sentencing, see Roberts, JV, (2003) 'Victim Impact Statements and the

Sentencing Process: Enhancing Communication in the Courtroom' 47 *Criminal Law Quarterly* 365.

11. See Wright, M and Galaway, B (eds), (1989) *Mediation and Criminal Justice: Victims, Offenders and Community* (London, Sage).

12. See, eg Morris, A, Maxwell, G and Robertson, JP, (1993) 'Giving Victims a Voice: a New Zealand Experiment' 32 *Howard Journal of Criminal Justice* 304; New Zealand Ministry of Justice, (1995), *Restorative Justice* (Wellington, New Zealand Ministry of Justice).

13. Braithwaite, J, (1989) *Crime, Shame and Reintegration* (Cambridge, Cambridge University Press), as applied in Braithwaite, J and Mugford, S, (1994) 'Conditions of Successful Ceremonies' 34 *British Journal of Criminology* 139. Cf Blagg, H, (1997) 'A Just Measure of Shame?' 37 *British Journal of Criminology* 481; Braithwaite, J, (1997) 'Conferencing and Plurality: Reply to Blagg' 37 *British Journal of Criminology* 502.

14. For a description of one of the earliest sentencing circles and a leading judgment on circles in general, see *R v Moses* (1992) 71 CCC (3d) 347; for discussion of the literature, see Roberts, JV and La Prairie, C, (1996) 'Sentencing Circles: Some Unanswered Questions' 39 *Criminal Law Quarterly* 69; Linker, M, (1999) 'Sentencing Circles and the Dilemma of Difference' 42 *Criminal Law Quarterly* 116.

15. For a good overview of restorative justice evaluation research, see Kurki, L, (2003) 'Evaluating Restorative Justice Practices' in A von Hirsch *et al* (eds), *Restorative and Criminal Justice: Competing or Reconcilable Paradigms?* (Oxford, Hart Publishing).

16. In one of the studies included in the review, the frequency of rearrest among offenders assigned to a restorative justice programme declined by 84 per 100 offenders—more than a comparable control group: see Sherman, L and Strang, H, (2007) *Restorative Justice: The Evidence* (London, The Smith Institute) 68.

Further Readings

Braithwaite, J, (1999) 'Restorative Justice: Assessing Optimistic and Pessimistic Accounts' 25 *Crime and Justice: A Review of Research* 1.

Dignan, J, (2005) *Understanding Victims and Restorative Justice* (Maidenhead, Open University Press).

Gavrielides, T, (2007) *Restorative Justice Theory and Practice: Addressing the Discrepancy* (Monsey, Criminal Justice Press).

Johnstone, G, (2002) *Restorative Justice. Ideas, Values, Debates* (Cullompton, Willan Publishing).

Shapland, J *et al*, (2007) *Restorative Justice: the Views of Victims and Offenders* (London, Ministry of Justice).

Sherman, L and Strang H, (2007) *Restorative Justice: the Evidence* (London, the Smith Institute).

Strang, H and Braithwaite, J (eds), (2000) *Restorative Justice: Philosophy to Practice* (Aldershot, Dartmouth).

Sullivan, D and Tifft, L (eds), (2008) *Handbook of Restorative Justice* (Abingdon, Routledge).

von Hirsch, A, Roberts, JV, Bottoms, AE, Roach, K and Schiff, M (eds), (2003) *Restorative and Criminal Justice. Competing or Reconcilable Paradigms?* (Oxford, Hart Publishing).

Weitekamp, E and Kerner, HJ (eds), (2003) *Restorative Justice in Context: International Practice and Directions* (Cullompton, Willan Publishing).

5.1

Conflicts as Property

NILS CHRISTIE

Full participation in your own conflict presupposes elements of civil law. The key element in a criminal proceeding is that the proceeding is converted from something between the concrete parties into a conflict between one of the parties and the state. So, in a modern criminal trial, two important things have happened. First, the parties are being *represented*. Secondly, the one party that is represented by the state, namely the victim, is so thoroughly represented that she or he for most of the proceedings is pushed completely out of the arena, reduced to the triggerer-off of the whole thing. She or he is a sort of double loser; first, *vis-à-vis* the offender, but secondly and often in a more crippling manner by being denied rights to full participation in what might have been one of the more important ritual encounters in life. The victim has lost the case to the state.

Professional Thieves

As we all know, there are many honourable as well as dishonourable reasons behind this development. The honourable ones have to do with the state's need for conflict reduction and certainly also its wishes for the protection of the victim. It is rather obvious. So is also the less honourable temptation for the state, or Emperor, or whoever is in power, to use the criminal case for personal gain. Offenders might pay for their sins. Authorities have in time past shown considerable willingness, in representing the victim, to act as receivers of the money or other property from the offender. Those days are gone; the crime control system is not run for profit. And yet they are not gone. There are, in all banality, many interests at stake here, most of them related to professionalisation.

Lawyers are particularly good at stealing conflicts. They are trained for it. They are trained to prevent and solve conflict. They are socialised into a sub-culture with a surprisingly high agreement concerning interpretation of norms, and regarding what sort of information can be accepted as relevant in each case. Many among us have, as laymen, experienced the sad moments of truth when our lawyers tell us that our best arguments in our fight against our neighbour are

From N Christie, "Conflicts as Property" (1977) 17 *British Journal of Criminology* 1.

without any legal relevance whatsoever and that we for God's sake ought to keep quiet about them in court. Instead they pick out arguments we might find irrelevant or even wrong to use . . .

Conflicts become the property of lawyers. But lawyers don't hide that it is conflicts they handle. And the organizational framework of the courts underlines this point. The opposing parties, the judge, the ban against privileged communication within the court system, the lack of encouragement for specialization—specialists cannot be internally controlled—it all underlines that this is an organization for the handling of conflicts. *Treatment personnel* are in another position. They are more interested in *converting the image of the case from one of conflict into one of non-conflict* . . .

One way of reducing attention to the conflict is reduced attention given to the victim. Another is concentrated attention given to those attributes in the criminal's background which the healer is particularly trained to handle. Biological defects are perfect. So also are personality defects when they are established far back in time—far away from the recent conflict. And so are also the whole row of explanatory variables that criminology might offer. We have, in criminology, to a large extent functioned as an auxiliary science for the professionals within the crime control system. We have focused on the offender, made her or him into an object for study, manipulation and control. We have added to all those forces that have reduced the victim to a nonentity and the offender to a thing. And this critique is perhaps not only relevant for the old criminology, but also for the new criminology. While the old one explained crime from personal defects or social handicaps, the new criminology explains crime as the result of broad economic conflicts. The old criminology loses the conflicts, the new one converts them from inter-personal conflicts to class conflicts. And they are. They are class conflicts—also. But, by stressing this, the conflicts are again taken away from the directly involved parties. So, as a preliminary statement: Criminal conflicts have either become *other people's property*— primarily the property of lawyers—or it has been in other people's interests to *define conflicts away* . . .

Conflicts as Property

Material compensation is not what I have in mind with the formulation "conflicts as property". It is the *conflict itself* that represents the most interesting property taken away, not the goods originally taken away from the victim, or given back to him. In our types of society, conflicts are more scarce than property. And they are immensely more valuable.

They are valuable in several ways. Let me start at the societal level . . . Highly industrialised societies face major problems in organizing their members in ways such that a decent quota take part in any activity at all. Segmentation according to age and sex can be seen as shrewd methods for segregation. Participation is such a scarcity that insiders create monopolies against outsiders, particularly with regard to work. In this perspective, it will easily be seen that conflicts represent a *potential for activity, for participation.* Modern criminal control systems represent one of the many cases of lost opportunities for involving citizens in tasks that are of immediate importance to them. Ours is a society of task-monopolists.

The victim is a particularly heavy loser in this situation. Not only has he suffered, lost materially or become hurt, physically or otherwise. And not only does the state take the compensation. But above all he has lost participation in his own case. It is the Crown that comes into the spotlight, not the victim. It is the Crown that describes the losses, not the victim. It is the Crown that appears in the newspaper, very seldom the victim. It is the Crown that gets a chance to talk to the offender, and neither the Crown nor the offender are particularly interested in carrying on that conversation. The prosecutor is fed-up long since. The victim would not have been. He might have been scared to death, panic-stricken, or furious. But he would not have been uninvolved. It would have been one of the important days in his life. Something that belonged to him has been taken away from that victim.

But the big loser is us—to the extent that society is us. This loss is first and foremost a loss in *opportunities for norm-clarification.* It is a loss of pedagogical possibilities. It is a loss of opportunities for a continuous discussion of what represents the law of the land. How wrong was the thief, how right was the victim? Lawyers are, as we saw, trained into agreement on what is relevant in a case. But that means a trained incapacity in letting the parties decide what *they* think is relevant. It means that it is difficult to stage what we might call a political debate in the court. When the victim is small and the offender big—in size or power—how blameworthy then is the crime? And what about the opposite case, the small thief and the big house-owner? If the offender is well educated, ought he then to suffer more or maybe less, for his sins? Or if he is black, or if he is young, or if the other party is an insurance company, or if his wife has just left him, or if his factory will break down if he has to go to jail, or if his daughter will lose her fiance, or if he was drunk, or if he was sad, or if he was mad? There is no end to it. And maybe there ought to be none

A Victim-Oriented Court

There is clearly a model of neighbourhood courts behind my reasoning. But it is one with some peculiar features, and it is only these I will discuss in what follows.

First and foremost; it is a *victim-oriented* organization. Not in its initial stage, though. The first stage will be a traditional one where it is established whether it is true that the law has been broken, and whether it was this particular person who broke it.

Then comes the second stage, which in these courts would be of the utmost importance. That would be the stage where the victim's situation was considered, where every detail regarding what had happened—legally relevant or not—was brought to the court's attention. Particularly important here would be detailed consideration regarding what could be done for him, first and foremost by the offender, secondly by the local neighbourhood, thirdly by the state. Could the harm be compensated, the window repaired, the lock replaced, the wall painted, the loss of time because the car was stolen given back through garden work or washing of the car 10 Sundays in a row? Or maybe, when this discussion started, the damage was not so important as it looked in documents written to impress insurance companies? Could physical suffering become slightly less painful by any action from the offender, during days, months or years? But, in addition, had the community exhausted all resources that might have offered help? Was it absolutely certain that the local hospital could not do anything? What about a helping hand from the janitor twice a day if the offender took over the cleaning of the basement every Saturday? None of these ideas is unknown or untried, particularly not in England. But we need an organization for the systematic application of them.

Only after this stage was passed, and it ought to take hours, maybe days, to pass it, only then would come the time for an eventual decision on punishment. Punishment, then, becomes that suffering which the judge found necessary to apply *in addition to* those unintended constructive sufferings the offender would go through in his restitutive actions *vis-à-vis* the victim. Maybe nothing could be done or nothing would be done. But neighbourhoods might find it intolerable that nothing happened. Local courts out of tune with local values are not local courts. That is just the trouble with them, seen from the liberal reformer's point of view.

A fourth stage has to be added. That is the stage for service to the offender. His general social and personal situation is by now well known to the court. The discussion of his possibilities for restoring the victim's situation cannot be carried out without at the same time giving information about the offender's situation. This might have exposed needs for social, educational, medical or religious action—not to prevent further crime, but because needs ought to be met. Courts are public arenas, needs are made visible. But it is important that this stage comes *after* sentencing. Otherwise we get a re-emergence of the whole array of so-called "special measures"— compulsory treatments—very often only euphemisms for indeterminate imprisonment.

Through these four stages, these courts would represent a blend of elements from civil and criminal courts, but with a strong emphasis on the civil side.

A Lay-Oriented Court

The second major peculiarity with the court model I have in mind is that it will be one with an extreme degree of lay-orientation. This is essential when conflicts are seen as property that ought to be shared. It is with conflicts as with so many good things: they are in no unlimited supply. Conflicts can be cared for, protected, nurtured. But there are limits. If some are given more access in the disposal of conflicts, others are getting less. It is as simple as that.

Specialization in conflict solution is the major enemy; specialization that in due—or undue—time leads to professionalization. That is when the specialists get sufficient power to claim that they have acquired special gifts, mostly through education, gifts so powerful that it is obvious that they can only be handled by the certified craftsman.

With a clarification of the enemy, we are also able to specify the goal; let us reduce specialization and particularly our dependence on the professionals within the crime control system to the utmost.

The ideal is clear; it ought to be a court of equals representing themselves. When they are able to find a solution between themselves, no judges are needed. When they are not, the judges ought also to be their equals.

5.2

Restoration and Retribution

RA DUFF

Crimes typically cause various kinds of 'harm', which we might then seek to 're-pair'. The simplest case is that of material harm: someone's property is destroyed or damaged or stolen. Three features of this case should be noted. First, such harm can usually be fully repaired: the property can be returned, or the damage made good, or a functionally equivalent replacement provided. Second, the harm can be under-stood as a harm independently of its causation by a criminal action: the same harm could be caused by an innocent action, or by natural causes (see Feinberg, 1970: 31). Third, the harm could in principle be repaired by anyone—by the victim, by other people, by the state or by the offender. It is just that the offender should pay for the repair if she has the resources to do so, since she culpably caused the harm: but it could be adequately provided by anyone.

Of course, even in property crimes, matters are not typically that simple: the 'harm' done is not limited to material damage to or loss of replaceable property. The property itself might not be reparable or replaceable: if the watch I inherited from my father is lost, a new watch cannot fully replace it. The victim might suffer psychological effects—anger, anxiety, loss of trust—which typically depend on how the harm occurred: the psychological effects of (what is perceived as) a crime typically differ from those of naturally caused harm. Such effects can spread beyond the immediate victim: his intimates might be distressed and angered on his behalf; those who know about the crime might be rendered anxious lest they become victims. We can also begin to talk here (as restorative theorists often talk) of damage to relationships: to the relationship between victim and offender, or between offender and wider community. We will need to look more carefully at the character of such 'damage', however, in particular at the question of whether it can be understood in empirical terms: is it just a matter of how the people concerned are now disposed to feel about and behave towards each other?

These points become even more obvious when we move from property crimes to other kinds of crime—especially those involving attacks on the person; the three features which characterised the case of simple material harm are no longer clearly present.

Adapted from A von Hirsch *et al* (eds), *Restorative Justice and Criminal Justice* (Oxford, Hart Publishing, 2003), 43–59.

First, it becomes less clear what, if anything, could count as 'fully repairing' the harm. This is true even when the crime causes a harm which can be identified as such independently of its criminal causation (a physical injury caused by an assault, for instance). Of course, many physical injuries can be repaired without long-term physical effects—but some cannot; and even with those that can, it is not clear that their 'repair' can (as the repair or restoration of property can) make it is as if they had never occurred. It is even more clearly true when we look at other kinds of harm—for instance, the emotional distress caused to victims of criminal attacks. The victims of such harms might still be offered, and accept, financial compensation: but we need to explain the sense in which money could 'repair' these kinds of harm, since it cannot repair them in the straightforward way in which it can repair financial loss or loss of functional property.

Second, it becomes harder, if not impossible, to identify the harm independently of the crime that caused it. Such independent identification is doubtful even when it seems possible: it is at least arguable that one whose property is stolen, or who is physically attacked, suffers a different harm from that suffered by one who simply loses her property or suffers a natural injury—the harm of being stolen from, or of being wrongfully attacked (see Duff, 2002). But it becomes more clearly impossible in other cases. If we are to understand the harm suffered by a rape victim, for instance, or by someone who is burgled, we might see it as manifest in their psychological distress: but to understand that, we must understand it as a response to the wrong that they suffered. The same is true of damage to relationships: even if we focus on the way in which the people concerned are now disposed to feel about and behave towards each other, we can understand those changed dispositions only as responses to a perceived wrong. I will return to this point shortly.

Third, whatever kind of 'repair' is possible, it is not clear that it is something that anyone other than the offender could provide. Others can, of course, do much for the victims of crime: friends and fellow citizens can offer material help and sympathetic support, of a kind that is sensitive to the fact that the victim suffered criminal, not merely natural, harm; the state can provide more formalised versions of such help, as well as financial compensation—though this again raises the question of how money can help to repair such harm. But once we move away from the straightforward repair or replacement of material property, the meaning and efficacy of reparative measures come to depend crucially on who offers them; and there may be kinds of repair that only the offender can provide. If, for instance, apology is an essential reparative measure, the offender must be involved: for whilst others might pay the financial compensation that I owe to the person I wronged, they cannot apologise for me.

These comments point towards something which should anyway be obvious enough: that any talk of 'restoration' in the context of crime must be sensitive to the fact that the victim of crime has been not just harmed, but wronged; he has suffered a wrongful, as distinct from a natural or merely unlucky, harm. Some restorative theorists reject the very concepts of crime and wrong: rather than talking of the 'wrong' the offender did or the 'crime' she committed, we should talk about the 'conflict' or 'trouble' that needs to be resolved. Others, however, rightly insist that we must retain the concept of crime (and the criminal law as providing an authoritative specification of criminal wrongs), and recognise that crimes typically involve a victim who is wronged.

This does not yet distinguish criminal law from tort law, which enables those who suffer wrongful loss to gain redress or compensation, by making those who caused the loss pay for it. I cannot pursue this issue in detail here, but can suggest two identifying features of the kinds of wrong that should be criminal rather than (merely) tortious.

First, in tort law the focus is on the loss or harm that was caused, which can typically be identified independently of its relation to any wrongful action. Fault becomes relevant only in deciding who should bear the cost of that loss: if it was caused by another's negligence, its cost can legitimately be transferred to her (see Ripstein, 1999). By contrast, criminal law focuses primarily on the wrong that was done. This is most obvious in the case of crimes that might cause no harm of a kind that could ground a tort claim, but that can still constitute serious criminal wrongs—such as attempts or crimes of endangerment (see Ashworth, 1993: 285)—but it is also true of crimes that cause such harm. The wrong done to the victim of rape, wounding burglary is in part constituted by, but also in part constitutes, the harm that she suffers: to understand such harm, we must understand it as a criminal harm—as a harm that consists in being wrongfully injured.

Second, it is often said that crimes are 'public' wrongs: but it is hard to explain the sense in which they are 'public' wrongs without denigrating the victim's standing by implying that they are wrongs against 'the public' rather than the victim. We could, however, say that they are 'public' in the sense that, while they are often wrongs against an individual, they properly concern 'the public'—the whole political community—as wrongs in which other members of the community share as fellow citizens of both victim and offender. They infringe the values by which the political community defines itself as a law-governed polity: they are therefore wrongs for which the polity and its members are part-responsible in the sense that it is up to them, and not just up to victim and offender as private individuals, to make provision for an appropriate response.

This brings us back, however, to the question of what an 'appropriate response' would be when such a wrong has been committed, and what the notion of 'restoration' could amount to in this context; and we can now see more clearly why the three features that characterised the simple case of material harm do not carry across to criminal wrongs.

First, it is not clear what could count as 'repair' or 'restoration', or whether there could be a complete repair or restoration. Property can be repaired or replaced; physical injuries can be healed; psychological suffering and distress might be assuaged, traumas eventually healed: but what can 'repair' or 'restore' the wrong that has been done? It is here that talk of apology, of shaming, even of 'confession, repentance and absolution', becomes appropriate: but I will argue that this brings us into the realm of punishment.

Second, we cannot separate the harm that needs repair from the wrong that was done: for the wrong partly constitutes the relevant harm. This is true even of crimes that involve some independently identifiable harm: the victim of wounding suffers not just the harm of physical injury, but the distinctive harm of being wrongfully attacked. It is also true when the harm is manifest in the victim's psychological suffering, or when we talk of damage to relationships. The victim's anger or fear expresses his understanding of what he suffered as a wrong, and it can be appraised as a reasonable or unreasonable response to that wrong—an appraisal which has implications for what we think is due to him by way of reparation. The damage done to the offender's relationships—with the victim, with others—might be described in apparently empirical terms: the victim, or others, no longer trust her, or feel at ease with her as a friend, or colleague, or fellow citizen. But it is crucial to a proper understanding of this kind of harm that these are reasonable responses to a wrong that was done—for instance, that they cease to trust her because she showed herself, by committing that wrong, to be untrustworthy. There is also a significant kind of damage to the offender's relationships that does not consist in and need not involve (though it might be recognised in) any such actual responses: she has by her crime violated the values that define her normative relationships with her victim and with her fellow citizens. If I betray my friend, my action is destructive of the bonds of friendship even if she never finds out, and even if we can maintain what looks like an undamaged friendship: for such an action denies the values, the mutual concern, by which a friendship is defined. So too, when I wrong a fellow citizen, my action damages the normative bonds of citizenship, which raises the question of how those bonds can be repaired.

Third, we must ask who could provide the kind of 'reparation' or 'restoration' that crime, as involving wrongdoing, makes necessary—but also to whom such reparation must be made. Where there is an identifiable victim, she is the obviously appropriate recipient of reparation, since it is she who was harmfully wronged: but the political community as a whole is also owed something, since it shares in the victim's wrong as a violation of its public values. The community can of course do something towards repairing or restoring the victim, by offering help, and sympathetic recognition of what she has suffered: but insofar as the harm consists in a wrong done to the victim, or damage to the normative relationship between offender and victim (and between offender and wider political community), there is a kind of 'repair' that only the offender can provide.

Since my claim is that we should seek restoration through retribution, I should say something about retribution, to ward off some likely misunderstandings. Talk of retribution conjures up in many minds the image of a vindictive attempt to inflict hardship—to 'deliver pain' (see Christie, 1981)—'for its own sake'; and who could argue in favour of that? I will argue, however, that the retributivist slogan—that 'the guilty deserve to suffer'—does express an important moral truth; and that in the case of the criminally guilty it is the state's proper task to seek to ensure that they suffer as they deserve.

The retributivist slogan says nothing about what the guilty deserve to suffer; the crucial task in making retributivism morally plausible is to explain this. Once we recognise that the offender has done wrong, we can identify two kinds of 'suffering' that he deserves in virtue of that wrong. First, he deserves to suffer remorse: he should come to recognise and repent the wrong that he did—which is necessarily a painful process. Second, he deserves to suffer censure from others—which might be a formal censure, or the angry, ferocious censure of the victim or her friends; this too, if taken seriously, must be painful. There is also a third kind of 'suffering', a third kind of 'burden', that might be appropriate, that of making reparation to the victim. Some restorative theorists argue that the hardship involved in making reparation is a side-effect of the restorative process, not its aim, thus seeking to distance themselves from any species of 'punishment' (eg Walgrave, 1994: 66): but I will argue that reparation must be burdensome if it is to serve its restorative purpose.

I can best develop my argument that the kind of restoration that crime makes necessary should involve the offender's punishment by contrasting two models of mediation—a 'civil' and a 'criminal' model: this will occupy the next section.

Mediation: Civil versus Criminal

For restorative theorists, the process is as important as (or more important than) the product: restoration is achieved as much by the process of discussion and negotiation between victim, offender and others as by whatever reparative measures flow from that process. That process takes a variety of different forms in different programmes. In particular, the range of people involved varies—as between, for instance, victim–offender mediation programmes in which individual victim and individual offender are the only lead players and group conferences that also involve their families, friends or 'supporters'. There is much to be said about who should participate (about who has responsibility, or standing, in the matter): but I will concentrate here on the simple case of victim–offender mediation, and on the contrast between two simple models of mediation.

Civil mediation is a matter of negotiation and compromise, aimed at resolving conflict. I am in conflict with my neighbour over her constant early morning DIY work; my complaints have proved fruitless. Rather than going to law, we try mediation to resolve our conflict: we must find a way to live together as neighbours; going to law would probably be an expensive way of failing to achieve that. The mediation process consists initially in mutual explanation, and complaint. I complain about her DIY work; she argues that I am exaggerating things, and accuses me of keeping her awake with my late night parties. However, we recognise that we must move beyond trading complaints and harping on past misdeeds.

Perhaps we should each admit that we have been variously in the wrong in the past, but now look to the future, to find a mutually acceptable modus vivendi. That will involve negotiating a compromise between our conflicting habits: we might agree that she will avoid noisy DIY work before 9.00 am, whilst I will hold no more than one late party a fortnight. We might also pay compensation for any past damage—damage to her hedge by my guests, to my walls by her building work; and we might exchange general apologies for any past wrongs. But the compensation will be focused purely on any material damage that was done; and the apologies might be formal (we do not aspire to the sort of friendship in which apologies are worthwhile only if sincere) and unfocused (we do not list every wrong).

Some such civil mediation process is often the appropriate way of dealing with conflicts, including many which involve criminal conduct. Perhaps my neighbour has committed what counts in law as criminal damage against me, as my guests have against her: but it would be stupid to call the police and demand that they press charges. This is partly because there have been similar, minor, wrongs on both sides, but also because our relationship is one of rough equality: neither has been oppressing the other. We have each failed to think carefully enough about our relationship, but we can remedy that through informal mediation.

Sometimes, however, such a process is inappropriate: if mediation is possible at all, what is required is *criminal* mediation, under the aegis of the criminal law.

Criminal mediation is focused on a wrong that has been done. A woman has been beaten by her husband, or her house has been burgled and vandalised; the parties agree to mediation. It matters, first, that the relevant facts be established, either before the mediation or as its first stage—that this was a serious criminal assault, or burglary and criminal damage. (Whereas in the civil case, it is less important or helpful thus to focus on the past.)

Second, the process will include discussion and mutual explanations of those facts: the victim can explain how the crime affected her; the offender might explain how he came to commit it. The offender's explanation might include mitigating factors: but he is not allowed to argue that his conduct was justified—that husbands have the right to 'chastise' their wives, for instance. For the criminal law, under whose aegis the process takes place, defines what counts as a crime and as a justification: whatever else is negotiable, the wrongfulness of the offender's conduct is not. (Whereas in civil mediation each party might initially seek to justify their own conduct, before realising that this is futile.)

Part of the aim of the process is precisely this communication between victim and offender: the victim has a chance to bring the offender to grasp the wrong he did her, and to understand his action from his perspective; the offender has the chance to explain himself, and to grasp more clearly what he has done. Censure is integral to this exercise: to try to bring the offender to grasp the wrong that he did involves at least implicitly condemning his action as wrongful (not to condemn it would be implicitly to deny that it was a wrong, or that its wrongfulness mattered); and if he comes to grasp it as a wrong, he will censure himself for doing it.

Third, however, the process also aims to reconcile offender and victim: but what does this involve? Minimally, the aim is to reconcile them as fellow citizens (if they had no closer relationship that could be salvaged): to repair or restore the normative relationship of fellow-citizenship, so that they can treat each other with the acceptance and respect that fellowship in the polity requires. The offender's crime violated the values which define that normative relationship, and was thus injurious to it; that injury must be repaired.

Now in civil mediation, reconciliation is achieved partly by a compromise between the conflicting interests of the parties concerned: but since the wrong-fulness of the crime is not negotiable, we cannot seek reconciliation in the criminal case through a similar compromise—for instance one that allows the husband to beat his wife occasionally. Nor can reconciliation be achieved merely by the kind of reparation that civil mediation can involve: for even if the independently identi-fiable harms suffered by the victim could be repaired, what is required is a response that addresses the wrong done to her. That must at least involve an apology, which expresses the wrongdoer's recognition of the wrong she has done, her implicit commitment to avoid such wrongdoing in future, and her concern to seek forgiveness from and reconciliation with the person she wronged. Apologies own the wrong as something that I culpably did, but disowns it as something that I now repudiate; they also mark my renewed recognition of the person I wronged as one to whom I owe a respect that I failed to display, and with whom I must reconcile myself by making up for what I did to her.

But a merely verbal apology might not be enough, for relatively serious wrongs. This is partly because verbal apologies can easily be insincere—mere words that lack depth or truth; but also because even sincere verbal apology might not do enough to address the seriousness of the wrong. We often need to give more than merely verbal expression to things that matter to us. We express gratitude for services done to us by gifts or, in the public realm, by public rewards or honours; we express our grief at a death through the rituals of a funeral. Such more-than-merely-verbal modes of expression have two purposes: they make the expression more forceful, and they help to focus the expresser's attention on what needs to be expressed.

Similarly, an apology is strengthened if it is given a more than merely verbal form—if I make some kind of material reparation to the person I wronged. Thus the mediation process typically aims to end with an agreement on what reparation the offender should make. This might consist in something superficially identical to the reparation to which civil mediation can lead: if I damaged another's property, I might pay for its repair, or even repair it myself. But such direct repair is not always possible: the wrongdoer might need to find some other benefit he can provide for the victim (or for others; the offender might agree to undertake some charitable activity). Furthermore, even if such direct repair is possible, it has a different meaning in the criminal case, as a forceful expression of the offender's recognition of his wrongdoing—a forceful apology.

One striking difference between reparation in the civil and in the criminal case concerns its burdensome character. Civil reparation can be burdensome, depending on what is required and on the repairer's resources: but it is not designed to be burdensome, and repairs the harm no less efficaciously if it is entirely unburdensome. Criminal reparation, by contrast, must be burdensome if it is to serve its purpose: only then can it express a serious apology for a wrong done; if it cost the wrongdoer nothing, it would mean no more than empty verbal apology.

I have spoken so far of how sincere apology can be adequately and forcefully expressed; and we could see the paradigm of moral reparation for a wrong as the voluntary undertaking of some designedly burdensome reparative task which will express the wrongdoer's sincerely remorseful apology. But life, especially of the kind that involves criminal mediation, is not always like that: what can I say about cases in which the offender is not sincerely apologetic, or in which the victim is not ready to accept such an apology? I will make two initial points about the former possibility at this point.

Part of the purpose of criminal mediation is, as I have noted, to bring the offender (if she needs bringing) to recognise her crime as a wrong—and thus to recognise the need for some apologetic reparation. But that might not happen; and the question is whether, on my account, there can then be any appropriate point to requiring her to undertake a reparative task, if it does not express a sincere apology. There is an appropriate point, in two ways.

First, the process of undertaking the reparation can help to induce what it is intended to express—the offender's repentant recognition of the wrong he has done. Just as the rituals of a funeral can serve both to express and to induce an understanding of the significance of the person's death by focusing the mourners' attention on it, so undertaking reparation can focus the wrongdoer's attention on the meaning of his wrongdoing, so inducing him to repent it as a wrong, and to see the reparation as an appropriate way of expressing that repentance.

Second, even if this does not happen, requiring the wrongdoer to undertake a reparative task serves a legitimate purpose. It makes it forcefully clear to him that he has done wrong, and that he owes this to his victim by way of apologetic reparation: we require him, in effect, to apologise to her in order to make clear to him why he ought to do so. It sends a message to the victim—that we recognise and take seriously the wrong she has suffered. There is also still a sense in which victim and offender are reconciled by the very ritual of reparation, even if it does not express a sincere apology. In more intimate relationships only sincere apologies have value: but in the more distant relationships in which we stand to each other simply as fellow citizens we can often make peace with each other by going through the ritual motions of making and accepting an apology without inquiring into its sincerity.

We can, I suggest, see criminal mediation and reparation as a kind of secular penance: as a burden undertaken by the wrongdoer, which aims to induce and express her repentant and apologetic understanding of the wrong she has done, and thus to secure reconciliation with those she has wronged. Religious penances are addressed to God, against whom the sinner has offended. Secular penances are addressed initially to the direct victim of the wrongdoing (when there is one), as the person to whom apology is most obviously owed; but they are also addressed to the wider community, against one of whose members the wrong was committed and whose values were violated. Crimes as public wrongs require public apology: an apology addressed to the whole community as well as to the individual victim.

We should also, I claim, recognise criminal mediation and reparation as punitive, indeed as a paradigm of retributive punishment.

Criminal Mediation and Punishment

Criminal mediation, as described here, certainly fits the standard definitions of punishment, as something intentionally painful or burdensome imposed on an offender, for her crime, by some person or body with the authority to do so—and, we can add, intended to communicate censure for that crime. It focuses on the offender and his crime: on what he must do to repair the moral damage wrought by his crime. It is intended to be painful or burdensome, and the pain or burden is to be suffered for the crime. The mediation process itself aims to confront the offender with the fact and implications of what he has done, and to bring him to repent it as a wrong: a process which must be painful. The reparation that he is then to undertake must be burdensome if it is to serve its proper purpose. The aim is not to 'make the offender suffer' just for its own sake: but it is to induce an appropriate kind of suffering—the suffering intrinsic to confronting and repenting one's own wrongdoing and to making reparation for it. Criminal mediation takes place under the aegis of the criminal law and the authority of a criminal court: a court must determine that the defendant committed the offence charged, supervise the mediation process, approve its outcome (the reparation the offender is to make), and deal with offenders who refuse to take part or to make the agreed reparation.

It might seem that criminal mediation and reparation still cannot constitute punishment, since punishment is imposed against or regardless of the offender's will, whilst mediation and reparation must be consensual: the offender must agree to enter mediation, and to undertake reparation. However, first, punishment can be self-imposed: an offender who willingly enters mediation and undertakes reparation can be said be punishing herself. Second, most of the punishments imposed by our courts are not strictly 'imposed' in the sense that the offender is simply their passive victim or recipient: more usually, they consist in requirements—to pay a fine, to undertake the specified community service, to visit the probation officer—which it is up to the offender to carry out for herself; and offenders could likewise be required to take part in the mediation process and to undertake the specified reparation. There are, of course, sanctions against offenders who fail to do what is required of them, which will involve, in the end, involve something strictly imposed on the offender: but restorative processes must also be backed up by ultimately coercive sanctions against offenders who fail to do what is required of them.

However, my claim that criminal mediation and reparation should be seen as punishment is not simply definitional: this process can serve the appropriate aims of criminal punishment.

First, mediation is a communicative process. The procedure consists in communication between victim and offender about the crime's implications, as a wrong against the victim; the reparation that the offender undertakes communicates to the victim and others an apology for that crime. But it is a process of punitive communication: it censures the offender for his crime, and requires some burdensome reparation for that crime. Criminal punishment must, I believe, be justified (if it can be justified at all) as a communicative enterprise between a state or political community and its members; criminal mediation is certainly such an enterprise.

Second, criminal mediation is retributive, in that it seeks to impose on (or induce in) the offender the suffering she deserves for her crime, and is justified in those terms. She deserves to suffer censure for what she has done: mediation aims to communicate that censure to her, in such a way that she will come to accept that she deserves it. She deserves to suffer remorse for what she has done: mediation aims to induce remorse in her, by bringing her to recognise the wrong she has done. She ought to make apologetic, burdensome, reparation to her victim: mediation aims to provide for such reparation. By seeing criminal mediation as punishment, we can thus make plausible sense of the retributivist idea that the guilty deserve to suffer, by showing what they deserve to suffer, and why. What they deserve to suffer is not just 'pain' or a 'burden', but the particular kind of painful burden which is integral to the recognition of guilt: they deserve to suffer that because it is an appropriate response to their wrongdoing; and criminal mediation aims precisely to impose or induce that kind of suffering.

Third, the reparation that the offender undertakes is a species of penal hard treatment: it is intentionally burdensome, making demands on his time, money or energies, independently of its communicative meaning. But we can now see how penal hard treatment can be justified as an essential aspect of a communicative penal process: the hard treatment that reparation involves is the means by which the offender makes apologetic reparation to the victim, and a vehicle through which he can strengthen his own repentant understanding of the wrong he has done.

Fourth, although criminal mediation is retributive, looking back to the past crime, it is also future-directed. It aims to reconcile victim and offender, through apologetic reparation by the offender. It aims to dissuade the offender from future crimes: to bring her to repent the wrong she has done is to bring her to see why she should not commit such wrongs in future. This is not, however, to posit a consequentialist 'general justifying aim' (see Hart, 1968) for criminal mediation or for punishment. On consequentialist accounts, the relationship between punishment and the good it aims to achieve is instrumental and contingent:

punishment is, as a matter of fact, an efficient technique for achieving that good. But the relationship between criminal mediation and the goods it aims to achieve is not merely instrumental. For the ends themselves determine the means which are appropriate to them: the reconciliation which is to be achieved must involve a recognition of and apology for the wrong that was done, and must therefore be achieved by a process which includes such recognition and apology; the offender is to be dissuaded from future crime by her recognition of the wrong she has committed.

Although I have argued that we should see criminal mediation of the kind described here as a paradigm of punishment, it might strike you that this process is still very different from the criminal punishments typically imposed under our existing penal systems; and so it is and should be. For although I believe that punishment is in principle a necessary and appropriate response to criminal wrong-doing, I am not seeking to justify our existing penal practices, or anything very like them. However, a criminal mediation process of the kind I have described will by no means always be possible or appropriate: I should therefore say something about how criminal mediation should fit into a larger system of criminal justice—a system that will also impose more familiar kinds of punishment; this will also involve some comments on the proper role of the criminal courts, and will thus address some further concerns of critics of the 'restorative paradigm'.

References

Ashworth, AJ, (1993) 'Some Doubts about Restorative Justice' 4 *Criminal Law Forum* 277.
Christie, N, (1981) *Limits to Pain* (London, Martin Robertson).
Duff, RA, (2002) 'Harms and Wrongs' 4 *Buffalo Criminal Law Review* 101.
Feinberg, J, (1970) 'The Expressive Function of Punishment' in J Feinberg, *Doing and Deserving* (Princeton, NJ, Princeton University Press).
Hart, HLA, (1968) 'Prolegomenon to the Principles of Punishment' in HLA Hart, *Punishment and Responsibility* (Oxford, Oxford University Press).
Ripstein, A, (1999) *Equality, Responsibility and the Law* (Cambridge, Cambridge University Press).
Walgrave, L, (1994) 'Beyond Rehabilitation: in Search of a Constructive Alternative in the Judicial Response to Juvenile Crime' 2 *European Journal on Criminal Policy and Research* 57.

5.3

Reparation and Retribution: Are They Reconcilable?

LUCIA ZEDNER

The arguments advanced for incorporating reparative elements into the criminal justice system are for the most part pragmatic and economic ones. At the most basic level, reparative justice is supported on the grounds that it is functional for the state to secure the payment of compensation or to support other ventures which seek to repair the damage done by crime. To the extent that reparative ventures are actually perceived by victims as having desirable effects, they reduce the possibility of a disgruntled victim taking the law into his or her own hands to seek redress. In the same vein, they lessen the likelihood that the victim will become so disaffected that they themselves turn to crime. Moreover, the prospect of reparation may encourage victims to report crimes, to cooperate with the police and to appear at trial, hence increasing the efficacy of the criminal justice process. Given that the vast majority of crimes are detected only with the aid of the general public, it must be desirable for these forms of co-operation to be encouraged . . .

Reparative sentences would, it is argued, not only lessen the burden of punishment on the offender but offer the possibility for constructive, forward-looking sentencing. Making good, whether via monetary compensation or other reparative endeavour, is also applauded as having psychological advantages over traditional retributive penalties. Reparation, it is argued, relieves the offender's feelings of guilt and alienation which may precipitate further crimes. The effect is said to be restorative not only to the victim but also to the offender, increasing their sense of self-esteem and aiding reintegration.[1]

These pragmatic purposes are largely uncontroversial, such controversy as exists arising mainly from doubts about the ability of reparation to achieve them. The theoretical reorientation posed by a fully developed reparative schema is more challenging. Such a schema would demand the abandonment of culpability of the offender as the central focus of sentencing and, in its place, pay much closer attention to the issue of harm. It would reconceive crimes less as the willed contraventions of an abstract moral code enshrined in law but, more importantly, as signals of social dysfunction inflicting harm on victims (and perhaps also offenders) as well as society. According to this view, criminal justice should be less preoccupied

From L Zedner, 'Reparation and Retribution: are they Reconcilable?' (1994) 57 *Modern Law Review* 228.

with censuring the code-breakers and focus instead on the process of restoring individual damage and repairing ruptured social bonds.[2] In place of meeting pain with the infliction of further pain, a truly reparative system would seek the holistic restoration of the community. It would necessarily also challenge the sole claim of the state to respond to crime and would instead invite (or perhaps demand) the involvement of the community in the process of restoration.

What is Reparative Justice?

"Reparation" is not synonymous with restitution, still less does it suggest a straight-forward importation of civil into criminal law. Reparation should properly connote a wider set of aims. It involves more than "making good" the damage done to property, body or psyche. It must also entail recognition of the harm done to the social relationship between offender and victim, and the damage done to the victim's social rights in his or her property or person. According to Davis, reparation "should not be seen as residing solely in the offer of restitution; adequate reparation must also include some attempt to make amends for the victim's loss of the presumption of security in his or her rights".[3] This way of thinking echoes, consciously or not, the concept of "dominion" developed by Braithwaite and Pettit.[4] For dominion to be restored, what is sought is some evidence of a change in attitude, some expression of remorse that indicates that the victim's rights will be respected in the future. Achieving such a change in attitude may entail the offender agreeing to undergo training, counselling or therapy and, as such, these may all be seen as part of reparative justice. A forced apology or obligatory payment of compensation will not suffice; indeed, it may even be counterproductive in eliciting a genuine change of attitude in the offender. But is "symbolic reparation" alone sufficient? According to Braithwaite, if reparation is not to come too cheap it must be backed up by material compensation. Accepting Braithwaite's view, the distinctions made between material and non-material or symbolic reparation tend to lose significance. It would seem that in most cases for full reparation to be achieved some mixture of the two will be required. Let us examine each in turn.

The most obvious and concrete form of reparative justice is compensation. Monetary compensation recognizes the fact that crime deprives its victim of the means to pursue life choices: it seeks to recognize that deprivation and to restore access either to those means which have been denied or to comparable alternative means . . .

In practice, compensation orders are set with reference to the ability of the offender to pay and, given that the majority of offenders are of limited means, they rarely result in complete restoration. In so far as reparation also seeks to promote the reintegration of the offender, it would surely be counterproductive to heap intolerable burdens on him. Although in seeking to embrace both reintegration and restoration simultaneously, reparative justice is necessarily riven by tensions, we should not see these aims as competing or necessarily in conflict: they are rather two sides of the same coin.

Less tangible but nonetheless important is what we might call "symbolic reparation". This might be an apology made by the offender to the victim or other attempts at reconciliation. The reparation here is "symbolic" in that it does not entail the return of money or material goods. Proponents of reparative justice argue that if the apology is not merely an empty gesture but one which conveys remorse and a genuine change of attitude, then such symbolic reparation is quite as important as more tangible returns. Mediation seeks to provide a way for parties to resolve disputes without recourse to the vagaries of the courts. It aims to allow both parties to retain control over the dispute and to voice their grievances under the supervision of a mediator, whether a trained professional or lay volunteer. In theory, the mediator acts only as a conduit and ideally any resolution is reached by the mutual agreement of the two parties. In practice, the form and organization of mediation schemes vary considerably . . .

Is Reparation Compatible with Punishment?

This is not the place to enquire into the philosophical foundations of the criminal law nor to explore at length theories of punishment. It is enough to recognize that certain basic elements of the prevailing paradigm must be fulfilled if reparation is to claim a place within it. These include: first, the imposition of "pain"; second, that the sanction is invoked in response to social wrongs (crimes); and, third, that it is applied against culpable offenders. Reparative justice must satisfy each of these elements if it is to escape the tag of "conceptual cuckoo". Let us examine them in turn.

(a) Punitive quality

Perhaps the most telling objection to reparative justice is that it has no intrinsic penal character and that to enforce civil liabilities through the criminal courts is not, of itself, to punish . . .

It is questionable, however, whether a compensation order can properly be seen as no more than a civil instrument riding on the back of a criminal trial. Unlike the French device of the *partie civile*,[5] compensation in English law is fully integrated into the criminal process and has the formal status of a penalty. . .

It is significant also that compensation orders extort money which, in the vast majority of cases, offenders would not otherwise have been required to pay. First, the action for recovery is brought about without financial cost to the victim. And, secondly, the state has the coercive mechanisms to ensure that repayment is actually made. In this sense, it may be said that the compensation order inflicts "pain" which is "additional" to that which civil law would otherwise exact. These factors also help to ensure that compensation orders are perceived both by offenders and society as "real" punishment. But the danger here is that to claim compensation orders operate as a punishment may lead us to the unhappy conclusion that for the offender the compensation order is undifferentiated from the fine and has little or no reparative quality. If the goal of restoring the recipient to a position akin to that which existed prior to the offence is obscured in the offender's mind by the punitive bite of the penalty, then it is unlikely that its avowed reintegrative aspects will be effective.

The objection that compensation lacks "penal value" becomes even more difficult to maintain in light of the fact that, since 1973, it has been possible to impose compensation as the sole penalty. Stigma attaches to conviction whatever the subsequent penalty and, where compensation is ordered alone, it too is accompanied by the shaming mechanism of the guilty verdict. We might do well to separate out notions of censure and sanction. It is possible to argue that the public drama of the trial, the naming of the defendant and, in particular, the formal attribution of guilt goes a long way toward fulfilling the requirements of censure. Once the demands of reproof have thus been met, is it not excessive to demand that penal sanctions also be endowed with censuring qualities?

In respect of mediation and reparation, the issue of punitive quality becomes more complex still. Purists might argue that the offender must enter into the process voluntarily and participate willingly in seeking an outcome. To the extent that participation is coerced, the reintegrative impact of mediation may be lost. But such a view is predicated upon reaching a resolution which is fully agreed upon by both parties. If the offender is a less than willing participant who agrees only reluctantly and under pressure, then it is more likely that he or she will fail to abide by the resolution reached. How, then, should enforcement be assured? Should mediation agencies have access to the full coercive powers of the court and, if they were to do so, would there not be a danger that the repara-tive potential would be undermined? Proponents of reparative justice might argue that discussion about enforcement is to miss the very point of mediation—that the outcome should be freely agreed and its terms willingly met. The experience of mediation in other areas (for example, the settlement of family disputes)[6] suggests that we would do well, however, to reflect further on what should happen if offenders fail to fulfil their part of the bargain. Should offenders be brought back to court, as would happen on breach of any other community disposal, and, if so, by whom and with what consequences?

(b) Recognition of social wrong

As we have seen, the original appeal to reparative justice was made through an evocation of a nostalgic vision of a bygone community in which disputes were settled by the parties to them.[7] Present mediation practice reflects this view and tends to treat crime as a personal issue between offender and victim. Not only does mediation take the private conflict as its sole object, but its organizational context sets it apart from the public symbolic processes of criminal justice. Most schemes promote mediation as an alternative to formal procedures, as a way of diverting the offender away from public prosecution, they host discussions between the immediate parties alone with only the mediator in attendance and shield their participants from media exposure. Whilst proponents might argue that all these measures are purposively designed to ensure that the parties retain a sense of ownership over "their" dispute, such tactics tend also to overlook the wider interests at stake. They tend also to strip the process of its power to signify public disapprobation and to inflict shame upon the offender. To this extent, it is arguable that reparation, narrowly conceived, fails to recognize that it is not only the victim but also society that has been wronged by the disregard shown for its norms and the general threat posed to public dominion. Another objection is that to make reparation to identifiable victims the primary aim of criminal justice would be effectively to decriminalize the mass of "victimless" offences. The model of mediating a dispute between two parties may operate with some plausibility in respect of interpersonal crimes of violence or theft, but offers little by way of resolution to crimes such as motoring violations, vandalism or public order offences.

It is surely possible, however, to put forward a broader conception of reparative justice which recognizes that the rights infringed by crime are not those of the victim alone but are held in common socially.[8] It is this social aspect which distinguishes crime from the private harms inflicted by torts. Thus, even where there is no identifiable victim, reparation to the wider community for actual harms or public "endangerment" is owed. Is it possible also for reparative forms of justice to fulfil the public functions (both recognition of the social wrong and public shaming) demanded by infringement of the criminal law? Proponents might legitimately argue that it is misplaced to look upon compensation and mediation as the only means to reparation and that penalties such as community service orders are better placed to make reparation to the wider community. One might then ask how far, or indeed whether, the community feels itself to be "repaired" by such activities. Until there is empirical research which offers evidence as to the psychological impact of "community service" on the community it purports to serve, it is probably unwise to make assertions about its wider reparative quality. Even to propose such research raises questions about the very entity of "community" and whether it actually refers to more than the geographical location in which mediation, reparation or community service orders take place.

If reparative justice, as currently conceived, fails to respond adequately to the social wrong which has been perpetrated, is it possible to envisage modifications which would allow it better to fulfil the public purposes of punishment? One would be to open up the mediation process, either by allowing the public to observe the proceedings or by permitting the media to report on both process and outcome. This would meet the requirement that the offender's offence be publicly known and censured. The danger in using the media as instruments of censure in this way is, however, that, as Dignan has pointed out, "the kind of shaming indulged in by much of the media is highly stigmatizing and might well make the process of reinte-gration all the more difficult".[9] A stronger and perhaps more controllable version of public participation would be to elevate the mediator from the position of go-between in an essentially bilateral negotiation to that of a third party repre-senting the public interest. If mediation is to respond adequately to the social wrong which has been done, then it must take due heed of the wider social purposes of the criminal trial. These include the reassertion of normative order, the re-estab-lishment of the rights and obligations of citizens, the interpretation and development of doctrinal law and of policy, and even the elaboration and mainte-nance of legal ideology. One may debate how and to what ends these goals should be pursued, but a system which wholly failed to acknowledge their place would scarcely merit the label of criminal justice.

Can Reparation Comply with the Principles of Punishment?

So far we have examined the capacity of reparative justice to mirror or incorporate the chief elements of punishment. If reparative justice is to claim a full place within the penal system, then it must also accord with the principles which delimit the intrusive powers of the state. Can reparation satisfy the requirements for fairness, consistency and proportionality which currently underpin and frame our penal sys-tem? Once again, let us look at each element in turn.

(a) Fairness

A primary criticism faced by the reparative approach is that it would create a system of penalties which would have little regard to the means of the offender and so impinge differently on rich and poor. At worst it might allow the very rich to "buy" their way out of punishment by paying off their victim for harms suffered . . .

In practice, in the interests of fairness to the offender, the amount payable in compensation is often scaled down below that which is proportional to the harm done. Critics of reparation would argue that it is right that fairness to the offender should take priority over that to the victim. But a pure restitutionist approach might insist that the harm be "made good" at whatever cost is necessary. Can it be right than an offender with meagre resources suffers, in real terms, a greater punishment than the wealthy offender for whom the payment is no burden at all? Is it desirable that an impoverished offender might work for years to pay off a compensation order (perhaps to a victim whose own wealth makes the sum received negligible)? All these factors clearly do considerable damage to the idea of fairness in criminal law. Yet one might argue that this conception of justice is predi-cated on being fair to the offender and that an alternative version might equally well be predicated on the rights or interests of the victim and be prepared to sacrifice fairness to the offender to this end.

(b) Consistency

The attempt made by desert theory to develop a coherent, structured approach to sentencing has been applauded as a move toward certainty and consistency. For the same reason Ashworth has objected to reparative justice on the grounds that it would allow the victim to influence sentencing, as happens in the United States through the use of victim-impact and victim-opinion statements. In so doing, it would be damaging to the pursuit of consistency.[10] If victims are given the right to influence the penalty, a twofold danger arises. Both the form of the penalty (be it reparative or retributive) and its size (be it monetary value or duration) may vary according to the temperament of the victim. But are such criticisms well-grounded?

First, there is a danger of presuming that the objective calculus posited by desert theory is in practice feasible or realistic. Individual sentences will always depend in part on subjective assessments regarding the gravity of the offence made by the sentencer. Thus, while just deserts may promise consistency, it cannot guarantee it. Second, Ashworth's objection makes certain assumptions about the reparative justice model which are questionable. It is not necessarily the case that reorientating the system around "making good" must inevitably entail allowing the victim to usurp the role of the state in determining the appropriate sentence. Reparation is owed not just to the victim but to all those whose interests are threatened, and the author would agree that it is not appropriate for the victim to determine the nature or extent of reparation. The harm suffered is a social one and it is for society to determine what is necessary to effect reparation. Just as the state now makes judgments about the seriousness of the offence and the severity of punishment deserved or, indeed, about the harm done and the quantum of compensation owed, so within a reparative model the state could retain the right to determine the penalty. One might even envisage a system which imports a standardized scale for determining the seriousness of harm analogous to that suggested by von Hirsch and Jareborg in their development of a "living standard analysis" for gauging criminal harm.[11] Whereas their model is backward-looking and concerned solely with "how much harm a standard act of burglary did", a reparative schema would need to furnish criteria for assessing what would be necessary to "make good" the harms done. Within this schema, victim-impact statements might furnish necessary information about the harm inflicted and the consequent needs of the victim upon which impartial judgments might be made about the reparation required. By developing a framework for making such judgments systematically, the risk that offenders would find themselves at the whim of vindictive or overly forgiving victims is surely overcome.

Conclusion: Can Reparation and Punishment be Reconciled?

Let us close by considering some points at which reparation and retributive punishment coincide. First, both retribution and reparation are predicated upon notions of individual autonomy. Unlike rehabilitative or "treatment" orientated models of justice, both reparation and retribution presume that offenders are rational individuals able to make free moral choices for which they may be held liable. The offender may thus be legitimately called to account, whether by making good or suffering a proportionate punishment. However, both approaches are open to the objection that they ignore the structural imperatives of deprivation and disadvantage under which many offenders act. Both assume that all offenders are rational, free-willed individuals despite the disproportionate incidence of mental illness and disorder, social inadequacy and poor education among our offending population.

Secondly, it might be argued that both reparation and retribution derive their "authority" from the offence itself and impose penalties according to the seriousness of the particular crime. Unlike the utilitarian aims of general deterrence or rehabilitation which import wider notions of societal good, both retribution and reparation exclude (or nearly exclude) consideration of factors beyond the particular offence. The offender's personal history, the social or economic causes of crime or the need to prevent future offending (all of which extend the limits of intrusion by the state under deterrent or rehabilitative theories) are here deemed irrelevant. As such, both retributive and reparative justice, it is said, impose strict constraints on the intrusion of the state into the lives of offenders. This apparent congruity is not, however, as close as it first seems. The seriousness of the offence is set according to two different sets of criteria. Retribution demands punishment proportional primarily to the intent of the offender, whereas reparative justice derives its "proportionality" from the harm inflicted on the victim. Whilst intent is generally focused on outcomes, and intent and harm may thus coincide, the two may point to very different levels of gravity. If reparation and retribution were to be wholly reconciled, then it would be necessary to devise a measure which integrated intent and harm in setting offence seriousness. A greater difficulty still is that, if reparative justice is to be more than a criminal analogue to civil damages, then it should go beyond the offence itself to enquire about its wider social costs and the means to making them good.

Finally, reparation and retribution have been described by Davis as each a "species of distributive justice, the root metaphor in each case is that of justice as balance, the object being to restore the distribution of rights which existed prior to the offence".[12] Whilst one seeks to restore equilibrium by depriving the offender of his rights, the other pursues the same goal by recompensing those whose rights were injured by the crime. This redistribution of rights is analogous to Ashworth's notion of criminal justice as a "form of social accounting".[13] In respect of mitigation, for example, laudable social acts by the offender are balanced against crimes to arrive at the appropriate penalty. Ashworth suggests that this calculus is based upon rehabilitative reasoning which sees the offender's subsequent conduct as evidence of his reform. Another possible view is that mitigation is justified here on the grounds that some restoration of the legal order has been made.

These "distributive" or "accounting" metaphors go some way to describing the common ethos of retributive and reparative justice. But they rely on a very narrow conception of reparative justice as solely restitutive in intent, seeking only to return to the preceding legal order.[14] Moreover, the legitimacy of a justification based on "restoring the balance of rights" is open to question on a number of counts. First, to use the criminal justice system solely as a means of restoring the balance of rights which existed prior to the offence is to condone the reinforcement of preexisting social inequality. Secondly, many of those activities defined as criminal and those groups identified as offenders reflect the interests and values of a socially dominant group. If reparation, with retribution, seeks to restore the values which criminalization underpins, it is likely not merely to recreate but to accentuate social inequality. Thirdly, as Davis has also argued, to demand that offenders bear the full burden of restoring the distribution of rights is to expect too much from that "unrepresentative and generally impecunious group of citizens who come to the attention of the criminal courts", both practically and as a matter of principle.[15] A powerful objection to the increased use of compensation orders, for example, is that they ignore the fact that very many offenders are in straitened financial circumstances. To impose further financial burdens upon impoverished offenders may simply be counterproductive.

In the light of these conceptual links, the concurrent re-emergence of retributive and reparative thinking is perhaps less surprising than it first appears. Ironically, however, the very points at which reparative and retributive justice coincide appear on closer inspection to be the points of greatest weakness within the reparative justice model. Its frailty is greatest in respect of its "redistributive" purposes which, while theoretically attractive, are predicated on a fictitious just society in which the only imbalance of rights is caused by crimes themselves. A truly reparative model might better recognize that much crime is not simply a cause but also the consequence of social injustice and that the victim, the community *and* the offender are probably in need of repair if criminal justice is to contribute toward a more reintegrated society.

We began with the questions "can and should" the penal system embrace both punitive and reparative goals: let us return to them by way of conclusion. From our discussion it would seem that while "making good" entails certain difficulties within a criminal justice system, reparation is quite capable of fulfilling the basic demands of punishment and, thus far, is reconcilable with retribution. The danger, however, is that the attempt to accommodate reparative justice to the rationale of punishment so perverts its underlying rationale as to strip it of much of its original appeal, not least its commitment to repairing ruptured social bonds. We are accustomed to seeing criminal justice as the repressive arm of the state, but might it not better be conceived as one end of a continuum of practices by which social order is maintained? Punishment has a very limited ability to control crime and, to the extent that it is disintegrative, it inflicts further damage on society. Given that the high profile "law and order policies" of the past decade have done little to stem spiralling crime figures, perhaps it is time to explore the integrative potential of reparative justice on its own terms.

Notes

1. J. Braithwaite, *Crime, Shame and Reintegration* (1989).
2. D. van Ness, "New Wine in Old Wineskins: Four Challenges of Restorative Justice", (1993) 4 *Criminal Law forum,* p. 251.
3. G. Davis *et al., Preliminary Study of Victim–Offender Mediation and Reparation Schemes in England and Wales* (1987), p. 7.
4. See P. Pettit and J. Braithwaite, "Not Just Deserts, Even in Sentencing", (1993) 4 *Current Issues in Criminal Justice* 222.
5. Or the German *Adhesionsverfahren*, though interestingly this device for attaching civil proceedings to the criminal process is rarely used: see Mueller-Dietz, "Compensation as a Criminal Penalty" in Kaiser, Kury and Albrecht (eds.), *Victims and Criminal Justice* (1992).
6. S. Roberts, "Mediation in Family Disputes", (1983) 46 *Modern L.R.* 537.
7. See Christie, Selection 5.1 above.
8. Watson, Boucherat and Davis, "Reparation for Retributivists", in M. Wright and B. Galaway (eds.). *Mediation and Criminal Justice* (1989); Pettit and Braithwaite, note 4 above.
9. J. Dignan, "Reintegration through reparation", in A. Duff, S. Marshall, R. E. Dobash and R. P. Dobash (eds.). *Penal Theory and Practice* (1994).
10. A. Ashworth, "Victim Impact Statements and Sentencing", [1993] *Crim.L.R.* 498.
11. See Selection 4.5 above.
12. G. Davis, *Making Amends: Mediation and Reparation in Criminal Justice* (1992), p. 11.
13. A. Ashworth, *Sentencing and Criminal Justice* (1992), p. 133.
14. They may also be inadequate for desert theory, which has moved away from the metaphor of "restoring the balance".
15. Davis, above n. 12, p. 12.

5.4

Normative Constraints: Principles of Penality

JIM DIGNAN

Debates about punishment tend to concentrate on two types of moral questions. The first asks *what justifies* the infliction of pain or suffering on a person, which raises a further question about *whom* we are entitled to punish. The second is concerned with the severity of punishment and asks *how much* punishment we are entitled to inflict? There is a third question, which is usually overlooked, or at any rate the answer to which is normally taken for granted: viz. *what kind* of punishment we are entitled to impose?

Restorative justice advocates need to be able to provide convincing answers' to the first two sets of questions if they are to allay the well-founded concerns of those who fear that, well-intentioned though it might be, restorative justice could all too easily result in unintended and unjust consequences for some. The response to these questions from most restorative justice advocates so far has not been entirely convincing, however. Some have appeared to question the need for such normative constraints, while others have failed to particularise the limits that they would be prepared to countenance, or even the principles by which such limits might be determined. In the sections that follow I will argue that there is ample scope for an accommodation to be reached which would meet the main concerns raised by just desert theorists without compromising the integrity of a restorative justice approach.

When it comes to the third question, relating to the *kind* of punishment we are entitled to impose, a restorative justice approach would in principle seem to be capable of generating a much more convincing set of answers than desert theory (or any other theory of punishment) has so far been able to come up with. Indeed, it may even have the potential to furnish the kind of 'replacement discourse' that Andrew Ashworth (1997) has called for, which could potentially change the terms of reference with which the debate about punishment is conducted. Or so I shall be arguing. But it will only do so if it stops assuming that the concept of restorative justice refers exclusively to a particular kind of process, and overcomes its reluctance to talk about what might count as just and unjust outcomes.

From J Dignan, 'Towards a Systemic Model of Restorative Justice: Reflections on the Concept, its Context and the Need for clear Constraints', in A Von Hirsch et al (eds), *Restorative Justice and Criminal Justice* (Oxford, Hart Publishing, 2003), 135. References and endnotes omitted.

1. The Need to Justify Restorative Justice Interventions

In response to the first question, relating to the justification for punishment, some restorative justice advocates (eg Wright, 1991: 15 and 1996: 27; Walgrave, 1999: 146) seem to deny that measures of a restorative nature stand in need of moral justification in the way that conventional forms of punishment do. Their argument is based on a purported distinction between 'punitive' measures that are intended to inflict pain or unpleasantness for its own sake, and 'restorative' interventions which 'cannot be defined as punishments' because their intended purpose is said to be constructive. However, this line of reasoning relies for its effect on the confusion of two distinct elements in the concept of intention. One relates to the motive for doing something, but the other refers to the fact that the act in question is being performed deliberately or wilfully. In the case of punishment (and all analogous practices), it is the fact that pain or unpleasantness is *deliberately* imposed on a person that calls for a moral justification, regardless of the motive for doing so. Restorative justice advocates would do well to recall that similar 'motivational' arguments were used by past generations of penal reformers in support of ostensibly more benevolent rehabilitative measures, and were also justifiably challenged on the grounds that they failed to provide adequate safeguards to protect offenders from being treated unjustly.

2. Limiting the Severity of Restorative Justice Interventions: The Inadequacy of 'Republican' Constraints?

Other restorative justice advocates (notably Braithwaite and Pettit, 1990; see also Braithwaite and Parker, 1999) have acknowledged that restorative justice interventions do stand in need of moral justification. And they have articulated a coherent and elaborate normative theory (based on the concept of 'dominion', or freedom as non-domination) that they claim is more likely to generate just outcomes than the rival 'just deserts' theory.

However, Braithwaite's republican theory of restorative justice has failed to convince just deserts theorists that he has an adequate answer to the second question, relating to the *amount* of punishment we are entitled to impose. This is largely because of his insistence (1999: 73) that restorative justice amounts to no more than a procedural requirement that 'the parties talk until they feel that harmony has been restored on the basis of discussion of all the injustices they see as relevant to the case'. Consequently, there can be no guarantee that even restorative justice conferences will be able to avoid unjust outcomes in which authoritarian figures like 'Uncle Harry' call the shots (Ashworth, 2000:8, commenting on Braithwaite, 1999: 66–7).

Braithwaite's response takes two forms, though neither has assuaged the concerns raised by his critics. One line of defence (Braithwaite and Parker, 1999: 109) is to rely on the moderating influence that a vigorous 'republican' political discourse is expected to exert on the deliberations that take place within restorative conferences, the effect of which should be to defend powerless minorities against the tyrannies of the majority. The problem with this argument is that it assumes the existence of a particular kind of polity within which restorative justice processes are most likely to produce acceptable outcomes. Where this is not the case, however (as will often be the case in practice), there are genuine concerns that even a partial switch to informal dispute-settlement processes could result in unjust outcomes being perpetrated at the hands of 'authoritarian' communities (Lacey and Zedner, 1995; Cavadino et al 1999; and Dignan and Lowey, 2000).

Braithwaite's second line of defence (1999:89) is to preserve an absolute right for the accused (and victims) 'to walk out of the restorative justice process and try their chances in a court of law'. The problem with this argument is that it leaves the parties exposed to the vagaries of a legal lottery. By equating restorative justice with a particular kind of informal dispute resolution process, and refusing to specify what might count as a just or unjust outcome, it is impossible for Braithwaite to assuage the concerns of those who fear that the kinds of punishments that are inflicted by the courts are themselves all too often excessive and unjust. Indeed, those concerns are heightened by Braithwaite's professed willingness to resort to more conventionally punitive strategies based on the principles of 'active deterrence' and incapacitation, both in cases where restorative justice has been tried repeatedly and failed, and also as an implicit threat, lurking in the background, to encourage a responsible restorative approach on the part of offenders.

3. Limiting the Severity of Restorative Justice Interventions: A 'Rights-Based' Approach

So how *might* restorative justice advocates respond to the legitimate question that has been posed by just deserts theorists regarding the amount of punishment we are entitled to impose, whether in the context of an informal restorative justice process (such as a restorative or community conference or victim offender mediation) or by a regular criminal court? Mick Cavadino and I have argued elsewhere (1997) in favour of a 'compromise' theory of punishment, which sets out a principled accommodation between a form of retributivism, as espoused by the 'justice model' that is associated with Andrew von Hirsch and Andrew Ashworth, and restorative justice. Our argument is based on a form of human rights theory (of the kind propounded by Ronald Dworkin (1978) and Alan Gewirth (1978)) and may be summarised as follows.

One of the most important human rights is the equal right of individuals to maximum 'positive freedom', by which we mean the right to make effective choices about their lives. Rights' theory insists that any kind of punishment (whatever form it takes, and whatever the motivation for imposing it might be) requires special moral justification, since it reduces the freedom of the person being punished. It is difficult to see how a purely retributive justification for punishment could be reconciled with the positive freedom principle. For if retribution was all that punishment achieved, the offender's freedom would be gratuitously diminished without doing anything to improve anyone's prospects for exercising choice. However, the theory allows for one person's right (including even the right to positive freedom) to be restricted in certain circumstances, *provided* this is justified on the basis of another person's 'competing rights' (Dworkin, 1978).

This provides a prima facie moral justification for two different types of response to a given offence. First, if the offence has resulted in harm to a victim, that person is likely to have experienced some reduction in positive freedom: to function free from physical or psychological pain or disability, or to choose how to use or dispose of their resources. And it is this 'special harm' that entitles victims to reparation at the hands of their offenders, even though *their* positive freedom may be diminished thereby. Rights' theory thus provides a principled justification for restorative justice processes that provide a forum in which victims and offenders may deliberate about the offence and its consequences, including the kind and amount of any reparation to which the victim may be entitled. Moreover, if victims are to be treated with *equal* concern and respect, which is also in line with a rights-based approach (Dworkin, 1978), then their entitlement to seek reparation should apply *irrespective* of the nature or seriousness of the offence in question. Indeed, the victim's entitlement to reparation should prevail even if the offender is unwilling to participate in an informal restorative justice process such as conferencing or victim offender mediation. However, the *kind* of reparation that an offender might be obliged to make in such a case would almost certainly be quite different from the kind of reparation that might be expected to emanate from such a process (see below).

Secondly, where it may plausibly be argued that punishing an offender does something to reduce the incidence of crime, and thereby prevents the diminution of some other people's positive freedom, this *may* also provide an independent prima facie justification for restricting the positive rights of an offender. However, the pursuit of *both* these punitive aims—the provision of appropriate reparation for victims and the reduction of offending—must be pursued in a manner that is consistent with the human rights of the offender.   .

Consequently, there would be no justification for punishing someone unless they had deliberately and wrongfully broken a just law, thereby exercising a freedom to which they are not entitled (because to do so has diminished or threatened to diminish other people's positive freedom). It also follows that the *amount* of punishment (of whatever kind) that we are entitled to impose is itself subject to limits. Although offenders are liable to forfeit certain of their rights (including, to some extent, their right of positive freedom) because of their infringement of the rights of others, the response to this infringement should not be excessively severe, taking into account the moral gravity of their offence (see below).

The human rights based precept of positive freedom is thus consistent with a general principle of proportionality in the maximum amount of punishment that is imposed on an offender. This is sometimes referred to as the principle of 'limiting retributivism' (as advocated by Morris, 1974: 75; and Morris and Tonry, 1990), which prescribes an upper limit for the response to an offence, whatever form this may take. At the other end of the scale, the principle of limiting retributivism may also (particularly in the case of more serious offences) be consistent with a lower limit for the response to an offence, whatever the parties may feel and agree is appropriate by way of reparation. However, it would be difficult to reconcile the principle of positive freedom for both offenders and victims with an insistence on the kind of strict proportionality that is favoured by just deserts advocates. I will return in a later section to the kind of proportionality constraints that might be appropriate in respect of restorative justice interventions. But in the meantime, it is necessary to turn to the remaining and frequently neglected question concerning the kind of punishment that we may be entitled to impose for a given offence.

4. What Kind of Punishment? The Limits of Just Deserts

Just deserts theorists deserve credit for focusing the minds of restorative justice advocates on such issues as the need for a defensible moral justification for restorative justice interventions, and the importance of determining acceptable limits on the degree of punitiveness that is warranted. However, the recent emergence of restorative justice as a distinctive philosophy and practice in its own right has focused attention on a third aspect of penality that has hitherto been sadly neglected, concerning the *kind of* punitive response that is appropriate and morally justifiable. And on this issue desert theory looks much more vulnerable in the face of the credible challenge that is posed by the theory and practice of restorative justice, particularly one that is founded on a rights-based approach of the kind sketched out above.

Hitherto, most debates about punishment have focused on the moral principles that either justify its imposition or regulate its distribution and severity without specifically addressing the equally important moral and practical question *how* we punish. Desert theorists (eg von Hirsch, 1993; Duff, 1996; 2000) have tended to simply assume the answer by taking for granted that punishment comprises two key elements: first 'censure' and second some form of 'hard treatment'. Both elements are highly problematic, however.

The 'censure' component suffers from three principal shortcomings, which relate to the form it takes, the forum in which it is administered, and its possible consequences. Although desert theorists contend that the institution of punishment is a valuable mechanism for conveying blame or censure, "this seems highly dubious for two main reasons. First, the rather crude form of instrumentalist reasoning that it relies on is unlikely to be the most effective method of communicating normative standards to offenders, or of eliciting compliance with those standards" (see Cavadino and Dignan, 2002: 198ff). And secondly, the moral attitudes of non-offending members of the public towards particular offences are equally unlikely to be affected by the severity of the punishment that is (or which they believe to be) inflicted (Walker and Marsh, 1984; cf. Tyler, 1990).

A second and related shortcoming relates to the court-based forum within which the censure is conveyed since this affords extremely limited opportunities for any meaningful censure-based communication to take place, and virtually no possibility of any constructive engagement on the part of either victim or offender (see also Walgrave, 2001). The third shortcoming is linked to Braithwaite's well-known critique of the potentially criminogenic consequences that may follow when the process of censuring an offender results in indelible, open-ended, stigmatic shaming.

In marked contrast, restorative justice processes that involve some form of dialogue between victims, offenders and other interested parties provide an opportunity for censure to be expressed in a normative way. They are based on a moralistic form of reasoning that offenders may find it harder to reject, and to which they may consequently be less likely to object. The forum in which this dialogue takes place is more likely to afford an opportunity in which both victims and offenders are able to participate constructively in the communicative enterprise. And, if handled sensitively, it may be possible for censure to be communicated in a non-stigmatising way that offers a better prospect for the offender's successful reintegration back into the community. In short, the challenge for desert theory that is presented by restorative justice processes is that they provide an alternative, and arguably far more effective form of normative discourse through which to convey censure without stigma.

The 'hard treatment' component within desert theory is also problematic on a number of counts. One major shortcoming is that it ties the expression of censure and denunciation to a relatively limited range of retributive-style punishments, the primary purpose of which is to inflict some form of deprivation on offenders. This has undesirable consequences from the victim's point of view because few such punishments do anything to redress the personal loss or injury that they may have experienced. Even those that do (such as compensation orders) are only capable of addressing part of the harm that is caused by an offence: comprising the physical injury or loss or damage to property. However, they are likely to do little to repair any emotional or psychological upset that is caused by an offence, or to restore the moral equilibrium that has been disturbed by undermining the victim's presumption of personal security (Watson et al 1989). Once again, the attraction of restorative justice processes is that they facilitate the negotiation of much more flexible forms of reparation that should, in principle, be capable of responding more appropriately to more of the particular harms that victims may have experienced.

Desert theory's insistence on the retention of 'hard treatment' as the only possible medium through which to express censure and denunciation also poses serious problems for penal reformers who support an overall lowering of penalty levels. One reason for this is that, as Ashworth (2000: 6) has pointed out, the 'parsimony principle' is not deducible from the bare bones of desert theory. This renders the theory especially vulnerable to political hi-jacking in pursuit of higher levels of punishment, even though its supporters may be right to maintain that this is by no means an inevitable process. A second problem relates to the fact that desert theory's unshakeable attachment to the principle of 'hard treatment' renders it manifestly incapable of furnishing the kind of 'replacement discourse' that Ashworth himself (1997) has called for. The latter calls for a new set of assumptions about the purposes of punishment and the confidence to articulate more constructive and less harmful ways of responding to and preventing crime than by imposing more imprisonment or by making community punishments ever more restrictive simply to enhance their 'credibility' in the eyes of the courts or public at large.

5.5

Restorative Justice: An Alternative to Punishment or an Alternative Form of Punishment?

GERRY JOHNSTONE

Some recent writers, most markedly Daly (2000) and Barton (1999; 2000), argue that to present restorative justice as an alternative to retributive justice is misleading and counterproductive (see also Zedner 1994). Without going into all the details of what is a complex debate, I deal here with certain aspects of it which are essential to a proper understanding and assessment of restorative justice. I look, very briefly, at whether the notion of a paradigm break between retributive justice and restorative justice is sustainable and at whether it is useful, for promotional purposes, to insist upon presenting restorative justice as an alternative to retributive punishment.

In certain respects, the image of retributive justice, which proponents of restorative justice criticize, is a caricature. This is particularly so when retributive justice is characterised as 'an elaborate mechanism for administering "just" doses of pain' (Zehr 1990: 75). It is, of course, quite true that in 'retributive justice' the immediate intention is to make things unpleasant for the offender. However, restorative justice proponents tend to imply that, in retributive justice, hurting offenders is either the whole *raison d'être* of punishment, or is intended as a crude form of deterrence.

There can be no doubt that many of those who advocate and support the idea of inflicting pain upon offenders do conceive of it in such terms. Others, however, advocate and seek to justify the practice of pain delivery in quite different terms. For example, classic exponents of a retributive theory of punishment, such as Immanuel Kant and Georg Hegel, defended the imposition of pain upon criminals as necessary to restore a metaphysical state of right which the criminal act had upset (Doyle 1969; Sorrell 1999; Brown forthcoming). Others retributivists see the imposition of pain as being the only way or the best way of expressing our indignation at cruelty or injustices which have been perpetrated, and they see indignation as quite distinguishable from the emotions underpinning revenge:

From G Johnstone, *Restorative Justice: Ideas, Values, Debates* (Portland, OR, Willan Publishing, 2001). Notes and references omitted.

Indignation against wrong done to another has nothing in common with the desire to avenge a wrong done to oneself.
(T. H. Green, cited in Moberly 1968: 83)

Most relevant of all, proponents of a moral education theory of punishment such as Jean Hampton (1984) and Herbert Morris (1981), regard the pain caused by punishment as neither an end in itself nor a simple disincentive to criminal actions, but as a method of conveying a larger message: that the offender's behaviour was morally wrong and should not be done for that reason (Hampton 1984:212). Moreover, they contend that the prime beneficiaries of this educative process are offenders (and potential offenders) themselves, should they listen to the message, since they will gain moral knowledge. Proponents of the moral education theory usually insist that if the imposition of pain is to perform its educative purposes, it must be done in accordance with retributivist principles, i.e. the pain must be shown to be deserved.

Among the latest in this line of penal philosophers who view retributive punishment as a (potential) communicative, educative and reintegrative act is Anthony Duff (1999a, 1999b). He argues that the proper aim of punishment should be to communicate censure and hence contribute to the offender's moral reform. Punishment should also, on his account, reconcile offenders with their victims and communities, and repair the damage to relationships which crime causes. The aim of punishment, he writes:

> should ideally be to bring the criminal to understand, and to repent, the wrong he has done: it tries to direct (to force) his attention onto his crime, aiming thereby to bring him to understand that crime's character and implications as a wrong, and to persuade him to accept as deserved the censure which punishment communicates—an acceptance which must involve repentance . . . by undergoing such penitential punishment the wrongdoer can reconcile himself with his fellow citizens, and restore himself to full membership of the community from which his wrongdoing threatened to exclude him.
> (Duff 1999a: 51–2)

According to Duff, if punishment is to perform these functions, the current style of punishment needs to be altered, with less emphasis on highly coercive and exclusionary sanctions such as imprisonment, and more on community-based communicative sanctions, involving reparation, of the kind which proponents of restorative justice recommend:

> Such communicative punishment is best exemplified, not by the kinds of long prison sentence which loom so large in penal discussion; nor by the fines which, though the penalty of choice for very many offenders, are usually ill-suited to this communicative purpose: but by such 'punishments in the community' as community service orders and probation (as well as by 'mediation' schemes whose aim is to bring the offender to recognise the nature and implications of what she has done, and thus make material or symbolic reparation for it).
> (Duff 1999a: 53)

Duff, along with Hampton and Morris and proponents of a reintegrative theory of punishment, such as Reitan (1996), are much closer in their thinking to proponents of restorative justice than they are to the likes of Thomas Carlyle, who justified punishment by appealing to the virtues of revenge and the natural hatred of scoundrels (Moberly 1968: 82), and to those who believe that the surest way of preventing crime is to make criminals suffer. Yet Duff and like-minded thinkers remain convinced that retributive punishment must be part of our response to offenders. They see the goals of retribution and restoration as compatible and even suggest that retributive punishment is essential to the achievement of restorative justice (Daly 2000).

It is quite clear, then, that many of those who advocate and support the practice of retributive punishment do not see pain delivery as an end in itself, nor as a crude form of deterrence, but regard it as an essential component (but only one component) of a more constructive, educative and reintegrative process. So, if the paradigm of retributive justice is to be rejected, it must be rejected simply on the grounds that it involves inflicting pain upon offenders. Those retributivists who are willing to inflict a minimal amount of pain upon offenders and to combine this with more positive educative and reintegrative measures must be condemned alongside those who take delight in making scoundrels suffer intense pain for their misdeeds and those who think that longer and harder prison sentences are the only solution to the crime problem.

Many proponents of restorative justice do seem to adopt such a position. They write as if any intentional infliction of pain upon offenders is to be expunged from our criminal justice system. Restorative justice is presented as an alternative to punishment; an alternative which eschews any intentional imposition of pain. Hence, restorative justice is distinguished sharply from even the most constructive versions of retributive justice.

However, if we subject the discourse of restorative justice to more rigorous scrutiny, the impression that it eschews intentional imposition of pain is revealed as, at best, wishful thinking. It is quite clear that undergoing a restorative justice process can be painful for offenders. Indeed, proponents of restorative justice are much concerned to reassure politicians and the public that it is not a soft option, that offenders will find it demanding. The fact that some offenders experience the restorative process as more arduous than a prison sentence is advertised as a point in its favour. More generally, most restorative justice processes aim to instil feelings of shame in offenders, and there can be no doubt that shame is a painful feeling (Nathanson 1992; Johnstone 1999). So why do proponents of restorative justice believe that, unlike the retributivists, they are not playing the pain game?

A common answer to this question is that of Lode Walgrave (2000: 166–7, 179). He concedes that restorative interventions may be painful. However, he insists that restorative interventions are not punishments because 'the pain is not deliberately inflicted' *(ibid*: 179). This seems disingenuous. Walgrave might be on sound ground when he states that, in restorative justice, the imposition of pain is 'subordinated to the aim of restoration' *(ibid*: 167). But this does not mean that pain is not deliberately inflicted. If pain is an inevitable, or even highly probable, consequence of restorative interventions, then (unless one adopts a perversely narrow interpretation of the term 'deliberately') somebody who purposely puts an offender through a restorative process, thereby causing them pain, deliberately inflicts pain on them. Whether causing pain is their primary intention, or something they desire, is immaterial. Or, at the very least, as we have seen, many supporters of retributive punishment could argue, with equal plausibility, that causing pain is not their primary aim nor something which they desire.

If both retributive punishment and restorative justice involve the deliberate imposition of pain, then the claim that there is a sharp distinction between them fails (to the extent that the distinction is drawn by reference to pain). Restorative justice, as Daly (2000) and others suggest, might be more accurately presented as an alternative form of punishment, rather than an alternative to punishment (see also Duff 1992). Daly argues, further, that there are practical advantages to dropping the retributive-restorative justice oppositional contrast (2000: 41). She sees the emphasis in restorative justice discourse on abandoning punishment for restorative justice as counterproductive. Offenders will treat the claim that they are not being punished (and hence do not need protection from unwarranted or excessive punishment) as hypocritical. Victims might see it as a denial of the validity of the 'retributive emotions' – such as indignation and resentment—which they feel towards the offender. And, the community might see it as trivialising crime. Hence, she maintains, there would be much to gain from recognising and portraying restorative justice as a more constructive use of the power to punish, rather than as something quite different from punishment.

An alternative to treatment?

We have seen that, as well as drawing a sharp distinction between retributive and restorative justice, many restorative justice proponents maintain with equal vigour that there is a sharp difference between restorative and therapeutic responses to offenders. Again, the image of treatment which proponents of restorative justice reject is largely a caricature. What they tend to attack is a highly 'medicalised' model of penal treatment, in which experts attempt to cure offenders of their criminal tendencies through psychiatric treatment and other techniques. What proponents of restorative justice seem to find most problematic about the 'treatment paradigm'—apart from the fact that it does little or nothing to meet the needs of victims—is that it assumes the offender to be a 'passive object' in need of expert intervention (Bazemore 1996: 40). Hence, an important point of contrast is that, in the restorative process offenders are required to play an active role and are expected to accept responsibility for their acts and for making reparation.

As I have argued elsewhere, many proponents of therapeutic interventions into the lives of offenders themselves reject such a highly medicalised model of treatment (Johnstone 1996a; 1996b). What they tend to prefer are socio-thera-peutic programmes in which offenders are encouraged to play a highly active role, rather than remain passive recipients of expert help, and to develop a sense of personal responsibility for their behaviour. If we examine these programmes and the assumptions which underpin them in detail, it becomes quite clear that they overlap in many ways with restorative interventions and that the two processes are more complementary than incompatible. Moreover, it is arguable that, in many cases, the goal of reintegrating offenders into the law-abiding community has a better chance of being achieved if both therapeutic and restorative interventions are employed, in a coordinated programme, rather than if we rely upon one to the exclusion of the other.

5.6

Specifying Aims and Limits for Restorative Justice:
A 'Making Amends' Model?

ANDREW VON HIRSCH, ANDREW ASHWORTH AND CLIFFORD SHEARING

Introduction

This paper explores the feasibility of clarifying aims and limits for Restorative Justice (hereafter, 'RJ'). It brings together three authors, two of whom (von Hirsch and Ashworth) have been associated with desert-oriented approaches to sentencing, and a third (Shearing) who has been exploring alternatives to traditional criminal-justice processes.

The essay proceeds by sketching a particular RJ model, which we shall term the 'making amends' model. We make no ambitious claims for this 'making amends' model: at best, it will reflect some (albeit not all) of the aims discussed in the RJ literature. Moreover, we are not ourselves advocating this model here; rather, we wish to make heuristic use of it, to suggest how RJ's aims and limits might be specified more clearly.

Our approach will mainly be conceptual: we will be examining RJ as a set of ideas about dealing with offending. None of the authors deem themselves expert on RJ practice in various jurisdictions, and it is theory not practice that primarily concerns us. Our theoretical emphasis reflects our view that it is the aims and limits of RJ that are particularly in need of clarification. Because of this theoretical emphasis, we will be dealing with 'ideal' models—that is, models that are designed best to reflect the chosen aims.

The model is responsive to the theme of criticism of RJ: its lack of coherent and consistent goals. Advocates of restorative justice have put forwards a variety of stated goals: that, for example, the victim be 'restored'; the offender be made to recognise his wrong; the 'conflict' between victim and offender be healed; the breach in the community's sense of trust be repaired; the community be reassured against further offending; and fear of crime be diminished. The goals may be ambitiously but vaguely formulated: for example, that the aim is to 'repair harm', but without considering whether this should address purely the consequential harms of the conduct, or should involve a normative response of some kind. Several

Adapted from A von Hirsch et al (eds), *Restorative Justice and Criminal Justice* (Oxford, Hart Publishing, 2003).

goals may be proposed simultaneously, without priorities among them specified. Some purported goals appear to have analogical rather than literal meaning. Restorative processes are supposed, for example, to resolve the 'conflict' between offender and victim; but crimes are different from disputes in that the offender seldom claims to be entitled to what he takes—so what 'dispute' is being resolved? RJ processes are said to 'restore' the bonds of community frayed through the offence, but it is not explained what kind of bonds have been damaged or how this restoration is to take place. Such over-breadth of purpose dilutes the guidance that RJ conceptions can provide. An injunction to seek numerous imprecisely delineated good ends tells us little about what particular purposes should be pursued, and how those ends should be achieved.

How might one respond to this critique? One way would be to try to specify aims and limits more clearly. What needs to be done is to develop a more coherent and consistent formulation of RJ's aims and related processes—that includes protections to help ensure that basic liberal democratic values are not compromised. Good reasons—ones suitable for the public sphere in a modern democratic society—need to be specified to justify RJ interventions. To see whether such a restatement of RJ is possible, we shall conduct a thought-experiment. It is to try to sketch a particular conceptual model for restorative justice.

An RJ Model: 'Making Amends'

The RJ model which we shall describe is one that involves the notion of 'making amends'. In the limited space available, our sketch will necessarily be incomplete but, we hope, sufficient to convey the concepts involved.

1. The 'Making Amends' Model

The 'making amends' model involves a response negotiated between the offender and his victim, which involves (1) the implicit or explicit acknowledgement of fault and (2) an apologetic stance on the part of the offender, ordinarily conveyed through having him undertake a reparative task.

The model differs from the conception of punishment developed by desert theorists (see von Hirsch, Selection 4.2 above). In a desert model, penal censure is *authoritatively* conveyed through the imposition of the punishment. Its aim, in part, is to convey blame which the offender, seen as a moral agent, may consider in evaluating his own conduct and deciding how to behave in future. That model involves a form of moral discourse but not a negotiated one: *A*, the punishing agent (usually the state), determines certain types of actions to be wrong, and adopts legal norms prohibiting such conduct and prescribing sanctions that convey disapproval for the conduct. If *B*, an actor, engages in the conduct, he will suffer the sanction and thereby be subjected to the disapproval. *B* and others may then take this into account in evaluating their own actions.

The 'making amends' model is also a form of moral discourse, but one which is closer in certain respects to informal moral discourse in everyday life. In this kind of response the victim's role is deemed central. The procedure is a *negotiated* process between offender and victim, leading to a response that conveys acknowledgement of fault and the undertaking of a reparative task reflecting that acknowledgement. The reparative features of the sanction do not literally heal or 'take back' the wrong. Rather, they constitute a way of showing concern for the victim's interests, on the part of a person (the offender) whose lack of respect and concern was expressed, precisely, in his act of wrongdoing.

While the negotiated and discursive character of this response differs from the authoritative model of deserved punishment, the model is 'retributive' in the sense that it is primarily responsive to *past* wrongdoing: making amends is a way of conveying an apologetic stance for a misdeed that has occurred. Granted, if the process works as intended, there will also be some consequential effects: a regretful offender may (and it is hoped will) come to feel more empathy for his victims and others, and be less inclined to offend in future; and the victim may become less resentful and less alienated from the offender. But these consequences are not the sole point of the exercise, so that the making-amends response does not fail whenever they do not materialise—just as an apology is no less appropriate because the offended individual is unwilling to accept it.

If 'making amends' were thus made the focus of RJ, would this have to be the exclusive aim? Not necessarily; other goals might also be pursued, so long as this were done consistently with the primary making-amends focus. (Providing support for the offender to help him avoid reoffending, for example, could be such a supplemental end—if this were done in a manner that comports with the appropriate making of amends for the offence.) How such supplemental goals could be taken into account would call for further analysis, however and could complicate the model somewhat. Thus for the sake of simplicity, and because of limitations of space, we shall limit our discussion to the aim of making amends.

2. The RJ Intervention as an Imposition

There is considerable divergence of view whether restorative responses are or are not 'punishments'. What should be clear, however, is that the making-amends model, even if it differs in significant respects from traditional punishment, is also one involving an *imposition*. It is so in two important respects. First, calling for acknowledgement of fault involves adverse judgements about the offender and his behaviour. Secondly, any disposition that results from the process may deprive the offender of important interests: of his property, if he pays compensation, of his freedom of action if he undertakes a reparative task, etc.

To say that an imposition is involved is no criticism; indeed, the adverse judgement and the burdens to be undertaken by the offender are central to the whole point of the process. Acknowledging that we are speaking of impositions means, however, that a burden of justification must be met: good reasons need to be supplied for why the offender must suffer these burdens, and fairness requirements need be observed to ensure that the burdens are justly imposed.

The character of making amends as an imposition cannot be avoided by pointing out that the offender's consent is required. The offender cannot choose simply to have nothing happen to him. If he refuses his consent, he will have to face whatever alternative sanctioning system awaits the non-consenting: a traditional criminal trial, or else possibly, Braithwaite's (1999) scheme of deterrent or incapacitative sanctions. He may have reason to fear that those latter responses would be (at best) no less unpleasant.

Where a negotiated procedure results in someone losing important interests, an imposition is involved—notwithstanding that the person agrees to participate in the negotiations. In simple contexts, this is obvious: being sentenced to prison as a result of a plea- and sentence-bargain obviously involves an imposition, and no less so because the person might have refused the bargain and faced the alternative legal consequences. The point holds also for restorative processes. So long as the offender engages in the process, it is that process—and not something else— which is responsible for any resulting deprivation of his interests. It does not matter that the offender could have withdrawn from the process, and faced an alternative sanctioning system.

3. Modalities and Guidance

The 'making amends' model represents a particular set of aims, which should influence the modalities of RJ intervention: only certain kinds of intervention are likely to be helpful in promoting the model's aims. Dispositions involving the making of restitution to the victim as a way of acknowledging fault appear to be legitimate ways of making amends. Purely unpleasant or humiliating sanctions might serve other (for example, deterrent) purposes, but not this purpose. There thus should be some explicit principles suggesting what kind of dispositions might be appropriate, and what kind might not be. Leaving this purely to the discretion of the particular group conference is likely to lead to dispositions which, if capable of being rationalised at all, would be so on grounds having little or nothing to do with the making of amends.

Even for those types of dispositions which appear generally to be appropriate to this model, it would be helpful to provide further guidance on specific means and techniques employed. What kind of apologetic ritual might help victim and offender understand that an expression of regret is involved? What kind is likely to bring the parties toward reconciliation and a better understanding? What kind of rituals and dispositions are likely to be counterproductive? As RJ programmes are tried and evaluated, there should develop some understanding on such matters, and individual decision-making groups should have available explicit guidance reflecting that knowledge. Calling for such guidance will mean that some rule-generating process needs to provide it, and will mean that the guidance will need to be set forth in some useful and readily available form.

4. Scope of Application of the Model

The making-amends model is addressed to a certain kind of case: one in which there is an identifiable person who is the offender, another identifiable person who is the victim, and a victimising act which infringes the latter's rights. A typical case which seems to suit this model is one where *A* unprovokedly vandalises *B*'s flat. Here, there is an act of wrongdoing against someone, which would seem to warrant an apologetic response by the actor to the victim, conveyed in some act of making of amends.

There are, however, a variety of cases which seem less well suited to this kind of response. One 'unsuitable' category, in our judgement, would consist of crimes in which there are no individual victims. If *A* is charged with tax evasion, there is no person to whom he can convey an apologetic stance via some kind of restitutionary act. Saying the 'community' is here the victim is not illuminating.

There are also types of cases in which the appropriateness of an RJ approach should be a matter for further analysis. An example are crimes in which an individual 'victim' has been injured or threatened with injury, but in which this is a response to comparable previous behaviour on the victim's part directed against the present perpetrator. *B* has beaten *A* up last Saturday night, and now *A* beats up *B* this Saturday night and is apprehended for that act and placed before a group conference. In such cases it is less clear who should apologise to whom; or whether mutual apologies would be desirable. Having a more clearly stated goal—in our suggested model of making amends—might help resolve whether a restorative approach is appropriate here.

5. The Role of Proportionality

There exists considerable disagreement, among RJ proponents, about the need for proportionality constraints. Some RJ advocates have suggested that these should be jettisoned entirely (Pettit and Braithwaite, 1993), although Braithwaite seems to have modified his position somewhat. Others, such as Dignan, suggest that there should be proportionality limits. However, the grounds for such limits have been little addressed in the RJ literature.

Outer proportionality requirements, that bar the use of very severe penalties for lesser crimes, are minimal requirements of fairness that any modern liberal state should observe. Indeed, a ban on grossly disproportionate penalties is constitutionally required in some jurisdictions.

The interesting question is whether there should be proportionality requirements going beyond these minimal ones. For a punishment system, the argument for proportionality requirements is straightforward enough: such a system utilises sanctions that involve *censure*. In such a sanctioning system, the severity of the sanction signifies the degree of censure conveyed. Consequently, the severity of sanctions should fairly reflect the degree of comparative blameworthiness of the conduct (see more fully, von Hirsch, Selection 4.2 above).

Could comparable themes be used to support proportionality requirements in a making-amends model? A possible argument might run as follows. An essential feature of the making-amends model is that the procedure and its sanction are designed to provide a moral evaluation of the conduct. The victim, it is assumed, has been *wronged* by the offender, and the procedure aims at giving adequate recognition to that wrongdoing. In tort law, there is no such aim: the point of tort is simply to decide who should bear the loss, the actor or the injured party; fault is deemed a ground—but not an exclusive one—for shifting the burden of loss to the actor. The making-amends model, however, is much more than a loss-shifting device: its point is to provide (through the imposition he undertakes to undergo) a method through which the actor can convey to his victim recognition of his wrongdoing. If such a moral evaluation of the conduct is thus centrally involved, the response should bear some reasonable relationship to how wrongful the conduct can fairly be characterised as being.

The foregoing point holds already for simple verbal apologies in everyday life. Suppose *A* negligently steps on *B's* toes, and says that he is sorry to have hurt him. Suppose, however, that *B* insists that this is not enough; that *A* must admit that his conduct has not merely been clumsy but extraordinary reprehensible. *A* would rightly be entitled to resist such a suggestion: to say that while he was wrong thus to have hurt *B*, the injury was not great, and his fault was one of mere negligence; and hence, that the wrong was relatively minor. *A's* apology should not be required to overstate his degree of fault.

This argument extends to the making-amends model, where what is to be negotiated is not just a verbal apology, but a burden undertaken by the offender that is designed to convey that apologetic stance. If the basis for the imposition lies in its recognition of wrongdoing, the degree of its onerousness necessarily conveys how reprehensible the conduct is treated as being. This implied valuation should, then, bear a reasonable relation to the actual degree of reprehensibleness of the conduct—that is, to its seriousness. The upshot is a requirement of proportionality. It should be noted, moreover, that this requirement has not been 'externally' derived from traditional criminal-justice principles; it derives from the logic of 'making-amends' itself.

In this kind of negotiated disposition, however, it would not seem feasible to impose the kind of rigorous ordinal-proportionality requirements that a desert model envisions for criminal punishments. (For a discussion of those requirements, see von Hirsch, Selection 4.2 above.) This is because considerable leeway would be needed for the parties to choose a disposition that they feel conveys regret in a satisfactory manner.

Is the 'Making Amends' Model Conceptually Coherent?

Our critique of RJ at the onset raised the question whether, as usually formulated, it is a meaningful rationale at all. RJ's multiple and unclear goals, its underspecified conception of means and modalities, its lack of dispositional standards and fairness limits, its dangling measures of success—these all seem to point to a lack of a coherent conception. The question we posed was whether an RJ model could be formulated that avoids these deficiencies, and we sketched our 'making amends' model as a possible way of doing so.

The making-amends model, in our view, does seem to provide a modicum of conceptual coherence. It seeks to achieve, not all conceivable desiderata, but a particular, interrelated, and mutually consistent set of them: namely, the conducting of a dialogue between offender and victim about the former's wrongdoing; the expression by the wrongdoer to his victim of a regretful stance, carried out through reparative sanction; and the opportunity given to the victim to accept that expression of regret and thus possibly to achieve some measure of reconciliation. This model resembles in important respects a kind of moral dialogue that is carried out in everyday life, and that can be described directly and without reliance on metaphors such as 'healing' and the like.

Adopting a model such as this one involves, however, certain tradeoffs—for the model focuses on some possible RJ goals, and not others. The making-amends model is victim/offender-focused: it is conceived as a certain kind of discursive interchange between them. As a result, other possible goals are given less emphasis, if any; the model is not explicitly aimed at maximising crime-control effects, or reducing fear of crime, or the like. This kind of trade-off is inevitable: trying to accomplish all goals simultaneously is tantamount to having no meaningful goals at all.

5.7

The Limits of Restorative Justice

KATHLEEN DALY

Restorative justice (RJ) is a set of ideals about justice that assumes a generous, empathetic, supportive, and rational human spirit. It assumes that victims can be generous to those who have harmed them, that offenders can be apologetic and contrite for their behavior, that their respective 'communities of care' can take an active role of support and assistance, and that a facilitator can guide rational discussion and encourage consensual decision-making between parties with antagonistic interests. Any one of these elements may be missing, and thus potentially weaken an RJ process. The ideals of RJ can also be in tension. For example, it may not be possible to have equity or proportionality across RJ outcomes, when outcomes are supposed to be fashioned from the particular sensibilities of those in an RJ encounter.

Achieving justice—whether RJ or any other form—is a fraught and incomplete enterprise. This is because justice cannot be achieved, although it is important to reach for it. Rather, drawing from Derrida, justice is an 'experience of the impossible' (Pavlich, 1996, p.37), 'an ideal, an aspiration, which is supremely important and worth striving for constantly and tirelessly' (Hudson, 2003, p.192).

This reading addresses a selected set of limits of RJ, those concerning its scope and its practices. I focus on RJ in youth justice cases because it currently has a large body of empirical evidence. However, as RJ is increasingly being applied in adult cases and in different contexts (pre- or post-sentence advice, for example, as is now the case in England and New Zealand), we might expect to see different kinds of limits emerging.

The Scope of RJ

Limit (1). There is no agreed-upon definition of RJ.

There is robust discussion on what RJ is or should be, and there is no consensus on what practices should be included within its reach. One axis of disagreement is

Adapted from D Sullivan and L Tifft (eds), *Handbook of Restorative Justice: A Global Perspective* (New York, Routledge, 2006).

whether RJ should be viewed as a process or an outcome (Crawford & Newburn, 2003). A second is what kinds of practices are authentic forms of RJ, what kinds are not, and what is in-between (McCold & Wachtel, 2002; *Contemporary Justice Review*, 2004). A third is whether RJ should be viewed principally as a set of justice values, rather than a process or set of practices (compare, e.g., Braithwaite, 2003 and Johnstone, 2002, with von Hirsch, Ashworth & Shearing, 2003), or whether it should include both (Roche, 2003). Finally, there is debate on how RJ can or should articulate with established criminal justice (CJ).

A lack of agreement on definition means that RJ has not one, but many identities and referents; and this can create theoretical, empirical, and policy confusion. Commentators, both advocates and critics, are often not talking about or imagining the same thing. Although the lack of a common understanding of RJ creates confusion, especially for those new to RJ, it reflects a diversity of interests and ideologies that people bring to the table when ideas of justice are discussed. A similar problem occurred with the rise of informal justice in the late 1970s. Informal justice could not be defined except by what it was not, i.e., it was not established forms of criminal justice (Abel, 1982). An inability to define RJ, or justice more generally, is not fatal. Indeed, it is a logical and defensible position: there can be no 'fixed definition of justice' because justice has 'no unchanging nature' and 'it is beyond definition' (Hudson, 2003, p.201).

Gerry Johnstone (2004) suggests that the RJ advocates have too narrowly focused their efforts on promoting RJ by claiming its positive effects in reducing re-offending and increasing victim satisfaction. Instead of taking this instrumental and technical tack, Johnstone argues that we should see RJ as a set of ideas that challenge established CJ in fundamental ways. There is much to commend in having this more expansive vision of RJ as a long term political project for changing the ways we think about 'crime,' 'being a victim,' 'responding to offenders,' among other categories nominated by Johnstone. However, I restrict my use of the term to a set of core elements in RJ practices. I do so not to limit the potential applicability of RJ to other domains or as a political project for social change, but rather to conceptualize justice practices in concrete terms, not as aspirations or values. As RJ takes shape and evolves, it is important that we have images of the social interactions being proposed. I identify these core elements of RJ:

- it deals with the penalty (or post-penalty), not fact-finding phase of the criminal process;
- it normally involves a face-to-face meeting with an admitted offender and victim and their supporters, although it may also take indirect forms;
- it envisions a more active role for victim participation in justice decisions;
- it is an informal process that draws on the knowledge and active participation of lay persons (typically those most affected by an offence), but there are rules circumscribing the behavior of meeting members and limits on what they can decide in setting a penalty;

- it aims to hold offenders accountable for their behavior, while at the same time not stigmatizing them, and in this way it is hoped that there will be a reduction in future offending; and
- it aims to assist victims in recovering from crime.

As we shall see, some (or all) of these elements may not be realized in RJ practices. For example, an RJ process aims to assist victims in recovering from crime, but this may be possible for some victims more than others. And although it is hoped that an RJ process will shift admitted offenders toward a law-abiding future, this too may occur for some, but not others. It should be emphasized that victims are not forced to meet an admitted offender in an RJ process. There can be other ways in which victims may engage an RJ process, including through the use of victim representatives or material brought into the meeting itself. In fact, some have proposed that victims have access to RJ processes when a suspect has not be caught for (or admitted to) an offence.

Limit (2). RJ deals with the penalty, not fact-finding phase of the criminal process.

There is some debate over whether RJ processes could be used in fact-finding, but virtually all the examples cited are of dispute resolution mechanisms in pre-modern societies, which rely on particular sets of 'meso-social structures' that are tied to kinship, geography, and political power (see discussion below by Bottoms, 2003; see also Johnstone, 2002). When we consider the typical forms of RJ practices, such as family group conferences (in New Zealand), family or community conferences (in Australia), police restorative cautioning schemes (in selected jurisdictions in England and North America), circles and sentencing circles (North America), or enhanced forms of victim-offender mediation (North America and some European countries), we see that all are concerned with what a justice practice should be *after* a person has admitted committing an offence. RJ does not address if a 'crime' occurred or not, or whether a suspect is 'guilty' of a crime or not. Rather, it focuses on 'what shall we do' after a person admits that s/he has committed an offence.

Ultimately, as I shall argue, we should view this limit as a strength of RJ. The reason is that it bypasses the many disabling features of the adversarial process, both for those accused of crime and for victim complainants. Without a fact-finding or investigating mechanism, however, RJ cannot replace established CJ. To do so, it must have a method of adjudication, and currently it does not. However, RJ can make in-roads into methods of penalty setting (in the context of court diversion or pre-sentence advice to judicial officers), and it may be effective in providing assurances of safety to individual victims and communities when offenders complete their sentences (in the context of post-sentence uses of RJ), but all of these activities occur only after a person has admitted committing an offence.

Several commentators point out that RJ differs from established CJ in that it is participatory and consensually-based, not adversarial. However, this muddles things greatly. The reason that established CJ is adversarial is that its adjudication process rests on a fundamental right of those accused to say they did not commit an offence and to defend themselves against the state's allegations of wrong-doing. There may well be better methods of adjudicating crime, and a troubling feature of established CJ is how long it takes for cases to be adjudicated and disposed; but surely, no one would wish to dispense with the right of citizens to defend themselves against the state's power to prosecute and punish alleged crime.

The focus of RJ on the penalty (or post-penalty) phase can be viewed as a strength. It enables us to be more imaginative in conceptualizing what is the 'right response' to offending behavior, and it opens up potential lines of communication and understanding between offenders, victims, and those close to them, when this is desirable (and it may not always be desirable). Communication and interaction are especially important elements because many victims want answers to questions, for example, about why *their* car was stolen, and not another person's car. They may be concerned about their security and seek reassurances from an offender not to victimize them again (although this may not stop an offender from victimizing others). There can be positive sources of connection between the supporters of offenders (say a mother or father) and victims or their supporters. All of this is possible because RJ processes seek a conversational and dialogic approach to responding to crime. Decisions are not made by a distant magistrate or judge, and an overworked duty solicitor and prosecutor with many files to process. In established CJ processes, research shows that in the courtroom, a defendant is typically mute and a victim is not present. State actors do all the work of handling and processing crime. The actual parties to a crime (the persons charged and victim-complainants) are bystanders or absent.

Some victim advocates who are critical of RJ think that it is 'outside' or not part of established CJ. Although a common perception, it is inaccurate. In all jurisdictions where RJ has been legislated in response to crime, it is very much 'inside' the established CJ process, as the police or courts make a decision about how to handle a case.

Restorative Justice Ideals and Practices

There is a gap between the ideals or aspirations for RJ and actual practices. This gap should not surprise us because the ideals for RJ are set very high, and perhaps too high. Advocates have made astonishing claims for what RJ can achieve, and what it can do for victims, offenders, their family members, and communities. Thus, a gap arises, in part, from inflated expectations for what RJ can achieve. There are deeper reasons for the gap, however.

First, as Bottoms (2003, p.109) argues, the 'social mechanisms of RJ' rest on an assumption that 'adequate meso-social structures exist to support RJ-type approaches.' By 'meso-social structures,' Bottoms refers to ordered sets of relationships that are part of pre-modern societies (for example, residence, kinship, or lineage). These relationships embed elements of 'intra-societal power' and coercion, which make dispute settlement possible (see also Merry, 1982). A second feature of relationships in pre-modern societies is that disputants are 'part of the same moral/social community.' They live in close proximity to one another or are related to one another, and typically wish to continue living in the community. These meso-social structures and 'thick' social ties, which are commonly associated with pre-modern (or *gemeinschaft*) societies, are not present in modern urban contemporary societies. Thus, as Bottoms (2003, p.110) suggests, 'a 'blanket' delivery of RJ . . . is always likely to achieve modest or patchy results in contemporary societies.'

Second, as I suggest (Daly, 2003, p.200), gaps emerge because those participating in an RJ process may not know what is supposed to happen, how they are supposed to act, nor what an optimal result could be. Participants may have an idea of what 'their day in court' might be like, but they have little idea of what 'their day in an RJ conference' would be like. Moreover, effective participation requires a degree of moral maturity and empathetic concern that many people, and especially young people, may not possess. Finally, we know from the history of established CJ that organizational routines, administrative efficiency, and professional interests often trump justice ideals (Daly, 2003, p.232). RJ is no exception. It takes time and great effort to create the appropriate contexts for RJ processes to work effectively, including a facilitator's contacting and preparing participants, identifying who should be present, coordinating the right time for everyone, running the meeting, and following up after it is over.

Some commentators argue that it is more appropriate to compare 'what restorative justice has achieved and may still achieve with what conventional justice systems have to offer' (Morris, 2002, p.601). This is a valid and important point. We know that substantial gaps exist between the ideals and practices of established CJ. Thus, for example, it would be relevant to compare the effects of the court's sentencing practices on victims, offenders, and others with their participation in penalty discussions in RJ meetings. Although court-conference comparative research can be illuminating and helpful, there is also a value to observing and understanding what happens in an RJ process itself, including the variable degree to which the aims of RJ are achieved. When we do that, several limits of RJ are apparent. It is important to bear in mind that these limits are not necessarily peculiar to RJ; they may have their analogy in established CJ as well. I draw from my research on youth justice conference in South Australia (the South Australia Juvenile Justice [SAJJ] project, Daly, 2000, 2005; see Daly et al., 1998, Daly, 2001b for SAJJ technical reports), along with other research, to elucidate these limits.

Limit (3). It is easier to achieve fairness than restorativeness in an RJ process.

Studies of RJ in Australia, New Zealand, and England often examine whether the observer-researcher, offender, and victim perceive the process and outcome as fair.

All published studies find high levels of perceived fairness, or procedural justice, in the process and outcome (see review in Daly, 2001a for Australian and New Zealand research; see also Hoyle, Young & Hill, 2002; Crawford & Newburn, 2003). For example, to questions such as 'were you treated fairly?,' 'were you treated with respect?,' 'did people listen to you?,' among other questions, a very high per cent of participants (80 per cent or more) say that they were. In addition, studies show that offenders and victims are actively involved in fashioning the outcome, which is indicative that laypeople are exercising decision-making power. Overall, RJ practices in the jurisdictions studied definitely conform to the ideals of procedural justice.

Compared to these very high levels of procedural justice, there appears to be relatively less evidence of 'restorativeness.' The measures of restorativeness used in the SAJJ project include the degree to which the offender was remorseful, spontaneously apologized to the victim, and understood the impact of the crime on the victim; the degree to which victims understood the offender's situation; and the extent of positive movement between the offender, victim, or their supporters. Depending on the variable, restorativeness was present in 30 to 60 per cent of the youth justice conferences studied. Thus, RJ conferences receive high marks for procedural fairness and victim and offender participation, but it may be more difficult for victims and offenders to resolve their differences or to find common ground in an RJ meeting (Daly, 2001a, 2003).

Why is fairness easier to achieve than restorativeness? Fairness is largely, although not exclusively, a measure of the behavior of the professional(s) (the facilitator and, depending on the jurisdiction, a police officer). As the professionals, they are polite, they listen, and they establish ground rules of respect for others and civility in the conference process. Whereas fairness is established in the relationship between the professionals and participants, restorativeness emerges in the relationships between a victim, an offender, and their supporters. Being polite is easier to do than saying you are sorry; listening to someone tell their story of victimization is easier to do when you are not the offender. Indeed, understanding or taking the perspective of the other may be easier when you are not the actual victim or the offender in the justice encounter.

Restorativeness requires a degree of empathic concern and perspective-taking; and as measured by psychologists' scales, these qualities are more frequently evinced for adults than adolescents. For example, from interviews with youthful offenders, the SAJJ project found that over half had not thought *at all* about what they would say to the victim. Most did not think in terms of what they might *offer victims*, but rather what they would be *made to do by others*. It is possible that many adolescents may not yet have the capacity to think empathetically, to take the role of the other (Frankenberger, 2000); they may be expected to act as if they had the moral reasoning of adults when they do not (Van Voorhis, 1985). And, at the same time, as we shall see in limits (4) and (5), victims may have high expectations for an offender's behavior in the conference process, which cannot be realized, or victims' distress may be so great that the conference process can do little to aid in their recovery.

Limit (4). A 'sincere apology' is difficult to achieve.

It is said that in the aftermath of crime, what victims want most is 'symbolic reparation, primarily an apology' (Strang, 2002, p.55, drawing from Marshall & Merry, 1990). Perhaps for some offences and some victims, this may be true; but I suspect that most victims want more than an apology. Fundamentally, victims want a sense of vindication for the wrong done to them, and they want the offender to stop harming and hurting them or other people. A sincere apology may be a useful starting point, but we might expect most victims to want more. In research on violent offences, for example, Cretney and Davis (1995, p.178) suggest that a 'victim has an interest in punishment,' not just restitution or reparation, because punishment 'can reassure the victim that he or she has public recognition and support.'

Let us assume, for the sake of argument, that a sincere apology is what victims mainly desire. What are the elements of a sincere apology, and how often might we expect this to occur in an RJ process?

Drawing from Tavuchis' work on the sociology of apology (1991), Bottoms (2003, pp.94–8) distils the 'experiential dynamics' of an 'ideal-typical apology:'

> In the fully-accomplished apology . . . we have first a *call* for an apology from the person(s) who regard themselves as wronged, or from someone speaking on their behalf; then the *apology* itself; and finally an expression of *forgiveness* from the wronged to the wrongdoer (p.94, emphasis in original).

Bottoms then says that 'each of these moves' in the fully-accomplished (or ideal typical) apology 'can be emotionally fraught' such that 'the whole apologetic discourse is (on both sides) 'a delicate and precarious transaction'' (quoting Tavuchis, 1991, p.vii).

It is important to distinguish between two types of apologies: an 'ideal-typical apology,' where there is an expression of forgiveness from a victim to an offender, and a 'sincere apology,' where there is a mutual understanding between the parties that the offender is really sorry, but there is no assumption of forgiveness. I make this distinction because we might expect a 'sincere apology' to occur in an RJ process, but we should not expect a victim to forgive an offender. In fact, I wonder if Tavuchis' formulation may be unrealistic in the context of a victim's response to crime. Tavuchis analyzes a range of harmful or hurtful behavior, not just crime; and I suspect that forgiveness may arise more often in non-criminal than in criminal contexts.

There is surprisingly little research on the character of apologies in RJ processes. From the RISE project, we learn that conference victims rated the offender's apology as 'sincere' (41 per cent), and a further 36 per cent rated it 'somewhat sincere' (Strang, 2002, p.115; 2004, personal communication). Hayes's (2006) summary of RISE observational and interview data on the apology process concludes that 'the ideal of reconciliation and repair was achieved in less than half of all cases.'

The SAJJ project explored the apology process in detail (see Daly, 2003, pp.224–5). When we asked the youth why they decided to say sorry to victims, 27 per cent said they did not feel sorry but thought they'd get off easier, 39 per cent said to make their family feel better, and a similar per cent said they felt pushed into it. However, when asked what was the *main reason* for saying sorry, most (61 per cent) said they really were sorry. When we asked victims about the apology process, most believed that the youth's motives for apologizing were insincere. To the item, the youth wasn't sorry, but thought they would get off easier if they said sorry, 36 per cent of victims said 'yes, definitely' and another 36 per cent said 'yes, a little.' A slim majority of victims believed that the youth said sorry either to get off more easily (30 per cent) or because they were pushed into it (25 per cent). Just 27 per cent of victims believed that the main reason that the youth apologized was because s/he really was sorry.

This mismatch of perception between victims and offenders was explored further, by drawing on conference observations, interview material, and police incident reports to make inferences about the apology process for all 89 conferences in the SAJJ sample (Daly, 2005). The results reinforce the findings above: they reveal that communication failure and mixed signals are present when apologies are made and received. Such communication gaps are overlaid by the variable degree to which offenders are in fact sorry for what they have done. In 34 per cent of cases, the offenders and victims agreed (or were in partial agreement) that the offender was sorry, and in 27 per cent, the offenders and victims definitely agreed that the offender was not sorry. For 30 per cent, there was a perceptual mismatch: the offenders were not sorry, but the victims thought they were (12 per cent); or the offenders were sorry, but the victims did not think so (18 per cent). For the remaining 9 per cent, it was not possible to determine. The findings show that a sincere apology may be difficult to achieve because offenders are not really sorry for what they have done, victims wish offenders would display more contrite behavior, and there are mis-readings of what the other is saying.

Hayes (2006) proposes an added reason for why sincere apologies are difficult to achieve. He suggests that there are 'competing demands' placed on youthful offenders in the conference process: they are asked both to explain what happened (or provide an 'account') and to apologize for what they did. Hayes surmises that 'offenders' speech acts … may drift from apologetic discourse to mitigating accounts and back again.' Victims may interpret what is said (and not said) as being insincere.

Limit (5). The conference process can help some victims recover from crime, but this is contingent on the degree of distress they experienced.

[Due to space constraints, the discussion of Limit (5) is deleted in this extract.]

Limit (6). We should expect modest results, not the nirvana story of RJ.

The nirvana story of RJ is illustrated by Jim Consedine (1995, p.9), who opens his book by excerpting from a 1993 New Zealand news story:

> The families of two South Auckland boys, killed by a car, welcomed the accused driver yesterday with open arms and forgiveness. The young man, who gave himself up to the police yesterday morning, apologised to the families and was ceremonially reunited with the Tongan and Samoan communities at a special service last night. The 20-year old Samoan visited the Tongan families after his court appearance to apologise for the deaths of the two children . . . The Tongan and Samoan communities. . . later gathered at the Tongan Methodist Church in a service of reconciliation. The young man sat at the feast table flanked by the mothers of the dead boys.

Later, in discussing the case, Consedine sees it as

> ample evidence of the power that healing and forgiveness can play in our daily lives . . . The grieving Tongan and Samoan communities simply embraced the young driver . . . and forgave him. His deep shame, his fear, his sorrow, his alienation from the community was resolved (Consedine, 1995, p.162).

This nirvana story of RJ contains elements that are not likely to be present in most RJ encounters: it was composed of members of racial-ethnic minority groups, who were drawn together with a shared experience of church, and there appeared to be 'meso-social structures' and 'thick' social ties between the families and kin of the offender and victims. These *gemeinschaft* qualities are atypical in modern urban life, and thus, we should expect 'modest and patchy results' (Bottoms, 2003, p.110) to be the norm, not the exception.

Conclusion

That there exist limits on what RJ can achieve should not be grounds for dispensing with it, nor for being disillusioned, once again, with a new justice idea. My reading of the evidence is that face-to-face encounters between victims and offenders and their supporters *is* a practice worth maintaining, and perhaps enlarging, although we cannot expect it to deliver strong stories of repair and goodwill most of the time.

In the penalty phase of the criminal process, both RJ and the established court process have limits. RJ is limited by the abilities and interests of offenders and victims to think and act in ways we may define as restorative. Established CJ is limited by the inability of formal legality to listen to the accounts of crime and their effects by those most directly involved. Legal professionals do the talking, and what is legally or administratively relevant takes precedence.

By recognizing the limits of both RJ and established CJ in the penalty (or post-penalty) phase of the criminal process, we more effectively grasp the nettle of justice as a promise, as something that may be partly, but never fully realized. As such, we see that all justice practices, including RJ, are limited.

References

Abel, R. (1982) Introduction. IN: Abel, R. ed. *The politics of informal justice: the American experience*. Vol. 1. New York, Academic Press, pp.1–13.

Bottoms, A.E. (2003) Some sociological reflections on restorative justice. In: von Hirsch, A., Roberts, J., Bottoms, A.E., Roach, K. & Schiff, M. eds. *Restorative justice and criminal justice: competing or reconcilable paradigms?* Oxford, Hart Publishing, pp.79–113.

Braithwaite, J. (2003) Principles of restorative justice. In: von Hirsch, A., Roberts, J., Bottoms, A.E., Roach, K. & Schiff, M. eds. *Restorative justice and criminal justice: competing or reconcilable paradigms?* Oxford, Hart Publishing, pp.1–20.

Consedine, J. (1995) *Restorative justice: healing the effects of crime*. Lyttelton, Ploughshares Publications.

Contemporary Justice Review (2004) Special issue 7 (1) on Restorative Justice and Community Justice.

Crawford, A. & Newburn, T. (2003) *Youth offending and restorative justice: implementing reform in youth justice*. Cullompton, Willan Publishing.

Cretney, A. & Davis, G. (1995) *Punishing violence*. London, Routledge.

Daly, K. (2000) Revisiting the relationship between retributive and restorative justice. In: Strang, H. & Braithwaite, J. eds. *Restorative justice: philosophy to practice*. Aldershot, Dartmouth/Ashgate, pp.33–54.

Daly, K. (2001a) Conferencing in Australia and New Zealand: variations, research findings, and prospects. IN: Morris, A. & Maxwell, G. eds. *Restorative justice for juveniles: conferencing, mediation and circles*. Oxford, Hart Publishing, pp.59–83.

Daly, K. (2001b) *South Australia Juvenile Justice (SAJJ) research on conferencing, technical report No. 2: research instruments in year 2 (1999) and background notes*. Brisbane, School of Criminology and Criminal Justice, Griffith University. Available from <http://www.aic.gov.au/rjustice/sajj.html>

Daly, K. (2003) Mind the gap: restorative justice in theory and practice. IN: von Hirsch, A., Roberts, J., Bottoms, A.E., Roach, K. & Schiff, M. eds. *Restorative justice and criminal justice: competing or reconcilable paradigms?* Oxford, Hart Publishing, pp.219–36.

Daly, K. (2005) A tale of two studies: restorative justice from a victim's perspective. In: Elliott, E. & Gordon, R. eds. *Restorative justice: emerging issues in practice and evaluation*. Cullompton, Willan Publishing, pp.153–74.

Daly, K., Venables, M., Mumford, L., McKenna, M. & Christie-Johnston, J. (1998) *SAJJ technical report No. 1: project overview and research instruments in year 1*. Brisbane, School of Criminology and Criminal Justice, Griffith University.

Frankenberger, K.D. (2000) Adolescent egocentrism: a comparison among adolescents and adults. *Journal of Adolescence*, 23 (3), pp.343–54.

Hayes, H. (2006) Apologies and accounts in youth justice conferencing: reinterpreting research outcomes. *Contemporary Justice Review*, 9 (4), pp.369–85.

Hoyle, C., Young, R. & Hill, R. (2002) *Proceed with caution*. Layerthorpe, York Publishing Services Ltd.

Hudson, B. (2003) *Justice in the risk society*. London, Sage Publications.

Johnstone, G. (2002) *Restorative justice: ideas, values, debates*. Cullompton, Willan Publishing.

Johnstone, G. (2004) *The idea of restorative justice*. Inaugural Professorial Lecture, University of Hull, 11 October.

Marshall, T. & Merry, S. (1990) *Crime and accountability: victim-offender mediation in practice*. London, HMSO.

McCold, P. & Wachtel, T. (2002) Restorative justice theory validation. In: Weitekamp, E. & Kerner, H.-J. eds. *Restorative justice: theoretical foundations*. Cullompton, Willan Publishing, pp.110–42.

Merry, S. (1982) The social organization of mediation in nonindustrial societies: implications for informal community justice in America. In: Abel, R. ed. *The politics of information justice: comparative studies*. Vol. 2. New York, Academic Press, pp.17–45.

Morris, A. (2002) Critiquing the critics: a brief response to critics of restorative justice. *The British Journal of Criminology*, 42 (3), pp.596–615.

Pavlich, G. (1996) *Justice fragmented: mediating community disputes under postmodern conditions*. New York, Routledge.

Roche, D. (2003) *Accountability and restorative justice*. Oxford, Clarendon Press.

Strang, H. (2002) *Repair or revenge: victims and restorative justice*. Oxford, Clarendon Press.

Strang, H. (2004) Email communication on RISE data, 24 November.

Tavuchis, N. (1991) *Mea culpa: a sociology of apology and reconciliation*. Stanford, Stanford University Press.

Van Voorhis, P. (1985) Restitution outcome and probationers' assessments of restitution: the effects of moral development. *Criminal Justice and Behavior*, 12 (3), pp.259–87.

von Hirsch, A., Ashworth, A. & Shearing, C. (2003) Specifying aims and limits for restorative justice: a 'making amends' model. In: von Hirsch, A., Roberts, J., Bottoms, A.E., Roach, K. & Schiff, M. eds. *Restorative justice and criminal justice: competing or reconcilable paradigms?* Oxford, Hart Publishing, pp. 21–41.

Structuring Sentencing Discretion

How can sentencing be organised effectively so that it achieves a single aim, or a carefully constructed hierarchy of aims? The question seems to have been little discussed until the last decades of the twentieth century. There was considerable debate about consistency in sentencing over 100 years ago in England and Wales, with calls in 1892 for an appellate court to review sentences. In fact, a Court of Criminal Appeal was created in 1907, but six years earlier Lord Chief Justice Alverstone had responded to public debate by overseeing the preparation of a 'Memorandum on Normal Punishments', a kind of informal sentencing tariff to which the High Court judges assented.[1] This debate did not, however, result in any clarification of the general aims or principles to be applied, and for most of the twentieth century, sentencing in England and Wales, and in the US, was characterised by wide judicial discretion. The notion of a sentencing 'system' was either not used or, if it was used, it would be applied to an agglomeration of sentencing powers provided by legislatures for courts. The normal approach in most jurisdictions was for the legislature to establish maximum penalties for offences, to create a range of sentencing options (including imprisonment) and then leave the courts to exercise discretion within the wide ranges provided.

In a few jurisdictions, most notably England and Wales, the availability of appellate review led to the development of some sentencing principles through case law. In many American jurisdictions, by way of contrast, there was virtually no authoritative guidance beneath the legislative maxima. The result was what Judge Frankel, in Selection 6.1, denounced as 'lawlessness in sentencing'. By this term he meant that decisions on sentence which concern the liberty interests of citizens—for example, whether those convicted of crimes should go to prison—were made in the seeming absence of the protections of the rule of law. No standards for sentencing existed, there was no requirement to give reasons and therefore no protection was provided from inconsistent or unprincipled decisions.

Structuring sentencing discretion represents one of the most significant challenges for a legislature. Allowing sentencers untrammeled discretion guided only by appellate review is likely to result in widespread disparity.[2] The other extreme, constraining judicial discretion to a very high degree by the use of mandatory minimum sentences, will generate an equally serious injustice, namely the treating of unlike cases in the same way. Most common law jurisdictions have elected to structure sentencers' discretion in a way that falls between the two extremes. However, even the middle ground contains a significant degree of variation. Some US states provide judges with sentencing guidelines that are purely advisory in nature; other states employ fairly rigid sentencing grids which allow little judicial discretion. In the second Selection (6.2), Andrew Ashworth describes the four principal techniques for reducing sentencing disparity. These include: judicial self-regulation; narrative style sentencing guidelines; statutory sentencing principles; and mandatory sentencing laws.

Over the last 20 years many countries have introduced or proposed reforms to structure the exercise of discretion at sentencing. In some jurisdictions, such as England and Wales, detailed guidelines for sentencers are now available for a wide range of offences.[3] New Zealand is the latest jurisdiction to introduce sentencing guidelines. At the time of writing the New Zealand Law Commission is developing comprehensive sentencing and parole guidelines.[4] It is now possible to identify a number of key factors in the process of structuring this discretion. Decisions must be taken on the *content* of guidance; on the *source* of guidance; on the *authority* by which it should be laid down; and on the *style* in which it should be formulated. Attention must also be paid to the *mechanics* of putting the guidance into practice. However, before introducing each of these topics, the constitutional dimensions of the subject need to be briefly explored.

In a system of state authority that has some attachment, however loose, to the doctrine of separation of powers, which organ of the state should have authority in matters of sentencing? It is widely accepted that the legislature has supreme authority over sentencing policy, at least to the extent that it may lay down maximum penalties for offences and may decide what forms of sentence are to be available to the courts.[5] It also seems that legislatures may provide for mandatory sentences or mandatory minimum sentences for any offence: mandatory sentences for murder are common to many jurisdictions, without any suggestion that they involve an unconstitutional exercise of power by the legislature, and mandatory minimum sentences have also been held constitutional.[6] However, when legislatures impinge on what was hitherto a wide sentencing discretion of the judiciary, this has led to claims that the judiciary has some quasi-constitutional right to discretion in matters of sentencing.

These claims, heard in many jurisdictions and at different times,[7] have sometimes been bolstered by suggesting that sentencing discretion is required by the constitutional principle of the independence of the judiciary. Such claims are dubious. If mandatory sentences and mandatory minimum sentences are accepted as constitutional, the only claim of the judiciary can be to whatever discretion the legislature leaves. The principle of judicial independence is surely designed to protect the impartiality of judges and their freedom from pressure, influence and bias[8]; it cannot be used to deny the propriety of legislatively authorized restrictions on sentencing, and therefore of legislative supremacy in sentencing matters.

Content of Guidance

Turning to the structuring of guidance for sentencers, an initial question concerns the *content* of the guidance. One of the consequences of the widespread discretion that has characterised sentencing for much of the twentieth century is that a whole variety of principles and policies have influenced sentencing, largely according to the inclinations of the particular sentencer. One of the aims of structuring discretion should be to ensure that it is exercised in a principled manner, and one essential step must be to decide upon a rationale for sentencing. A choice should be made between deterrence, rehabilitation, incapacitation, reparation or desert as the leading aim of the system. Once the leading aim is chosen, a decision should be taken about whether any other aim or aims should be allowed to influence sentences, to what degree and in what types of case. Unless decisions of principle are taken on priorities and spheres of application of two or more sentencing aims, the resultant uncertainty would be a recipe for disparity: Selections 6.2 and 6.3 show how these points have been accepted and acted upon in England and in Sweden, respectively.

There are other decisions of principle to be taken into consideration too. One concerns the promotion of principles such as equality before the law, particularly if there has been evidence of discriminatory sentencing in the past: a declaration that courts may not have regard to such factors as race, colour, gender, employment status and religion might be a first step toward this goal. Another issue concerns the use of imprisonment: if there is to be a policy of restraint in the use of imprisonment, this may be implemented, for example, by means of specific legislative declarations or by introducing a prison capacity constraint into the fixing of the sentencing guidance itself (as in Minnesota; see Selection 6.4 by Richard Frase).

What should be the *source* of any guidance on sentencing? If guidance is to be given, who should undertake the inquiries necessary to decide upon and formulate the guidance most appropriate to a particular system? The typical English approach, in times of legislative abstention, used to be for the senior judiciary in the Court of Appeal to develop guidance through their judgments. Since 1999, however, there has been a form of sentencing guideline system in England and Wales, as described by Andrew Ashworth in Selection 6.2. In several other jurisdictions, governments entrusted the task to a specially appointed drafting committee as a prelude to legislation (as in Sweden); or to a commission acting with legislatively delegated rule-making authority (as in Minnesota, for example). The membership of such bodies can be broadly based, drawing upon the experience of some judges and also including others with wider correctional and criminal justice experience.

Once proposals for the structuring of sentencing have been drawn up, there is the question of the *authority* by which they should be promulgated. Should all the standards be contained in legislation, or should use be made of some other form of regulation? Some jurisdictions, such as California, have placed all the detailed guidance in primary legislation; this might appear to ensure maximum control by a democratically elected institution, but it brings the danger that a carefully conceived scheme of guidance can be distorted by individual and piecemeal amendments, often proposed for political gain. Another approach, adopted in Minnesota and Oregon, is for the legislature to set out some basic principles in primary legislation, and to establish a rule-making commission to formulate detailed guidance in the form of regulations, which will then take effect unless the legislature resolves otherwise. In England and Wales the Sentencing Guidelines Council is empowered to issue definitive sentencing guidelines, once it has completed the required consultation process. Much depends here on the competence and sense of commitment of the commission, and its ability to devise a coherent system of guidance which sentencers can be persuaded to adopt. The traditions and legal culture of the jurisdiction will clearly be a significant factor. A third approach would be for the primary legislation to set out the basic principles, and leave the judiciary to develop the detailed guidance through appellate judgments. This approach, adopted in the 1988 Swedish sentencing law (see Selection 6.3), depends for its success on the judiciary's willingness to take the principles seriously and to develop them sympathetically. In Selection 6.5 Cyrus Tata notes some of the limitations of appellate review in the area of sentencing.

The next question is what *style* of guidance should be chosen. Mandatory minimum sentences for certain crimes have become increasingly attractive to politicians in recent decades: the UK Parliament has followed the example of others, such as the US and Singapore, by introducing mandatory sentence types (eg life imprisonment for certain offences) and mandatory minimum prison sentences of specified numbers of years (eg a three-year minimum sentence for burglary). There is little evidence that mandatory minimum sentences have any effect on crime rates. Moreover, sentencers often strive to avoid the injustice of having to treat different cases as if they were the same; these and other criticisms are noted by Cassia Spohn in Selection 6.6.

Numerical Sentencing Guidelines

Perhaps the best known style of guidance in recent times in the USA has been numerical guidelines. In Minnesota, these take the form of a two-dimensional grid of normally prescribed sentence ranges. The two dimensions of the grid represent the seriousness of the crime and the prior record of the offender. Departures from sentence length ranges contained in the grid are possible, but reasons must be given and these 'departure' sentences are subject to appellate review. The sentencing guidelines created and implemented in the US have attracted extended scholarly commentary over recent years. At the federal level, the sentencing guidelines became mandatory in 1984 with passage of the Sentencing Reform Act. The federal guidelines have been greatly criticised over the years. In 2005, the status of the guidelines changed significantly following a judgment of the US Supreme Court. In

United States v Booker[9] the court held that, since the guidelines required judges rather than juries to find facts that would result in a harsher sentence, the guidelines constituted a violation of the sixth amendment. The effect of this ruling was to render the guidelines advisory rather than mandatory in nature.[10] Scholarly reaction has been more positive with respect to the Minnesota guidelines. The Selection (6.4) by Richard Frase summarises the guideline system used in the state of Minnesota. The Minnesota sentencing guidelines are generally acknowledged as being one of the success stories of the guidelines movement.

Guidance in the Form of Statutory Directions to Courts

Another approach, adopted in some European countries, is that of setting out in legislation detailed principles, including guidance on how to resolve conflicts of principles. Courts are left to translate these principles into specific dispositions: this is the approach of Swedish law, described in Selection 6.3(a) by Andrew von Hirsch and supplemented by a translation of the law in Selection 6.3(b).

These various styles of guidance differ in the extent to which they reduce judicial discretion, but it would be wrong to assume that the pursuit of principled sentencing means that the most constraining approach is necessarily the best. The point is that there will inevitably be questions of detailed application that can be answered differently by different sentencers, so that, even if all sentencers were conscientiously pursuing the same aim or set of aims, inconsistencies could result. For example, if the overall aim of the system were incapacitation, it would still be important to have guidance on the types of offence and offender for whom predictive restraint might be justified, on whether limits should be placed on sentences in certain types of cases, and on whether class- or race-related factors such as employment history might be taken into account. If the overall aim is desert, it would be important to have parameters for determining the relative seriousness of different crimes, and for deciding how much weight to give to an offender's prior record. Beyond that, the choices are familiar. Much will depend, in practice, on what is deemed appropriate in the context of the legal and political culture of the jurisdiction.

Devising guidance is insufficient to achieve the structuring of decisions on sentence. Whatever the content, source, authority and style of sentencing guidance, it will only be worthwhile if it operates in practice in the way intended. It is abundantly clear that compulsion may not bring this about: the experience of courts circumventing mandatory minimum sentences is sufficient to substantiate this.[11] Where the degree of compulsion is reduced and courts are given the opportunity to depart from guideline sentences upon giving reasons, there may be substantial compliance; but the experience of 'adaptive behaviour' by both judges and prosecutors in Minnesota demonstrates that the element of flexibility may be exploited to some extent.[12] Appellate review of sentences may be expected to contribute to the practical enforcement of sentencing guidance, but the extent of its contribution will depend on three points. First, the appeal court will need to take a strong line against unwarranted deviations from guidance by lower court. Secondly, its decisions should not merely decide the particular case, but serve as precedents for later cases. And thirdly, it must be willing to address issues of principle in its judgments.

Another approach to promoting consistency is the introduction of technical aids for sentencers, such as computerised systems with databases that can help the judge to discover the relevant laws, policies and current practice relating to a particular type of case. Information systems of this kind may be useful in collating and presenting relevant guidance from different sources, for example, legislation, judicial decisions and common practice.[13] Various jurisdictions, including Canada and Scotland, have created sentencing information systems for courts. In Selection 6.7 Marc Miller discusses the issues surrounding these systems.

Having surveyed a range of possible methods for structuring sentencing, so as to bring practice into conformity with the rationales and principles of a given sentencing system, it remains to emphasise that sentencing forms only a part of the criminal justice process. Any structuring would therefore need to be related to the stages of the criminal process occurring before and after the sentencing decision. This is not the place to develop these arguments in detail,[14] but a few examples can be given. Clearly those cases that come before the courts for sentence are those selected for prosecution by the police and public prosecutors, such as the Crown Prosecution Service in England and Wales, who have powers to 'divert' cases from the courts and who do so in considerable numbers. Likewise, the offence labels attached to the conduct for which courts pass sentence stem from those earlier prosecutorial decisions and from any bargains struck by prosecution and defence in relation to guilty pleas and the reduction of charges. Moving to the post-sentence phase, the impact of sentences may be affected by the decision of the parole authorities in jurisdictions which still employ a discretionary release mechanism. It follows from these examples that any approach to sentencing guidance that fails to take into consideration the stages of decision-making before and after sentence would be limited in its effect. At the least, there should be an attempt to ensure congruity with prosecution guidance and parole guidance.

JVR

Notes

1. See Radzinowicz, L and Hood, R, (1990) *The Emergence of Penal Policy in Victorian and Edwardian England* (Oxford, Clarendon Press) 755–8.
2. Empirical research over the past 40 years has demonstrated the existence of unwarranted disparity when courts impose sentence in the absence of any formal sentencing

guidelines: see, eg Hogarth, J, (1971) *Sentencing as a Human Process* (Toronto, University of Toronto Press); Palys, T and Divorski, S, (1986) 'Explaining Sentence Disparity' 28 *Canadian Journal of Criminology* 347.

3. See Ashworth, A, (2006) 'The Sentencing Guideline System in England and Wales' 19 *South African Journal of Criminal Justice* 1.

4. See Young, W and Browning, C, (2008) 'New Zealand's Sentencing Council' 4 *Criminal Law Review* 287.

5. For further discussion of the constitutional aspects, see Munro, C, (1992) 'Judicial Independence and Judicial Functions' in C Munro and M Wasik (eds), *Sentencing, Judicial Discretion and Training* (London, Sweet & Maxwell); Ashworth, A, (1992) 'Sentencing Reform Structures' in N Morris and M Tonry (eds), *Crime and Justice*, vol 16 (Chicago, IL, Chicago University Press) 181–241.

6. *Palling v Corfield* (1970) 123 CLR 52, a decision of the High Court of Australia.

7. For example, the statement of Lord Halsbury, as Lord Chancellor, in 1890, quoted by Radzinowicz and Hood, above n 1, 754. A century later a similarly vigorous assertion may be found in a memorandum of the judges of Victoria (Australia) on sentencing: see Victorian Sentencing Committee, (1988) *Sentencing*, vol 3 (Melbourne, Victorian Sentencing Committee), app 1.

8. See the declaration of the United Nations, *Basic Principles on the Independence of the Judiciary*, adopted at the Seventh United Nations Crime Congress, 1985, paras 1 and 2: 'The independence of the judiciary shall be guaranteed by the State and enshrined in the constitution or law of the country—The judiciary shall decide matters before them with impartiality on the basis of facts, in accordance with the law, without any improper influences or pressures'.

9. *United States v Booker* (2005) 543 US 220.

10. For a clear and concise discussion of the federal sentencing guidelines in the post-Booker era, see Berry III, W, (2007) 'Discretion without Guidance: The Need to Give Meaning to s 3553 after Booker and its Progeny' 40 *Connecticut Law Review* 631.

11. See Tonry, M, (1996) *Sentencing Matters* (Oxford, Oxford University Press) ch 5.

12. For evidence from Minnesota, see Parent, D, (1989) *Structuring Criminal Sentencing* (Stoneham, MA, Butterworth) p184; see more generally Tonry, M, (1996) above n 11, ch 6.

13. For developments in Scotland, see Hutton, N, Paterson, A, Tata, C and Wilson, J, (1996) *A Sentencing Information System for the Scottish High Court of Justiciary* (Edinburgh, Scottish Office, Central Research Unit); earlier systems are reviewed by Ashworth, above n 3, 227–30.

14. For a detailed discussion of pre-trial processes, see Ashworth, A, (1998) *The Criminal Process*, 2nd edn (Oxford, Oxford University Press); for post-sentence processes, see Richardson, G, (1993) *Law, Process and Custody: Prisoners and Patients* (London, Weidenfield & Nicolson).

Further Reading

Ashworth, A, (2006) 'The Sentencing Guideline System in England and Wales' 19 *South African Journal of Criminal Justice* 1.

Criminal Law Review (2008) Special Issue on Sentencing Guidelines, April.

Doob, AN, (1995) 'The United States Sentencing Commission: If You Don't Know Where You Are Going, You Might Not Get There' in C Clarkson and R Morgan (eds), *The Politics of Sentencing Reform* (Oxford, Clarendon).

Freiberg, A, (2001) 'Three Strikes and You're Out! It's Not Cricket: Colonization and Resistance in Australian Sentencing' in M Tonry and R Frase (eds), *Sentencing and Sanctions in Western Countries* (New York, Oxford University Press).

Reitz, K, (2001) 'The Disassembly and Reassembly of U.S. Sentencing Practices' in M Tonry and R Frase (eds), *Sentencing and Sanctions in Western Countries* (New York, Oxford University Press).

Roberts, JV and Baker, E, (2007) 'Sentencing in Common Law Jurisdictions' in S Shoham, O Beck and M Kett (eds), *International Handbook of Penology and Criminal Justice* (New York, Routledge).

Tata, C, (2002) 'Accountability for the Sentencing Decision Process—Towards a New Understanding' in C Tata and N Hutton (eds), *Sentencing and Society: International Perspectives* (Aldershot, Ashgate).

Tonry, M, (2002) 'Setting sentencing policy through guidelines' in S Rex and M Tonry (eds), *Reform and Punishment: The Future of Sentencing* (Cullompton, Willan).

Tonry, M and Frase, R (eds), (2001) *Sentencing and Sanctions in Western Countries* (New York, Oxford University Press).

Young, W and Browning, C, (2008) 'New Zealand's Sentencing Council' 4 *Criminal Law Review* 287.

6.1

Lawlessness in Sentencing

MARVIN FRANKEL

The common form of criminal penalty provision confers upon the sentencing judge an enormous range of choice. The scope of what we call "discretion" permits imprisonment for anything from a day to one, five, 10, 20, or more years. All would presumably join in denouncing a statute that said "the judge may impose any sentence he pleases". Given the mortality of men, the power to set a man free or to confine him for up to 30 years is not sharply distinguishable.

The statutes granting such powers characteristically say nothing about the factors to be weighed in moving to either end of the spectrum or to some place between. It might be supposed by some stranger arrived in our midst that the criteria for measuring a particular sentence would be discoverable outside the narrow limits of the statutes and would be known to the judicial experts rendering the judgements. But the supposition would lack substantial foundation. Even the most basic sentencing principles are not prescribed or stated with persuasive authority. There is, to be sure, a familiar litany in the literature of sentencing "purposes": retribution, deterrence ("special" and "general"), "denunciation", incapacitation, rehabilitation. Nothing tells us, however, when or whether any of these several goals are to be sought, or how to resolve such evident conflicts as that likely to arise in the effort to punish and rehabilitate all at once. It has for some time been part of our proclaimed virtue that vengeance or retribution is a disfavoured motive for punishment. But there is reason to doubt that either judges or the public are effectively abreast of this advanced position. And there is no law—certainly none that anybody pretends to have enforced—telling the judge he must refrain, expressly or otherwise, from trespassing against higher claims to wreak vengeance.

Moving upward from what should be the philosophical axioms of a rational scheme of sentencing law, we have no structure of rules, or even guidelines, affecting other elements arguably pertinent to the nature or severity of the sentence. Should it be a mitigating factor that the defendant is being sentenced upon a plea of guilty rather than a verdict against him? Should it count in his favour that he spared the public "trouble" and expense by waiving a jury? Should the sentence be more severe because the judge is convinced that the defendant perjured himself on the witness stand? Should churchgoing be considered to reflect favourably? Consistent

From ME Frankel, 'Lawlessness in Sentencing' (1972) 41 *Cincinnati Law Review* 1.

with the first amendment, should it be considered at all? What factors should be assessed—and where, if anywhere, are comparisons to be sought—in gauging the relative seriousness of the specific offence and offender as against the spectrum of offences by others in the same legal category? The list of such questions could be lengthened. Each is capable of being answered, and is answered by sentencing judges, in contradictory or conflicting, or at least differing, ways. There is no controlling requirement that any particular view be followed on any such subject by the sentencing judge.

With the delegation of power so unchannelled, it is surely no overstatement to say that "the new penology has resulted in vesting in judges and parole and probation agencies the greatest degree of uncontrolled power over the liberty of human beings that one can find in the legal system". The process would be totally unruly even if judges were superbly and uniformly trained for the solemn work of sentencing.

The *kadi*, unfettered by rules, makes his decrees swiftly and simply. But we learned long ago that the giving of reasons helps the decision-maker himself in the effort to be fair and rational, and makes it possible for others to judge whether he has succeeded. And so we require our federal district judges and many others to explain themselves when they rule whether a postal truck driver was at fault in crumpling a fender and, if so, how much must be paid to right the wrong.

There is no such requirement in the announcement of a prison sentence. Sometimes judges give reasons anyway, or reveal in colloquy the springs of their action. The explanations or revelations sometimes disclose reasoning so perverse or mistaken that the sentence, normally unreviewable, must be invalidated on appeal. Most trial judges (to my impressionistic and conversational knowledge, at least) say little or nothing, certainly far less than a connected "explanation" or rationale of the sentence. Many, sharing a common aversion to being reversed, are perhaps motivated by the view (not unknown on trial benches) that there is safety in silence. It is likely that the judge, not expected to explain, has never organized a full and coherent explanation even for himself. Some judges use the occasion of sentencing to flaunt or justify themselves by moral pronunciamentos and excoriations of the defendant. This has no relation to the serious and substantial idea that the community's "denunciation" is a—possibly the— chief aim of sentencing. It is, in any event, not kin to the reasoned decisions for which judges are commissioned.

The state I have described as lawlessness calls for some immediate, if not immutable, remedies by law-making. At least some principles of sentencing should by now be attainable. Both by substantive controls and through procedural revisions the unchecked powers of the untutored judge should be subject to a measure of regulation. The vague, indefinite, and uncritical use of indeterminate sentences calls for restriction through meaningful definitions and discriminating judgements. Matters like the "apportionment of punishment" and its "severity" are peculiarly questions of legislative policy. Believing it has been time long since to start abhorring the vacuum that exists in this area, I propose here to suggest only some beginnings, leaving for wiser heads and fuller time the continuous task of completion and betterment.

Despite all the philosophizing on this most fundamental of subjects in scholarly works and random judicial opinions, we have virtually no meaningful or specific legislative declarations of the principles justifying criminal sanctions.

Beyond dealing with the bedrock subject of sentencing purposes a new code of sentencing should begin to weigh and decide numerous issues of mitigation or aggravation on which judges are now free to go their disparate ways. It is not acceptable to leave for the normally unspoken and diverse judgements of sentencing courts such questions as: whether a plea of guilty should be considered in mitigation; whether (what is not the converse) standing trial should be considered aggravating; whether waiving a jury or seemingly lying on the stand should be taken into account; whether disruptive behaviour and tactics at trial should be considered aggravating; or whether "co-operation" with the prosecutor (furnishing evidence for other investigations, testifying against codefendants, etc.) should be considered mitigating. In addition to such matters of in-court behaviour, there are, of course, more fundamental questions touching the criminal acts and the general character and history of the defendant. Students of the subject recall, and generally scorn these days, the efforts of scholars in times past to catalogue such factors—the relative gravity of the specific offence, the cruelty or stealth or deliberateness of the behaviour, defendant's age, prior record, character traits, etc.—and evolve a kind a calculus for computing sentences. The short answer to such proposals for detailed sentencing codes has been the familiar, and weighty, aversion to illusory certainty bought at the cost of inflexible laws that torture disparate people and events into identical molds. But, like other short answers, this one is too short. There has not yet been a sufficient investment of energy and imagination in the attempt to codify precise, detailed factors governing sentences. Until the attempt has been made, with at least a measure of the resources and attention befitting a moon-voyaging society, the vague, futile, helpless wailing about disparity remains hypocrisy. Believing this, and risking the misunderstanding likely to greet a proposition conceded to be rudimentary and tentative, I mean to outline (a) the reasons for a detailed sentencing code and (b) the general nature of the contents and uses of such a code.

(a) The argument for codifying sentencing criteria is, very simply, that they now exist and operate, whether we like this or not, in an arbitrary, random, inconsistent, and unspoken fashion. Factors I have repeatedly mentioned—guilty pleas, prior record, defendant's age and family circumstances—are considered every day by sentencing judges, but in accordance with uncontrolled and divergent individual views of what is, after all, the "law" each time it applies. Every factor of this kind calls for a judgement of policy, suited exactly for legislative action and surely not suited for random variation from case to case. It is not a question, then, of seeking out and attempting to apply artificial criteria. It is a question of making explicit and uniform what is now tacit, capricious, and often decisive.

Making such determinations, a detailed sentencing code would eliminate some of the obscurity and the futility now attending the subject. Counsel would have some basis for knowing what to do and how to argue. The sentencers—the single judge or a group, as well as probation officers— would face a task similarly defined and capable of similarly focused appraisal. The defining of concrete issues would lead in turn to the possibility of meaningful appellate review.

(b) To posit at least a theoretical ideal, subject to revision of all kinds in the pursuit, I suggest the goal of codification might be conceived as a fairly detailed calculus of sentencing factors, including such use of arithmetical weightings as experimental study might reveal to be feasible. Again, I disclaim anything beyond the crude diagramming of a preliminary hypothesis. The hypothesis begins with the thought that every sentence under the code, as heretofore urged, would be classified in accordance with its basic purpose or purposes—as deterrent, rehabilitative, etc. For each such category, the code might contain some initial or tentative sentencing guides—for example, that a purely deterrent sentence should presumptively fall (subject to aggravating factors) in the lowest quartile of the sentencing range for the particular crime, or that a rehabilitative sentence might be categorized initially in terms of the denned need and proposed form of treatment.

Thereafter, within each broad sentencing category or group of categories, particular factors of mitigation or aggravation would be enumerated in the proposed code. Where possible, as I have suggested, numerical weights or ranges would be assigned—as, for example, for the relative gravity of the offence, the defendant's past criminal record, the favourable or unfavourable character of the defendant's work history and abilities. However unromantic numbers sound, or however misleading they may be in foolish hands, their proper uses may guide and regulate judgement. The physician who speaks of a grade 3 heart murmur may not be reporting a measurement as precise as the number of feet in a yard. But he says a meaningful thing that gives information and guidance to others professionally trained. Similarly, at least over time, a score of 5 on a scale of 1 to 5 for "gravity of particular offence" would help to tell what the sentencing judge thought and to test whether his thoughts made sense for the particular case.

For lack of time and competence, I have not attempted to think through how far a scheme of quantification might be carried. Depending upon the resolution of this basic problem, the aim of the sentencing code would be a sentencing form or chart giving possibly an overall "score" or, more likely, a profile of factors and their weights. The end product thus recorded by the sentencing tribunal could be preceded by proposed forms on charts submitted by counsel, probation officers, and others seeking to affect or determine the sentence. All, as I have urged, would have concrete things to aim at and talk about. All would have bases for comparison in assessing differences of ultimate judgement.

If this sounds crass and mechanical, I press it nonetheless as a goal preferable to the void in which we now operate. Outside the sombre field of sentencing, it has not been our way to make a fetish of vagueness. Whether numbers and scores are useless is a judgement that ought to follow, not precede, earnest study.

The aspects of sentencing that strike me as most flawed and most urgently in need of law revision have led to the few, somewhat scattered suggestions for legislative reform outlined above. There are needs, however, for action of a more thorough and continuous nature. Ignorance being one of the greatest problems, there is a need to marshal resources and talent for research and experimentation. Because the subject of sentencing is not steadily exhilarating or profitable to political officials, there is a need to fill the gaps in attention between sporadic moments of concern in times of crisis. Another aspect of the same essential point is the lack of political power suffered not only by convicted persons but by their keepers as well. Finally, the need for revision of the law is not a one-time thing: the gross inadequacies of the existing situation require continuing study and reform.

Thoughts along these lines lead to the very possibly impractical but earnest final recommendation of this paper. I propose that there be established a national commission charged with permanent responsibility for (1) the study of sentencing, corrections, and parole; (2) the formulation of laws and rules to which the results of such study may lead; and (3) the actual enactment of rules subject to congressional veto. When I suggest details of the commission's proposed composition and functions, it will be to invite thought rather than to claim anything like certainty or finality. With these caveats I sketch the proposal and its rationale.

Starting with the latter, I have mentioned the need for continuous and prestigious attention to problems of sentencing. The commission, properly launched and populated, could serve in a sense as a lobby within the government of those sentenced and for those charged with their custody and treatment. Other interests, politically significant, have such representation. Agriculture, labour, business, investors, and others have their spokesmen in various departments and agencies. Lately, reflecting a variety of things we seem to care about as a nation, the consumer is elbowing his way into the power structure. Prisoners and jailers, like the poor and others who seemed so distant a while ago, are headed for participation unless we mean to deflect sharply the lines of our recent development. But whether or not that is so, the stakes of everyone in a system of rational sentencing are too great for contentment with the dishevelled status quo. The improvements needed will not be achieved through fitful bursts of activity. The task requires the continuous attention of a respected agency.

Membership of the commission would be a matter for discussion. Obvious possibilities suggest themselves—lawyers, judges, criminologists, penologists, more generally-based sociologists, psychologists, and, not least but least traditional, former or present prison inmates. This is not to stump for government of prisoners by consent. It is to say we have gone too long without paying much attention to the actual impact upon the recipients of our well-intentioned but ineffectual "treatment" programmes.

The commission would not pretend to supersede existing scholarly efforts in universities and elsewhere. Like other agencies of government, the commission would draw upon such enterprises, generate additional ones, and engage in its own study programmes. Early in its career, the commission would chart a programme of inquiry and action and would set priorities. From this would follow decisions on the commissioning of outside studies and the organization of the agency's own projects.

I envision a highly prestigious commission or none at all. The calibre of those to be sought as commissioners would be a crucial concern. Their roles would be as philosopher-statesmen, charged with both basic scholarship and the formulation of rules, but leaving administrative and operating responsibilities to others. It is conceived, however, that the commission would have significant impact upon the shape and functioning of the affected administrative institutions. It may well be, for example, that the commission would want to consider whether there is any sound reason why the attorney general, the chief prosecutor, should have the Bureau of Prisons and Board of Parole under this jurisdiction. The phrasing here, if it implies a view as to the answer, is accurately revealing, but the commission might discover two sides to the question. The list of provocative possibilities could be extended, but the result might not be to enhance the palatability of my basic suggestion.

Sentencing is today a wasteland in the law. It calls, above all, for regulation by law. There is an excess of discretion given to officials whose entitlement to such power is established by neither professional credentials nor performance. Some measures already in existence—such as sentencing councils and appellate review—seem desirable because they operate to channel the exercise of discretion. On the other hand, the evil of unbounded discretion is enhanced by the uncritical belief that a beneficent "individualization" is achieved through indeterminate sentencing. Indeterminancy in its most enthusiastic forms takes on its literal dictionary quality of vagueness; it means the conferring of power to extend or terminate confinement where the grounds of the power have been misconceived and the occasions for its exercise are not ascertainable. Some aspects of sentencing and the treatment of convicted persons call for prompt legislative attention—in the choice of basic substantive principles, the prescription of basic procedures, and provisions for appellate review. The entire subject, however, is one for study and a steady process of law revision led by an imminent and permanent federal commission.

6.2

Techniques for Reducing Sentence Disparity

ANDREW ASHWORTH

This essay offers a brief examination of a range of techniques for increasing consistency in sentencing decisions. It begins with a distinctive English contribution to the structuring of sentencing and the development of judicial guidance and guidelines, followed by the revised English approach of narrative sentencing guidelines. It then turns to the Scandinavian approach of articulating statutory sentencing principles; American numerical guideline systems; and mandatory sentencing regimes. In conclusion, the 1992 recommendations of the Council of Europe are outlined.

Judicial Self-regulation

For many years the English courts regulated their own sentencing practices, within the boundaries set by the legislature. Since the latter part of the nineteenth century, Parliament had done little more than lay down maximum penalties, leaving a broad judicial discretion with few restrictions on what courts might and might not do. However, the Court of Criminal Appeal, now the Court of Appeal, began to lay down various general principles of sentencing in its judgments on appeals against sentence, occasionally in the early years and more frequently from the 1960s onwards. That was a slow and essentially reactive way in which to develop sentencing principles, but in the 1980s the Court of Appeal began to develop a more active role. Periodically, the Lord Chief Justice would select a particular appeal case in which to deliver a guideline judgment, setting out the parameters of sentencing for a whole range of variations of the crime in question—the first being a drugs case, in which the Court gave guidelines for sentencing for importation, supply and possession of class A, B and C drugs.[1]

This approach had the advantage of providing judges with a framework within which they can locate the individual case, without depriving them of the discretion to deal differently with a case which has unusual features. The guidance is also narrative, having the familiar form of an appellate court's judgment rather than presenting a stark table of numbers. This kind of self-regulation through appellate review has also been used to some extent in other jurisdictions, such as Scotland,

This is a modified version of Selection 5.2 published in the previous (2nd) edition of this book.

Ireland, Canada, New Zealand and Australia, and there are other common law countries in which the appeal court's decisions constitute binding precedents for other judges. Guideline judgments were welcomed by most English judges, largely because they were constructed by judges for judges, and also because they were seen as providing a common framework while preserving flexibility for individual cases.

The disadvantages were that guideline judgments tended to be sporadic, there was no overall strategy and many frequently occurring offence types (such as burglary) were hardly covered at all. Moreover, whilst such judgments clearly created sentencing policy, only judges had an input. Recognition of these disadvantages prompted the reforms dealt with in the next paragraph. But at least the guideline judgments disposed of one much-trumpeted judicial objection to sentencing guidance: that each case is unique and has its own individual combination of factors, and therefore guidelines will invariably be crude and unhelpful. This is often the last line of defence for those who favour unfettered judicial discretion in sentencing, and yet the guideline judgments showed that sentencing structures can have an effect.

Narrative Sentencing Guidelines

In 1998 the English system modified its reliance on the Court of Appeal by introducing a Sentencing Advisory Panel.[2] The main arguments in favour of this development were that: (i) although discretion in sentencing is essential, greater attention should be paid to the rule of law and to the articulation of common principles and standards of sentencing; (ii) this would be best achieved through a coordinated set of sentencing guidelines to bring greater consistency of approach to sentencing, a task for which the Court of Appeal had insufficient time and resources; and (iii) the task is one of policy creation and therefore not only judges and sentencers from all levels, but also those with experience of other aspects of the criminal justice system, should play a part in the creation of such guidelines. The Panel, with a diverse membership including judges, academics, criminal justice professionals and lay members, was empowered to prepare draft guidelines on various offences, consult widely on them and then send a written advice to the Court of Appeal proposing guidelines for that offence. The Court retained the power to accept, modify or reject the Panel's advice. In practice, it usually accepted the advice and subsequently, when a convenient case arose, incorporated the proposals (with or without modifications) into a guideline judgment. The authority of those judgments stood on the same foundations as that of earlier guideline judgments devised by the Court itself.[3]

In 2003, Parliament altered the system: it was thought that the Court of Appeal was not the most suitable body for creating guidelines by incorporating them into its judgments on appeals, and the Sentencing Guidelines Council (SGC) was created to develop a system of guidance for sentencing (having first consulted government ministers and a parliamentary committee). The SGC has the power to issue definitive sentencing guidelines; judges must 'have regard to' them when sentencing, and must give reasons for any departure.[4] The details of the operation of these two separate bodies (SAP and SGC) need not be described here. Notable, however, is the fact that the style of guidance has been developed from the two models that were previously in use in England: the narrative approach of Court of Appeal guidelines and the more structured approach of the special guidelines for magistrates' courts.

The guidelines issued by the SGC for various offences tend to consist of a first part, which discusses the features of the offence and factors that might increase or decrease its seriousness, somewhat similar to parts of 1999–2003 Court of Appeal judgments based on the Panel's advice; and a second part, which sets out three or four levels of seriousness of the offence and assigns a sentencing range to each of them. The first part can be described as narrative; the second part consists chiefly of a sentencing table for the offence. Some of the tables are quite elaborate: for example, the table for the offence of causing death by careless driving when under the influence or alcohol or drugs contains nine separate sentence ranges.[5] A somewhat simpler example is that for the offence of robbery for adult offenders (Table 1).[6]

The guideline includes a narrative discussion of the table and its levels of seriousness in the preceding pages, and a list of aggravating and mitigating factors appears beneath the table. However, these tables should not be confused with American-style sentencing grids: not only do those grids tend to cover many types of offence and specify narrower ranges, but a major characteristic is that they have two axes (levels of offence seriousness presented vertically, and 'criminal history scores' presented horizontally) and thereby incorporate previous convictions into the grid itself.

The most recent definitive guidelines issued by the SGC include a single page

Table 1

Type/nature of activity	Starting point	Sentencing range
The offence includes the threat or use of minimal force and removal of property	12 months' custody	Up to 3 years' custody
A weapon is produced and used to threaten, and/or force is used which results in injury to the victim	4 years' custody	2–7 years' custody
The victim is caused serious physical injury by the use of significant force and/or the use of a weapon	8 years' custody	7–12 years' custody

Source: Sentencing Guidelines Council (available at www.sentencing-guidelines.gov.uk).

headed 'The Decision Making Process', which sets out an eight-stage structure for deciding sentence in the light of the guideline.[7] The proper relationship between the appropriate starting point, range, and aggravating and mitigating factors is also explained in each guideline.[8] However, the English tables are significantly less constraining than the American grids, in four major respects. First, as just noted, the English tables do not incorporate enhancements for previous convictions: the starting points and ranges are based on a first offender convicted after pleading not guilty, so the amount of increase for any previous conviction(s) is left to the court's judgment.[9] Secondly, many offenders are being sentenced for more than one offence, and when there are several offences the court may not simply add all the sentences up together, but must apply a 'totality principle' to reduce the overall sentence. The relationship between this and the guideline is unspecified. Thirdly, courts are allowed to move the sentence up or down from the appropriate starting point in order to take account of aggravating and mitigating factors, and, where one such factor is very strong, the court may be justified in sentencing outside the range. The weight given to these factors is for the court's judgment and is not specified in the guidelines. Fourthly, the current English legislation requires a court only to 'have regard to' the guidelines and to give reasons for departing from them. These formulae, together with the amply wide ranges, leave courts with considerable flexibility.

Opinions will differ as to whether these four differences are strengths or weaknesses of the current English system. Some will argue that they strike the right balance between (i) the structuring effect of definitive guidelines, the need for which derives from the notion of rule of law, and (ii) a leeway for the court to impose a sentence outside the guidelines where its judgment is that the features of a particular case require it, the need for which flows from the duty to do justice. Others may argue that they leave too much flexibility and therefore compromise consistency and the rule of law to too great an extent: this is an argument, not for moving towards American-style grids, but for tightening the existing English approach. As this volume goes to press in July 2008, a Sentencing Commission Working Group will be reporting on this and related issues, and further changes in the English system will be under discussion.

As indicated above, the SGC's general approach to sentencing guidelines is not the only one being adopted in England and Wales. There is a history of separate guidelines for magistrates' courts (which chiefly use part-time lay magistrates with a legal adviser, and which are limited in powers to 6 months' imprisonment or an absolute maximum of 12 months' imprisonment for two or more offences). These guidelines have not hitherto had the force of law, but they have now been reworked by the SAP and SGC, and have been issued as a definitive system of standards.[10] The result is a large document that covers hundreds of offences, and its style differs from that of other SGC guidelines. Its aim is to present for each offence a single page that sets out the starting point and a structured decision-making process. The guidelines for the magistrates' courts therefore do not have much narrative about varying levels of seriousness for each offence, although elsewhere in the document there is a large amount of narrative about general sentencing factors such as previous convictions, racial aggravation, the use of compensation orders, and so forth. Table 2 provides an example from the Magistrates' Court Sentencing Guidelines.

Table 2: Example of Magistrates' Court Guidelines

Drugs – class B and C – possession	Misuse of Drugs Act 1971, s.5(2)

Triable either way:
Maximum when tried summarily: Level 4 fine and/or 3 months (class B); level 3 fine and/or 3 months (class C)
Maximum when tried on indictment: 5 years (class B); 2 years (class C)

Offence seriousness (culpability and harm)		
A. Identify the appropriate starting point		
Starting points based on first time offender pleading not guilty		
Examples of nature of activity	Starting point	Range
Possession of a small amount of class B drug for personal use	Band B fine	Band A fine to low level community order
Possession of large amount of class B drug for personal use	Band C fine	Band B fine to 12 weeks custody

Offence seriousness (culpability and harm)	
B. Consider the effect of aggravating and mitigating factors	
(other than those within examples above)	
Common aggravating and mitigating factors are identified in the pullout card –	
the following may be particularly relevant but these lists are not exhaustive	
Factor indicating higher culpability 1. Offender exercising or acting in position of special responsibility **Factor indicating greater degree of harm** 1. Possession of drugs in a public place or school	**Factors indicating lower culpability** 1. Possession of Class C rather than Class B drug 2. Evidence that use was to help cope with a medical condition
Form a preliminary view of the appropriate sentence, then consider offender mitigation Common factors are identified in the pullout card	

Consider a reduction for a guilty plea

Consider ancillary orders, including forfeiture and destruction of drug Refer to pages 168-174 for guidance on available ancillary orders

Decide sentence Give reasons

Source: Magistrates' Court Sentencing Guidelines.

Overall, it can still be said that the English approach depends to a considerable extent on narrative elements of the guideline documents, but that the actual guidelines—both those specifically for the magistrates' courts and the general ones—appear in the form of tables for each offence. The English guidelines also include different kinds of guidance, such as guidelines on matters of general principle[11] and guidelines on new forms of sentence.[12] Two questions remain unresolved: have the guidelines been successful in increasing the consistency of approach? Do guidelines of this type strike an appropriate balance between the structuring of discretion, so as to ensure that general principles and starting points are adopted, and the room for judgement that is essential if justice is to be done in individual cases?

Statutory Sentencing Principles

This approach was pioneered by Finland. In 1976, that country adopted a system of statutory principles with a single main rationale: that of proportionality. These statutory principles are set forth in Article 6 of the Finnish Penal Code. The most important provision declares that:

> Punishment shall be measured so that it is in just proportion to the damage and danger caused by the offence and to the guilt of the offender manifested in the offence.

(Other jurisdictions, such as Germany, also have legislative declarations of sentencing aims, but these are multiple and sometimes conflicting in character.) The Finnish sentencing statute not only articulates a primary rationale (proportionality), but also contains a list of aggravating and mitigating factors, and a provision on the role of previous convictions, which relate to that aim. The application of this system of guidance in individual cases is left to the courts.

A more sophisticated version of the same approach is to be found in the Swedish Penal Code, as revised in 1988. The new chapters of the Code identify proportionality (desert) as the primary rationale for sentencing, and require the judge to assess the 'penal value' (ie seriousness) of the offence. Some aggravating and mitigating factors are specified, as are other factors that the court may take into account. There is also guidance on the choice among forms of sentence. The Swedish law is discussed in Selection 6.3 below.[13]

The Finnish and Swedish approaches are notable in that they leave the judge to apply and individuate the general norms declared in the legislation. In one sense the judges have considerable discretion, because they are subject to few legislative restrictions. In another sense the discretion is structured, because they are expected to evaluate the factors in individual cases by reference to the principles of sentencing declared in the legislation—they are not free to impose exemplary deterrent sentences, for example, because that would be inconsistent with those stated principles. Moreover, legal argument on sentencing can now be related to the legislative principles. The structuring of discretion is therefore achieved through an approach which ties patterns of reasoning to particular aims and principles, rather than through numerical guidance of the kind used in some US systems.

Numerical Guideline Systems

In the US, the most notable approach to guidance on sentencing (in those states which have opted for guidance at all) has been to adopt numerical guidelines, usually in the form of a sentencing grid. Several variations on this approach may be found in different American jurisdictions: they vary in their format, in the presence or absence of overall aims or policies, and in the degree of latitude left to courts in individual cases. The best-known system is that of Minnesota, which has been adapted for use in other states. This will be contrasted with the distinctly less successful federal guidelines, issued by the US Sentencing Commission.

The sentencing commission in Minnesota began work in the late 1970s.[14] One of its earliest determinations was to decide upon a primary rationale for sentencing: desert. It then went on to make some crucial policy decisions. Sentences for property offenders were to be made less severe, and those for violent offenders correspondingly more severe. A prior criminal record was to be less influential than the seriousness of the offence. And overall sentence levels were to be calculated so as to ensure that the numbers sentenced to imprisonment remained within the capacity of the prisons.[15] The Commission then divided all serious offences into 11 categories of relative gravity, and developed a seven-point scale for calculating the seriousness of an offender's criminal history. The result was Minnesota's 'Sentencing Guidelines Grid', in operation since 1981, which enables a judge to find the presumptive sentence for each case by placing the offence within the appropriate category, calculating the offender's criminal history score, and then locating the cell where the two intersect. The judge is obliged to impose a sentence within the range of presumptive sentences unless there are substantial and compelling circumstances in the individual case warranting a departure from that range. In such circumstances, the departure is permitted upon the court's giving reasons, and the guidelines include a list of factors which may and factors which may not be used as reasons for departure (see Table 3).

Table 3: Minnesota Sentencing Guidelines Grid

MINNESOTA SENTENCING GUIDELINES GRID

(Presumptive Sentence Lengths in Months)

Italicized numbers within the grid denote the range within which a judge may sentence without the sentence being deemed a departure. Offenders with non-imprisonment felony sentences are subject to jail time according to law.

SEVERITY LEVEL OF CONVICTION OFFENSE (Common offenses listed in italics)		CRIMINAL HISTORY SCORE						
		0	1	2	3	4	5	6 or more
Murder, 2nd Degree (intentional murder; drive-by- shootings)	XI	306 *261-367*	326 *278-391*	346 *295-415*	366 *312-439*	386 *329-463*	406 *346-480*	426 *363-480*
Murder, 3rd Degree Murder, 2nd Degree (unintentional murder)	X	150 *128-180*	165 *141-198*	180 *153-216*	195 *166-234*	210 *179-252*	225 *192-270*	240 *204-288*
Assault, 1st Degree Controlled Substance Crime, 1st Degree	IX	86 *74-103*	98 *84-117*	110 *94-132*	122 *104-146*	134 *114-160*	146 *125-175*	158 *135-189*
Aggravated Robbery, 1st Degree Controlled Substance Crime, 2nd Degree	VII I	48 *41-57*	58 *50-69*	68 *58-81*	78 *67-93*	88 *75-105*	98 *84-117*	108 *92-129*
Felony DWI	VII	36	42	48	54 *46-64*	60 *51-72*	66 *57-79*	72 *62-84²*
Controlled Substance Crime, 3rd Degree	VI	21	27	33	39 *34-46*	45 *39-54*	51 *44-61*	57 *49-68*
Residential Burglary Simple Robbery	V	18	23	28	33 *29-39*	38 *33-45*	43 *37-51*	48 *41-57*
Nonresidential Burglary	IV	12¹	15	18	21	24 *21-28*	27 *23-32*	30 *26-36*
Theft Crimes (Over $5,000)	III	12¹	13	15	17	19 *17-22*	21 *18-25*	23 *20-27*
Theft Crimes ($5,000 or less) Check Forgery ($251-$2,500)	II	12¹	12¹	13	15	17	19	21 *18-25*
Sale of Simulated Controlled Substance	I	12¹	12¹	12¹	13	15	17	19 *17-22*

 Presumptive commitment to state imprisonment. First-degree murder has a mandatory life sentence and is excluded from the guidelines by law.

☐ Presumptive stayed sentence; at the discretion of the judge, up to a year in jail and/or other non-jail sanctions can be imposed as conditions of probation.

Effective August 1, 2007

The Minnesota system has been reasonably successful in attaining its objectives. Sentencing consistency has been improved, property offenders have been sent to prison less frequently, and the state's Supreme Court has developed a jurisprudence of permissible and impermissible departures. On the other hand, the division of all serious offences into only 11 categories is rather crude, and the elements of discretion remaining in the Minnesota system have enabled judges and prosecutors to circumvent some of the guidelines.[16] The possibility of adjusting the guidelines so as to conform to prison capacity has been established. In recent years some of the policies underlying the original guidelines have been altered for political reasons, but the structure remains the same.

The Minnesota model has been adopted or adapted successfully in several other states, such as Oregon, Virginia and North Carolina.[17] Further states have opted for similar guideline structures that are 'voluntary', in the sense that they are not enforced by strict requirements ('substantial and compelling reasons' for departure) backed by appellate review, but only require judges to give their reasons for departure. Those reasons may be scrutinised on appeal, but often with a more permissive 'light touch'.

The most recent jurisdiction to adopt the voluntary approach, Washington D.C., notes that some states with voluntary guidelines report substantial compliance rates, and concluded that any additional compliance produced by formal enforcement mechanisms would be outweighed by the cost of those mechanisms and the concomitant loss of judicial flexibility.[18]

The approach of the US Sentencing Commission was different, as have been the consequences of the guidelines they drafted. The Commission was established by the federal Sentencing Reform Act of 1984 and was directed to draft, within certain legislative constraints, guidelines for the sentencing of federal offences. The guidelines became law in 1987, but from the outset their structural defects were manifest in practice. Four areas of difficulty might be mentioned briefly.

First, the Commission declined to declare a primary rationale for sentencing, and instead opted for a scheme with an indiscriminate mixture of rationales. This is not a mere matter of academic elegance; it is a matter of fundamental practical importance when it comes to deciding what factors should aggravate or mitigate and how judges should exercise the discretion left to them by the system. Without an explicit and well-articulated guiding aim, consistency is a forlorn hope.

Secondly, the Commission declined to adopt a principle of restraint in the use of imprisonment, despite a reference to resource constraints in the Sentencing Reform Act. This position has been worsened by the mandatory and mandatory minimum sentences enacted by Congress, particularly for drug offenders and career criminals. Federal imprisonment rates are high, and the mandatory sentences (to which many judges are opposed) have had a further distorting effect on the guidelines.

Thirdly, the federal guidelines are high on complexity and low on clarity. The Commission's 'Sentencing Table' has some 43 'offence-levels' on one axis and six 'criminal history categories' on the other. For each type of offence a 'base level' is indicated by the guidelines; then there are various 'enhancements', for which the judge must raise the offence level if these are present; and there are also some factors such as 'acceptance of responsibility' (an ambiguous and practically troublesome reference to a plea of guilty) which reduce the offence level where they are present. A practical example may be used to show how the guidelines operate.[19] Robbery carries a base level of 18 on the scale. The amount stolen increases this, so that if $100,000 or more was taken, this would add three points to the offence level. There are further enhancements if a weapon was involved: if a gun was brandished but not used, for example, this would add three further points. Then if the judge thought that the offender's plea of guilty showed acceptance of responsibility, the offence level would be reduced by two. Next the judge would turn to the offender's prior record: the calculation takes account not only of the number of previous convictions but also of their seriousness.[20] There are also augmentations for 'career criminals'. The result of this should lead the judge to a cell in the 'Sentencing Table' indicating the appropriate range of sentences. Courts may depart from the range wherever it seems 'reasonable' to do so. The guidelines specify some factors which may and others which may not justify departures, and there are also certain 'policy statements' whose authority has at times caused judicial confusion.

A fourth difficulty is that the apparent rigidity of the guidelines in practice (with a compliance rate of some four-fifths of cases) resulted, as the Federal Courts Study Committee found in 1990,[21] in a transfer of considerable power to federal prosecutors. Although this is a natural consequence of rigidly drafted guidelines, the situation has been more complex because of the uncertainty about sentencing discounts for guilty pleas. Nevertheless, early research found a significant degree of guideline evasion through plea bargaining.[22]

The federal guideline system has been subject to an extraordinarily voluminous amount of judicial and academic criticism, much of it predictable in view of the defects inherent in the original conception.[23] Much of the criticism concerned the tight constraints that it imposed on sentencers, and those have now been loosened by a series of Supreme Court decisions.[24] Among the state systems, the amount of flexibility and the breadth of ranges are usually greater than under the federal guidelines, and in some states considerably greater.[25]

Mandatory and Mandatory Minimum Sentences

One of the difficulties in US federal sentencing has been the increasing number of mandatory and mandatory minimum sentences for which Congress has legislated, adding to the restrictiveness of the guidelines themselves. Mandatory sentences have proved attractive to legislatures across the world in recent years, and examples are to be found in several jurisdictions such as South Africa,[26] Australia,[27] Canada,[28] and England and Wales.[29]

The proclaimed purposes of enacting mandatory (minimum) sentences are usually twofold—to reduce crime, through increased deterrence and public protection; and to reduce judicial discretion, so as to increase certainty of punishment. Are these objectives achievable by this technique? From the detailed study by Michael Tonry,[30] four principal problems can be identified. First, 'there is little basis for believing that mandatory penalties have any significant effects on rates of serious crimes'. This is a firm inference from the various US initiatives,[31] and one obvious reason is that low detection rates would tend to offset any expected increase in deterrent effect. In respect of drugs, an influential criminological view holds that other approaches which target a reduction of demand are likely to be far more effective in reducing crime rates than higher sentences. In respect of the 'serious offences' targeted by the mandatory minimum penalties enacted in England by the 1997 Crime (Sentences) Act, little evidence has been found that these penalties have a significant incapacitative effect.[32]

Secondly, mandatory sentences and mandatory minimum sentences have considerable potential for injustice: 'such laws sometimes result in the imposition of penalties in individual cases that everyone involved believes to be unjustly severe'. In this respect, much depends on whether the relevant legislation provides an 'escape clause' and, if so, whether it is narrow ('exceptional circumstances, 'substantial and compelling reasons') or broad ('unjust in all the circumstances'), although a broad escape clause would mean that the law is hardly mandatory.

Thirdly, the potential for injustice often leads prosecutors and judges to find ways of circumventing the mandatory provisions. The US studies cited by Tonry show all kinds of 'adaptive behaviour' by judges and others, in order to avoid outcomes which are agreed to be unjust. A more recent study of the Californian 'three strikes law' shows that it was applied in only 10 per cent of eligible cases.[33]

Fourthly, a related but distinct effect is that there are fewer guilty pleas where the penalty is mandatory. Thus Tonry reports that 'the U.S. Sentencing Commission found that trial rates were two-and-a-half times higher for offences bearing mandatory minima than for other offences', and there were similar effects in state jurisdictions. This both increases anxiety for victims and other witnesses, and acts as a further drain on resources in a criminal justice system already under strain. Some might be prepared to accept this if a substantial deterrent or incapacitative effect were likely to follow from the mandatory sentences: but, as we saw earlier, the prospects for this seem poor.

Despite these manifest weaknesses of mandatory sentencing, it continues to hold considerable political attraction for officials and legislators. Many US states have enacted mandatory or mandatory minimum sentences for drugs or gun offences. A number of these have introduced 'three strikes' laws, which impose a long mandatory sentence on those who commit a third felony. A constitutional challenge to the California statute was brought in *Lockyer v Andrade*,[34] arguing that a total of 50 years' imprisonment (twice 25 years) for two offences of theft involving a total of 11 blank videotapes was so disproportionate as to amount to 'cruel and unusual punishment'. The challenge failed.

Conclusions

Disparity of sentencing occurs when similar cases are dealt with differently, and where different cases are treated without reference to those differences. Whilst disparity is a manifest form of injustice, the choice of techniques to reduce disparity and to promote consistency is not a simple matter. Much will depend on the political climate and on the legal tradition of the country or state. Any sentencing reform should be formulated and promulgated in the most appropriate way for each jurisdiction, and it must be applied faithfully by the judiciary if it is to achieve its objectives.

Judicial self-regulation offers an excellent basis for the development of principles that are highly sensitive to the practical problems of sentencers and, because the guidance is in narrative form and emanates from other judges, it is likely to have the support of sentencers. As a technique of guidance, judicial self-regulation is likely to be best received in those jurisdictions where the appellate courts are experienced at delivering principled judgments. However, judicial self-regulation is not a suitable means for deciding and specifying the overall aims of sentencing, or for determining the policies to be pursued with respect to imprisonment, victims, and so on; whether it can deliver consistency of approach is debatable, and it is unlikely to be an effective engine of change.

On matters of overall policy, there is a need for both institutional change and a refinement in the techniques of guidance. The design of an appropriate machinery should be adjusted to the legal traditions of the jurisdiction, but there are strong arguments in favour of it being independent of the executive and the judiciary, and against it having an inbuilt judicial majority.[35] The question of the most appropriate technique for ensuring that sentencing complies with the rule of law principles also depends to some extent on legal traditions. In some countries the enactment of statutory principles, formulated after appropriately wide consultation and presented as a framework for judicial sentencing, will be helpful in bringing about consistency of approach. A firmer structure might be achieved through the kind of narrative guidelines, with sentencing tables, developed in England and Wales and proposed for New Zealand.[36] Greater control over sentencing decisions may be exerted through a numerical guideline system based on a sentencing grid, on what might be termed the Minnesota model, an approach that can be more or less restrictive and could be adapted so as to provide principled guidance without undue compulsion.

In 1992 the Council of Ministers of the Council of Europe approved a recommendation on 'Consistency of Sentencing' that sets out a number of principles for the structuring of sentencing in member states.[37] The first point is that legislation ought to articulate the basic principles of sentencing and, where more than one such principle is enunciated, it should state the order of priority among those principles. Whilst the Finnish, Swedish and English legislation complies with this recommendation—for example, the Swedish law allows deterrent sentencing for the offence of drink-driving while maintaining proportionality as the leading criterion elsewhere—other examples (such as Australia) show that legislatures sometimes proclaim several inconsistent principles without prescribing much in the way of an order of priority or separate spheres of application.[38] The Council of Europe's recommendations go on to declare various principles of sentencing: the principle of proportionality between the seriousness of the offence and the sentence, the principle of humanity, and the principle of non-discrimination. Perhaps the most innovative recommendation relevant to this chapter is set forth in the following passages from the Council's report:

[1] Wherever it is appropriate to the constitution and traditions of the legal system, some further techniques for enhancing consistency of sentencing should be considered.

[2] Two such techniques which have been used in practice are 'sentencing orientations' and 'starting points'.

[3] *Sentencing orientations* indicate ranges of sentence for different variations of an offence, according to the presence or absence of various aggravating or mitigating factors, but leave courts with the discretion to depart from the orientations.

[4] *Starting points* indicate a basic sentence for different variations of an offence, from which the court may move upwards or downwards so as to reflect aggravating and mitigating factors.

[5] In particular for frequently committed or less serious offences or offences which are otherwise suitable, consideration may be given to the introduction of some form of orientations or starting points for sentencing as an important step towards consistency in sentencing.

[6] Wherever it is appropriate to the constitution or the traditions of the legal system, one or more of the following means, among others, of implementing such orientations or starting points may be adopted:
  i) legislation;
  ii) guideline judgments by superior courts;
  iii) an independent commission;
  iv) Ministry circular;
  v) Guidelines for the prosecution.

The Council of Europe's recommendations proceed to deal with a range of issues, including previous convictions, custodial sentencing, aggravation and mitigation. But the above proposals on approaches to structuring sentencing, which studiously avoid any giving prominence to the term 'guidelines' because of its American association with numbers, deserve serious consideration.

Notes

1. See Aramah (1982) 4 *Criminal Appeal Reports (Sentencing)* 407.
2. Crime and Disorder Act 1998 (UK), ss 80–1.
3. For discussion of the details on the English system, see Wasik (2003, 2008) and Ashworth (2006).
4. Criminal Justice Act 2003 (UK), ss 167–73; for discussion, see the reference in n 6, and the critical appraisals in Tonry (2004), ch 5, and Ashworth (2005), 33–5 and 54–7.
5. This is to be found in SGC, *Causing Death by Driving* (definitive guideline, 2008). All guidelines, drafts and consultation papers from the SGC and SAP can be accessed at www.sentencing-guidelines.gov.uk.
6. SGC, *Robbery* (definitive guideline, 2006), 11.

7. SGC, *Assault and Other Offences Against the Person* (definitive guideline, 2008), 11.
8. *Ibid*, 10.
9. For the relevant English law, see Ashworth (2005), ch 4.
10. SGC, *Magistrates' Court Sentencing Guidelines* (definitive guideline, 2008).
11. Eg SGC, *Overarching Principles: Seriousness* (2004, currently under revision), and SGC, *Reduction in Sentence for a Guilty Plea* (revised guideline, 2007).
12. SGC, *New Sentences: Criminal Justice Act 2003* (definitive guideline, 2005).
13. For further details, see Jareborg (1995).
14. For the history and the experience of the early years, see Parent (1989).
15. For detailed analysis and discussion, see von Hirsch (1987).
16. See Knapp (1987).
17. For a survey and analysis of state guideline systems, see Frase (2005).
18. Frase (2005), 1220–1.
19. For another practical example, with greater detail, see the essay by Doob (1995), 218–26.
20. For discussion of issues relating to previous convictions, see Selection 4.6 above.
21. Federal Courts Study Committee (1990).
22. Schulhofer and Nagel (1990).
23. Among these, see eg the criticisms of Freed (1992), Doob (1995) and Tonry (1996).
24. The most important of these were *Blakely v Washington* (2004) 124 S Ct 2531 and *US v Booker* (2005) 125 S Ct 738. The literature on these decisions is enormous, but for assessments of the implications of the jurisprudence, see Reitz (2005) and Berman (2007).
25. Eg North Carolina, discussed by Wright (2002).
26. van Zyl Smit (2000).
27. Morgan (1999) and Warner (2007).
28. Crutcher (2001).
29. Ashworth (2005), 206–10.
30. Tonry (1996), ch 5, from which all quotations in this paragraph are taken.
31. *Ibid*.
32. For a careful study, see Hood and Shute (1996).
33. Zimring *et al* (2001).
34. (2003) 123 S Ct 1166; see also *Ewing v California* (2003) 123 S Ct 1179.
35. Tonry (2004), ch 5.
36. Young and Browning (2008).
37. Council of Europe (1993).
38. Eg the Sentencing Act 1991 in Victoria, Australia, discussed by Freiberg (1995).

References

Ashworth, A, (2005) *Sentencing and Criminal Justice*, 4th edn (Cambridge, Cambridge University Press).
—— (2006) 'The Sentencing Guideline System in England and Wales' 19 *South African Journal of Criminal Justice* 1.
Berman, DA, (2007) 'Claiborne and Rita—Booker Clean-up or Continued Confusion?' 19 *Federal Sentencing Reporter* 151.

Council of Europe (1993) *Consistency of Sentencing*, Recommendation No R (92) 17 (Strasbourg, Council of Europe).

Crutcher, N, (2001) 'Mandatory Minimum Penalties of Imprisonment: an Historical Analysis' 44 *Criminal Law Quarterly* 279.

Doob, A, (1995) 'The United States Sentencing Commission Guidelines' in C Clarkson and R Morgan (eds), *The Politics of Sentencing Reform* (Oxford, Oxford University Press).

Federal Courts Study Committee (1990) *Report* (Washington, DC, US Government Printer).

Frase, R, (2005) 'State Sentencing Guidelines: Diversity, Consensus and Unresolved Policy Issues' 105 *Columbia Law Review* 1190.

Freed, D.J, (1992) 'Federal Sentencing in the Wake of the Guidelines' 101 *Yale Law Journal* 1681.

Freiberg, A, (1995) 'Sentencing Reform in Victoria: a Case Study' in C Clarkson and R Morgan (eds), *The Politics of Sentencing Reform* (Oxford, Oxford University Press).

Hood, R and Shute, S, (1996) 'Protecting the Public: Automatic Life Sentences, Parole and High Risk Offenders' *Criminal Law Review* 788.

Jareborg, N, (1995) 'The Swedish Sentencing Reform' in C Clarkson and R Morgan (eds), *The Politics of Sentencing Reform* (Oxford, Oxford University Press).

Knapp, K, (1987) 'Implementation of the Minnesota Guidelines: Can the Innovative Spirit be Preserved?' in A von Hirsch, K Knapp and M Tonry (eds), *The Sentencing Commission and its Guidelines* (Boston, MA, Northeastern University Press).

Morgan, N, (1999) 'Capturing Crims or Capturing Votes? The Aims and Effects of Mandatories' 22 *University of New South Wales Law Review* 267.

Parent, DG, (1989) *Structuring Criminal Sentences* (Stoneham, MA, Butterworths).

Reitz, K, (2005) 'The New Sentencing Conundrum: Policy and Constitutional Law at Cross-Purposes' 105 *Columbia Law Review* 1082.

Schulhofer, S and Nagel, I, (1990) 'Negotiated Pleas under the Federal Sentencing Guidelines' 27 *American Criminal Law Review* 231.

Tonry, M, (1996) *Sentencing Matters* (New York, Oxford University Press).

—— (2004) *Punishment and Politics* (Cullompton, Willan).

Van Zyl Smit, D, (2000) 'Mandatory Sentences: a Conundrum for the New South Africa' 2 *Punishment and Society* 197.

Von Hirsch, A, (1987) 'Structure and Rationale: Minnesota's Critical Choices' in A von Hirsch, K Knapp and M Tonry (eds), *The Sentencing Commission and its Guidelines* (Boston, MA, Northeastern University Press).

Warner, K, (2007) 'Mandatory Sentencing and the Role of the Academic' 18 *Criminal Law Forum* 321.

Wasik, M, (2003) 'Sentencing Guidelines—Past, Present, and Future' 56 *Current Legal Problems* 239.

—— (2008) 'Sentencing Guidelines in England and Wales—State of the Art?' *Criminal Law Review* 253.

Wright, RF, (2002) 'Counting the Cost of Sentencing in North Carolina, 1980–2000' 29 *Crime and Justice* 39.

Young, W and Browning, C, (2008) 'New Zealand's Sentencing Council' *Criminal Law Review* 287.

Zimring, F, Hawkins, G and Kamin, J, (2001) *Punishment and Democracy: Three Strikes and You're Out* (New York, Oxford University Press).

6.3

The Swedish Sentencing Law

6.3(a) The Principles Underlying the New Law

ANDREW VON HIRSCH

[This first extract describes the principles underlying the Swedish reforms, and was written at the time when they were proposed. The actual law as enacted in 1988, which differs little from the proposals, is set out and explained in Selection 6.3(b)—eds.]

The Rise of Swedish "Neoclassicism"

In the decades after the Second World War, Sweden became internationally noted for its interest in penal rehabilitation. Actually, it did not go so far as foreigners imagined: the idea of a graded tariff of penalties retained considerable influence. Indeterminate sentences were used only for special offender categories, such as youthful offenders, and habitual criminals. The Swedish Penal Code did not have much to say on choice of sentence for offenders outside these narrow categories. It mentioned rehabilitation and general prevention in broad terms, but provided scant advice on how those aims should be implemented by the courts.

During the 1970s and 1980s, Sweden witnessed growing disenchantment with its law and conceptions of sentencing. The Penal Code, it was felt, gave insufficient guidance for choosing the sanction. It began to be recognized that only limited capacity exists to fashion sentences for rehabilitative effect. Questions were raised about the fairness of basing sanctions on supposed responsiveness to treatment or on likelihood of future offending. There was a strong revival of interest in the idea of proportionality—of punishments that fairly comport with the seriousness of the defendant's criminal conduct.

The new thinking received considerable stimulus with the publication in 1977 of A *New Penal System: Ideas and Proposals*.[1] This report, written for the Swedish National Council on Crime Prevention by a working group of judges and penologists, attracted widespread debate and comment. The report emphasized ideas of

From A von Hirsch, 'Guiding Principles for Sentencing: The Proposed Swedish Law' (1987) *Criminal Law Review* 746, with some textual changes.

structuring sentencing discretion and proportionate sanctions. Similar ideas—sometimes referred to as "neoclassical"— were echoed in an influential essay collection that appeared three years later. Such ideas continued to surface in the Swedish literature, affected in part by Finnish writings and by English-language writings on "just deserts".

Writing the Proposed Law

The Swedish neoclassicists' first success was in their campaign against the indeterminate sentence. We have, they asserted, neither the capacity to identify persons who are long-term risks nor the ability to treat such persons, that these measures assumed. Above all, they argued, indeterminacy was unfair, in its potential disregard of the seriousness of the offender's conduct in deciding whether and how long to confine. Indeterminate confinement for youths was abolished in 1979, and "internment" for adults eliminated in 1981.

The next step was to address the Penal Code's general provisions on sentencing. In 1979, the Swedish minister of justice appointed a study commission, the Committee on Imprisonment *(Fangelsestraffkommitten)* to examine the matter. The Committee issued its report, *Sanctions for Crimes,* six years later, in the spring of 1986. The report, among other things, recommended a lowering of the statutory maxima and minima for many crimes, an expansion of the system of unit fines, and changes in the rules on parole release. Its most notable proposal, however, concerned the principles governing the choice of sentence. The Committee put forward two wholly new draft chapters of the Penal Code, dealing with the subject. The chapters emphasize notions of proportionality in sentencing.

As is customary with study commissions in Sweden, the Committee circulated its proposals to a wide group of scholars, judges, prosecutors, lawyers, correctional administrators, union officials, and other interested parties. The provisions on choice of sentence received generally favourable comment—and early in 1987 the Ministry of Justice, after reviewing the responses, tentatively decided to support those proposals. Ministry support means that the proposed new chapters—after some technical amendments to reflect comments received—will became a government bill, with reasonably good chances for passage. [In fact they were enacted in 1988 and came into force in 1989: the key provisions are set out in Selection 6.3(b), which follows—eds.]

How Much Guidance?

The previous provisions of the Swedish Penal Code, as I mentioned, provided little guidance to sentencing judges. The so-called penalty scales (that is, the ranges between the statutory maxima and minima) were fairly wide, especially for the more serious crimes—albeit not as wide as they have been in the USA. The Penal Code provided that sentences should (1) promote general obedience to law and (2) foster the defendant's rehabilitation. It is far from clear, however, how the courts are to accomplish these potentially conflicting aims—especially given the paucity of effective treatments and the tenuous connection between general law-abidingness and the sentence in any particular case. The Code failed to suggest what features of the offender or his offence should ordinarily be given emphasis. And it left important issues unaddressed—especially, the issue of proportionality between the gravity of crimes and the severity of punishments. Guidance was thought necessary, therefore, to supply a coherent policy for sentencing: to help choose which penal aim should predominate, and thereby to help decide what features of the offender or his offence should be given most weight.

How much guidance should there be, and who should supply it? The Imprisonment Committee considered various solutions. At one extreme was the traditional English approach—of leaving the task of guidance to the appellate courts, without substantial assistance provided by statute or regulation. At the other was Minnesota's approach of a numerical sentencing grid that prescribes specific terms or narrow ranges as the normally recommended sentences. The Committee adopted an intermediate solution: the legislation should provide general principles but no numbers. The courts are then to apply those principles in deciding the quantum of sentence.

The Swedish Imprisonment Committee's proposals on choice of sentence consist, therefore of *principles*. The primary factors to be considered in deciding the sentence are set forth, not the actual sentencing outcomes. The proposed statute thus provides that the seriousness of the crime should be given principal emphasis, directs how seriousness ("penal value") should be judged, and gives general directives on the use of imprisonment and lesser sanctions. The numbers—the actual quanta of sentences—are to be evolved later by the courts. This is designed to permit the statute to focus on what is most important: the *policy*. The Imprisonment Committee's proposals offer a general policy: since the seriousness of the crime should count most, lesser offenders with long criminal records ordinarily should not receive the severe sanction of imprisonment. Such a general statute need not specifically address the extraordinary cases: what should happen if the offender's criminal record is extremely long—for instance, the case of the person convicted of a routine theft for the twentieth time. The courts would deal with such extraordinary cases, bearing the statute's general principles in mind. The drafters did not need to distort the general principles to supply a politically "acceptable" solution for the special cases.

Rationale

The proposed statute—as the Imprisonment Committee's report makes clear—rests on the idea of proportionality: that the offender's punishment should be fairly proportionate in its severity with the seriousness of the criminal conduct for which he stands convicted.

Why should punishments comport with the gravity of crimes? The idea of proportionate punishments presupposes no deep "metaphysical" notions of requital for evil or of guilt and atonement. There is, instead, a simpler explanation. Punishment is a *condemnatory* institution. The difference between a criminal and a civil sanction lies, generally, in the fact that the former levies censure on the actor. Penalties should, in fairness, be allocated consistently with their blaming implications.

Swedish neoclassicists tended also to feel that proportionality in punishment might serve general preventive aims. American and some English general preventionists have focused on deterrence, that is, the intimidating effect of punishment—a notion which may offer little support for principles of commensurability and desert. Scandinavian neoclassicists have taken a different tack: their discussion of general prevention focused on punishment's "moral" and "educational" effects in reinforcing people's inhibitions against criminal behaviour. People's sense of moral self-restraint, the authors of A *New Penal System* argued, might well be enhanced if they are treated as responsible for their conduct, and are sanctioned in a proportionate manner that reflects an ordinary persons sense of justice.

Penal Value

How, then, should proportionate sentences be determined? The proposal's central concept is that of a crime's penal value, and the draft begins with a general definition: "The penal value *(straffvarde)* of a crime is determined by its seriousness". To determine a crime's seriousness, the statute goes on to state, special regard should be given to (1) the harmfulness of the conduct and (2) the personal culpability of the actor. This definition—of seriousness in terms of the conduct's harm and culpability—is standard in the recent literature on desert.

Harm

That harm is an important element in a crime's seriousness should be obvious. Murder is more serious than assault because the harm characteristic of such conduct is greater: death instead of injury or attempted injury. Harm has always been important in determining the statutory penalty scales—which is why the legal maximum and minimum for murder are so much higher than those for assault. What the proposed law would do is to direct the judge to give more careful consideration to the conduct's harmfulness *within* the applicable scale: that is, to try to distinguish among types of assaults in terms of the degree of actual or potential injuriousness.

Giving harm this central role should stimulate the development of more sophisticated doctrines on how to assess harm.

Culpability

It is a peculiarity of the Swedish language that the word "culpability" does not exist. Hence the drafters had to resort to the more old-fashioned term "guilt". While the word "guilt" may for some readers evoke theological connotations, those are *not* intended. When the draft speaks of "the offender's guilt manifested in the conduct", it is *not* referring to an elusive evil state in the criminal's soul which the conduct reflects. The draft is referring, instead, to what in English would be denoted by the more neutral word culpability: the degree of intent, recklessness, or negligence involved, the presence of partial excuses, and so forth.

Criteria for Choice of Sanctions

The proposal sets forth, for the first time in Swedish law, criteria for the use of imprisonment. These criteria indicate when imprisonment ordinarily is to be imposed, in preference to the lesser sanctions of probation or conditional sentence. The criteria—when read together with the draft's other provisions—prescribe imprisonment in two main kinds of cases. The first is where the crime of conviction is serious: in the words of the draft, where it has "considerable penal value". The courts will have to assess which crimes thus qualify as serious, but crimes of violence such as armed robbery would be included, as would major economic offences. Those convicted of such crimes could expect to be imprisoned, unless they were able to establish mitigating circumstances indicating reduced culpability for the crime. The fact that the defendant was a first offender would *not* justify withholding imprisonment. The rationale is plain enough. If punishment is to reflect the gravity of the conduct, then the system's most severe type of sanction, imprisonment, becomes appropriate for the worst conduct.

The second type of case where imprisonment would be invoked concerns the criminal record. The Committee's proposals generally attempt to restrict the role of the prior record: serious offenders would be confined even if not previously convicted, and lesser offenders would be given noncustodial sanctions even if recidivists. However, the prior record would continue to play a role with respect to offences in the middle range of seriousness, such as, perhaps, burglary. Offenders convicted of such crimes would ordinarily be imprisoned only after having accumulated a significant criminal record.

The draft contains parallel provisions on the use of non-custodial penalties. The fine would continue to be the sanction most extensively utilized. It would be the sanction of choice for crimes of low penal value. It would also be so for crimes of intermediate penal value except where the defendant's prior criminal record was extensive. The more substantial fines would be unit fines, scaled according to the offender's income.

Between the fine, below, and actual imprisonment, above, would be the two other alternatives—conditional sentence and probation. To ensure that these sanctions are more onerous than a fine alone, they could be supplemented by monetary penalties.

Supplementary Principles

A few other provisions of the proposed statute are worth noting:
1. The draft contains a list of aggravating and mitigating circumstances, as noted already. These are generally desert-related—concerning increased or decreased harm or culpability of the conduct.
2. The draft calls also for reduced sanctions when special circumstances make the penalty uncharacteristically onerous. Ill health or advanced age are included. So, more controversially, are situations where specially adverse employment consequences are involved. The rationale still is one of proportionality—these questions bear (albeit indirectly) on the severity of the sanction. The employment provision may present problems of implementation, however, since punishment can so readily have employment consequences.
3. The draft authorizes deterrent penalties (in excess of what the conduct's penal value would indicate) for certain crimes, such as drinking and driving. This authorization, however, is restricted to conduct which the Swedish Parliament has found (a) to have unusually harmful consequences and (b) to be more than usually amenable to deterrence. The imposition of such sanctions is treated as a departure from the normal standards, for which a special burden of justification must be met.

These supplemental principles would permit the court to address, in sophisticated fashion, a variety of issues that have long been of concern to courts in other countries. Only now, the applicable principles would be spelled out, and would reflect a consistent set of purposes. Mitigation of sentence, for example, would no longer have to be treated ad hoc. Instead, the courts would have statutory guidance in developing coherent doctrines of extenuation.[3]

Notes

1. Brottsforebyggande Radet, NyK *Straffsystem: Ideer och Forslag* (1977). For english summary, National Swedish Council for Crime Prevention: *A New Penal System: Ideas and Proposals* (1978).
2. For discussion of such hybrid systems, see Selection 4.4 above.

3.   For discussion of the implementation of the statute since enactment, and for further detail on the law itself, see Nils Jareborg, "The Swedish Sentencing System", in C. M. V. Clarkson and R. Morgan, *The Politics of Sentencing Reform* (Oxford: Clarendon, 1995).

6.3(b) The Details of the New Law

ANDREW VON HIRSCH AND NILS JAREBORG

The proposed Swedish law, with certain changes, was enacted in June 1988, to take effect in the following year. The statute consists of two main parts. Chapter 29 addresses "punishments". In Swedish legal tradition, only two sanctions are termed "punishments": fines and imprisonment. Where an offender qualifies for a fine, only the provisions of this chapter apply. If the case is somewhat more serious and a fine alone is not appropriate, then the reader must turn also to the next chapter, chapter 30. This chapter addresses the choice between (1) actual imprisonment and (2) substitutes for imprisonment—viz., conditional sentence or probation.

The statute thus creates three graded levels of sanction. The lower level is the fine—which includes unit fines levied as a proportion of income. The next level is conditional sentence or probation—which may be supplemented by monetary penalties. The highest level is incarceration in a penal institution.

The distinctions are significant, because the statute becomes confusing when they are overlooked. There are, for example *two* provisions governing prior criminal record. Chapter 29, § 4, addresses how prior record affects the choice between fines and imprisonment and how it affects the amount of fines or imprisonment. Chapter 30, § 4, governs how prior record affects the choice between probation or conditional sentence and actual imprisonment.

Swedish legal tradition permits (indeed, requires) the courts to consult legislative history in interpreting a statute. The statute, therefore, needs to be read in the light of the report of the Committee on Imprisonment, and of the Ministry of Justice's report accompanying submission of the bill. Those texts clarify certain language that may appear ambiguous on the statute's face:

1. Reasons for Imprisonment (Chap. 30, § 4). This section addresses the choice between imprisonment and its substitute sanctions, probation and conditional sanction. It has applicability, therefore, only to the higher-ranking offences—for which fines would not be the sanction of choice. For these crimes, according to the section's second paragraph, imprisonment may be invoked in three kinds of situations. The first is where the crime has a high penal value—that is, is quite serious—

From A von Hirsch and N Jareborg, 'Sweden's Sentencing Statute Enacted' (1989) *Criminal Law Review* 275, with some textual changes.

irrespective of whether the offender has a record. The second is where the penal value (seriousness) is of the upper-middle range (that is, high enough to preclude a fine alone) and the person has a significant criminal record. The third (referred to by the "nature of the criminality" clause) is a restricted authorization for deterrent penalties for certain crimes—an important instance being drinking and driving.

2. *Predicted Risk.* (chap. 30, § 7). The statute generally rules out predictive sentencing: proportionality is sacrificed when those defendants who seem good risks are given substantially less punishment than equally culpable offenders who seem bad risks. The objection diminishes, however, when prediction is used to change the character of the penalty but not its severity by much. This provision thus allows the sentencing judge, when choosing between a conditional sentence and probation, to opt for conditional sentence—if the offender appears unlikely to offend again. Probation with its supervision of the offender, may be unnecessary for low-risk offenders—and is not much more severe than a conditional sentence. However, this provision is *not* intended to permit the court to substitute conditional sentence for imprisonment on predictive grounds, as those sanctions differ so greatly in their severity.

Changes in the Final Version of the Law

The law, as proposed by the Ministry of Justice and enacted by the Swedish Parliament, contains certain changes from the recommendations of the Committee on Imprisonment (described in Selection 5.3 (a) above). However, those changes are of limited scope.

1. *Definition of "Penal Value"* (chap. 29, § 1). The seriousness of a crime depends on the harmfulness (or risk of harm) of the conduct and the culpability of the actor. The Swedish language lacks the term "culpability", so the Committee on Imprisonment used the old-fashion term "guilt". That term's connotations evoked objections, so the law has substituted, "What the accused realized or should have realized . . . and the intentions and motives of the accused". However, no substantive change is intended, and the idea remains what is denoted in English by "culpability".

2. *Prior Record* (chap. 29, § 4). The Committee on Imprisonment proposed narrow restrictions on considering the criminal record. For upper-middle level crimes, as noted, a criminal record would be grounds for invoking actual imprisonment, instead of conditional sentence or probation. It would also affect the severity of fines. However, the record could not be used to affect the duration of imprisonment. The Ministry's proposals, and the statute as enacted, have relaxed this latter restriction, so that the record could affect the duration of imprisonment to a limited degree.

3. *Rehabilitation* (chap. 30, § 9). The Committee on Imprisonment's draft authorized reduction of sentence in situations where "through the offender's own efforts,

a considerable improvement has occurred in his personal and social situation that bears on his criminality". The intention, apparently, was to qualify the statute's general emphasis on proportionality, in order to permit treatment-based sentences in the most plausible and sympathetic-seeking kind of case, viz., where the change was wrought by efforts of the offender himself or herself. The enacted version eliminates the reference to the offender's own efforts. The legislative history, however, makes clear that any departures from the statute's proportionality requirements on rehabilitative grounds should be quite sparingly invoked.

The Statute

The text of the statute is as follows:

"Chapter 1   *On Crimes and Sanctions* . . .

§ 3 In this code, sanctions for crime are the punishments of fine and imprisonment, as well as conditional sentence, probation, and commitment to special care . . .

§ 5 Imprisonment is to be regarded as a more severe punishment than a fine.
   The relation between imprisonment and conditional sentence and probation is regulated in chapter 30, § 1.

§ 6 No one may be sentenced to a sanction for a crime he committed before he has reached fifteen years of age . . .

Chapter 29   *On the Measurement of Punishment and Remission of Sanctions*

§ 1 The punishment shall be imposed within the statutory limits according to the penal value of the crime or crimes, and the interest of uniformity in sentencing shall be taken into consideration.
   The penal value is determined with special regard to the harm, offence, or risk which the conduct involved, what the accused realized or should have realized about it, and the intentions and motives of the accused.

§ 2 Apart from circumstances specific to particular types of crime, the following circumstances, especially, shall be deemed to enhance the penal value:

1. whether the accused intended that the criminal conduct should have considerably worse consequences than it in fact had,
2. whether the accused has shown a special degree of indifference to the conduct's adverse consequences,
3. whether the accused made use of the victim's vulnerable position, or his other special difficulties in protecting himself,
4. whether the accused grossly abused his rank or position or grossly abused a special trust,

5. whether the accused induced another person to participate in the deed through force, deceit, or abuse of the latter's youthfulness, lack of understanding, or dependent position, or

6. whether the criminal conduct was part of a criminal activity that was especially carefully planned, or that was executed on an especially large scale and in which the accused played an important role.

§ 3 Apart from what is elsewhere specifically prescribed, the following circumstances, especially, shall be deemed to diminish the penal value:

1. whether the crime was elicited by another's grossly offensive behaviour,

2. whether the accused, because of mental abnormality or strong emotional inducement or other cause, had a reduced capacity to control his behaviour,

3. whether the accused's conduct was connected with his manifest lack of development, experience, or capacity for judgement, or

4. whether strong human compassion led to the crime.

The court may sentence below the statutory minimum when the penal value obviously calls for it.

§ 4 Apart from the penal value, the court shall, in measuring the punishment, to a reasonable extent take the accused's previous criminality into account, but only if this has not been appropriately done in the choice of sanction (see chap. 30, § 4) or revocation of parole (see chap. 34, §4). In such cases, the extent of the previous criminality and the time that has passed between the crimes shall be especially considered, as well as whether the previous and the new criminality is similar, or whether the criminality in both cases is especially serious.

§5 In determining the punishment, the court shall to a reasonable extent, apart from the penal value, consider

1. whether the accused as a consequence of the crime has suffered serious bodily harm,

2. whether the accused according to his ability has tried to prevent, or repair, or mitigate the harmful consequences of the crime,

3. whether the accused voluntarily gave himself up,

4. whether the accused is, to his detriment, expelled from the country in consequence of the crime,

5. whether the accused as a consequence of the crime has experienced or is likely to experience discharge from employment or other disability or extraordinary difficulty in the performance of his work or trade,

6. whether a punishment imposed according to the crime's penal value would affect the accused unreasonably severely, due to advanced age or bad health,

7. whether, considering the nature of the crime, an unusually long time has elapsed since the commission of the crime, or

8. whether there are other circumstances that call for a lesser punishment than the penal value indicates.

If, in such cases, special reasons so indicate, the punishment may be reduced below the statutory minimum.

§ 6 The punishment is to be remitted entirely when, with regard to circumstances of the kind mentioned in § 5, imposition of a sanction is manifestly unreasonable.

§ 7 If someone has committed a crime before the age of 21, his youth shall be considered separately in the determination of the punishment, and the statutory minimum may be disregarded.

Life imprisonment is never to be imposed in such cases.

Chapter 30   *On the Choice of Sanctions*

§1 In choosing sanctions, imprisonment is considered as more severe than conditional sentence and probation.

Provisions on the use of commitment to special care are set forth in another chapter.

§ 2 Unless otherwise provided, no one is to receive more than one sanction for the same crime.

§ 3 Unless otherwise provided, someone convicted of more than one crime is to be given one sanction.

If there are special reasons, however, the court may combine a fine for some criminal conduct with another sanction for other conduct, or combine imprisonment for some conduct with conditional sentence or probation for other conduct.

§ 4 In choosing the sanction, the court shall especially pay need to circumstances that suggest a less severe sanction than imprisonment. In so doing, the court shall consider circumstances referred to in chapter 29, § 5.

As a reason for imprisonment the court may consider, besides the penal value and the nature of the criminality, the accused's previous criminality.

§ 5 For a crime committed by someone before the age of 18, imprisonment may be imposed only if there are extraordinary reasons.

For a crime committed by someone between the age of 18 and the age of 21, imprisonment may be imposed only if there are, with respect to the penal value of the crime or other grounds, special reasons.

§ 6 For a crime committed by someone under the influence of mental disease, mental deficiency, or other mental abnormality of such a substantial nature as to be comparable to mental disease, the court may only impose commitment to special care, a fine, or probation.

If no such commitment or sanction should be imposed, the accused shall be free from sanction.

§ 7 In choosing sanction, the court shall consider, as a reason for conditional sentence, whether there is no special reason to fear that the accused will relapse in criminal conduct.

§ 8 Conditional sentence shall be combined with day fines, unless a fine would be unduly harsh, considering the other consequences of the crime, or there are other special reasons that militate against imposition of a fine.

§9 In choosing sanction, the court shall consider, as a reason for probation, whether there is reason to suppose that such sanction can contribute to the accused's not committing crimes in the future.

   As special reasons for probation the court may consider.

> 1. whether a considerable improvement has occurred in the accused's personal or social situation that bears upon his criminality,
> 2. whether the accused is being treated for abuse or other condition that bears upon his criminality, or
> 3. whether abuse of addictive substances, or other special condition that calls for care or other treatment, to a considerable degree explains the criminal conduct and the accused has declared himself willing to undergo adequate treatment, in accordance with an individual plan that can be arranged in connection with the execution of the sentence.

§ 10 In judging whether probation should be combined with day fines, the court shall consider whether this is called for with regard to the penal value or nature of the criminal conduct or the accused's previous criminality.

§ 11 Probation may be combined with imprisonment only if it is unavoidably called for, with regard to the penal value of the criminal conduct or the accused's previous criminality . . .

Chapter 34 Certain Provisions concerning Concurrence of Crimes and Change of Sanction

§ 4 ... In judging whether parole should be revoked and in deciding on duration of reconfinement on revocation, it shall be considered whether the previous criminality and the new criminality are similar, whether the criminality in both cases is serious, and whether the new criminality is more or less serious than the previous criminality. In addition, the time that has passed between the crimes shall be considered.

6.4

Sentencing Policy Development under the Minnesota Sentencing Guidelines

RICHARD S FRASE

Introduction to Minnesota Guidelines Sentencing

This part of the chapter introduces Minnesota and its Guidelines system by explaining the political and social climate of the State, the overall structure of Minnesota's sentencing laws, and the scope and operation of the Guidelines.

The Political and Social Context

Since the 1970s Minnesota has generally been a politically liberal State, consistently voting Democratic in Presidential elections, but it has become considerably more moderate in recent years (for example, the three Governors elected since 1990 have all been Republicans or Independents). In the late 1970s, when the Guidelines were formulated and implemented, the State's political culture was described as one in which "citizens tended to view government as a means to achieve a good community through positive political action" (Martin, 1984, p 28). The consensus needed to achieve major sentencing reform was facilitated by Minnesota's relatively small population (about four million in 1970), its substantial degree of ethnic and cultural homogeneity (98 per cent of the State population in 1970 was White, mostly of northern European ancestry) and its "tradition of citizen participation in government, including the involvement of interest groups in policymaking" (Martin, 1984, pp 28–9). Reform consensus – and in particular, the decision to delegate guidelines formulation to an independent sentencing commission – was further encouraged by the Legislature's tradition (up to that time, at least) of non-partisanship with respect to criminal justice policy issues (Martin, 1984, p 61 n 180). Political and public consensus may also have been facilitated by the moderate tone of the State's principal news media. Neither of the two papers with State-wide circulation can be characterised as a "tabloid" although these papers do occasionally publish sensational crime stories and features.

Adapted from A Freiberg and K Gelb (eds), *Penal Populism, Sentencing Councils and Sentencing Policy* (Cullompton, Willan Publishing, 2008). References and endnotes omitted.

Sentencing reform consensus and moderation have also been encouraged by the generally non-partisan nature of Minnesota's judicial system. Judges serve six-year terms and run for election or re-election without political party endorsement (Martin, 1984, p 30). In practice, most judges are initially appointed by the Governor to fill an unexpired term and then are routinely re-elected in uncontested elections; they usually retire during their terms so that their successors can likewise be appointed. Chief prosecutors in each county are also chosen in non-partisan elections, but (unlike judges and public defenders) they are "a well-organised and active political force" (Martin, 1984, p 30).

Although Minnesota's population remains quite homogeneous in comparison to others in the United States, the State has become much more ethnically diverse since the 1970s. Minnesota's Black population more than tripled from 1980 to 2000 (Frase, 2005b, p 201) and there have also been major increases in the State's Asian population, due primarily to an influx of refugees after the end of the Vietnam war. The State has relatively few Hispanic residents (less than 4 per cent in 2005, compared to over 14 per cent for the nation: Frase, 2006b). The growing diversity of Minnesota's population is reflected in the State's criminal case loads: from 1981 to 2005 the proportion of non-Hispanic Whites among convicted felons declined from 82 per cent to 62 per cent, and there were substantial increases in all non-White categories except American Indians – Blacks increased from 11 per cent in 1981 to 24 per cent in 2005; Hispanics went from 1.6 to 5.5 per cent; and Asians went from 0.2 to 2.0 per cent (Minnesota Sentencing Guidelines Commission, 2006c, p 10).

Minnesota was a low-incarceration State in the 1970s and remains so today. In 1978, when the Guidelines enabling statute was enacted, Minnesota's State prison incarceration rate was 49 per 100,000 State residents; Massachusetts had the same rate, and only two States had lower rates (Bureau of Justice Statistics, 1980, p 4). By 2005 Minnesota's prison rate had risen to 180 per 100,000, but the State still had the second lowest rate in the country (Bureau of Justice Statistics, 2006b, p 4). Minnesota's low prison incarceration rate is due in part to its relatively low rate of violent crime and also to the State's heavy use of local jail sentences. However, even when jail inmates are included, Minnesota's total incarceration rate (300 per 100,000 residents) is still the second lowest in the nation (Bureau of Justice Statistics, 2006a, p 9).

Overview of Minnesota Sentencing Laws

There have been many changes in Minnesota's Guidelines and other sentencing laws since 1980, but the general features of the sentencing system have remained the same. The following overview is therefore focused on the current Guidelines (Minnesota Sentencing Guidelines Commission, 2006a) and laws to provide a framework for the historical and contemporary material presented in later parts of this chapter.

The Guidelines apply to all felonies except those punishable with life in prison (the most serious murder and rape offences). For lesser crimes (misdemeanours and gross misdemeanours, punishable with maximum terms of 90 days and one year, respectively), there are no guidelines, and judges retain full sentencing discretion.

As to felonies (all of which are punishable by statute with State prison sentences of more than one year), the Guidelines specify the recommended sentences that are presumed to be correct for most cases. These recommendations include both the duration of imprisonment and the "disposition" – whether the prison term should be executed (immediately carried out) or stayed (suspended); in the latter case the offender is normally placed on probation under various conditions, which may include confinement in a local jail or workhouse for up to one year. The Guidelines provide some general, non-binding policies but no specific guidelines concerning the conditions of a stayed sentence or subsequent decisions to revoke the stay.

Except for life sentences, there is no parole release discretion and prison terms may be reduced only by earned good time (up to a one-third reduction of the prison term). Some life sentences are without possibility of parole. For parole-eligible offenders, release is decided by the Department of Corrections (Minnesota Statutes Chapters 243, 244), not a separate parole board, and there is no public membership on the decision-making body. The Department holds hearings on parole release issues that the victim (or if deceased, the victim's spouse or next of kin) may attend. Parole-eligible murderers may not be released until the offender has served 30 years; the minimum terms for life sentences in rape cases are determined by the Guidelines (prison term, less earned good time) and a few mandatory minimum statutes. Subject to these limits, parole release is discretionary and there are no guidelines for these decisions. However, the paroling authorities are directed to consider community sentiments toward the inmate at the time of offence and of proposed release (Minnesota Statutes Section 244.05 Subdivision 5(b)).

How the Guidelines Work

Recommended Guidelines sentences are based primarily on two factors: the severity of the offender's most serious current offence and the number and type of .prior convictions. The specific recommendations are contained in two grids, one for sex offenders and one for all other felons. Offence severity (the vertical axis, with 11 severity levels on the main grid) is based on the Commission's own rank-order assessments of crime seriousness. The defendant's criminal history score (the horizontal axis, with seven columns on the main grid) consists primarily of previous felony convictions which are weighted by their severity levels (for example, two points for each prior conviction at level nine or higher; half a point each for convictions at levels one and two); limited additional points are added for prior misdemeanour convictions, juvenile delinquency adjudications, and "custody status" (whether the offender was in custody or on some form of conditional release at the time of the current offence).

The Guidelines specify the sentence that is presumed to be correct for each combination of offence severity and criminal history. Judges may "depart" from the presumptive sentence only if they cite "substantial and compelling circumstances". Offenders with low to medium criminal history scores convicted of lower severity offences presumptively receive a stayed (suspended) prison term of a specified number of months; for more serious offences or criminal history scores, the presumptive sentence is an executed prison term within a specified range. Defendants with executed prison terms serve their entire term, less a credit of up to one-third for good conduct in prison. The boundary between presumptive stayed and presumptive executed prison terms is shown on the grid by a heavy black line (the "disposition line"). Cases in the shaded area below the line have presumptive stayed sentences (except for a few cases – mostly involving recidivists or the use of a dangerous weapon – that are subject to mandatory minimum prison terms provided in State statutes).

Additional rules specify permissible and impermissible bases for departure from presumptive disposition and durational rules. In extreme cases, upward durational departures may go all the way up to the statutory maximum prison term for the offence. The prosecution and defence each have the right to appeal the sentence, on the grounds that the departure (or refusal to depart) was improper. Finally, the Guidelines suggest a wide variety of possible conditions of stayed prison sentences, which judges may select in their discretion: up to one year of confinement in a local jail or workhouse; treatment (residential or out-patient); home detention (with or without electronic monitoring); probation (with "intensive", regular or no supervision); fines; restitution; victim-offender mediation; and community service. In felony cases the duration of the stay (that is, the length of probation) may be any period up to the maximum prison term that could have been imposed, or four years, whichever is longer.

The Commission's Early Work

In carrying out its statutory mandate, the Minnesota Sentencing Guidelines Commission made several critical policy decisions. One of the earliest decisions was to adopt a "prescriptive" rather than a "descriptive" approach to guidelines development (Minnesota Sentencing Guidelines Commission, 1980, pp 2–3; 1984, pp v, 8–14) – the Guidelines were not designed simply to model past judicial and parole decisions (or the average of those decisions). Although prior practices were studied and taken into account as required by the enabling statute, the Commission made a number of independent decisions about which offenders ought to go to prison and for how long, and what the primary purposes of punishment ought to be. The Commission's most important prescriptive changes in pre-existing sentencing policy related to the following issues:

1. Identification and prioritising of permissible sentencing purposes under the Commission's "modified just deserts" theory (Minnesota Sentencing Guidelines Commission, 1980, p 9) – sentencing was to be proportional to both offence severity and the seriousness of the offender's prior conviction record.
2. Rejection of "real-offence" sentencing. Recommended prison commitment and duration rules, and suggested departure criteria, were based almost entirely on elements of the crime or crimes of conviction and the offender's prior conviction record (Parent & Frase, 2005, pp 13-14).
3. Rank-ordering of offence severity based on the Commission's own sense of the seriousness of each crime (Minnesota Sentencing Guidelines Commission, 1980, pp 6-7).
4. Definition and weighting of criminal history. In particular, the Commission gave limited weight to prior juvenile felony-level adjudications and to prior adult misdemeanour and gross misdemeanour convictions (Minnesota Sentencing Guidelines Commission, 1980, p 7).
5. Recognition of the goal of socio-economic as well as racial and gender neutrality. The Commission explicitly prohibited consideration of the defendant's education, marital status, and employment status at the time of the offence or at sentencing (Minnesota Sentencing Guidelines Commission, 2006a, Section 1(1)), even though employment at sentencing had been a significant factor in prior court decisions when choosing whether to impose prison or probation (referred to in Minnesota as "dispositional" decisions) (Minnesota Sentencing Guidelines Commission, 1980, p 5).
6. Explicit prioritising of prison use – in particular, sending more low-criminal history "person" offenders to prison and fewer recidivist property offenders (Minnesota Sentencing Guidelines Commission, 1980, pp 9–10, 15; 1984, pp 10–14, 21).
7. Matching sentencing severity with prison capacity. The Commission gave great weight to the statutory directive to take existing correctional resources into substantial consideration; accordingly, the Guidelines were designed to produce State prison populations that remained well within (no more than 95 per cent of) current and projected (fully funded) prison capacity. A detailed, computerised projection model was developed and used throughout the drafting process to test the expected prison population that would result from each proposed guidelines rule or procedure. The Commission's "capacity constraint" and its prison population projections forced members of the Commission, as well as outside constituencies and interest groups, to confront the reality of limited prison resources and the need to set priorities in the use of those resources; any member, constituency or interest group that proposed greater severity for one group of offenders was asked to identify other offenders who could receive correspondingly reduced severity (Martin, 1984, pp 46, 54 n 150, 101, 104; Parent, 1988, pp 6–7, 40-5, 92–3). Minnesota was the first jurisdiction to use this approach, which became feasible due to the greater predictability of guidelines sentencing.

This policy has helped Minnesota to avoid the problems of prison overcrowding that have plagued most other jurisdictions in the United States in the past several decades. Resource-matching policies were subsequently adopted in some form by almost all State guidelines systems, and the capacity to implement such a policy has become one of the most important reasons leading States to adopt guidelines sentencing (Frase, 1995, p 175).

8. Preference for guidelines rules that are simple to apply and narrow in scope. The Commission recognised that highly complex sentencing rules are difficult for the public and offenders to understand, more costly and time-consuming for practitioners to apply and likely to produce error and new forms of disparity (Frase, 2005b, pp 132, 206). The Commission also chose not to exercise its option to develop guidelines for non-prison sentences (although it did make a number of non-binding recommendations as to such sentences), and it also did not develop, or request a mandate to develop, guidelines for probation revocation, charging and plea bargaining, and misdemeanour sentencing (Frase, 2005b, pp 209–10).

The Evolution of the Guidelines

Since their inception in 1980 there have been many changes in the Minnesota Guidelines and related sentencing laws, although the basic structure and operation of the Guidelines remain the same. As I have discussed at greater length in prior writings (Frase, 1997; 2005b), the mix of purposes under Minnesota's hybrid, "modified just deserts" approach has shifted somewhat; greater emphasis is now being given to crime-control purposes and individualised assessments of risk and amenability to treatment, with a corresponding decrease in emphasis on retributive and uniformity goals. The Guidelines and related laws have become more complex, but remain fairly easy to apply. The goal of matching sentencing policy to available correctional resources is still given substantial weight; Guidelines sentencing remains sufficiently predictable to permit accurate forecasts of resource impacts, and the Commission and the Legislature take these forecasts seriously and tailor their proposals to limit State and local resource impacts. As a result, the State's prison population, although growing rapidly, has grown more slowly than in many other States over the past 26 years and has almost always remained within rated capacity.

6.5

Institutional Consistency: Appeal Court Judgements

CYRUS TATA

Scholars of legal doctrine have been concerned to describe and explain the use of sentencing discretion by analysing Appeal Court Judgements. This has been a rich source of academic commentary and the attempt to try to extract more general even universal 'principles' about how sentencing can and should operate. Indeed, over the last 15 years or so the Court of Appeal of England and Wales may arguably have begun to try to present some kind of observable jurisprudence of sentencing involving 'Guideline' judgements intended to provide sentencers with starting points in similar cases (Thomas 1995). However, two main inter-related limitations of this method to explain and enhance the structure of sentencing discretion have been identified. These two limitations are: weak impact of Appeal Court judgements on first instance sentencing, and secondly, deficiency in principled coherence ofAppeal Court behaviour.

Limitation one: weak impact of appeal court decisions on first instance sentencing Ascertaining knowledge about the influence of Appeal Court 'policy' on first instance sentencing practice is problematic. Although Appeal Court judgements are collated together with academic commentaries in sentencing texts (e.g. Nicholson 1992; Walker and Padfield 1996; Kelly 1993), or, as part of an on-going digest, these are essentially case-by-case presentations of Appeal Court sentencing rather than 'normal'sentencing practice in 'similar cases'. For example, commenting on Thomas' sagacity about the England and Wales Court of Appeal, von Hirsch (1987, p. 194) carefully observed that it is "not certain to what extent trial courts and magistrates actually follow the Court of Appeal's opinions in unappealed cases, and the extent of such compliance or non-compliance has not been systematically measured". More recently, Ashworth (1998) notes that there has been no research into the effectiveness of the England & Wales Court of Appeal Guidelines in fostering consistency of approach with Appeal Court Guidance. Although Tonry (2001, p. 24) generously concedes that "many English judges and informed observers believe that guideline judgements do influence sentencing patterns", he has to point out that "there is no credible evaluation literature" of their impact.

From C Tata and N Hutton (eds), *Sentencing and Society: International Perspectives* (Aldershot, Ashgate Publishing, 2002). References omitted.

However, there are a number of reasons to expect that compliance is limited. First, Appeal Courts are reluctant to 'interfere' with first instance sentencing even if that original sentence is not one which the Appeal Court itself would have imposed. Writing about sentencing in Canada, Brodeur (1989, p. 28) has observed that ". . . unless a Court of Appeal sees reason at least to double the sentence or cut it by half, it will generally uphold the decision of the trial judge". Similarly, Doob (1990, p. 10) noted that Appeal Court judges try not to "tamper with sentences unless they are more than twice as long or less than half as long as they should be". In the South African context, Hutton (1998, p. 320) suggests that the previous reluctance of the Appeal Court to intervene in a first instance sentence, unless it was held to be "shocking or startlingly inappropriate" is unlikely to change under the new regime.

Secondly, Doob (1990, p. 10) shows that this reluctance to 'interfere' (which is meshed with individual judicial 'ownership' of sentencing), can easily provide sentencers with a false sense of security. Appeal Court permissiveness encourages first instance sentencers to draw a false comfort in the conclusion that because very few of his/her sentences are appealed, and even fewer successfully, the sentencer is 'in line' with normal practice (e.g. Tata and Hutton 1998).

Thirdly, given their sense of distance from the Appeal Court and the unlikelihood of appeal first instance sentencers may not necessarily wish to emulate the view of the Appeal Court, if it is believed by first instance sentencers to lead to substantive injustice.

Fourthly, Guideline Judgements in England and Wales, (the jurisdiction to have pursued the technique with more vigour than any other), are very limited in scope. They remain "clustered around serious offences which tend to attract substantial prison sentences" rather than areas of everyday sentencing - notably burglary, theft etc. (Ashworth 2001, p. 74).

Limitation two: deficient in 'principled coherence' A second main limitation has been popularised by academic criminal lawyers who have advocated greater systematisation and coherence in Appeal Court decision-making (e.g. Henham 1995, 1996; 1998b; Ashworth 1995; Fox 1994). Appeal Courts in common law jurisdictions have tended to stress the limits of extrapolation of the judgement to other cases. Either it is argued that the judgement cannot be compared with other cases; or, in 'leading' or 'guideline' judgements the court has said that a tariff can be established but that it can only apply when cases share the specific combination of 'facts'. The fundamental problem with this approach is in the inherent interpretability of legal 'facts' (Ashworth et al. 1984). Thus as long as Appeal Courts hold to the fiction that because each individual case is unique (in some sense) therefore sentencing each case is a 'unique' exercise, first instance sentencing will elude attempts to systematise the extrapolation of Appeal Court Guideline.

On the basis of Appeal Court (including 'Guideline') Judgements, it tends to be difficult to identify clearly any overall systematic pattern, or, attempt to structuring of sentencing overall. Academic lawyers have repeatedly called for greater overall coherence based on some kind principled reasoning (e.g. Ashworth 1995; Henham 1995, 1996; Fox 1994; Stith and Cabranes 1998). Yet, why does this incoherence of Appeal Court Judgements persist? The conventional explanation is that incoherence is due to a lack of penal philosophical consensus: different judges pursuing diverging penal philosophies. However, this hypothesis cannot, in itself, fully explain the lack of philosophical coherence in a single Appeal Court judgement, or, indeed the diverging philosophies expressed by a single judge from one case to another.

6.6

Criticisms of Mandatory Minimums

CASSIA SPOHN

Although the primary objection to mandatory penalties, particularly those for drug offenses, is their excessive severity, opponents also criticize their inflexibility. They charge that mandatory statutes turn Judges into sentencing machines: The type of drug plus the amount of drugs equals the sentence. As noted above, in sentencing a defendant convicted of an offense carrying a mandatory minimum sentence, the Judge is not supposed to consider anything other than the type and amount of drugs involved. Thus, "It matters not at all whether the offender is a 17-year-old transporting drugs from one location to another (a 'mule'), the battered girlfriend of a small-time distributor, or a genuine 'drug kingpin.'" State and federal Judges echo these criticisms (see Box 6.2). Large majorities disapprove of mandatory minimums, want mandatory penalties for drug offenses eliminated, and support changes designed to increase the discretion of the Judge.

Critics also charge that mandatory minimum sentencing statutes, like presumptive sentencing guidelines, shift discretion from the sentencing judge to the prosecutor. Because sentencing for offenses carrying mandatory penalties is, by definition, nondiscretionary and because the application of a mandatory minimum sentence depends on conviction for a charge carrying a mandatory penalty, prosecutors, not judges, determine what the ultimate sentence will be. If, in other words, a defendant is convicted of a drug offense carrying a mandatory minimum sentence of 5 years in prison, the judge's hands are tied: He or she must impose the mandatory 5-year term. The prosecutor, on the other hand, is not required to charge the defendant with the drug offense carrying the mandatory term. If the prosecutor does file the charge, he or she can reduce it to an offense without a mandatory penalty if the defendant agrees to plead guilty. By manipulating the charges that defendants face, prosecutors can circumvent the mandatory penalty statutes.

A study conducted by the USSC confirmed that prosecutors often did not file charges carrying mandatory minimum penalties when the evidence indicated that such charges were warranted. In fact, prosecutors did not file the expected charges in about a fourth of the cases. To avoid the mandatory minimum penalty,

Extracted from C Spohn, *How do Judges Decide? The Search for Fairness and Justice in Punishment* (London, Sage Publications, 2002). References and footnotes omitted.

BOX 6.2

MANDATORY MINIMUM SENTENCES:
JUDICIAL EXASPERATION AND DESPAIR

In 1993, Bill Langston, who was on probation for driving while intoxicated, and a friend were stopped by the police as they were transporting chemicals used to manufacture PCP. He was convicted of conspiracy to manufacture 70 kilograms of PCP after a DEA agent testified that Billy had admitted he was going to use the chemicals to make PCP.

Billy Langston's codefendant, who provided information to the government to help convict the man who was to receive the chemicals, received a 60-month sentence. The alleged recipient received probation. Billy Langston, who contended that he had played only a minimal role in the crime and maintained that his codefendant bought the chemicals, was sentenced to 30 years in prison.

At the sentencing hearing, U.S. District Court Judge David V. Kenyon stated that "there is no question that this is an unjust, unfair sentence"; he lamented the fact that his hands were tied by the mandatory minimum sentencing statute. As he stated from the bench, "it is clear that what's going on here is a far greater sentence than what this man deserves. But there's nothing I can do about it, at least that I can figure out."

Judge Kenyon's comments were echoed by the prosecuting attorney, who stated that "the 30-year sentence in this case, which is mandated, is extraordinarily heavy. I don't think that it's anything that anyone feels good about. I certainly don't."

SOURCE: "Victims of MMS," Families Against Mandatory Minimums, available on the World Wide Web at http://www.famm.org

---

prosecutors filed drug charges that did not specify the amount of drugs or that specified a lower amount than appeared supportable, failed to file charges for mandatory weapons enhancements, and did not request increased minimums in cases involving offenders with prior convictions. Plea-bargaining decisions also had an impact. A substantial proportion of the defendants who were charged with mandatory minimum offenses pled guilty to offenses that carried lower mandatory minimum sentences or no mandatory minimums at all. The USSC study also found that 40 percent of the defendants received shorter sentences than would have been warranted under the applicable mandatory minimum statute.

The commission acknowledged that prosecutors might have legitimate reasons for not filing charges that carried mandatory penalties or for allowing defendants to plead guilty to lesser offenses. Nonetheless, they concluded that the results of their study indicated that mandatory minimums were not working. As they noted, "Since the charging and plea negotiation processes are neither open to public review nor generally reviewable by the courts, the honesty and truth in sentencing intended by the guidelines system is compromised." According to the USSC, "There are a number of ways in which Congress effectively can shape sentencing policy without resorting to mandatory minimum provisions." (See Box 6.3 for a discussion of the "safety valve" provision.)

Evaluations of mandatory minimum sentences in New York, Massachusetts, and Michigan also revealed high levels of noncompliance and circumvention. An examination of the impact of New York's Rockefeller Drug Laws, touted as the "nation's toughest drug laws," found that the proportion of felony arrests that resulted in indictment declined, as did the percentage of indictments that led to conviction. Although the likelihood of incarceration and the average sentence imposed on offenders convicted of drug felonies did increase, the lower rates of indictment and conviction meant that the overall likelihood that someone arrested for a drug felony would be sentenced to prison remained about the same. A similar pattern was observed in Massachusetts and Michigan, which adopted mandatory sentencing provisions for carrying or using a firearm. For offenses targeted by these gun laws, the rate at which charges were dismissed increased and the conviction rate decreased. In all three states, as in the federal system, prosecutors and judges devised ways to avoid application of mandatory penalties.

21st-Century Backlash?

In 1996, Michael Tonry, a staunch critic of mandatory penalties, predicted that "sooner or later, the combination of chronic prison overcrowding, budgetary crises,

---

BOX 6.3

MANDATORY MINIMUMS AND THE "SAFETY VALVE"

In 1994, the Department of justice issued a report that revealed that 1 in 5 federal prisoners were low-level drug offenders with no records of violence, no involvement in sophisticated criminal enterprises, and no prior sentences to prison. Among federal prisoners locked up for drug offenses, over a third were low-level offenders.

Publication of these findings led Congress to search for ways to revise, but not repeal, mandatory minimum penalties for drug offenses. Senator Strom Thurmond (R-SC) and Senator Alan Simpson (R-WY) cosponsored legislation establishing a "safety valve" for nonviolent drug offenders. Under this provision, first-time, nonviolent offenders would be exempt from mandatory penalties if they met specified criteria.

Although the safety-valve provision was attacked by conservative legislators, the National Rifle Association (which claimed, incorrectly, that the provision would eliminate mandatory minimums for gun crimes), and the National Association of U.S. Attorneys, it was included in the final version of the Omnibus Crime Control Act of 1994.

---

a. Mauer (1999). *Race to Incarcerate*. New York: The New Press.

and a changed professional climate will make more public officials willing to pay attention to what we have long known about mandatory penalties."

By the late 1990s, it appeared that Tonry might be correct. Prison populations continued to grow even as the crime rate declined, and mandatory minimum sentencing statutes came under increasing criticism. In July of 1998, Michigan Governor John Engler signed a law reforming Michigan's "650 Lifer Law." Under the old law, anyone convicted of possessing, delivering, or intending to deliver more than 650 grams of cocaine or heroin received a mandatory life sentence without the possibility of parole. The new law requires a sentence of "life or any term of years, not less than 20" for future offenders. A companion bill made the change applicable to offenders sentenced under the old law. In February of 1999, DeJonna Young became the first person released from prison as a result of the legal changes. She had been sentenced to life in prison without parole in 1979 after she and her boyfriend were stopped by the police, who found 3 pounds of heroin in her car. Young, who was 24 years old at the time of her arrest, maintained that she didn't know the drugs were in her car.

New York's draconian Rockefeller Drug Laws also came under attack. In early 2001, New York Governor George Pataki proposed changing the laws. He recommended shorter mandatory terms, treatment instead of incarceration in some cases, and enhanced sentencing discretion for judges. Although state legislators were generally supportive of the governor's recommendations, the New York State District Attorneys Association came out against the changes. The president of the association stated, "We can't live with a system that takes out of prosecutors' hands the right to send predatory drug dealers to prison."

Federal officials also are questioning the wisdom of mandatory mini-mums, particularly for drug offenders. In the spring of 2000, for example, the House Subcommittee on Criminal Justice, Drug Policy, and Human Resources held hearings on mandatory minimum drug sentences. After hearing testimony regarding the quadrupling of the federal prison population since 1980, Representative Elijah Cummings (D-MD) stated, "It appears the only thing that mandatory minimums have accomplished is growth in the federal prison system." Both former Attorney General Janet Reno and Supreme Court Chief Justice William Rehnquist also called for reexamining mandatory minimums. Rehnquist, who characterized mandatory penalties as "the law of unintended consequences," said that "these mandatory minimums impose unduly harsh punishment for first-time offenders and have led to an inordinate increase in the prison population."

These direct attacks on mandatory minimums, coupled with the drug court movement and the increasing emphasis on drug treatment rather than incarceration, suggest that state and federal officials are willing to rethink mandatory minimum sentencing statutes, particularly for nonviolent, low-level drug offenders. Although it is unlikely that mandatory penalties will be repealed, there appears to be growing consensus that reform is needed.

6.7

Sentencing Information System (SIS) Experiments

MARC MILLER

The central idea of a sentencing information system is fairly simple: judges should be provided with sufficient information to place an offender into a larger context, and the most useful context for judges is how other offenders like that offender have been sentenced before—by the same judge, by other judges in the same court-house, or by other judges in the same state or country. A separate question is what judges then do with that information—whether and how it might constrain their authority beyond general statutory sentencing limits.

Despite the existence of several SIS experiments over the past 20 years, only a modest amount is known about sentencing under sentencing information systems. The three most widely reported efforts are in Canada, Scotland, and New South Wales, Australia. An early and ultimately failed experiment in several Canadian provinces suggests some of the difficulties in creating and more importantly in using an SIS (Doob and Park 1987). In Scotland, a five-year experiment was only adopted for all 32 judges on the high court in late 2002. An SIS has been operating in New South Wales, Australia, since 1988, and the Scottish judge who took the lead in developing the Scottish SIS learned about the concept from New South Wales. The Israeli system has also been described as an SIS (Schild 2000), and there is fragmentary information about an SIS in Holland (van der Vinne, van Zwol, and Karnekamp 1998). Recently, there has been a call by English senior appeal court judge Robin Auld for development of an SIS in England in a major report, and work has begun on an SIS for magistrates' courts (Auld 2001).

There do not appear to have been many substantial U.S. experiments with sentencing information systems: computerized sentencing "application" software that leads users through guideline systems does not provide information about the actual operation of the system or decisions of judges, and therefore is of a funda-mentally different (and less interesting) character than any SIS (Simon, Gaes, and Rhodes 1991; Fino 1987). The most interesting effort in the United States to develop a sentencing information system has been a county-level system spurred by a Portland, Oregon (Multnomah County) state judge, Michael Marcus, and focuses

From M Tonry (ed), *The Future of Imprisonment* (Oxford, Oxford University Press, 2004). References omitted.

not on inputs but on information about available sanctions and recidivism (Marcus forthcoming; see http://www.smartsentencing.com).

The Canadian experiment operated for six years in the late 1980s in four provinces. The Canadian system emerged as part of the same efforts and discussions that led to early guideline systems. In 1978, before the implementation of the first modern guideline system in Minnesota and a decade before the implementation of the U.S. federal system, Anthony Doob of the Centre of Criminology at the University of Toronto spent a sabbatical at the Institute of Criminology at Cambridge, where he developed the idea that sentencing reform to address sentencing disparities might come from the judges in Canada, if they knew more about what their fellow judges were doing in similar cases (Doob 1990). Doob found Canadian judges in several provinces interested and willing to participate in the experiment, and found public and private funding (Doob 1990; Doob and Park 1987; Hogarth 1971).

Doob worked with judges to develop the relevant categories of sentencing information and ultimately developed a "workable" system where judges first selected an offense (from among 34 offenses), and then added information about six other "dimensions," including criminal record, involvement of the offender in the offense, seriousness of the offense, impact on the victim, and prevalence of the offense in the community (Doob 1989). A judge would then be given a distribution of sentences from "like" cases. Contrary to initial expectations by Doob and from judges, judges did not find the system helpful, and the experiment ceased in the early 1990s. The Canadian experiment failed according to Doob because most judges in most cases turned out not to be interested in knowing about the practices of other judges (Doob 1989; Hutton, Tata, and Wilson 1994).

> [I]t is clear that the kind and amount of information that decision makers want about sentencing in the current climate is quite different from what we had originally thought . . . Judges do not, as a rule, care to know what sentences other judges are handing down in comparable cases . . .
>
> [J]udges do not appear to feel a need to seek out information . . . about sentences in "normal" cases . . . [J]udges . . . tend to have a lot of experience sentencing a small number of common offences. For these offences, there may be a lot of inter-judge disparity. But, when judges are reasonably confident, rightly or wrongly, about their own sentences, why would they want to examine others' decisions, especially if they knew (or thought) that these other judges have different approaches? (Doob 1989, pp. 4–6, 10)

Doob has also suggested that the Canadian experiment failed because of a lack of institutional authority (Doob 1989). Doob noted that if judges were required by the Parliament of Canada to assess "guideline ranges," then the response might have been different (Doob 1989). The failure of the voluntary exchange of sentencing information in Canada, and the corresponding absence of any indication (or expectation) that the information actually shaped sentencing decisions, offers lessons and hypotheses for other SIS efforts, but, given the further development of sentencing reform demands and experiences, may not be entirely predictive of even similar efforts today.

The Scottish SIS has been described in a series of published and government publications, most written by Neil Hutton and Cyrus Tata. The Scottish SIS was born in the shadow of two modern reform movements, the use of sentencing guidelines, mostly in the United States, and the development of a tradition of appellate court sentencing guidelines in England. In the early 1990s, the Scottish judges—led by one senior judge in particular—wanted to respond to the reform sentiments pushing many systems towards greater regulation and guidance of sentencing decisions, while at the same time maintaining substantial judicial independence. The main motivation was not so much to introduce reform for its own sake as a desirable rationalization of sentencing but rather to head off what was seen as potential political intervention in the form of sentencing guidelines that would restrict discretion. The Scottish SIS, therefore, emerged from the courts. The Scottish experiment includes no additional restrictions on what judges must do with the information they receive. There is no appellate review of a sentencing judge's use of the SIS (though appeals remain on other grounds, including occasional appeals of sentencing decisions).

Judges participated in the design of the Scottish system, including specification of the relevant offense and offender categories (Hutton, Paterson, Tata, and Wilson 1996; Hutton, Tata, and Wilson 1994). The explicit goal of the Scottish system was to assist judges at sentencing: "The aim of [the SIS] project was ... to provide judges with a form of support which they thought would assist them in their sentencing work. [T]he SIS was conceived as a practical tool for sentencers" (Hutton and Tata 2000b). The Scottish SIS was developed for the High Court, which hears about 1,000 cases a year, including the most serious matters, and covering about 1 percent of all caes brought before the criminal courts. Before the development of the Scottish SIS high court judges received little sentencing guidance. Most Scottish criminal offenses are common law offenses for which no legislative maximum penalty has been specified (Hutton and Tata 2000a).

The system was designed starting in 1993, with a prototype in 1995, and a first stage of implementation, to about half of the 32 judges on the high court, in 1997. As of the end of 2002, the Scottish SIS has been extended to all judges, and is now operating with a database of 13 years and 13,000 cases.

A judge faced with a new case can specify various offense and offender characteristics. Information is entered through a simple set of forms with drop-down lists for each type of information. For any combination of factors, the system will depict the range of sentences imposed. Because Scotland has a uniform system, results are portrayed for all cases in the system. By adding or removing facts, or making different hypothetical determinations, a judge can compare the outcomes for a set of case scenarios. Hutton and Tata describe the operation of the system as follows:

> The easiest way to describe how the SIS works is to imagine a sentencer faced with a sentencing decision in a particular case who wishes to use the system to see the range

of penalties passed by the High Court for similar cases. For example let us take a case where a 19 year old male offender, with no previous convictions, has been convicted of a robbery from a shop using a knife where there was no injury to the shopkeeper. What counts as a "similar" case in this instance? Is it all robberies using a weapon or just a knife? Does the sentencer only want to look at sentences passed for 19 year old offenders or should older offenders be included? Is the absence of injury important or should the sentencer also look at cases where there was slight injury? There could be many more questions. The point here is that it is impossible to construct an objectively settled definition of similarity. The system is flexible and allows users to vary the set of specified characteristics . . .

[T]he system can be used to show penalty distributions for bundles of cases which are similar to the one at hand although each definition of similarity is different. . . . The flexibility of the system is a strength: it permits the sentencer to gain a subtle picture of the previous sentencing practices of the courts for broadly similar cases. (Hutton and Tata 2000a, p. 44)

In other words, judges can add or subtract facts and see the results. Generally, fewer factors will portray a wider range of outcomes, based on a larger number of cases. A system could easily include defaults or options for different time periods and different jurisdictional subunits, including prior sentences by the individual judge. A sentencing information system is also not necessarily limited to information that can be quantified (Tait 1998). Indeed, judges who participated in the initial implementation of the Scottish SIS requested more case-specific information (Hutton and Tata 2000b). The system was modified by allowing judges to enter narrative information about each case. This development had a parallel in the Canadian experiment, where Doob and Park noted the importance of including textual case summaries and access to trial or appellate decisions (Doob and Park 1987, p. 68).

Although the New South Wales system has been in operation for almost 15 years, there is no published evaluation of the system (Hutton and Tata 2000a). Indeed, it appears that none of the current sentencing information systems have been "subject to rigorous analysis and evaluation" (Lovegrove 1999). The system has been said to be the product of public reports on wide sentencing variation for drug offenders (Chan 1991). The New South Wales SIS was designed "to show a sentencer the range of penalties imposed in past cases *which are similar along the main legal dimensions of interest*" (Chan 1991, p. 139).

In contrast to the Scottish system, the New South Wales system was the product of both executive and judicial calls for reform, and the particular reform was the product of legislation. Like the Scottish system, the New South Wales legislation specified that "[n]othing in this section limits any discretion that a court has in determining a sentence" (Chan 1991, p. 138). The variables in the New South Wales system were developed from prior appellate decisions, research, and a survey of all judges and magistrates in New South Wales. The designers favored factors that were more objective over those that were more subjective or harder to measure. As in the Scottish high court, the New South Wales system displays the range of prior sentences for judge-specific combinations of offense and offender facts.

Experts at the Judicial Commission of New South Wales, created to develop the SIS, claim it is "one of the most sophisticated yet unobtrusive systems of its kind in the world" (Potas et al. 1998, p. 100; Auld 2001). The New South Wales system combines sentencing statistics, full text opinions (3,500 cases) and factual case summaries (an additional 2,500 cases), a database structured around sentencing "principles" (including multiple logical entry points, such as offenses and offender characteristics, and including sentencing trends and changes over time), available punishment facilities (resources), current and proposed legislation, and access to various publications (Potas et al. 1998, pp. 106–111; see http://www.judcom.nsw.gov.au/). Notably, the New South Wales system includes appellate review for reasonableness and proportionality (Potas et al. 1998).

The initial experiences with sentencing information systems confirm several important points. First, sentencing information systems are by no means simply a technical matter, nor are they value neutral. Doob and Park put it this way in describing the Canadian experience:

The absence of clear [sentencing] principles creates a distinct difficulty for anyone interested in providing information to judges about sentencing. [O]ne does not know what information should be provided. No information system on sentencing can be completely neutral with respect to principles of sentencing. (Doob and Park 1987, pp. 55–56)

A related problem was the difficulty of getting more factors like criminal history to capture more subjective information relevant to judges such as whether prior offenses were "minor" or "serious" or whether the offender had a "long but non-violent" criminal history (Doob and Park 1987, pp. 62–63).

If information systems are not neutral, who should define the relevant categories and principles? The experiences in Canada, Scotland, and Australia suggest that sentencing information systems are more likely to succeed if judges are actively involved in their creation and implementation (Tata 1998). Since none of these systems have evaluated the ability of information systems to shape sentencing behavior, the claim here is modest: judicial involvement may be essential in shaping categories if the system is to work at all. But the larger point may hold as well: judges will be more likely to have their decisions guided by the patterns of decisions by other judges if the information fits with the way that judges assess offenders and offenses.

It is clear that an SIS alone is not the "answer" to all sentencing problems. To the extent that an SIS is intended to be an alternative to guidelines, it should be combined with some process or tradition of decision making. At the least this should include narrative explanations by sentencing judges of their decisions (Miller 1989). An SIS that encouraged a practice of narrative sentencing decisions would also encourage reflection on the relationship between quantitative data and sentencing narratives. Narrative descriptions might be used to test or question the adequacy of the data categories. An SIS that included both sentencing decisions and appellate sentencing decisions might provide the foundation for the common law of sentencing that Morris and others have hoped for over the years, but which has yet to emerge (Sweet, Van Hook, and Di Leilo 1996, p. 946; Miller 1989).

The current systems in Scotland and New South Wales, the earlier experiment in Canada, and the occasional references to sentencing information systems elsewhere have yet to prove the viability of the SIS approach alone at meeting the modern goals of sentencing reform. Perhaps in the absence of underlying agreement about purposes and other foundational principles, sentencing information systems might perpetuate a "false justice" (Lovegrove 1999, p. 71). At the very least, however, the early experiments suggest the practicability of such systems and offer a source of expertise and a place for further study by judges, reformers, and scholars.

Sentencing Information Systems and the Purposes of Sentencing Reform

How does providing information on sentencing patterns respond to concerns about unjustified disparity, resource allocation, "truth in sentencing" or reveal the basis for sentencing in each case?

Sentencing information systems have some hope of addressing disparity concerns, but it is harder to see how an SIS alone would be likely to account for resource concerns. Indeed, the difficulty if not impossibility of accounting for system-wide resource constraints in a "bottom up" fashion is one of the greatest weaknesses in the idea of an SIS alone as a substitute or full competitor to the commission and guidelines model.

Any explanation, including one built around statistical norms, may provide more transparency than a traditional indeterminate system, but an SIS, like some guideline systems, runs the risk of appearing to provide more information while not revealing enough of the judge's thought process to allow observers (defendants, lawyers, scholars, and other judges) to really understand the judge's thought process in each case.

One of the modern reforms that probably can be joined to information systems is the abolition or severe restriction on parole—often referred to as the goal of "truth in sentencing" (this phrase has also been co-opted and abused by the U.S. Congress, which has required a particular and severe form of "truth in sentencing" from states that wish to receive certain federal monies).

The Canadian, Scottish, and New South Wales systems did not try to respond to the full range of modern sentencing reform goals, but focused on the aim of reducing unwarranted disparity (Lovegrove 1999, p. 32). In theory, the Scottish judges believe that if judges saw the range of sentences imposed by other judges, it would lead them to sentence the next offender in a more reasoned fashion, in line with prior sentences. The New South Wales approach did not intend "to curtail discretion, but to better inform it" (Potas et al. 1998, p. 99).

In theory, the availability alone of sentencing information might produce both more consistent and more principled and visible sentences. However, the literature on non-binding or voluntary guidelines raises questions about the necessary and sufficient conditions for non-binding systems to "work" in the sense that they actually shape judicial decisions (Tonry 1996; Berman 2000, p. 28). Twenty years ago scholars and reformers would probably claim that non-binding or voluntary guidelines could not work. The last several decades of experience in a range of guideline systems, however, suggests that the language of "binding" and "voluntary" are too crude, and that many finer gradations of guidance have emerged in practice and turn on such things as the kinds of social norms and degree of acceptance among judges (Miller and Wright 1999).

Perhaps the availability of information would have a more powerful shaping power than the availability of rules: the information is the product of the actual decisions of judges, while rules are typically (though not necessarily) the product of a panel or commission. There does not appear to be any direct evidence on the impact of the Scottish SIS, even though the fact that some judges used the system while others did not would offer an unusual opportunity to test the impact of the system.

Although the literature is modest, with the current adoption of the SIS across all Scottish high court judges, it is reasonable to expect more attention and analysis in the future. During the five years the prototype system has been in place, the judges have not allowed external access to the available data by lawyers or scholars. As Hutton and Tata note, the underlying information comes from public records, and it is reasonable to hope that greater confidence on the part of judges and public expectations will encourage greater access to this information over time (Hutton and Tata 2000a).

The options for making a voluntary or non-binding SIS into one that could more plausibly match the shaping power of commission-bred guidelines—assuming that changing sentencing patterns to produce greater consistency and responsiveness to resource constraints are in fact goals—include developing or requiring sentencing explanations or opinions, perhaps backed up by some appellate review. Resource management is a question that requires some source of external information for judges to add into the sentencing calculus in each case and across cases. Another possibility would be to join presumptive rules to the sentencing range—rules that might be set wholly internally to the judiciary or with external input, for example accounting for prison space and other resources—but to allow the SIS to define the available size of the range for a mix of factors.

If judges are allowed to pick and choose which factors apply to each case without any standards or principles for identifying which factors should be relevant, it is hard to see how such an SIS would lead to more consistent and principled sentencing. However, there are many options for structuring sentencing within sentencing information systems. Judges might be told that they had to identify four basic kinds of information (offense, harm, prior record, and mode of adjudication). More likely, judges would be required to specify a sufficient number of categories or factors, including a time factor, that would produce a meaningful number of cases (e.g., 30, 50, or 100 cases). The system might include even more formal tests of confidence in the meaning and reliability of the information (its significance).

One very attractive option, after a proper "pool" of sufficiently "like" cases had been identified, would be to allow judges to sentence within one standard deviation above or below the mean without exceptional justification, but to require such justification, perhaps subject to more sweeping appellate review, beyond that range. Note that in such a system the size of the presumptive range would vary. Where sentences clumped for a particular kind of offense and offender, judges would have less discretion. For other combinations of offense and offender, the range would be wide as many additional factors (the proper subject of judicial discretion) would guide the actual sentence.

Among the many questions that do not appear to have been faced by the early SIS experiments is the relevance of geographic variation. A judge might want to know what his or her courthouse neighbors did, even if there was no formal jurisdictional line at stake. The jurisdictions that have experimented with SIS are relatively small and cohesive. But sentencing information systems also offer the possibility of illuminating sentencing variation beyond jurisdictional boundaries and in both directions—California judges might find what Washington State or North Carolina judges do of interest, U.S. judges might find Canadian and English sentences of interest, and judges on the new International Criminal Court might find the sentences of many countries of interest. The question is whether systems should allow factors and distinctions that should not have any binding weight, but which might nonetheless inform a judge or a system. A sentencing information system that created some procedures and presumptions about how the information should be used could more easily distinguish between shaping, informing, and irrelevant information.

Another puzzle for information systems is how to encourage the use of similar definitions within each information category. One familiar and serious problem is whether judges restrict themselves to offenses that have been proven beyond a reasonable doubt, or also look at various kinds of "real offense" information, which may include unproven aspects of a conviction offense, or facts proven at sentencing by lesser standards of proof, -and in some systems information about uncharged, dismissed, and even (shockingly, and not in most guideline systems) information underlying acquittals (Reitz 1993; Yellen 1993; Tonry 1997).

It is interesting to contrast a sentencing information system with a commission-produced guidelines model. For example, some guideline systems, including the federal system, are developed based on statistical models of prior sentencing decisions (Breyer 1988). How different would sentences look when they are modeled at one time or constantly remodeled over time?

A set of rules modeled on prior sentencing practice and a statistical portrait of prior sentencing practice might at first glance seem similar. But on closer examination they are distinct conceptually and practically. A critical factor for any structured system is its language and grammar—the operative concepts involving the offense and offender and their relationships that shape final sentencing choices. Systems, such as the federal system, that allegedly model their rules retrospectively, based on prior practice, must take records designed for one purpose (such as pre-sentence investigation reports prepared by probation officers in the pre-guidelines federal system) and superimpose (or try to superimpose) the categories the rule-designers later choose. An SIS can and should be designed pro-spectively, with careful thought to the sentencing categories, and then fact-finding and record keeping should be done in accordance with those categories.

In practice, the retrospective modeling of available sentencing information is ripe for manipulation, as the U.S. federal experience shows (Miller and Wright 1999). A prospective system is less susceptible to such manipulation. Retrospective modeling can be more or less sophisticated, but the U.S. federal experience suggests a tendency to opt for the medians and means of prior sentences, given various (available) offender and offense facts. The goal of drafting sentencing "guidelines" may contribute to this excessive tendency to average almost everything, at least if the presumptively available sentences are restricted to some fairly narrow range.

In contrast, sentencing information systems should portray the full range of sentences applicable to a given set of factors. Moreover an SIS can continue gradually to take account of changing social norms. Guideline systems can also take account of changing social norms through the promulgation of revised guidelines.

Changing norms could come in the form of new legislation or popular movements such as recent efforts in several states to change presumptive punishments for low-level nonviolent drug offenders. Another source of variation and change over time could be "local conditions" (Sifton 1993; Raggi 1993; Braniff 1993; Broderick 1993). Sentencing information systems might be slower than commission-driven guidelines systems to respond to legislative changes such as changing the maxima or minima for particular offenses. But an SIS could take account of local variation and variation over time more easily than top-down guidelines.

Guideline systems, at least in the United States, do not seem to produce standard narratives about offenses and offenders. (The appellate guideline practice in England may do a much better job at laying out what makes a set of cases more or less serious for the same general type of offense.) Instead, some U.S. guideline systems (and notably the federal system) focus courts, participants, and critics on particular factors, isolated from a picture of the offender and offense as a whole—for example, was the offender an "organizer," what quantity of drugs were involved, or was a gun used in the offense. Sentencing information systems offer the possibility of suggesting different narratives that vary by key facts, and that may in theory span a range of seriousness as reflected in the distribution of sentences actually imposed. Neil Hutton and Cyrus Tata explained that the SIS was designed on the assumption that judges sentenced with narratives in their mind.

> Cases are necessarily simplified, standardized, interpreted and reinterpreted to conform to typified and familiarized patterns of behavior and character. [Judges] are aware that there are other judges making decisions about similar cases, and there is a history of these decisions and that such decisions will be made in the future . . . Judges are also aware that . . . their decisions are unavoidably part of the continuing public debate about punishment and, more broadly, about law and order . . . Sentencers do not view each case . . . as if it were a completely distinctive and fresh set of circumstances. They experience cases as more or less familiar and predictable narratives or "Typical Whole Case Stories," and their sentencing decisions need to be made against this background. (Hutton and Tata, 2000b, p. 309)

Potential virtues of a complete SIS compared to the U.S. federal sentencing guidelines include the capacity to identify offense and offender mixes requiring a wider range of sanctions to satisfy sentencing purposes, the possibility of gradual explicit and implicit evolution in severity and choice of sanction, and the possibility of constructing relatively coherent sentencing narratives and variations.

One substantial puzzle of modern commission and guideline sentencing reforms is the proper role for the sentencing judge. Most guideline systems include statements retaining a central role for the sentencing judge. But in the federal system, the judicial role seems largely to be one of either fact-finding (including calculation of sentences, often with the aid of a probation officer) or of validating bargains (often including fact bargains) reached by the parties. Judges have been forced to this more limited role by narrow sentencing ranges and restrictive departure standards, with many cases especially in the dominant drug category governed by mandatory sentences or by sentences sufficiently severe that the de facto federal system is one of specific sentences, not sentencing ranges.

Honoring the role of the sentencing judge both as decision maker in individual cases and in shaping guideline systems has been one of the greatest weaknesses of the federal commission. Most legislatures and commissions have asserted that the opinions and suggestions of judges (formal and informal) will be used as feedback to improve the system, and some states seem to have done a much better job at living up to this goal (Reitz 1997; Wright 2002).

Sentencing information systems offer a dramatically different way of depicting the sentencing judge's role and could perhaps help to achieve the promise of more principled sentencing while maintaining a central role for sentencing judges. In the spirit of Morris's 1953 essay, judges would be provided with much more information about the decisions of their fellow judges. Sentencing information systems respond to the actual decisions of judges rather than directing judges how to sentence. Even with stronger rules and presumptions than in the SIS in Scotland or New South Wales, judges should retain a much stronger individual and collective role in such systems than in current commission and guideline systems. Sentencing information systems would not rely on the input of judge members of commissions to capture systematic judicial insights about sentencing.

Sentencing information systems might echo traditional common law systems in some ways: indeed an SIS might help to nurture the common law development of sentencing principles. But the common law rides the crest of precedent, while an SIS with some "bite" (one that is not wholly voluntary or where judicial social norms create strong pressures to match sentences to prior sentencing patterns) should ride the crest of group action, but with no strong binding force to the act of any one prior court.

The appeal of an SIS and principles that allow for expanding and contracting presumptive ranges based on combinations of factors has some similarities to the appeal of markets more generally. A well-designed SIS would allow in effect for market pricing of sanctions (albeit a market constrained—as other markets are often constrained—by some degree of legislative superstructure, and perhaps constrained as well by some resource pressures on the default rules). The contrast with the dominant commission and guidelines model is revealing: in comparison, the dominant model has the character not of a market for proper principles and punishments but of an economy designed by "command and control." Sentencing information systems need not be solely "ground up"; as with the varying degrees of authority and constraint in different guideline systems, different mixes of ground-up and top-down rules and case-level decision making are possible.

While an SIS, at least with some process or principles beyond the mere provision of information, may offer an alternative path to the reduction of unwarranted disparity and might offer a major alternative to sentencing guidelines, it is not clear, in the absence of some addition rule or process, how an SIS that merely provides information can answer the critique of indeterminate sentencing that called for more legal principle and regulation to guide each sentencing decision. Nor is it clear how SIS can respond to important resource allocation concerns, at least in the absence of some "top down" or centralized guidance, whether from a legislature, the executive branch, or a sentencing commission.

7

Sentencing Young Offenders

> The concept of the young offender, with all that it implies for penal policy, is a Victorian creation. Until well into the nineteenth century there were no differentiations according to age in the method of bringing offenders to trial, in the form of the trial itself, in the punishments that could be imposed or, generally, in the way in which they were enforced.[1]

For at least a hundred years there has been a belief, growing quickly at first, but more recently wavering in strength, that the sentencing of youth offenders calls for principles that differ from those applicable to the sentencing of adults. Not only have different procedures and courts for young defendants become commonplace, and different forms of sentence developed, but the very rationales for imposing censure and punishment on the young have been questioned. In parallel to this, the children's rights movement was developing, and this has given rise to important international instruments, such as the United Nations Standard Minimum Rules for the Administration of Juvenile Justice 1985 (known as the Beijing Rules; see Selection 7.1) and the United Nations Convention on the Rights of the Child 1989 (Selection 7.2; UNCRC). The primary purpose of this introduction is to examine the justifications for approaching the sentencing youth offenders differently from the sentencing of adults. Four issues are singled out for discussion—first, questions of responsibility and agency; secondly, rationales for punishing the young; thirdly, separate procedures for the young; and fourthly, separate sanctions for the young.

Questions of Responsibility

It is widely accepted that children are, on the whole, less responsible than adults for their actions. But in order to make this into a meaningful proposition which can have clear implications for the sentencing of youth offenders, considerable groundwork needs to be accomplished. Can we be more precise about the nature and causes of the reduced responsibility of children? In Selection 7.3 Franklin Zimring posits three main reasons for the diminished moral and emotional capacity of youth offenders. The first is the lack of fully developed cognitive abilities: younger children have 'obvious gaps in both information and the cognitive skills to use it'. As Archard has argued, the diminution lies not merely in underdeveloped cognitive skills but also in the inability to realise the full significance and implications of an act:

> a child may know that its actions will result in harm being occasioned to another child but, nevertheless, not really grasp the importance of that harm being done to another.[2]

The second reason identified by Zimring is the lack of developed control mechanisms: for many people, self-control is a capacity that has to be developed, and in young people that development may not yet be complete. The third reason is a susceptibility to peer pressure. Zimring shows that a large proportion of violent crimes by young people are committed in groups, and argues that many youths have a strong desire to impress their peers and an underdeveloped capacity to resist peer group pressure.

These arguments about moral and emotional immaturity, taken together, suggest that many young offenders have a form of diminished culpability; but this is not yet a convincing reason for treating all young offenders differently from adult offenders. As Andrew von Hirsch argues (Selection 7.4), the normative force comes from a conception of what we should reasonably demand of young people, given the degree to which their understanding of the consequences and significance of acts 'depends on experience, learning and capacities for moral reasoning that need to develop in adolescence over time'. Similarly, reduced self-control should reduce culpability for young offenders because it is not reasonable to expect more:

> self-control, as other aspects of moral development, is a learned capacity, and childhood and adolescence is the period during which it is learned.

Thus it is not enough simply to state general facts about the immaturity of the young; it is also necessary to link those facts to justifications for reducing the level of penal response.

The structure of the preceding arguments is that throughout childhood a development towards adulthood is taking place; and from this it would seem to follow that young people close to adulthood—sometimes termed adolescents—are likely to have only a slightly reduced level of responsibility whereas much younger children are likely to have a significantly reduced level of responsibility. Since those statements refer to 'likelihood', one approach might be to provide for an assessment of each individual defendant's level of responsibility, to determine to what extent (if any) he or she falls below the minimum level to be expected of an adult. However, it is important again to move from the merely descriptive to the normative: the key is what should reasonably be expected of young people, and expectations should surely increase as the young person comes closer to the age of majority.

Expectations should correspondingly be lower for younger juveniles, and this raises the question of the appropriate minimum age for criminal responsibility. The age of criminal responsibility varies considerably across jurisdictions. The minimum is 13 in France, 14 in Germany, 15 in the Scandinavian countries, and 16 in Spain and Portugal. Some US states have similarly high minima, whereas others are as low as 12 or 10. In England and Wales the minimum age is still 10.[3] This low age has been the subject of criticism from the UN Committee on the Rights of the Child, which has recommended that the UK government should 'considerably raise the minimum age for criminal responsibility'.[4] But at what age ought it, ideally, to be set?

The commentary to the Beijing Rules argues that there should be

> a close relationship between the notion of responsibility for delinquent or criminal behaviour and other social rights and responsibilities (such as marital status, civil majority etc).[5]

In the UK there is no such closeness: not only is the age of majority 18, but that is also the age at which tort liability begins (beneath that age it is presumed that someone else is responsible for allowing young people to cause the relevant damage). The age of consent to sexual familiarities is 16, and the Sexual Offences Act 2003 (UK) includes a number of offences against children under 16 designed to protect them from themselves (even if they give their *de facto* consent to the activity). In respect of medical interventions, the age of capacity is more flexible, depending on an assessment of the individual child's understanding.[6] However, the age at which children are treated as responsible agents and thought to have sufficient understanding of behaviour and its consequences seems to be either 16 (consent to sexual activity, driving a motorcycle), 17 (driving a car) or 18 (civil capacity, right to vote)—all a long way above the age of 10.

In 1969 the British Parliament enacted that the age of criminal responsibility should be raised to 14,[7] but that statutory provision was never brought into force. Although some argue that this provision should be reinstated, the logic of the arguments above points towards a minimum age of 16 for criminal responsibility. However, any increase in the age would be controversial, largely because of the way in which 'young criminals' have been demonised by some politicians and media in England and Wales, particularly since the murder of James Bulger in 1993 and the subsequent conviction of boys aged 10 at the time of the killing.[8] To keep the age at 10 for England and Wales is to 'responsibilise' children unduly, and to fail to take proper account of the diminished culpability of young offenders and the responsibility borne by the family and the wider community.[9] Raising the age would be in line with international standards and with the urgings of the UN Committee on the Rights of the Child,[10] and it is a step that should be taken.

One consequence of raising the age of criminal responsibility would be that the relatively small number of children beneath the chosen age who are now dealt with in the criminal justice system would be transferred to the children's services. The relevant departments would need to be adequately prepared, trained and resourced to take over this role, and several questions (such as the use of secure accommodation) would need to be tackled with care in order to ensure that the new system was more, rather than less, compatible with international standards.

Rationales for Punishing the Young

What rationales should determine the imposition of compulsory measures on young people who offend? The next section will discuss possible differences in the approach to choice of sanctions, but at this stage the enquiry is at a deeper level. Is it appropriate to punish the young at all? If so, is the case for any of the rationales for punishment considered in previous chapters (rehabilitation, deterrence, desert, incapacitation or restorative justice) any stronger in relation to sentencing youth offenders than in relation to the sentencing of adults?

It may be argued that the state has a different relation to children than to adults: the state ought to have a responsibility to provide support, or to reinforce institutions (such as the family) which provide support, for the proper development and socialisation of children. This is not necessarily to take a position on the contested issue of children's rights[11]; rather, it is to suggest that state authorities, as well as parents, are responsible for ensuring that certain basic needs of children are provided for, that they are given opportunities to develop their potential towards that of an adult citizen, and that as they develop towards adulthood they are consulted about major decisions. Thus the UN Convention on the Rights of the Child (Selection 7.2) states in Article 3 that 'the best interests of the child shall be a primary consideration in all actions concerning children', and follows this with the requirement that a youth justice system should treat its subjects in a way that is appropriate for 'the child's age and the desirability of promoting the child's reintegration and the child's assuming a constructive role in society'.

Should this rule out punishment of the young? It can be argued that, since desert theory is founded on the notion of individuals as rational, moral agents (see Chapter 4 above), and thus on responding to offences proportionately to their seriousness, there is insufficient basis for punishing those below the age of majority. By definition, they are not yet recognised as full moral agents, and cannot be expected to respond as such.

It has to be recognised, however, that the alignment of criminal responsibility with the age of civil and political majority is rare in the modern world. Desert theorists, like others, have to deal with the fact that there is usually an age band in which young offenders are above the age of criminal responsibility but below the age of majority. In respect of these young offenders, there is inevitably a strong degree of paternalism in the role of the state, although international standards maintain the principle of proportionality between offence and degree of compulsory measures.[12]

The paternalist thrust of sentencing young offenders has tended to lead to emphasis on a rehabilitative rationale, within proportionality constraints. However, the rehabilitative rationale has taken a particular direction in respect of young offenders. This has come to be known as the welfare approach, which developed through the twentieth century and is characterised by the belief that most young people in trouble are the products of poor social conditions, particularly multiple deprivation. On this approach, the prevention of child poverty and other improvements in social conditions are the most fruitful ways to tackle the problem of child offending.[13] Moreover, the role played by such social factors would suggest that whether a child offends or not, or is caught offending or not, should not be a principal determinant of the state's response. The logic of this approach would be to deal with young offenders as one element of a social system that also caters for children who need care or protection.

Thus, in the Scottish system, the criminal courts play only a limited part in dealing with children under 16 who offend, and that is to determine whether an offence has been committed (in cases where that is contested).[14] Otherwise, the central feature is the children's hearing, which decides whether any compulsory intervention is required in order to further the child's best interests. The commission of an offence is insufficient ground for referring a child to a hearing, since there must also be a demonstrable need for compulsory supervision measures. The child may address the hearing, and if (for example) it is concluded that the parents can properly ensure the child's development, no order may be made. In other cases, the hearing may decide to make a compulsory order—for care or for education, for example. Among the acknowledged problems of this welfare-based system is that it continues only until the age of 16, after which youth offenders are exposed to the full range of adult measures; and that it has not coped well with a small minority of persistent youth offenders (although that is true of many youth justice systems).

Similar in some respects but different in others—but still a species of rehabilitative approach—is the developmental approach to youth crime. The essence of this is that the principal sources of support and control for young people are in the home and the school, that any compulsory intervention should aim to strengthen those sources, and that any intervention that fails to strengthen the roles of family and the school and instead seeks to displace them should be regarded as exceptional and calling for compelling justification.[15] All these prescriptions were linked to criminological findings such as the age–crime curve, which shows that most children who offend will 'grow out of crime', and to labelling theory in criminology, which advances an explanation for the fact that almost 9 out of 10 youth offenders sentenced to detention reoffend quickly. These 'criminological facts' do not themselves encompass all cases—not all official interventions in young offenders' lives are deleterious, not all children who offend have an 'adolescence-limited' criminal career[16]—but they have sufficient generality to suggest that the arguments of the developmental theorists should not be lightly dismissed.

Thus Zimring argues that, since offending amongst 'adolescence-limited' teenage offenders is

> a more or less normal adolescent phenomenon, a by-product of the same transitional status that increases accident risks, rates of accidental pregnancy and suicidal gestures,

responses to offending in this age group 'should be a part of larger policies towards youth' (Selection 7.3). Zimring's argument is that the principal strategy for dealing with this age group should be the management of risks, by a variety of techniques, with criminal sanctions as a last resort—and, moreover, with sanctions that are suitably muted (compared with those for adults) so that they do not compromise the longer-term interests of the young people. Those remarks relate only, of course, to youth offenders with 'adolescence-limited' careers. It remains, here as under the welfare approach, to reach a decision on how to respond to the more intractable group of 'life-course-persistent' offenders, provided that they can be reliably identified as such.

Restorative justice is a third approach that, like the rehabilitative and welfare approaches, is presented as consistent with the idea of a supportive and paternalistic state. More is said about the general strengths and weaknesses of this rationale in Chapter 5. The reason why it is often advanced as particularly appropriate for young offenders is that it has reintegrative purposes and also seeks to address the cognitive deficit associated with young offenders. On the first point, the aim of restorative justice is often said to be to reintegrate the offender into the family and the wider community. It is therefore inclusive rather than exclusive in its objectives, and consistent with the ideals of the Convention on the Rights of the Child. It also allows the young person to participate in the process of restorative justice, recognising that he or she may wish to contribute to the discussion of the crime and its aftermath.

On the second point, restorative processes should bring the young offender to understand the full consequences of the crime committed, supplementing the bare cognitive proposition ('I broke his car window'; 'I punched him') with an appreciation of the physical, psychological and social ramifications for the victim and family. As argued in the opening paragraphs of this introduction, the difference between a bare cognitive understanding and a fuller appreciation of the significance of an act is one of the reasons for maintaining lower expectations of young people.

We have reviewed three ways of ensuring that any penal response to youth offending is consonant with the state's responsibility towards the young—rehabilitation, the developmental approach and restorative justice—but it is important to recall that Article 40.4 of the UNCRC (Selection 7.2) rightly declares that all penal responses to the young should remain proportionate. There are two aspects to the principle of proportionality in relation to juveniles. First, not only do the justifications set out in Chapter 4 above have resonance here, but it is also important to the moral development of the young that the degree of penal response should be seen to correspond to the seriousness of their wrongdoing. Proportionality is also a necessary safeguard against the excesses of beneficence, which might in some cases lead to unduly lengthy interventions in the lives of young offenders, especially in pursuit of rehabilitative aims.

Secondly, there are strong reasons for ensuring that the application of the principle of proportionality to young offenders is more muted than to adults. As von Hirsch argues (Selection 7.4), we should recognise that punishments are generally more onerous for the young because they impinge on important developmental interests, in terms of education and socialisation, for which the teenage years are a crucial phase. Proportionality theory thus requires that sentence levels be significantly lower than those for adults, and Article 41.4 of the UNCRC (Selection 7.2) recognises that account should also be taken of the circumstances of the particular young offender.[17]

Certain countries do not always observe these proportionality constraints. Some argue that the movement in England and Wales in the last decade, for example, has been to place greater emphasis on deterrence, incapacitation and populist punitiveness: the trend is 'away from rehabilitative and transformative optimism towards greater surveillance, regulation and, ultimately, punishment'[18]—and this in a system that still has 10 as the minimum age of criminal responsibility. However, even in those jurisdictions that accept the proportionality principle and, within it, pursue other goals, such as rehabilitation or restorative justice, there remain significant pockets of controversy.

Three may be mentioned briefly here. First, any reintegrative or rehabilitative goal is likely to be much more difficult to achieve once the characteristics of the typical young offender who is convicted are taken into account—a background of 'family poverty, disruption and difficulty', together with 'experience of public care and poor educational experience'.[19] This suggests that even treating such offenders within general child policy is likely to encounter difficulties unless considerable additional resources are put into social policy, housing, education and the relief of poverty.

Secondly, there remains the category of 'life-course-persistent' young offenders, who are so persistent in their offending as to cross the boundaries of tolerance. If the offences are not major violent or sexual crimes, there is a strong argument for trying to contain them without resorting to custody. But there will inevitably be some who will not be so contained, even by a curfew with electronic monitoring and support through supervision.

What is important, however, is to distinguish them from the third group—those who commit very serious victimising offences of a violent or sexual nature. Those in this group who are below the age of responsibility must be dealt with through the social services, as is done in other jurisdictions. A further question, for those in this group over the age of criminal responsibility, is whether the proportionality principle ought to be subject to an exception for public protection. The usual arguments (discussed in Selections 3.3 and 3.4 above) might be marshalled in favour of a limited exception to deal with a small number of extreme cases, but, set against that, in the case of young offenders there is the probability that incapacitative detention would significantly reduce their chances of rehabilitation and reintegration. This is a strong reason for keeping this category much smaller and more exceptional than for adults, and separate from the second group above.

Separate Sanctions for the Young

The arguments of the previous two sections—in support of expecting less of young offenders on account of their diminished responsibility, and the state's obligation to assist them towards mature citizenship—suggest that different considerations should apply when devising sanctions for the young. Although adolescence is a time when offending rates tend to be higher, it is also a time when the greatest efforts are necessary in order to strengthen the bonds between young people and the family, school and wider community. It is therefore appropriate to try to ensure that sanctions for youth offenders are so constructed as to reduce the harmful side effects. This principle has two widely accepted implications, in favour of diversion and the minimum use of custody.

The aim of diversionary practices is to ensure that as many young offenders as possible are diverted away from the criminal justice system towards less formal responses. The rationale is that the formal system labels offenders, stigmatises them and makes it more likely that they will continue to offend (perhaps because they come to identify themselves as offenders) than if they had been dealt with in another way. The principle of diversion is supported by Article 40(3)(b) of the UNCRC, which obliges states to promote 'whenever appropriate and desirable measures for dealing with such children without resorting to judicial proceedings'. This approach is also supported by findings that young offenders subjected to the English diversionary approach of 'cautioning' had lower rates of subsequent conviction than those convicted and sentenced.[20]

However, there are at least three major qualifications to be borne in mind. First, the definition of diversion must be applied carefully. The term is widely used, and should properly be confined to methods of dealing with offenders outside the formal criminal justice process. In England and Wales many young offenders were 'cautioned' prior to 1998, a semi-formal process organised by the police. Since 1998 there has been a scheme of reprimands and warnings for young offenders which are, at the very least, closely linked to the formal criminal justice process, if not actually part of it. There is no 'resort to judicial proceedings' in these cases, but they are certainly part of a formal process that may lead to such proceedings. A second qualification is that diversion must be genuine and not merely a means of widening the net: in other words, diversion must apply to young offenders who would otherwise be subjected to formal procedures and not to those who would otherwise have received a less formal response (such as a few words of warning from the police). A third qualification is that diversion must not be used as a way of avoiding proper safeguards. Thus, when Article 40 of the UNCRC refers to dealing with young offenders 'without resorting to judicial proceedings', it adds: 'providing that human rights and legal safeguards are fully respected'. The use of diversionary measures often depends on the offender's readiness to admit guilt, and this may lead to the exertion of pressure—admit the offence and we will divert you; deny it and we will prosecute, and conviction is likely to result in a more severe outcome—which may lead to consequences that are not necessarily in the young offender's best interests. Insofar as it is possible, legal safeguards against such pressure must be maintained.

The principle of the minimum use of custody for young offenders is also widely accepted. Article 37(b) of the UNCRC provides that:

> detention or imprisonment of a child shall be used only as a measure of last resort and for the shortest appropriate period of time.[21]

The rationale for this principle is partly connected with the developmental theory, which maintains that it is best in the long run to keep a young person close to the family, the school and the community in which he or she must live, and partly connected with the adverse effects of institutionalisation, mixing with other young offenders in conditions that are often less than constructive and sometimes quite brutal. Certainly in England and Wales the reconviction rate of young offenders aged 14–17 discharged from detention is over 80%,[22] which indicates that such institutions rarely exert any significant rehabilitative effect and might indeed have a negative impact on future behaviour.

However, the principle itself is indeterminate in its wording. The phrase 'measure of last resort' can easily be emptied of significance by suggesting that, if the courts have already tried community-based sanctions and the youth has continued to offend, detention may therefore be used as a last resort. Such reasoning could lead to detention for persistent thieves or others well down the scale of offending. Similarly, the 'shortest appropriate period' is a fine phrase, but is open to the response that 'we always select the shortest appropriate period when dealing with a youth offender'. No doubt many English sentencers would affirm this, even though England and Wales have the highest rate of young offender detention in Europe and have received international criticism on this account.[23] The principle of minimum use of custody therefore requires greater sharpness of definition if it is to have the desired effect. It should be clearly stated that any period of loss of liberty that is held to be justified should be significantly shorter than for an adult, in view of the interruption of normal education and the probability that juveniles are less able to deal with the deprivations of penal custody.

One possibility would be to incorporate a restriction to serious offences of violence or sexual violation, or a tightly worded dangerousness restriction. Another possibility would be to adopt or adapt the approach taken in Canada's Youth Criminal Justice Act 2002, discussed by Nicholas Bala and Julian Roberts in Selection 7.5. This Act introduced a range of new sentencing principles, designed (among other objectives) to reduce the use of custody for young offenders. Although some of the Act's provisions are not greatly limiting—as, for example, the provisions for custody for non-compliance with non-custodial sentences—the overall effect appears to have been to change the sentencing culture in Canada, and the use of custody for young offenders has shown a substantial decline since 2003. Thus, in the first two years following implementation the average number of young persons in custody in Canada declined by 60%, with all jurisdictions showing a significant decline.[24]

Stepping away from the extremes of diversion and incarceration, attention must be given to the provision of community-based measures for young offenders. The challenge is to devise non-custodial measures that respond effectively to the special needs of the young. As with all sanctions for the young, the challenge is increased by the fact that a large proportion of sentenced young offenders come from distinctly disadvantaged and disturbed backgrounds, and may well continue to offend whatever official response results. In most cases it would be more appropriate and possibly more effective to deal with these young people through educational and social services rather than the criminal justice system.

Even if the age of criminal responsibility were 16 in most countries, there would still be questions about the provision for young offenders aged 16 and 17. The current trend is towards the 'what works' approach (see Chapter 1 above), with 'evidence-based' policies grounded in evaluations of programmes. However, there are considerable doubts about the rigour of many of the British evaluations and the uses to which they have been put, as noted in Chapter 1. It remains important to invest considerable effort in the development of effective programmes for young offenders, whether rehabilitative or restorative or whatever, and to ensure that they can be fitted into a community order that is no longer or more demanding than is proportionate to the offence.

Separate Courts for the Young

Although the movement towards separate treatment of juveniles in the penal system had begun in the nineteenth century, it was not until the Illinois Juvenile Court Act 1899 that the idea of separate courts received recognition. This was followed in England and Wales by the Children Act 1908, establishing the juvenile court. Behind these developments lay recognition of the need for different modes of thinking about the punishment of young offenders, the need for specialist sentencers trained to deal with these cases and the importance of separating young offenders from their adult counterparts not only during the sentence itself but also at the court stage. Although these ideals are still maintained today in many countries, Barry Feld (Selection 7.6) demonstrates how 'public safety' arguments and other political considerations have led to a regression from juvenile courts in many US jurisdictions.[25] A further aim is that of speedy procedures when dealing with young offenders, whose sense of time may be underdeveloped: as rule 20 of the Beijing Rules affirms (Selection 7.1), it is important to ensure a close temporal link between the offending behaviour and the official response.

The Scottish system differs from many others in having a separate tribunal to determine what compulsory measures (if any) are appropriate. The case will go to court if there is a plea of not guilty; otherwise it will go to the children's hearing if the child is under 16, and that body will reach its decision based on its view of the best interests of the child.[26] However, this system applies only until the age of 16, which means that youths aged 16 and 17 are dealt with in the adult court. This raises the question of how the age limit for the special court should relate to the age of criminal responsibility. In principle, the minimum age of criminal responsibility has the effect of consigning all cases of offending beneath that age to civil and social measures. Special courts and special penal measures should be available to deal with the next stage of adolescence, up to the age of majority at least. Thus, if the age of criminal responsibility is 16, ought not special youth courts be available at least to 18, and probably to 20 or 21?

Where the age of criminal responsibility is lower than 16, and particularly where it is as low as 10 (as in England and Wales), questions arise about the ability of a young defendant to follow the proceedings. English law provides that a child under 14 who is accused of murder or manslaughter should appear at the Crown Court, not in a youth court. Thus, following the killing of James Bulger in 1993, two boys (then aged 11) were tried for murder in the Crown Court. Some modifications of procedure were made, but the European Court of Human Rights held that the trial still failed to meet the standards of a 'fair hearing' within Article 6 of the European Convention.[27] The Court received evidence from psychologists about the traumatic effect of the trial proceedings and widespread publicity on the defendants and on their inability to follow the proceedings. In a subsequent judgment the European Court elaborated on a young defendant's right to effective participation in the criminal trial:

> it is essential that he be dealt with in a manner which takes full account of his age, level of maturity and intellectual and emotional capacities, and that steps are taken to promote his ability to understand and participate in the proceedings, including conducting the hearing in such a way as to reduce as far as possible his feelings of intimidation and inhibition.[28]

These are the right principles, but they have been enunciated in response to a legal system that has a manifestly low age of criminal responsibility. If international pressure is unable to bring about change in that regard, then at least it might be more definite in insisting that such cases be heard in tribunals having some specialised knowledge of juvenile justice, and not in courts dealing chiefly with serious cases. In the meantime, as Barry Feld argues in Selection 7.6, the ideology of the juvenile court has suffered a transformation in most US states, with a trend in the 1990s towards facilitating the transfer of many youth defendants to adult courts, where they are liable to be sentenced as adults. This runs against most of the arguments above, and against the international standards set out in Selections 7.1 and 7.2.[29]

AA

Notes

1. Radzinowicz, L and Hood, R, (1986) *The Emergence of Penal Policy* (London, Stevens) 133.
2. Archard, D, (2001) 'Philosophical Perspective on Childhood' in J Fionda (ed), *Legal Concepts of Childhood* (Oxford, Hart Publishing) 49.
3. The former presumption of *doli incapax*—that a child under 14 was presumed incapable of knowing that the act was 'seriously wrong' unless the prosecution proved this—was abolished in 1998. For discussion of minimum ages and the presumption of *doli incapax*, see Fionda, J, (2005) *Devils and Angels: Youth Policy and Crime* (Oxford, Hart Publishing) 9–19.
4. United Nations Committee on the Rights of the Child, (2002) *Concluding Observations of the Committee on the Rights of the Child: United Kingdom of Great Britain and Northern Ireland*, para 59.
5. United Nations Standard Minimum Rules for the Administration of Juvenile Justice, (1985) Official Commentary to Rule 4.
6. *Gillick v West Norfolk and Wisbech Area Health Authority* [1986] AC 112.
7. Children and Young Persons Act 1969, s 4.
8. One of the many arguments addressed to the European Court of Human Rights in *T and V v United Kingdom* (2000) 30 EHRR 121 was that it amounted to 'inhuman or degrading treatment', contrary to Art 3 of the European Convention on Human Rights, to hold children as young as 10 to be criminally responsible. The Court found no breach of Art 3, by a majority of 12 to 5, holding that there was such diversity among the age of criminal responsibility in different European countries that it could not be said that the age of 10 differed disproportionately from the other ages (mostly higher, but a few lower).
9. English law does provide for the taking of penal measures against parents for the offending of their children: on this, see Zedner, L, (1998) 'Sentencing Young Offenders' in A Ashworth and M Wasik (eds), *Fundamentals of Sentencing Theory: essays in honour of Andrew von Hirsch* (Oxford, Clarendon Press) 176–81.
10. Above n 4.
11. On which see, eg MacCormick, N, (1976) 'Children's Rights: a Test-case for Theories of Rights' 62 *Archiv für Rechts und Sozialphilosophie* 305; O'Neill, O, (1992) 'Children's Rights and Children's Lives' 98 *Ethics* 445; Fortin, J, (2003) *Children's Rights and the Developing Law*, 2nd edn (London, LexisNexis) ch 1.
12. See further van Bueren, G, (1995) *International Law on the Rights of the Child* (Dordrecht, Martinus Nijoff) ch 7.
13. See Zedner, above n 9.
14. For a brief explanation of the Scottish system of juvenile justice, see Fionda, above n 3, 245–52; for fuller discussion, see Bottoms, AE and Dignan, J, (2004) 'Youth Justice in Great Britain' in M Tonry and A Doob (eds), *Youth Crime and Youth Justice: Crime and Justice, a Review of Research*, vol 31 (Chicago, IL, University of Chicago Press) 21; Stevenson, R and Brotchie, R, (2005) *Getting it Right for Every Child* (Scottish Executive, Edinburgh).
15. See, eg Rutherford, A, (1986) *Growing Out of Crime* (Harmondsworth, Penguin Books) ch 1.
16. Cf Moffitt, T, (1993) 'Adolescent-limited and Life-course-persistent Antisocial Behaviour: a Developmental Taxonomy' 100 *Psychological Review* 674; and the discussion by Bottoms and Dignan, above n 14, 33–3, 169 and 171.

17. Cf Zedner, above n 9, 173–4.
18. Goldson, B and Muncie, J, (2006) 'Rethinking Youth Justice: Comparative Analysis, International Human Rights and Research Evidence' 6 *Youth Justice* 91, 99; compare the various policy statements of the Youth Justice Board, at www.yjb.gov.uk.
19. Waterhouse, L *et al*, (2000) *The Evaluation of Children's Hearings in Scotland, vol 3: Children in Focus* (Edinburgh, CRU) 95, quoted by Bottoms and Dignan, above n 14, 70.
20. Ashworth, A, (2005) *Sentencing and Criminal Justice*, 4th edn (Cambridge, Cambridge University Press) 363.
21. For discussion of the genesis of this text, and related international instruments, see van Bueren, above n 12, 184.
22. Social Exclusion Unit, (2002) *Reducing Re-offending by Ex-prisoners* (London, Social Exclusion Unit) Annex D, puts the figure at 84% for those discharged in 1997.
23. Committee on the Rights of the Child, above n 4; Office of the Commissioner for Human Rights, *Report by Mr Alvaro Gil-Robles, Commissioner for Human Rights, on his visit to the United Kingdom* (Comm DH (2005) 6) paras 105–7.
24. Calverly, C, (2007) 'Youth Custody and Community Services in Canada, 2004/05' 27 *Juristat* No 2.
25. This is not true of countries like Sweden, for example, where young offenders are sentenced in adult courts according to the same general principle of proportionality but with a separate and less severe set of sanctions: see Jareborg, N, (1995) 'The Swedish Sentencing Reform' in C Clarkson and R Morgan (eds), *The Politics of Sentencing Reform* (Oxford, Clarendon Press).
26. On the Scottish system, see the references at n 14 above.
27. *T and V v United Kingdom* (2000) 30 EHRR 121.
28. *SC v United Kingdom* (2004) 40 EHRR 226, para 28.
29. The United States has not ratified the UN Convention on the Rights of the Child.

Further Reading

Feld, B, (1999) *Bad Kids: Race and the Transformation of the Juvenile Court* (New York, Oxford University Press).
Fionda, J, (2005) *Devils and Angels: Youth Policy and Crime* (Oxford, Hart Publishing).
Junger-Tas, J and Decker, S (eds), (2006) *International Handbook of Juvenile Justice* (Dordrecht, Springer).
Scott, E, (2000) 'Criminal Responsibility in Adolescence: Lessons from Developmental Psychology' in T Grisso and R Schwartz (eds), *Youth on Trial: A Developmental Perspective on Juvenile Justice* (Chicago, IL, University of Chicago Press).
Tonry, M and Moore, M (eds)(1998) *Youth Violence: Crime and Justice, a Review of Research*, vol. 24 (Chicago, University of Chicago Press).
Tonry, M and Doob, A (eds), (2004) *Youth Crime and Youth Justice: Crime and Justice, a Review of Research*, vol 31 (Chicago, IL, University of Chicago Press).
van Bueren, G, (1995) *International Law of the Rights of the Child* (Dordrecht, Martinus Nijhoff).
Weijers, I and Duff, RA (eds), (2002) *Punishing Juveniles. Principle and Critique* (Oxford, Hart Publishing).

7.1

United Nations Standard Minimum Rules for the Administration of Juvenile Justice ("The Beijing Rules")
Adopted by General Assembly resolution 40/33 of
29 November 1985

PART ONE

GENERAL PRINCIPLES

1. Fundamental perspectives

1.1 Member States shall seek, in conformity with their respective general interests, to further the well-being of the juvenile and her or his family.

1.2 Member States shall endeavour to develop conditions that will ensure for the juvenile a meaningful life in the community, which, during that period in life when she or he is most susceptible to deviant behaviour, will foster a process of personal development and education that is as free from crime and delinquency as possible.

1.3 Sufficient attention shall be given to positive measures that involve the full mobilization of all possible resources, including the family, volunteers and other community groups, as well as schools and other community institutions, for the purpose of promoting the well-being of the juvenile, with a view to reducing the need for intervention under the law, and of effectively, fairly and humanely dealing with the juvenile in conflict with the law.

1.4 Juvenile justice shall be conceived as an integral part of the national development process of each country, within a comprehensive framework of social justice for all juveniles, thus, at the same time, contributing to the protection of the young and the maintenance of a peaceful order in society.

1.5 These Rules shall be implemented in the context of economic, social and cultural conditions prevailing in each Member State.

1.6 Juvenile justice services shall be systematically developed and coordinated with a view to improving and sustaining the competence of personnel involved in the services, including , their methods, approaches and attitudes . . .

4. Age of criminal responsibility

4.1 In those legal systems recognizing the concept of the age of criminal responsibility for juveniles, the beginning of that age shall not be fixed at too low an age level, bearing in mind the facts of emotional, mental and intellectual maturity.

Commentary

The minimum age of criminal responsibility differs widely owing to history and culture. The modern approach would be to consider whether a child can live up to the moral and psychological components of criminal responsibility; that is, whether a child, by virtue of her or his individual discernment and understanding, can be held responsible for essentially antisocial behaviour. If the age of criminal responsibility is fixed too low or if there is no lower age limit at all, the notion of responsibility would become meaningless. In general, there is a close relationship between the notion of responsibility for delinquent or criminal behaviour and other social rights and responsibilities (such as marital status, civil majority, etc.).

Efforts should therefore be made to agree on a reasonable lowest age limit that is applicable internationally.

5. Aims of juvenile justice

5.1 The juvenile justice system shall emphasize the well-being of the juvenile and shall ensure that any reaction to juvenile offenders shall always be in proportion to the circumstances of both the offenders and the offence.

Commentary

Rule 5 refers to two of the most important objectives of juvenile justice. The first objective is the promotion of the well-being of the juvenile. This is the main focus of those legal systems in which juvenile offenders are dealt with by family courts or administrative authorities, but the well-being of the juvenile should also be emphasized in legal systems that follow the criminal court model, thus contributing to the avoidance of merely punitive sanctions. (See also rule 14.)

The second objective is "the principle of proportionality". This principle is well-known as an instrument for curbing punitive sanctions, mostly expressed in terms of just deserts in relation to the gravity of the offence. The response to young offenders should be based on the consideration not only of the gravity of the offence but also of personal circumstances. The individual circumstances of the offender (for example social status, family situation, the harm caused by the offence or other factors affecting personal circumstances) should influence the proportionality of the reactions (for example by having regard to the offender's endeavour to indemnify the victim or to her or his willingness to turn to wholesome and useful life).

By the same token, reactions aiming to ensure the welfare of the young offender may go beyond necessity and therefore infringe upon the fundamental rights of the young individual, as has been observed in some juvenile justice systems. Here, too, the proportionality of the reaction to the circumstances of both the offender and the offence, including the victim, should be safeguarded.

In essence, rule 5 calls for no less and no more than a fair reaction in any given cases of juvenile delinquency and crime. The issues combined in the rule may help to stimulate development in both regards: new and innovative types of reactions are as desirable as precautions against any undue widening of the net of formal social control over juveniles.

6. Scope of discretion

6.1 In view of the varying special needs of juveniles as well as the variety of measures available, appropriate scope for discretion shall be allowed at all stages of proceedings and at the different levels of juvenile justice administration, including investigation, prosecution, adjudication and the follow-up of dispositions.

6.2 Efforts shall be made, however, to ensure sufficient accountability at all stages and levels in the exercise of any such discretion.

6.3 Those who exercise discretion shall be specially qualified or trained to exercise it judiciously and in accordance with their functions and mandates.

Commentary

Rules 6.1, 6.2 and 6.3 combine several important features of effective, fair and humane juvenile justice administration: the need to permit the exercise of discretionary power at all significant levels of processing so that those who make determinations can take the actions deemed to be most appropriate in each individual case; and the need to provide checks and balances in order to curb any abuses of discretionary power and to safeguard the rights of the young offender. Accountability and professionalism are instruments best apt to curb broad discretion. Thus, professional qualifications and expert training are emphasized here as a valuable means of ensuring the judicious exercise of discretion in matters of juvenile offenders. (See also rules 1.6 and 2.2.) The formulation of specific guidelines on the exercise of discretion and the provision of systems of review, appeal and the like in order to permit scrutiny of decisions and accountability are emphasized in this context. Such mechanisms are not specified here, as they do not easily lend themselves to incorporation into international standard minimum rules, which cannot possibly cover all differences in justice systems.

7. Rights of juveniles

7.1 Basic procedural safeguards such as the presumption of innocence, the right to be notified of the charges, the right to remain silent, the right to counsel, the right to the presence of a parent or guardian, the right to confront and cross-examine witnesses and the right to appeal to a higher authority shall be guaranteed at all stages of proceedings . . .

11. Diversion

11.1 Consideration shall be given, wherever appropriate, to dealing with juvenile offenders without resorting to formal trial by the competent authority, referred to in rule 14.1 below.

11.2 The police, the prosecution or other agencies dealing with juvenile cases shall be empowered to dispose of such cases, at their discretion, without recourse to formal hearings, in accordance with the criteria laid down for that purpose in the respective legal system and also in accordance with the principles contained in these Rules.

11.3 Any diversion involving referral to appropriate community or other services shall require the consent of the juvenile, or her or his parents or guardian, provided that such decision to refer a case shall be subject to review by a competent authority, upon application.

11.4 In order to facilitate the discretionary disposition of juvenile cases, efforts shall be made to provide for community programmes, such as temporary supervision and guidance, restitution, and compensation of victims . . .

14. Competent authority to adjudicate

14.1 Where the case of a juvenile offender has not been diverted (under rule 11), she or he shall be dealt with by the competent authority (court, tribunal, board, council, etc.) according to the principles of a fair and just trial.

14.2 The proceedings shall be conducive to the best interests of the juvenile and shall be conducted in an atmosphere of understanding, which shall allow the juvenile to participate therein and to express herself or himself freely . . .

16. Social inquiry reports

16.1 In all cases except those involving minor offences, before the competent authority renders a final disposition prior to sentencing, the background and circumstances in which the juvenile is living or the conditions under which the offence has been committed shall be properly investigated so as to facilitate judicious adjudication of the case by the competent authority . . .

17.1 The disposition of the competent authority shall be guided by the following principles:

(a) The reaction taken shall always be in proportion not only to the circumstances and the gravity of the offence but also to the circumstances and the needs of the juvenile as well as to the needs of the society;

(b) Restrictions on the personal liberty of the juvenile shall be imposed only after careful consideration and shall be limited to the possible minimum;

(c) Deprivation of personal liberty shall not be imposed unless the juvenile is adjudicated of a serious act involving violence against another person or of persistence in committing other serious offences and unless there is no other appropriate response;

(d) The well-being of the juvenile shall be the guiding factor in the consideration of her or his case.

17.2 Capital punishment shall not be imposed for any crime committed by juveniles.

17.3 Juveniles shall not be subject to corporal punishment.

17.4 The competent authority shall have the power to discontinue the proceedings at any time.

Commentary

The main difficulty in formulating guidelines for the adjudication of young persons stems from the fact that there are unresolved conflicts of a philosophical nature, such as the following:

(a) Rehabilitation versus just desert;

(b) Assistance versus repression and punishment;

(c) Reaction according to the singular merits of an individual case versus reaction according to the protection of society in general;

(d) General deterrence versus individual incapacitation.

The conflict between these approaches is more pronounced in juvenile cases than in adult cases. With the variety of causes and reactions characterizing juvenile cases, these alternatives become intricately interwoven.

It is not the function of the Standard Minimum Rules for the Administration of Juvenile Justice to prescribe which approach is to be followed but rather to identify one that is most closely in consonance with internationally accepted principles. Therefore the essential elements as laid down in rule 17.1, in particular in subparagraphs (a) and (c), are mainly to be understood as practical guidelines that should ensure a common starting point; if heeded by the concerned authorities (see also rule 5), they could contribute considerably to ensuring that the fundamental rights of juvenile offenders are protected, especially the fundamental rights of personal development and education.

Rule 17.1 (b) implies that strictly punitive approaches are not appropriate. Whereas in adult cases, and possibly also in cases of severe offences by juveniles, just desert and retributive sanctions might be considered to have some merit, in juvenile cases such considerations should always be outweighed by the interest of safeguarding the well-being and the future of the young person.

In line with resolution 8 of the Sixth United Nations Congress, rule 17.1 (b) encourages the use of alternatives to institutionalization to the maximum extent possible, bearing in mind the need to respond to the specific requirements of the young. Thus, full use should be made of the range of existing alternative sanctions and new alternative sanctions should be developed, bearing the public safety in mind. Probation should be granted to the greatest possible extent via suspended sentences, conditional sentences, board orders and other dispositions.

Rule 17.1 (c) corresponds to one of the guiding principles in resolution 4 of the Sixth Congress which aims at avoiding incarceration in the case of juveniles unless there is no other appropriate response that will protect the public safety . . .

19. Least possible use of institutionalization

19.1 The placement of a juvenile in an institution shall always be a disposition of last resort and for the minimum necessary period . . .

20. Avoidance of unnecessary delay

20.1 Each case shall from the outset be handled expeditiously, without any unnecessary delay . . .

7.2

United Nations Convention on the Rights of the Child
Adopted and opened for signature, ratification and accession by
General Assembly resolution 44/25 of 20 November 1989
entry into force 2 September 1990, in accordance with article 49

Article 1

For the purposes of the present Convention, a child means every human being below the age of eighteen years unless under the law applicable to the child, majority is attained earlier.

Article 2

1. States Parties shall respect and ensure the rights set forth in the present Convention to each child within their jurisdiction without discrimination of any kind, irrespective of the child's or his or her parent's or legal guardian's race, colour, sex, language, religion, political or other opinion, national, ethnic or social origin, property, disability, birth or other status.

2. States Parties shall take all appropriate measures to ensure that the child is protected against all forms of discrimination or punishment on the basis of the status, activities, expressed opinions, or beliefs of the child's parents, legal guardians, or family members.

Article 3

1. In all actions concerning children, whether undertaken by public or private social welfare institutions, courts of law, administrative authorities or legislative bodies, the best interests of the child shall be a primary consideration.

2. States Parties undertake to ensure the child such protection and care as is necessary for his or her well-being, taking into account the rights and duties of his or her parents, legal guardians, or other individuals legally responsible for him or her, and, to this end, shall take all appropriate legislative and administrative measures.

3. States Parties shall ensure that the institutions, services and facilities responsible for the care or protection of children shall conform with the standards established by competent authorities, particularly in the areas of safety, health, in the number and suitability of their staff, as well as competent supervision . . .

Article 37

States Parties shall ensure that:

(a) No child shall be subjected to torture or other cruel, inhuman or degrading treatment or punishment. Neither capital punishment nor life imprisonment without possibility of release shall be imposed for offences committed by persons below eighteen years of age;

(b) No child shall be deprived of his or her liberty unlawfully or arbitrarily. The arrest, detention or imprisonment of a child shall be in conformity with the law and shall be used only as a measure of last resort and for the shortest appropriate period of time;

(c) Every child deprived of liberty shall be treated with humanity and respect for the inherent dignity of the human person, and in a manner which takes into account the needs of persons of his or her age. In particular, every child deprived of liberty shall be separated from adults unless it is considered in the child's best interest not to do so and shall have the right to maintain contact with his or her family through correspondence and visits, save in exceptional circumstances;

(d) Every child deprived of his or her liberty shall have the right to prompt access to legal and other appropriate assistance, as well as the right to challenge the legality of the deprivation of his or her liberty before a court or other competent, independent and impartial authority, and to a prompt decision on any such action . . .

Article 40

1. States Parties recognize the right of every child alleged as, accused of, or recognized as having infringed the penal law to be treated in a manner consistent with the promotion of the child's sense of dignity and worth, which reinforces the child's respect for the human rights and fundamental freedoms of others and which takes into account the child's age and the desirability of promoting the child's reintegration and the child's assuming a constructive role in society.

2. To this end, and having regard to the relevant provisions of international instruments, States Parties shall, in particular, ensure that:

(a) No child shall be alleged as, be accused of, or recognized as having infringed the penal law by reason of acts or omissions that were not prohibited by national or international law at the time they were committed;

(b) Every child alleged as or accused of having infringed the penal law has at least the following guarantees:

(i) To be presumed innocent until proven guilty according to law;

(ii) To be informed promptly and directly of the charges against him or her, and, if appropriate, through his or her parents or legal guardians, and to have legal or other appropriate assistance in the preparation and presentation of his or her defence;

(iii) To have the matter determined without delay by a competent, independent and impartial authority or judicial body in a fair hearing according to law, in the presence of legal or other appropriate assistance and, unless it is considered not to be in the best interest of the child, in particular, taking into account his or her age or situation, his or her parents or legal guardians;

(iv) Not to be compelled to give testimony or to confess guilt; to examine or have examined adverse witnesses and to obtain the participation and examination of witnesses on his or her behalf under conditions of equality;

(v) If considered to have infringed the penal law, to have this decision and any measures imposed in consequence thereof reviewed by a higher competent, independent and impartial authority or judicial body according to law;

(vi) To have the free assistance of an interpreter if the child cannot understand or speak the language used;

(vii) To have his or her privacy fully respected at all stages of the proceedings. 3. States Parties shall seek to promote the establishment of laws, procedures, authorities and institutions specifically applicable to children alleged as, accused of, or recognized as having infringed the penal law, and, in particular:

(a) The establishment of a minimum age below which children shall be presumed not to have the capacity to infringe the penal law;

(b) Whenever appropriate and desirable, measures for dealing with such children without resorting to judicial proceedings, providing that human rights and legal safeguards are fully respected.

4. A variety of dispositions, such as care, guidance and supervision orders; counselling; probation; foster care; education and vocational training programmes and other alternatives to institutional care shall be available to ensure that children are dealt with in a manner appropriate to their well-being and proportionate both to their circumstances and the offence . . .

7.3

Rationales for Distinctive Penal Policies for Youth Offenders

FRANKLIN E. ZIMRING

Little has been written about the substantive reasons that support a separate policy toward crimes committed by young offenders for a variety of reasons. Part of the problem is that juvenile and criminal court issues were usually considered separately, so that there was little pressure exerted to examine the same questions across different procedural settings. A further deterrent to substantive analysis is that separate treatment of children seemed intuitively right in a way that did not invite farther scrutiny from its advocates. Of course, kids who violate laws should be differently treated; should we imprison six-year-olds? Legal nuance and complexity might seem beside the point in this context. For all these reasons, no sustained analysis of the factors that justify separate treatment of adolescent offenders is in the literature to measure against the known facts on serious youth violence.

Some years ago, I suggested two general policy clusters that were at work in youth crime policy: diminished capacity due to immaturity, and special efforts designed to give young offenders room to reform in the course of adolescent years (Twentieth Century Fund 1978, pp. 78–81). The issues grouped under the "diminished capacity" heading relate to the traditional concerns of the criminal law, so that these matters tell us why a criminal lawyer might regard a younger offender as less culpable than an older offender. The cluster of policies under the heading of "room to reform" are derived from legal policies toward young persons in the process of growing up. They are the same policies we apply to young drivers, teen pregnancy, and school dropouts.

A. Dimensions of Diminished Responsibility

To consider immaturity as a species of diminished responsibility has some historic precedent but little analytic pedigree. Children below seven were at common law not responsible for criminal acts by reason of incapacity, while those between seven and fourteen were the subject of special inquiries with respect to capacity. But

From FE Zimring, 'Toward a Jurisprudence of Youth Violence' in M Tonry and M Moore (eds), *Youth Violence: Crime and Justice, a Review of Research*, vol 24 (Chicago, IL, University of Chicago Press, 1998), 447–501.

capacity in this sense was an all-or-nothing matter like legal insanity rather than a question of degree. Yet diminished-capacity logic argues that, even after a youth passes the minimum threshold of competence that leads to finding capacity to commit crime, the barely competent youth is not as culpable and therefore not as deserving of a full measure of punishment as a fully qualified adult offender. Just as psychiatric disorder or cognitive impairment that does not render a subject exempt from the criminal law might still mitigate the punishment justly to be imposed, so a minimally competent adolescent should not be responsible for the whole of an adult's desert for the same act . . .

What characteristics of children and adolescents might lead us to lessen punishment in the name of immaturity? An initial distinction needs to be drawn between diminished capacities and the poor decisions such impairments encourage. Most teenaged law violators make bad decisions, but so do most adults who commit major infractions of the criminal law. The Anglo-American criminal law is designed to punish bad decisions full measure. But persons who for reasons not their own fault lack the capacity observed in the common citizen to appreciate the difference between wrong and allowable conduct or to conform their conduct to the law's requirements may be blameless because of the incapacity. Even when sufficient cognitive capacity and emotional control is present to pass the threshold of criminal capacity, a significant deficit in the capacity to appreciate or control behavior would mean the forbidden conduct is not *as much* the offender's fault, and the quantum of appropriate punishment is less.

How might fourteen- and fifteen-year-olds who commit crimes be said to exhibit diminished capacity in moral and legal terms? There are three different types of personal attributes that influence decisions to commit crimes where adolescents may lack full adult skills and therefore also full adult moral responsibilities when the law is violated.

1. *Cognitive Abilities.* First, older children and younger adolescents may lack fully developed cognitive abilities to comprehend the moral content of commands and to apply legal and moral rules to social situations. The lack of this kind of capacity is at the heart of infancy as an absolute defense to criminal liability. This ability to comprehend and apply rules in the abstract requires a mix of cognitive ability and information. A young person who lacks these skills will not do well on a paper-and-pencil test to assess knowledge about what is lawful and unlawful behavior and why. Very young children have obvious gaps in both information and the cognitive skills to use it. Older children have more subtle but still significant deficits in moral reasoning abilities.

2. *Self-Control.* The capacity to pass paper-and-pencil tests in moral reasoning may be one necessary condition for adult capacity of self-control, but it is by no means a sufficient condition. A second skill that helps transform cognitive understanding into the capacity to obey the law is the ability to control impulses. This is not the

type of capacity that can be tested well on abstract written or oral surveys. Long after a child knows that taking candy is wrong, the capacity to resist temptation when a taking is the only available route to the candy may not be fully operational.

To an important extent, self-control is a habit of behavior developed over a period of time, a habit dependent on the experience of successfully exercising self-control. This particular type of maturity, like so many others, takes practice. While children must start learning to control impulses at a very early age, the question of how long the process continues until adult levels of control are achieved is an open one. Impulse control is a social skill not easily measured in a laboratory. We also do not know the extent to which lessons to control impulses are generalized or how context-specific are habits of self-control. Kids must learn not to dash in front of cars at an early age. How much of that capacity to self-control carries over when other impulses—say, the temptation to cheat on a test—occur in new situations? The empirical psychology of self-control is not a thick chapter in current psychological knowledge. The developmental psychology of self-control is practically nonexistent. There may also be an important distinction between impulse control in the context of frustration and impulse control in temptation settings. If so, the frustration context may be the more important one for study of the determinants of youth violence.

To the extent that new situations and opportunities require new habits of self-control, the teen years are periods when self-control issues are confronted on a series of distinctive new battlefields. The physical controls of earlier years are supplanted by physical freedoms. New domains—including secondary education, sex, and driving—require not only the cognitive appreciation of the need for self-control in a new situation but also its practice. If this normally takes a while to develop, the bad decisions made along the way should not be punished as severely as the bad decisions of adults who have passed through the period when the opportunity to develop habits of self-control in a variety of domains relevant to the criminal law has occurred. To the extent that inexperience is a condition of reduced capacity, this inexperience is partially excusable in the teen years, whereas it is not usually understandable in later life.

3. *Peer Pressure.* The ability to resist peer pressure is yet another social skill that is a necessary part of legal obedience and is not fully developed in many adolescents. A teen may know right from wrong and even may have developed the capacity to control his or her impulses if left alone to do so, but resisting temptation while alone is a different task than resisting the pressure to commit an offense when adolescent peers are pushing for the adolescent to misbehave and witnessing whether or not the outcome they desire will occur. Most adolescent decisions to break the law or not take place on a social stage where the immediate pressure of peers urging the adolescent on is often the real motive for most teenage crime. A necessary condition for an adolescent to stay law-abiding is the ability to deflect or resist peer pressure. Many kids lack this crucial social skill for a long time.

Consider the percentage of juvenile defendants who were accused of committing a crime with at least one confederate in the New York City Family Courts in 1978. These offenders were all under sixteen at the time the act was committed. The percentage of total defendants who acted with a confederate ranged from 60 percent for assault to 90 percent for robbery.

The cold criminological facts are these: the teen years are characterized by what has long been called "group offending." No matter the crime, if a teenager is the offender, he is usually not committing the offense alone. When adults commit theft, they usually are acting alone. When kids commit theft, they usually steal in groups. When adults commit rape, robbery, homicide, burglary, or assault, they usually are acting alone. When adolescents commit rape, robbery, homicide, burglary, or assault, they usually commit the offense accompanied by other kids (Zimring 1981). The setting for the offenses of adolescents is the presence of delinquent peers as witnesses and collaborators.

No fact of adolescent criminality is more important than what sociologists call its "group context" (Reiss 1988). And this fact is important to a balanced and worldly theory of adolescent moral and legal responsibility for criminal acts.

When an adult offender commits rape, his motive may be rage or lust or any number of other things. When a teen offender in a group setting commits rape, the motive may well be "I dare you" or its functional equivalent "Don't be a chicken." When an adolescent robs, steals, breaks into a house, or shoots another youth in the company of co-offenders, the real motive for his acts may be the explicit or implicit "I dare you" that leads kids to show off and that deters kids from withdrawing from criminal acts. Fear of being called chicken is almost certainly the leading cause of death and injury from youth violence in the United States.

"I dare you" is the core reason young persons who would not commit crimes alone do so in groups. "I dare you" is the reason that "having delinquent friends" both precedes an adolescent's own involvement in violence and is a strong predictor of fature violence (Elliott and Menard 1996; Howell and Hawkins 1998).

That social settings account for the majority of all youth crime suggests that the capacity to deflect or resist peer pressure is a crucially necessary dimension of being law-abiding in adolescence. Dealing with peer pressure is another dimension of capacity that requires social experience. Kids who do not know how to deal with such pressure lack effective control of the situations that place them most at risk of crime in their teens. This surely does not excuse criminal conduct. But any moral scheme that gives mitigational recognition to other forms of inexperience must also do so for a lack of peer-management skills that an accused has not had a fair opportunity to develop. This is a matter of huge importance given the reality of contemporary youth crime as group behavior.

I do not want to suggest that current knowledge is sufficient for us to measure the extent of diminished capacity in young offenders or to express in detail the types of understanding and control that are important parts of a normative developmental psychology. We have an awful lot of social psychology homework ahead of us before achieving understanding of the key terms in adolescent behavioral controls relevant to criminal offending.

B. Room to Reform in Youth Development Policy

The notion that children and adolescents should be the subject of special legal rules pervades the civil as well as the criminal laws of most developed societies. There are a multiplicity of different policies reflected in different legal areas and also important differences throughout law in the treatment of younger and older children. Under these circumstances, to refer to "youth policy" generally risks misunderstandings about both the subjects of the policies and the policy objects of the rules.

The policies I refer to in this section concern adolescence, a period that spans roughly from ages eleven or twelve to about age twenty. This is also the only segment of childhood associated with high rates of serious crime. This span has been described as a period of increasing semiautonomy when kids acquire adult liberties in stages and learn their way toward adult freedoms (Zimring 1982).

At the heart of this process is a notion of adolescence as a period of "learning by doing" when the only way competence in decision making can be achieved is by making decisions and making mistakes. For this reason, adolescence is a period that is mistake-prone by design. The special challenge here is to create safeguards in the policies and environments of adolescents that reduce the permanent costs of adolescent mistakes. Two goals of legal policy are to facilitate "learning by doing" and to reduce the hazards associated with expectable errors. One important hallmark of a successful adolescence is survival to adulthood, preferably with the individual's life chances intact.

There is a currently fashionable theory of the classification of youth crime in legal policy that provides a rationale for a room-to-reform policy. The theory is that the high prevalence of offense behavior in the teen years and the rather high rates of incidence for those who offend are often transitory phenomena associated with a transitional status and life period. Even absent heroic interventions, the conduct that occurs at peak rates in adolescence will level off substantially if and when adolescents achieve adult roles and status. With regard to youth violence, the distinction is drawn between "adolescence-limited" and "life-course-persistent" adolescent violent offenders (Moffitt 1993).

The adolescence-limited assumption may carry three implications. First, it regards criminal offenses as a more or less normal adolescent phenomenon, a by-product of the same transitional status that increases accident risks, rates of accidental pregnancy, and suicidal gestures. This view of youth crime tells us, therefore, that policy toward those offenses that are a by-product of adolescence should be a part of larger policies toward youth.

A second implication of the notion that high rates of adolescent crimes can be outgrown is that major interventions may not be necessary to reorient offenders.

The central notion of what has been called "adolescence-limited" offending is that one cure for youth violence is growing up (Moffitt 1993; Howell and Hawkins 1998).

Related to the hope for natural processes of remission over time is the tendency for persons who view youth crime policy as a branch of youth development policy to worry that drastic countermeasures that inhibit the natural transition to adulthood may cause more harm than they are worth. If a particular treatment risks severe side effects, it usually should only be elected if failure to use would risk more cost. Those who regard youth crime as a transitional phenomenon see problems of deviance resolving themselves without drastic interventions and thus doubt the efficacy of high-risk interventions on utilitarian grounds. So juvenile justice theories with labels like "radical nonintervention" and "diversion" are a natural outgrowth of the belief that long-term prospects for most young offenders are favorable.

But what about the short term? The current costs of youth crime to the general community, to other adolescents, and to the offending kids are quite large. How would enthusiasts for juvenile court nonintervention seek to protect the community? Is a room-to-reform policy inconsistent with *any* punitive responses to adolescent law violation?

The emphasis in youth development policy is on risk management over a period of transitional high danger. As we have seen, the theory that adolescents are not fully mature allows a larger variety of risk-management tactics than is available for dealing with adults. Minors cannot purchase liquor, acquire handguns, buy cigarettes, or pilot planes. Younger adolescents are constrained by curfews and compulsory education laws. There are special age-graded rules for driving motor vehicles, entering contracts, and establishing employment relationships. Many of these rules are to protect the young person from the predation of others. Many are to protect the young person from herself. Many are to protect the community from harmful acts by the young. So there is a rich mixture of risk-management strategies available to reduce the level of harmful consequences from youth crime.

Does this mix of strategies include the punishment of intentional harms? The answer to this question is yes from all but the most extreme radical noninterventionists, but attaching negative consequences to youthful offenders is good policy in this view only up to a point. Youth development proponents are suspicious of sacrificing the personal interests of a young person in order to serve as a deterrent example to other youth if the punished offender's interests are substantially prejudiced. And punishing a young offender in ways that significantly diminish later life chances compromises the essential core of a youth protection policy. There may be circumstances where drastic punishment is required, but such punishments always violate important priorities in youth development policy and can be tolerated rarely and only in cases of proven need. In this view, punishment begins to be suspicious when it compromises the long-term interests of the targeted young offender . . .

General Conclusions

There are two clusters of reasons criminal acts by immature offenders are treated differently from the same acts committed by adults. Concerns about diminished responsibility come from a criminal law concern about punishment in just proportion to culpability. Concerns about preserving the future life chances of young offenders come from general policies that provide special support to adolescents in the transition to adulthood. Diminished-responsibility doctrines seek to reduce the amount of punishment that is appropriate. Room-to-reform policies address not so much the amount of punishment imposed but the kind of punishment. and the kind of consequences that should be avoided. The orientation of these policies is qualitative rather than quantitative.

References

Elliott, D.S., and Menard, S. (1996), 'Delinquent Friends and Delinquent Behaviour', in J.D. Hawkins (ed). *Delinquency and Crime: Current Theories* (Cambridge: Cambridge U.P.)
Howell, J.C., and Hawkins, J.D. (1998), 'Prevention of Youth Violence', in N. Tonry and M. Moore (eds), 24 *Crime and Justice: a Review of Research* (Chicago: Chicago U.P.).
Moffitt, T. (1993), 'Adolescent-Limited and Life-Course-Persistent Antisocial Behaviour: a Developmental Taxonomy', *Psychological Review* 100: 674.
Reiss, A. (1988), 'Co-Offending and Criminal Careers', in M. Tonry and N. Morris (eds), 10 *Crime and Justice: an Annual Review* (Chicago: Chicago U.P.)
Twentieth Century Fund (1978), *Confronting Youth Crime* (New York: Holmes and Meier).
Zimring, F. (1981), 'Kids, Groups and Crime: Some Implications of a Well-Known Secret', *Journal of Criminal Law and Criminology,* 72: 867.

7.4

Reduced Penalties for Juveniles: the Normative Dimension

ANDREW VON HIRSCH

The thesis to be defended is that, in applying a policy of proportionate sentencing to juveniles, substantial overall penalty reductions are called for, with the amount of those reductions graded according to the young offender's age.[1] The issue then becomes *why* there should be such severity-reductions for juveniles. The available literature refers to three kinds of reasons, relating to (1) juveniles' lesser culpability; (2) criminal sanctions' greater 'punitive bite' when applied to juveniles; and (3) the notion of adolescence as a 'time of testing'. Each of these three purported reasons will be examined in the light of desert theory.

Culpability

One argument for reduced punishments concerns juveniles' lesser degree of culpability. If a 15-year old commits burglary, or if a 35-year old commits it, the harmful consequences of the act are the same; but what may be different is the ascription of culpability: the juvenile appears to act with less personal fault in committing the act, making the behaviour less serious. Thus there should be less punishment for the crime, because it becomes less serious compared to the same criminal act committed by an adult.

The question then becomes, *why* is culpability reduced? Two kinds of arguments have been put forward: (1) a *cognitive* claim, that juveniles have less capacity to assess and appreciate the harmful consequences of their criminal actions; and (2) a claim concerning *volitional controls,* that they have had less opportunity to develop impulse control and resist peer pressures to offend. This provides a useful general framework, but more analysis is needed of *why* these factors should be permitted to count as culpability-reducing. For a legally competent adult, insufficiently developed appreciation-of-consequences or impulse-controls are not ordinarily considered grounds for ascribing reduced culpability. Why should it be otherwise for juveniles?

From A von Hirsch and A Ashworth, *Proportionate Sentencing* (Oxford University Press, 2005), 34–49.

Cognitive Factors

The cognitive claim relates to juveniles' more limited capacity to grasp the harmful consequences of their actions. Adolescents, it is said, 'have not acquired the capacity to realise as fully as adults the consequences of their actions'.[2] But what kind of capacities are being referred to here?

This deficiency of knowledge would not ordinarily concern those consequences that constitute the defining elements of the crime. Many commonplace offences committed by juveniles are *mens rea* crimes, requiring purpose or knowledge on the part of the defendant. Knowledge of the defining elements, for such crimes, is a prerequisite of criminal liability. For residential burglary, for example, a person satisfies the conduct-requirements of the offence if he enters the dwelling of another as a trespasser and takes items of personal property belonging to that person. He must, however, be aware that the dwelling and those items are not his own; and must, when entering the dwelling, have had the intention to steal or commit another offence.[3] If he does not understand such matters, he is not committing burglary at all. However, simple knowledge of this kind is something that most juveniles are capable of having. A 15-year old, when he breaks into a flat and steals a television set, can easily grasp that the flat is someone else's and that the television is not properly his for the taking.

In what other respects, then, might the juvenile be said to have less comprehension of a criminal act's harmful consequences? Perhaps, the reduced awareness concerns the character and importance of the interests which the prohibition is designed to protect – interests which often are not specified as defining elements of the crime. The offence of residential burglary is defined in terms of unauthorized entry into the dwelling of another for purposes of committing a theft or other offence. But what interests are thereby protected? Prevention of theft could not be the sole aim, as that is dealt with by other criminal prohibitions. Prevention of trespass into the homeowner's real property also cannot be a sufficient explanation, as trespass is not itself a criminal offence in most English-speaking jurisdictions. The paramount interests relate instead to the occupant's personal privacy and the sense of personal security.[4] It is with respect to consequences of this kind that juveniles' understanding may be partially inadequate. While the 15-year old house burglar may know that he enters his victim's flat unlawfully and wrongfully takes that person's television set, he may well have less grasp of how those actions affront the person's legitimate sense of the dwelling as personal space, and of how his entry might make that person feel vulnerable and insecure. And even if he grasps these matters intellectually, he still may not properly *appreciate* them – that is, have a sense of (say) what it might feel like to have one's privacy thus invaded.

What remains to be explained, however, is why this kind of incomplete understanding of the relevant interests should affect the ascription of culpability. For adults, it usually is not considered exculpating or even mitigating: the 25-year old house burglar who thinks he is merely trespassing and stealing items of property is not considered to merit less punishment in virtue of the fact that he fails to understand or appreciate the character of the privacy invasion that his conduct involves. We demand of a competent adult a minimal general understanding of other persons' basic interests, and of how various kinds of criminal conduct intrude upon such interests.[5] Lack of understanding of such matters constitutes just a failure to have the relevant moral standards, and should not be extenuating; the house burglar who lacks this kind of comprehension would not be regarded as preferable, morally speaking, to the burglar who does understand and enters and steals anyway.

If the conclusion should be different for juveniles, it must be because we ought to have different normative expectations for them. Young adolescents, the argument runs, cannot reasonably be expected to have a fully fledged comprehension of what other people's basic interests are and how typical crimes affect those interests – because achieving this kind of understanding is a *developmental* process. It takes a greater degree of moral sophistication to appreciate how house burglary affects someone's sense of privacy, than to know that it is impermissible to take that person's TV set. Developing that understanding calls for cognitive skills and capacities for moral reasoning which develop over time – precisely during the period of adolescence with which we are concerned. A 14 or 15-year old has had less opportunity to develop the understanding of other people's interests that we reasonably may demand of an adult.

This brings us to the critical point of whether these cognitive arguments are descriptive or normative ones. If descriptive, then claims to reduced culpability would depend on empirical evidence of a juvenile offender's reduced comprehension of consequences.[6] But that degree of understanding varies greatly within a given age group: a clever 15-year old will have a better grasp of such matters than a dull one – or even, than a dull adult. A descriptive approach thus would lead to diverse treatment of young persons of the same age, and would call making elusive judgements about the degree of moral insight a given adolescent has.[7] It would also lead to the strange result of punishing children with greater moral sophistication more severely,[8] a difficulty that had been apparent already in the application of the (now repealed) English rule of *doli incapax*. Above all, a purely descriptive approach would fail to explain why limited understanding of consequences *should* affect culpability.

The claim of reduced culpability must thus be one that has normative elements. It is not just that adolescents tend in fact to have a less full understanding of criminal acts' harmful consequences; but, rather, that this should be reflected in what we may reasonably demand of them, given the degree to which such understanding depends on experience, learning, and capacities for moral reasoning that need to develop in adolescence over time.

In such an account, it is appropriate to employ age-based gradations. Because opportunities to develop cognitively are related to age, fuller comprehension may be expected of 17-year old adolescents than of 14-year olds. A graded scale may thus be established in which there would be a reduction in severity based on age, and it would be greatest for those nearest to the minimum age of responsibility (say,

14).[9] What such a scale reflects are moral expectations, not actual patterns of development among individuals. There will be variations in how much a particular 14-year old, vis-à-vis a particular 17-year old, actually grasps the typical harmful consequences of burglarizing someone's home. But more may be demanded of the 17-year old, because he has had more time to grow toward adulthood.

Volitional Controls

The other aspect of culpability concerns *volitional controls*. Adolescents tend to be less able to postpone gratification, to restrain themselves from acting out of feelings of anger and aggression, and to resist peer pressures.[10] It is harder to say 'No' to peers, when one is only 14 or 15.

With respect to this dimension, however, the relevant normative expectations become still more important: it must be asked why lesser self-control *should* be culpability-reducing. For adults, this characteristic should not ordinarily serve to mitigate fault. Were an adult criminal defendant to assert that his penalty should be diminished because of his deficient command of his impulses, we ordinarily would regard this to be a moral failing which did not render his conduct any less reprehensible. It is only if these deficiencies are based on significant mental or emotional disabilities that a claim for mitigation of punishment could be sustained.[11] Why should the conclusion be otherwise for adolescents?

Self-control, as other aspects of moral development, is a *learned* capacity, and childhood and adolescence is the period during which it is learned. Angels might have self-discipline from the moment of their creation, but we should not expect children to be born with similar virtues. It is through cognitive and emotional growth, interaction with others, and exposure to social norms that such capacities are gained; and this can be expected to develop not just in childhood, but also throughout adolescence. The adolescent who offends has had less time and opportunity to develop impulse-control and ability to resist the urgings of peers than the adult man or woman, which is why these factors properly should bear on the degree of culpability ascribed to him or her. And as with the cognitive dimension discussed previously, the expectations we should have should vary with age. As the adolescent approaches the age of adulthood, it is right to expect a higher level of self-control.

Youth 'Discount' or Individualized Assessment?

If culpability factors suggest reduced penalties for juveniles, should this involve categorical penalty reductions or individual determinations of culpability? The principle we have suggested earlier is one of categorical, age-related reductions. While actual appreciation of consequences varies considerably among youths of the same age, the degree of appreciation that we *should* demand should depend on age: we may rightly expect more comprehension and self-control from the 17-year old youth than a 14-year old, so that the 17-year old's penalty reduction would be smaller. The principle is thus one of gradually diminishing sentence reductions, as the age of adulthood approaches.[12]

Aside from the categorical, age-related reductions, juveniles should also be entitled to individualized claims in mitigation of kinds that adults could assert. A young offender may, for example, merit punishment somewhat below the level normally appropriate for his age if he was provoked by the victim's own misconduct.

What requires further exploration is whether there should be any special, individualized grounds for sentence reduction that hold for adolescents only. Even if we should not try generally to make individualized assessments of moral development, certain particular types of situations might be recognized where children have been confronted with unusually grave impediments to developing comprehension or self-control. Taking such an approach would necessitate further reflection on what kinds of special circumstances should warrant such mitigation; and whether these should be treated as culpability-reducing or as compassion-based 'equity' concerns.

Punitive Bite

A second line of argument for penalty reductions that appears in the literature relates to 'punitive bite'. A given penalty is said to be more onerous when suffered by a child than by an adult. Young people, assertedly, are psychologically less resilient, and their punishments interfere more with opportunities for education and personal development.[13]

Such claims, however, raise the question of what conception of punitive bite should be used . . . What makes punishments more or less severe is not so much identifiable sensations (that may vary considerably from person to person) but, rather, the extent to which those sanctions interfere with important interests that people have. Interests are not merely subjective: they consist of resources over which persons have legitimate claims . . .

Young people, it may be argued, have certain special interests; and punishments are more onerous for them because of their intrusion upon those interests. There are, first, certain *developmental interests*. Ordinarily, there are critical opportunities and experiences that need be provided between the ages of 14 and 18. A youth requires adequate schooling and learning opportunities; needs to be in a reasonably nurturing atmosphere such as that of a family; requires exposure to adequate role models; and needs to be able to begin to develop ties to friends and associates who can be trusted. These are not mere preferences, but real interests: a young person *should* have such resources in order to mature adequately. Punishments are thus more onerous for adolescents because of the way they tend to compromise these kinds of interests. This is most obviously true of imprisonment – which tends to stunt learning opportunities, provide a hostile rather than a nurturing atmosphere, offers few role models or destructive ones; and fosters attitudes of distrust. If punishments are thus more onerous when undergone by juveniles, proportionality would require that they be reduced.

A second kind of interest relates to *capacity for self-esteem*. Given the censuring connotations of punishment, being punished is hard on a person's self-esteem. It is difficult for anyone to undergo being punished without having his sense of self adversely affected; but the difficulty is greater for juveniles, especially as they enter adolescence. It is characteristic of adolescents that their self-esteem, their sense of self as worthwhile persons having the potential for a better future, tends to be more fragile (and can reasonably be expected to be more fragile) than that of adults. Again, this is a normative and not just a descriptive matter. Developing a robust conception of self, one that is resilient yet capable of coping with the criticism of others, is a product of maturation and experience. It is thus appropriate to expect, for juveniles, a lesser degree of psychological resilience in the face of being punished than we should be able to expect of adults. Such normative judgements, again, are age-related. The younger the offender is, the less resilience can reasonably be demanded of him.

A Special 'Tolerance' for Juveniles?

The literature on proportionate sanctions for juveniles touches mainly upon the foregoing issues of culpability and punitive bite. Juveniles are to be punished less because they are less culpable, and because punishments are more onerous for them. This still assumes, however, that the conventions linking severity and seriousness are unchanged. Where the crimes (adjusting for culpability factors) have similar seriousness-ratings, and where the penalties (adjusting for juveniles' greater vulnerability) should have the same severity-ratings, then juveniles and adults would receive equivalent punishments.

But might a further step be worth taking? Might not there be different conventions linking severity of punishment with seriousness of crimes for juveniles than for adults? That would constitute a real claim that young persons warrant less: that there should be different and milder punishment conventions for juvenile offenders, even after one has taken into account differences in culpability and in punitive 'bite'. For the reasons to be elaborated next, we believe that there is a justification within proportionality theory for arguing that adolescents should thus have less punishment . . .

The notion of adolescence as a time of testing provides another reason for granting a partial tolerance. Why does it do so? It is not just that adolescents are more liable to overstep legal limits, but rather, that the situation in which they are placed – of being encouraged to begin making autonomous choices – prompts experimentation on their part and hence the overstepping of bounds. If young persons are supposed to 'try out' making their own decisions, notwithstanding the harmful choices that may foreseeably ensue, then there should be some sympathy for failures, and those should be judged by a less stringent standard.

A few features of this argument are worth noting. First, it is different from the claim made earlier in this chapter that juvenile offenders are less culpable. This tolerance argument is not reducible to claims, for example, about lesser understanding of consequences. It is rather that young persons, when given the opportunity of trying to live autonomously, may often make the wrong choices – including wrongs for which they know the harmful consequences, and which they could well have avoided making. Learning to make choices carries with it the risk of making *bad* choices.

Second, the tolerance should *generally* be available to youthful offenders; it should not be the kind of mitigation which is accorded to this youthful offender and denied to that one, because one attracts our sympathies more than another. Any youth, in virtue of the status of adolescence, faces the predicaments of learning to live in freedom, and all should be entitled to a degree of sympathy for transgressing the limits.

Third and critically, the tolerance is *temporary*. It should be greatest in early adolescence and gradually diminish with the approach of the age of majority. This comports with the underlying rationale – that adolescence is a time for learning to live in freedom. When adulthood is reached, the person will already have had his or her opportunity to test limits, and should be treated as an adult – that is, held fully accountable.

What does this account have to do with Zimring's thesis about youth as a time for testing? His arguments are concerned with the consequences for juveniles. What was needed, in order to justify penalty reduction under a proportionalist sentencing rationale, was a retrospectively-oriented reason – and that we believe we have supplied by the tolerance argument. Our thesis is that scaling down punishments is not just a matter of avoiding undesirable consequences to juveniles in the future. Rather, it is appropriate to judge juveniles by a less stringent standard, in view of the predicaments they face when learning how to live autonomously.

Notes

1   Such a general approach, of proportionate sanctions but with age-related reductions in sentence levels, is also recommended by B. Feld, *Bad Kids: Race and the Transformation of the Juvenile Court* (1998), ch. 8.

2   C. Ball, K. McCormac and N. Stone, *Young Offenders: Law, Policy and Practice* (1995), 115; see also Feld (above, n.l), 306-312.

3   For the elements of the offence of burglary, see e.g. American Law Institute, *Model Penal Code* (1962), sec. 221.1(1).

4 A. von Hirsch and N. Jareborg, 'Gauging Criminal Harm: a Living-Standard Analysis', (1991) 11 *Oxford Journal of Legal Studies* 1.

5 D. Husak and A. von Hirsch, 'Culpability and Mistake of Law' in S. Shute, J. Gardner and J. Horder (eds). *Action and Value in Criminal Law* (1993), 163–5.

6 For discussion of psychological studies of reduced comprehension, see Feld (above, n. 1) 306–314.

7 As Feld points out, 'developmental psychology does not possess reliable indicators of moral development that equate readily with criminal . . . accountability': B. Feld, 'Juvenile and Criminal Justice Systems' Response to Youth Violence' in M. Tonry and M. Moore (eds), *Youth Violence: Crime and Justice, a Review of Research*, 24: 248.

8 Such a result seems strange because a youth's degree of appreciation of the harmful consequences of his conduct may depend not only on his innate abilities and his opportunities but (at least to some degree) also on his own efforts at learning to comprehend others' interests. To the extent that he succeeds in increasing his comprehension, it seems odd to penalize his efforts by holding him to a higher fault standard and thus punishing him more severely.

9 Gradations of response based on age are also suggested by Feld (above, n. 1), 315–320.

10 See Feld (above, n. 1), 308–313, and F.E. Zimring, 'Toward a Jurisprudence of Youth Violence', in M. Tonry and M. Moore (eds), *Youth Violence: Crime and Justice, a Review of Research*, 24: 447, at 487–490.

11 Thus under Swedish sentencing law, it is deemed a mitigating factor that the defendant '. . . because of mental abnormality or strong emotional inducement or other cause, had a reduced capacity to control his behaviour': Swedish Penal Code, ch. 29, s. 3.2.

12 How this should be accomplished would depend on the type of sentencing system: see Ch. 6 below.

13 Ball, McCormac and Stone (above, n. 2), 116; L. Zedner, 'Sentencing Young Offenders' in A. Ashworth and M. Wasik (eds), *Fundamentals of Sentencing Theory* (1998), 173.

7.5

The Transformation of the American Juvenile Court

BARRY C FELD

Within the past three decades, judicial decisions, legislative amendments, and administrative changes have transformed the juvenile court from a nominally rehabilitative social welfare agency into a scaled-down second-class criminal court for young people. Politicians and the public have repudiated the court's original rehabilitative premises and endorsed punishment of young offenders. Judicial opinions and statutory changes have rejected procedural informality and incorporated imperfectly many of the safeguards of criminal courts. These substantive and procedural reforms have converted the historical ideal of the juvenile court as a welfare agency into a quasi-penal system that provides young offenders with neither therapy nor justice.

The Progressive reformers who created the juvenile court conceived of it as an informal welfare system in which judges made dispositions in the 'best interests' of the child, and the state functioned as *parens patriae*, as a surrogate parent. In 1967 the Supreme Court in *In re Gault* granted juveniles some constitutional procedural rights in delinquency hearings and provided the impetus to modify juvenile courts' procedures, jurisdiction, and purposes (387 U.S. 1[1967]). The ensuing procedural and substantive convergence between juvenile and criminal courts eliminated virtually all the conceptual and operational differences in strategies of social control for youths and adults. Even proponents reluctantly acknowledge that juvenile courts often fail either to 'save' children or to reduce youth crime. In short, the contemporary juvenile court constitutes a conceptually and administratively bankrupt institution with neither a rationale nor a justification.

Social structural and cultural changes fostered both the initial creation and contemporary transformation of the juvenile court. Ideological changes in cultural conceptions of children and in strategies of social control during the nineteenth century led Progressive reformers to create the Juvenile court in 1899. Rapid industrialization and modernization, immigration and urbanization, social change and intellectual ferment provided the impetus for the juvenile court. Reformers combined new theories of criminality, such as positivism, with new ideas about childhood and adolescence to construct a social welfare alternative to criminal

From BC Feld, *Bad Kids: Race and the Transformation of the Juvenile Court* (New York, Oxford University Press, 1999), 3–10.

courts. They designed juvenile courts to respond flexibly to youths' criminal and noncriminal misconduct, to assimilate and integrate poor and immigrant children, and to expand control and supervision of young people and their families. The Juvenile court reformers removed children from the criminal justice and corrections systems, provided them with individualized treatment in a separate system, and substituted a scientific and preventive alternative to the criminal law's punitive policies. By separating children from adults and providing a rehabilitative alternative to punishment, juvenile courts also rejected criminal law's jurisprudence and its procedural safeguards, such as juries and lawyers. Juvenile courts' flexible and discretionary strategies enabled its personnel to differentiate and discriminate between their own children and 'other people's children,' those of the poor and immigrants.

A century later, social structural changes have modified the cultural conceptions of young people and the strategies of social control that juvenile courts employ. These changes leave the juvenile court, as an institution, searching for a new policy foundation and legal rationale. Since *Gault*, social structural, demographic, and legal changes have altered dramatically juvenile courts' structure and functions, the characteristics of their clientele, and the crime and social welfare issues that they confront. The internal migration of African Americans from the rural South to the urban North and West in the decades before and after World War II greatly increased the minority populations in urban ghettos and placed race on the national legal and public policy agendas. By the 1960s the Warren Court embarked upon its civil rights and due process revolutions in constitutional jurisprudence. Responding to the issues of race, the Supreme Court scrutinized and invalidated many discriminatory laws, biased public policies, and abusive law enforcement practices. The Court's decisions modified the practices of many criminal justice, administrative, and social service agencies, including juvenile courts. By the 1970s and 1980s, the structural transition from an industrial and manufacturing to an information and service economy and the migration of many white people and employment opportunities from cities to suburbs further increased the social isolation and concentration of poverty of the urban minority population. Macrostructural changes within the past two decades resulted in the deindustrialization of the urban cores in which most African Americans live, eroded the employment opportunities for lower skilled and less well educated young black males, and fostered the emergence of a structural 'underclass.' By the late 1980s, the 'crack cocaine' epidemic exacerbated the historical relationships among urbanism, poverty, race, and youth crime. In inner-city areas of intense racial segregation, concentrated poverty, industrial decline, and weakened family and community social controls, young black men entered the violent drug economy and youth homicide rates soared. In media depictions and in the public mind, a close linkage exists between minority youths, escalating violence, and crime. Since the 'baby boom' increases in youth crime that began in the late 1960s, 'law-and-order' politicians have responded to these social structural and racial demographic changes with 'get-tough' policies to 'crack down' on crime. Increasingly, punitive Juvenile justice policies impose harsh sanctions disproportionately on minority youths and foster the growing procedural and substantive convergence between Juvenile and criminal courts.

Throughout these analyses, I trace the relationships between social changes and legal changes. In the language of the social sciences, the Juvenile court constitutes the dependent variable, and social structural, economic, racial, demographic, and other legal changes constitute independent variables. A century ago, the processes of modernization and industrialization fostered a particular ideological conception of *childhood* and *positive criminology*, which, in turn, provided the impetus to create the 'rehabilitative' Juvenile court. More recent social structural and macro-economic changes provide the catalyst to transform the Juvenile court into a more punitive agency. From the Juvenile court's inception, the social control of ethnic and racial minority offenders has constituted one of its most important functions. The Progressives created the Juvenile court to assimilate, integrate, and control the children of the eastern European immigrants pouring into cities of the East and Midwest at the turn of the century. In postindustrial American cities today, Juvenile courts function to maintain social control of minority youths, predominantly young black males. The current, more punitive Juvenile Justice policies reflect the changing character and complexion of Juvenile courts' clientele. Fear of other people's children, especially minority youths charged with crimes, provides the impetus to transform the Juvenile court from a welfare agency into a second-rate criminal court for young offenders.

Writing about race, crime, and social control policies produces intensely charged ideological debates about the causes of minority youths' demonstrable overrepresentation in the Juvenile Justice system. For example, does their dis-proportional presence reflect a subculture of violence or social structural in-equality? Does it reflect differential involvement in criminal behavior or discriminatory decision making by Justice system personnel? Unfortunately, even to pose these questions or to analyze the relationships between race, crime, and Juvenile Justice administration exposes one to the dangers of being misunderstood or labeled a racist. Despite these hazards, one cannot understand current Juvenile Justice policies and practices in isolation from their broader social context, especially the role of race in American society. The macro-structural transformation of cities—deindustrialization, racial segregation, and concentration of poverty— fostered an increase in youth violence and, especially, murders committed with guns by young black men. The visibility of young black men in media depictions of crime promoted public and political perceptions that juvenile courts deal primarily with violent minority delinquents. Public hostility toward other people's children, especially minority and poor children, provides the catalyst for more punitive juvenile justice policies. As African Americans became urban Americans and the public attributed increases in crime primarily to urban black youths, race and crime intersected to produce more punitive juvenile justice policies.

Public officials couch their get-tough policy changes in terms of 'public safety' rather than racial repression. But, ambivalence about young people and conceptual contradictions embedded in the *ideas of childhood* and *social control* readily facilitated the rapid reformulation of juvenile justice practices from rehabilitation to retribution and from support to suppression. Policies toward young offenders balance precariously between America's century-old experiment with the paternalistic, rehabilitation-oriented juvenile court and the more modern movement to punish youthful offenders as if they were adults. Proponents of special procedures for young offenders argue that 'kids are different' and less blameworthy than adults, that youth policies should protect and enhance troubled children's life chances, and that adult sentences are too harsh to inflict on young people. Others, by contrast, insist that serious youth crime and violence are just as harmful and damaging as serious adult crime and violence, and public protection requires harsh punishments even for younger offenders.

American cultural and legal conceptions of young people contain two competing images of youth that also facilitate the transformation of the juvenile court. On the one hand, the legal culture views young people as innocent, vulnerable, fragile, and dependent *children* whom their parents and the state should protect and nurture. On the other hand, the legal culture perceives young people as vigorous, autonomous and responsible *adultlike* people from whose criminal behavior the public needs protection. From its inception, the juvenile court attempted to reconcile the fundamental ambivalence and conflicted impulses engendered by these competing images when a child is a criminal and the criminal is a child.

Progressive reformers attempted to harmonize the dissonance created by the *child* and the *criminal* by constructing a binary opposition between the juvenile and criminal justice systems. They did so by situating the juvenile court on several unstable cultural and criminological fault lines that embodied the binary constructs of *childhood* and *social control*. They conceived of the juvenile court as a welfare agency to *treat children* rather than as a criminal court to *punish adults*. Thus, the *ideas* of the juvenile court implicate many cultural and criminological tensions: positivism versus classicism, determinism versus choice, child versus adult, dependence versus independence, treatment versus punishment, offender versus offense, forward- versus backward-looking responses to crime, welfare versus just deserts, discretion versus rules, procedural informality versus formality, social welfare versus social control, and the like. Across these various dimensions, Progressive reformers emphasized the first element of each juxtaposed pair, obscured its polar opposite with euphemisms and good intentions, but left the foundation of the juvenile court vulnerable and unstable.

The recent escalation of serious youth crime challenges these dichotomous constructs. Currently, juvenile justice jurisprudence, law, policy, and practice emphasize increasingly the second element of each binary pair, for example, punishment rather than treatment, rules rather than discretion, adult rather than child, and crime control rather than social welfare. These changes question and implicitly reject the traditional ideas of childhood and benevolent social control on which the Progressives founded the juvenile court. Characterizing delinquents as responsible young offenders rather than as misguided, troubled children abets juvenile courts' transformation from a rehabilitative to a punitive institution. Juvenile courts' reorientation from social welfare to crime control and reconfiguration of youths from being dependent to being responsible reflect broader cultural and legal changes. Progressive reformers asserted a public obligation to provide for the welfare and control of children. More recent punitive policies reduce the state's duty to intervene affirmatively and make youths more responsible and accountable for their own conduct regardless of their social circumstances.

Judicial decisions and legal policies selectively choose between these two competing cultural conceptions and legal formulations of young people— responsible and autonomous or vulnerable and dependent—in order to maximize their social control. From the juvenile court's inception, Progressive reformers designed juvenile courts to enable them to respond differently to other people's children than to their own. In the last three decades, this administrative flexibility enables juvenile courts to intervene disproportionally in the lives of minority youths.

Recent changes in juvenile courts—increase in procedural formality, diversion of status offenders, waiver of serious young offenders to the adult system, and harsher punishment of delinquents—constitute a form of criminological 'triage' to distinguish between 'our children' and 'other people's children.' In so doing, these policies erode the theoretical and practical differences between the juvenile and criminal justice systems. The triage strategy selectively manipulates the alternative conceptions of young people as dependent and vulnerable or as autonomous and responsible to remove many middle-class, white, and female noncriminal status offenders from the juvenile justice system to the private social service systems; to consign persistent, violent, and disproportionally minority youths to criminal court for prosecution as adults; and to impose increasingly punitive sanctions on those middle-range delinquents who remain within the jurisdiction of the juvenile court. By shedding the 'soft' and 'hard' ends of its client spectrum, these legal changes have transformed the juvenile court into a second-class criminal court. The macrostructural changes in urban America and the public and political linkages between race and serious youth crime coincide with these moves toward increased punitiveness in juvenile courts. The triage policies enacted by law-makers and implemented by juvenile justice practitioners separate 'our children' from 'other people's children' and cull the salvageable from the hopeless. In short, the transformation of the juvenile court occurs within the broader structural context of the racial metamorphosis of urban America.

The shortcomings of the juvenile court stem from its conceptual bankruptcy, rather than simply from its failures of implementation, profound though they may be. Juvenile courts *do* lack adequate resources to address child welfare needs, at least in part because of the gender, socioeconomic class and racial characteristics of their clients. But even more fundamental obstacles prevent the juvenile court from successfully implementing its 'rehabilitative ideal.' The juvenile court's creators envisioned a social service agency in a judicial arena and attempted to fuse its social welfare mission with the power of state coercion. The *idea* that judicial clinicians successfully can combine social welfare and criminal social control in one agency constitutes the juvenile court's inherent conceptual flaw. Progressives created an irreconcilable conflict by asking the juvenile court simultaneously to enhance child welfare and to control youths' violations of criminal law. The hostile impulses people experience toward other people's threatening children undermine benevolent aspirations and elevate crime control concerns. Juvenile courts inevitably subordinate social welfare considerations to crime control concerns because of their built-in penal focus. Every state's juvenile code defines juvenile courts' jurisdiction based on a youth's committing a crime, a prerequisite that detracts from a compassionate response. Because juvenile courts define eligibility for 'services' on the basis of criminality, they highlight those aspects of youth that rationally elicit the least sympathy and ignore social conditions that might evoke a greater desire to help. Recent changes in juvenile court waiver and sentencing laws to emphasize punishment, 'accountability,' and personal responsibility further reinforce juvenile courts' penal foundations and reduce support for humanitarian assistance.

If we separate social welfare from penal social control, then no need remains for a separate juvenile court for young offenders. Systematically uncoupling social welfare from criminal social control can lead to greater conceptual clarity, improved justice for young offenders, and broadened support for child welfare. If criminal social control is the 'real' reason why states refer youths to juvenile courts, then we can abolish juvenile courts and try younger offenders in criminal courts alongside their adult counterparts. But if the criminal is a child, then states must modify their criminal justice system to accommodate the youthfulness of some defendants. The physical and psychological immaturity and lesser culpability of younger defendants require criminal courts to make certain substantive and procedural modifications. Developmental psychological research and jurisprudential policies provide rationale to grant greater procedural safeguards to youths and to sentence younger offenders less severely than older offenders for their misdeed simply because they are young. Trying and sentencing all offenders in one integrated court recognizes that adolescents do not differ from adults to nearly the degree that traditional legal dichotomies imply. Rather, young people mature and criminal careers emerge along a developmental continuum, and youths do not graduate from irresponsible childhood one day to responsible adulthood the next except as a matter of law. Taken in combination, these substantive and procedural modifications can avoid the 'worst of both worlds,' provide youths with protections functionally equivalent to those accorded adults, and do justice in sentencing. Uncoupling social welfare from social control also avoids many of the constraints that providing for child welfare through a juvenile court imposes. If we frame child welfare policy proposals in terms of child welfare rather than as a response to crime, then opportunities to intervene creatively and proactively in the lives of all young people expand greatly.

I critically analyze the *idea* of the juvenile court and its sustaining ideologies of *childhood* and *social control* for several purposes. The earlier *idea of* a rehabilitative juvenile court combined a theory of delinquency with a policy prescription, for example, troubled children required treatment. However, contemporary public and political pressures to get tough repudiate rehabilitation, foster the convergence between juvenile and criminal courts, and require a different rationale for the social control of youths. The *idea* of youthful partial responsibility provides a rationale and a policy prescription for sentencing young offenders in an integrated criminal justice; youthful reduced culpability deserves a mitigated sentence. Because states already sentence many youths as adults, the *idea* of youthfulness as a mitigating factor in sentencing has considerable contemporary salience whether or not states abolish juvenile courts in their entirety.

The transformation of the juvenile court also provides a metaphor of the changing social construction and legal status of youth. The current schizophrenic formulations of youth—dependent and vulnerable or independent and responsible—enable states to selectively choose between the two constructs to manipulate young people's legal status, to maximize their social control, and to subordinate their freedom and autonomy. Reexamining the social construction of adolescence through a lens of partial responsibility may facilitate the formulation of social policies that foster greater autonomy, equality, and realism in young people's transition to adulthood.

Finally, the transformation of the juvenile court forces us to confront the issue of race in American society. The increasing and explicit punitiveness of juvenile and criminal justice policies emerge against the backdrop of the structural transformation of cities, the deindustrialization of the urban core, and the emergence of a threatening black 'underclass' living in racial isolation and concentrated poverty. A century ago, Progressive reformers had to choose between either initiating social structural reforms that would reduce inequality and ameliorate criminogenic forces or ministering to the young people damaged by those adverse conditions. 'Child saving' satisfied Progressives' humanitarian impulses without engendering more fundamental social changes. A century later, we face similar choices between either rehabilitating 'damaged' individuals in a criminal justice system or undertaking more fundamental changes that address the issues of racial and social inequality. Unfortunately, neither juvenile court judges nor any other criminal justice agencies realistically can ameliorate the social ills that afflict young people or significantly enhance their life chances. On the other hand, uncoupling criminal social control from social welfare enables us to make societal commitment to the welfare of all children regardless of their criminality and to expand the possibilities of positive intervention for all young people. Public policies to provide all young people with a hopeful future and to reduce racial and social inequality require a political commitment to the welfare of children that extends far beyond the resources or competencies of any juvenile justice system.

7.6

Restraining the Use of Custody for Young Offenders: The Canadian Approach

NICHOLAS BALA AND JULIAN V ROBERTS

Section 38(2) of the Youth Criminal Justice Act 2002 (YCJA) articulates a number of principles to govern youth sentencing, of which the most important is that in s. 38(2)(c) that any sentence must be "proportionate to the seriousness of the offence and the degree of responsibility of the young person for the offence." This reinforces the statement in s. 38(1) that the purpose of youth sentencing is to hold young persons "accountable" for their criminal acts.

Section 3(l)(b)(ii) of the YCJA makes clear, however, that the accountability of youths must reflect their "limited maturity," and hence youth sentences will normally be less severe than sentences imposed on adults in similar circumstances. Section 38(2)(a) reinforces this limitation on the severity of youth sentencing: the sentence imposed on a youth "must not result in a punishment that is greater that would be appropriate for an adult . . . convicted of the same offence committed in similar circumstances."

The statement of sentencing principles also makes clear that the YCJA is intended to reduce the use of custody, with s. 38(2)(d) stating that "all available sanctions other than custody that are reasonable in the circumstances must be considered" before a sentence is imposed on a youth. Further, s. 38(2)(e) provides that "the sentence must be the least restrictive sentence that is capable of achieving the purpose [of sentencing]."

Sections 38 and 39 reflect the policy position taken by the government that the use of custody in youth courts under the YOA was excessive. Under the YOA, over one-third of youth sentences resulted in a term of custody, a similar percentage as at the adult level (Sanders, 2000). In many other countries, the rate of custody is lower for adolescents than for adults. In addition, comparative research suggested that the incarceration rate for youth in Canada was one of the highest in the world, even higher than the rate in the USA (Hornick et al. 1995). One reason for the relatively high incarceration rate is that youth courts have used custody for crimes of relatively low seriousness. For example, statistics revealed that under the YOA

From N Bala and JV Roberts, 'Canada's Juvenile Justice System: Promoting Community-Based Responses to Youth Crime' in J Junger-Tas and SH Decker (eds), International Handbook of Juvenile Justice (New York, Springer-Verlag, 2006), 52–55.

approximately half the youth court convictions for theft over $5,000 resulted in a term of custody (DeSouza, 2002).

While the YCJA principles restrict the use of custody, in appropriate cases, especially those involving violence, a proportionate response may require a custodial sentence, especially where a youth has a prior record that indicates that community-based response will not have a rehabilitative effect.[33] If the offence causes sufficient harm, a custodial sentence will normally be appropriate to hold a youth accountable.

The Declaration of Principle makes references to the special social and legal status of Aboriginal youth. Thus s. 38(2)(b) requires a judge to pay "particular attention to the circumstances of aboriginal young persons" when considering a custodial sentence. The reason for this provision is that Aboriginal youth in Canada are significantly overrepresented in the prison population. In 2000/2001, at the juvenile level, Aboriginal persons accounted for 5% of the general population, but one quarter of admissions to youth custody (Marinelli, 2002). It has, however, been stressed by appeal courts that Aboriginal youth must also be held accountable and that judges need to be realistic about their prospects for rehabilitation.[34]

Restrictions on the Imposition of a Custodial Sanction

Section 39 of the YCJA gives effect to the more general statements of principle, placing significant restraints on the use of custody for young offenders:

A youth justice court shall not commit a person to custody unless

1. the young person has committed a violent offence;
2. the young person has failed to comply with noncustodial sentences;
3. the young person has committed an indictable offence for which an adult would be liable to imprisonment for a term of more than 2 years and has a history that indicates a pattern of findings of guilt; or
4. in exceptional cases where the young person has committed an indictable offence, the aggravating circumstances of the offence are such that the imposition of a noncustodial sentence would be inconsistent with the purpose and principles set out in s. 38.

A considerable amount of research in Canada (and elsewhere) has now accumulated to suggest that harsher criminal sanctions for youth, such as imprisonment are no more effective in preventing recidivism than community-based sanctions.[1] The restrictions in the YCJA on the use of custody in youth justice courts in Canada are reducing the usc of this expensive sanction, and resulting in more use of less expensive, less intrusive and equally or more effective community alternatives. In the first year that the YCJA was in effect, there was a 37.2% decline on the number of custodial sentences imposed.

While it is difficult to determine precisely how much s. 39 has reduced the use of custody, under the previous law there were significant numbers of youth who were imprisoned but who could not receive a custodial sentence under the YCJA. In particular, it is noteworthy that a youth can only receive a custodial sentence for breach of probation, and there has been a breach of previous community-based sentence. Under the previous law one charge in eight was for breach of probation, and almost 40% of these charges resulted in a custodial sentence.[2]

Further, apart from "exceptional circumstances" and cases where a youth has a history of noncompliance with noncustodial sentences, a nonviolent offence can only result in a custodial sentence if the offence is reasonably serious (an offence for which the maximum adult sentence is greater than 2 years) *and* there is a "history that indicates a pattern of findings of guilt," words that suggest there must have been at least three previous findings of guilt.

Additional Restrictions Regarding the use of Custody

If the case before a youth court satisfies one of the four conditions in s. 39(1), a number of other principles must still be considered before a court can imprison the young offender. There is a clear reminder to judges in s. 39(2) of the principle of restraint in the use of custody, even if one of the conditions of s. 39(1) is satisfied: "if [one of the criteria for custody] apply, a youth justice court shall not impose a custodial sentence . . . unless the court has considered all alternatives to custody raised at the sentencing hearing that are reasonable in the circumstances, and determined that there is not a reasonable alternative, or combination of alternatives, that is in accordance with the purpose and principles of sentencing at the youth court level."

Another provision in s. 39 is intended to discourage judges from escalating the severity of the sentence in response to subsequent offending. Having imposed an alternative to custody for one offence, some judges shift to custody if a youth reappears before the court, reasoning that the first sentence was insufficient to discourage the offender. Section 39(4) addresses this judicial reasoning, providing:

> The previous imposition of a particular noncustodial sentence on a young person does not preclude a youth justice court from imposing the same or any other non-custodial sentence for another offence.

While s. 39(4) does not prohibit judges from following the "step principle" logic at sentencing, the provision makes it clear that the same alternative may be imposed on separate occasions.

A common justification for the imposition of a term of custody in some cases under the previous law was that the judge could see no other way of providing necessary social intervention for an adolescent at risk. Under the new youth justice statute, this justification for the imposition of custody is eliminated, as s. 39(5) of the YCJA explicitly states that a youth court "shall *not*" use custody as a substitute for a child protection, mental health, or other social measures. Hopefully, needed services will be provided under provincial child welfare or mental health laws, there may be situations in which homeless or mentally ill may simply not receive needed help due to the absence of appropriate resources under provincial law.

There are also procedural provisions that are intended to limit the use of custody. Section 39(6) provides that a youth court is generally obliged, prior to imposing a custodial sentence, to consider a pre-sentence report as well as any sentencing proposal made by the young offender or his or her counsel. Further, s. 39(9) imposes on youth court judges who impose a term of custody an obligation to provide reasons why "it has determined that a non-custodial sentence is not adequate" to achieve the purpose of sentencing ascribed to the youth court system.

References

1   Solicitor General Canada (2002) 'The Effects of Punishment on Recidivism' 7 *Corrections Research and Development* No 3.
2   Statistics Canada (2002) 'Youth Court Statistics 2002–03' 24 *Juristat* No 2.

8

Doing Justice to Difference: Diversity and Sentencing

This chapter explores two problems related to diversity and discrimination—disproportionate involvement of certain populations in criminal justice, and differential impact of criminal sanctions—and addresses the question of how, if at all, sentencing systems should respond to those problems. One or other of these problems affects many groups in society, such as persons with disabilities, women, lower socio-economic groups and ethnic minorities; the focus here will be on race and gender, with some references to wider equality issues. In this introduction, we describe the nature of the problems, before going on to consider the normative framework for possible responses.

Disproportionate Involvement

It is well known that the individuals appearing for sentencing do not constitute a representative sample or cross-section of society in general. Convicted offenders are more likely than the general population to be members of an ethnic or social minority, to report lower than average incomes, to be unemployed or to come from a socially disadvantaged background. Ultimately this means that the demographics of the sentenced population, and to an even greater extent the demographics of the prison population, bear little correspondence to the general population. Visible minorities and offenders from disadvantaged backgrounds are clearly over-represented in prison statistics, relative to their numbers in the general population. For example, black Americans are highly over-represented in prison populations across the US: African Americans are incarcerated at nearly six times the rate of whites.[1] The over-representation of minorities can also be observed in England and Wales: recent statistics show that the proportion of black prisoners relative to the general population was five times higher than for whites.[2] In countries with a significant indigenous or aboriginal population, such as Australia, New Zealand and Canada, these ethnic groups are also over-represented in the sentenced population and in the prison populations.[3] These patterns of disproportionate involvement in sentencing and in prison populations exist in all jurisdictions in which statistics are collected.[4]

Differential Impact

In addition to the over-representation problem, legal punishments do not have a uniform impact on all offenders upon whom they are imposed. Any custodial sentence imposed on a person with a disability is likely to have a greater impact.[5] A lengthy custodial term imposed on a single parent will cause disproportionate suffering to both the offender and his or her child or children. Female offenders account for about one-fifth of crimes in England and Wales and a smaller minority of all sentenced cases,[6] yet their needs are very different from their male counterparts.[7] Carlen and Worrall note that approximately two-thirds of female prisoners have dependent children.[8] And, of course, custody has a disproportionately severe impact upon the lives of young offenders, an issue which is explored in Chapter 7 above. These empirical trends have not escaped the attention of sentencing scholars, particularly those who identify the patriarchal assumptions about women and crime that may be influential in shaping the responses of sentencers and others.[9] Some argue that human diversity should be taken into account in sentencing decisions. This can mean different things: it may mean considering the differential impact of the sentence on individuals of diverse backgrounds, accepting an argument that culpability is reduced in cases of social disadvantage or attempting to rectify a disproportionality problem by reconfiguring existing sentencing principles or policies.

Principles of Equality

At the centre of the normative framework for assessing the differences mentioned in the two foregoing paragraphs is the principle of equality or non-discrimination. One enunciation of the principle may be found in Article 15(1) of Canada's Charter of Rights and Freedoms 1982, which provides:

> Every individual is equal before and under the law and has the right to equal protection and equal benefit of the law without discrimination and, in particular, without discrimination based on race, colour, religion, sex, age or mental or physical disability.

Similar provisions can be found in other bills of rights and constitutional documents, for example, section 9 of the South African Bill of Rights.[10] The European Convention on Human Rights declares a more restrictive right in Article 14, that being a right not to be discriminated against in the exercise of another Convention right. However, Protocol 12 of the Convention now provides for a general prohibition on discrimination. The protocol was opened for signature in 2000, and only binds those Member States that ratify it.

What implications does a general principle of equality before the law have for sentencing? The principle should apply throughout the law, and its specific application to sentencing would lead to a principle in this form:

> No person should be sentenced more severely on account of their race, national or ethnic origin, colour, gender, sexual orientation, religion, age, mental or physical disability, or similar factor.

To this principle of non-discrimination should be added a principle of equal impact, along the following lines:

> No sentence should be imposed that may be expected to have a more severe impact on an offender on account of the offender's race, national or ethnic origin, colour, religion, gender, sexual orientation, age, mental or physical disability, or similar factor.

These two principles derive from the general principle of equality before the law, and apply its general philosophy to two specific problems of discriminatory treatment that may occur through sentencing.

Forms of Discrimination

Before drawing the inference that disproportionate numbers or differential treatment amounts to discrimination, it is important to explore the meaning and varying forms of discriminatory treatment. At least three forms of discrimination may be distinguished: *intentional* discrimination, where a sentencing decision is taken in the full knowledge and intention that it will result in an offender being treated more severely on account of race, national or ethnic origin, colour, religion, sex, age, or mental or physical disability. A more likely form of discrimination in most jurisdictions is *direct but unintentional* discrimination. This would consist of 'actions, processes and outcomes based on unconscious racial (not "racist") stereotypes';[11] and *indirect* discrimination, which occurs 'when a rule or practice that is framed as general, in fact applies differentially to particular groups of persons'.[12] Cases of intentional discrimination are likely to be relatively infrequent in the sentencing process. Cases of direct but unintentional discrimination stem from the influence of stereotypical views about different kinds of people. Barbara Hudson provides the example of gender-role stereotypes, whereby 'employment for men and domestic responsibilities for women operate as constraints on imprisonment'[13] but greater punishment is likely to flow from the opposite characteristics. Coretta Phillips and Ben Bowling cite the example of different stereotypes for members of different ethnic minorities, contrasting the 'unjustified heightened suspicion of black people' with the 'stereotype of Asians as passive, conformist and self-regulating' and concluding that this stereotyping often led to different criminal justice responses to members of the two groups, until recent anxiety about terrorism gave rise to increased suspicions about Asian people.[14]

Turning to indirect indiscrimination, two examples in the sentencing context would be the sentence reduction for pleading guilty, which leads to more severe sentences for black offenders because they are less likely to plead guilty, and the so-called war on drugs in the US and in Britain, which leads to a higher rate of black offenders being sanctioned because they are more likely to select controlled drugs as their drug of choice whereas white people are more likely to select alcohol.

Sentencing Rationales and the Principle of Equal Treatment

How do these possibilities of discrimination relate to the different sentencing rationales? Are certain sentencing rationales more likely to produce discrimination than others?

Predictive approaches to sentencing take offender variables into account if there is reliable evidence that they relate to risk of reoffending. Thus the main concern of the predictive approach inherent in the incapacitative rationale is the assessment of risk: an unemployed defendant, living in a high-crime area and who has a long-standing drug addiction, might well be assessed as presenting a high risk, and would therefore be an obvious target for an incapacitative sentence.[15] Those who support incapacitation, whether as a general rationale or (more plausibly) as a rationale for offenders classed as 'dangerous', will therefore find it difficult to avoid a discriminatory sentencing regime. The whole basis of incapacitation and public protection lies in assessing the risk of further serious offences, as argued in Chapter 3 above, and the risk factors may be directly or indirectly discriminatory.

Risk assessments are also increasingly prominent in rehabilitative approaches to sentencing, although the main elements of this rationale are the use of programmes or individual interventions in order to reduce reoffending. The rehabilitative approach is not discriminatory by nature, unlike the incapacitative approach. But it does open up the possibility of discriminatory applications, and there is long-standing evidence that members of certain ethnic minorities are less likely to be given certain forms of community sentence (particularly probation supervision) than are other offenders.[16]

In respect of deterrent rationales, much depends on the extent to which they take account of risk factors of the kind discussed earlier in the context of incapacitation. General deterrence is hardly likely to have a discriminatory element to it, unless it is adopted as the sentencing approach for a type of crime that has a disproportionate number of women or members of an ethnic minority among the offenders to be sentenced. Calculations of individual deterrence may take account of assessments of the risk of reconviction, however, and those assessments may also include indirectly discriminatory elements. Restorative justice, on the other hand, ought not to be concerned with risk assessments of the participants, and may be thought to be a propitious way to deal with any underlying conflicts relating to the offending behaviour: see Chapter 5 above.

The approach of desert theories stands in contrast to all the others. Desert theories can plausibly claim that the principle of equal treatment forms part of their rationale: sentences should be determined chiefly by the seriousness of the offence, and matters such as the race, class or gender of the offender have no bearing on that variable. Some US guideline systems explicitly prohibit consideration of variables such as employment status and race. However, it remains unlikely that this eliminates all possibility of indirect discrimination, or even of direct but unintentional discrimination. For example, different conceptions of offence seriousness are possible, and a ranking that places robbery and drug crimes high on the list might well be regarded as indirectly discriminatory against visible minorities.

For those desert-based systems that do not restrict the range of mitigating factors, it is possible for stereotyping to have a considerable influence on the construction of mitigation. Hudson refers to the need for women offenders to be presented in a particular light if they are to obtain a sentence reduction, and argues that

> for women, their crimes are dissolved into their characteristics and lifestyles; for black offenders, their characteristics and lifestyles are dissolved into their crimes.[17]

Hudson also argues (in Selection 8.4) for a broader conception of culpability at the sentencing stage, and urges consideration of whether the fact that an offender has been subject to acute social deprivation, or to overt racism, should result in them being assessed as less culpable for their actions.

Responding to Discrimination

At the level of policy and practice, how should sentencing systems respond to departures from the principle of equal treatment such as those identified above? Consider, for example, the over-representation of aboriginal persons in the prison populations of certain jurisdictions. Some countries have introduced statutory provisions that direct courts to consider the aboriginal status of the defendant at sentencing, particularly when contemplating the imposition of custody. In Canada, section 718.2(e) of the Criminal Code states that

> All available sanctions other than imprisonment that are reasonable in the circumstances should be considered for all offenders, with particular attention to the circumstances of aboriginal offenders.

The Supreme Court of Canada interpreted this provision to mean that

> the jail term for an aboriginal offender may be less than the term imposed on a non-aboriginal offender for the same offence.[18]

Similar provisions can be found in other jurisdictions, such as New Zealand.[19] The purpose of such legislative directions to courts seems clear: to reduce the over-representation of aboriginal persons in correctional populations. A laudable goal, but does this involve a violation of the principle of equality of treatment?[20] If it does, is that favourable treatment justifiable?

Research suggests that the over-representation of visible minorities in prison statistics is largely a consequence of higher offending rates (themselves a product of social deprivation) rather than of direct discrimination by courts. Although research by Roger Hood in England and Wales[21] uncovered limited evidence of discriminatory sentencing in some English courts, the disproportionate number of blacks in prison cannot be explained by directly discriminatory sentencing.[22] However, it has been argued that elements of the sentencing process have an *indirect* discriminatory effect, notably the discount offered to defendants to who plead guilty.[23] The discount can be significant, particularly if the defendant enters a guilty plea at the earliest opportunity. It may reduce the length of a custodial sentence by a third, or it may make the difference between a custodial sentence and community service. Research has found that visible minorities are less likely to plead guilty[24] and are therefore less likely to benefit from the discount. This sentencing practice, ostensibly neutral to the race of the offender, operates in a discriminatory way. If it cannot be adjusted so as not to have this effect, should it be abolished or curtailed? In Selection 8.1 Michael Tonry argues that we should abandon this sentencing practice. Removing the guilty plea discount would eliminate this differential application, but could lead to harsher overall sentencing levels. Might this not be a classic case of throwing out the baby with the bathwater? Should the principle of equal treatment be given such a powerful effect, or are there other powerful considerations that outweigh it?

In the second Selection (8.2) Tonry suggests that allowing courts greater flexibility to mitigate sentences will help to reduce racial disparities in prison populations. The goal would be to mitigate the punishment of all offenders appearing before the courts and in particular those who have had to endure exceptional hardships in life. In Selection 8.3 Ian Brownlee responds to Tonry's proposal by arguing that allowing judges this wide margin for evaluating character may be counterproductive and, more substantially, that it is questionable whether those who overcome adverse social or other conditions should receive mitigation of sentence on that ground.

Whether, and to what extent, there is discrimination towards some women in the sentencing process is a matter for debate.[25] Although overall sentencing statistics suggest that women are treated less severely than men, even after taking account of their offences and previous convictions, research has demonstrated how some women who do not fit particular models of 'the ideal woman' may receive more severe sentences.[26] Recent reported 'surges' in the conviction rate of women and young women for offences of violence may evoke some such preconceptions at the sentencing stage. In Selection 8.4 Barbara Hudson takes the view that the sentencing process is insufficiently sensitive to the diversity of people appearing for sentence. She argues that the differential life experiences of defendants should be considered at sentencing. In order to 'do justice to difference' a court may have to adopt a defendant-centric approach to establishing culpability.[27] Hudson makes the point that these individuals typically have had very different life experiences from most of those imposing sentence, and proposes that sentencers should adopt a broader concept of (reduced) culpability. These different life experiences include certain factors that have not received emphasis in the paragraphs above, particularly poverty, unemployment and relative social deprivation. These are factors that often apply to both women and members of ethnic minorities who come up for sentence. It is well known that they influence many earlier decisions in the criminal process: to what extent, if at all, should the sentencing decision attempt to compensate or make allowances for these factors?

AA

JVR

Notes

1. Mauer, M and King, R, (2007) *Uneven Justice: State Rates of Incarceration by Race and Ethnicity* (Washington, DC, The Sentencing Project).
2. Home Office, (2006) *Race and the Criminal Justice System: An Overview to the Complete Statistics 2004–2005* (London, Home Office).
3. For example, although Aboriginal persons represent 3% of the general population in Canada, in 2004/2005 they accounted for 22% of federal admissions to custody: see Beattie, K, (2005), 'Adult Correctional Services in Canada, 2004/2005' 26 *Juristat* No 5.
4. See Tonry, M (ed), (1997) *Crime and Justice, vol 21: Ethnicity, Crime and Immigration: Comparative and Cross-National Perspectives* (Chicago, IL, University of Chicago Press).
5. Committal of a severely disabled person to prison was found to be a violation of the European Convention of Human Rights in *Price v United Kingdom* (2001) 34 EHRR 1285.
6. Heidensohn, F and Gelsthorpe, L, (2007) 'Gender and Crime' in M Maguire, R Morgan and R Reiner (eds), *Oxford Handbook of Criminology*, 4th edn (Oxford, Oxford University Press) 391.
7. Walklate notes that a recent survey of the prison population in England and Wales found that 60% of female prisoners were mothers: Walklate, S, (2004) *Gender, Crime and Criminal Justice*, 2nd edn (Cullompton, Willan).
8. Carlen, P and Worrall, A, (2004) *Analysing Women's Imprisonment* (Cullompton, Willan).
9. See, eg Walklate, above n 7; Heidensohn and Gelsthorpe, above n 6.
10. Constitution Act 1996 (South Africa), s 9; see also the Constitution of Ireland 1937, Arts 40(1) and 45.
11. Tonry, M, (2004) *Punishment and Politics: Evidence and Emulation in the Making of English Crime Control Policy* (Cullompton, Willan) 77.

12. Hudson, B, (1998) 'Doing Justice to Difference' in A Ashworth and M Wasik (eds), *Fundamentals of Sentencing Theory: Essays in Honour of Andrew von Hirsh* (Oxford, Clarendon Press) 223.
13. *Ibid*, 231.
14. Phillips, C and Bowling, B, (2007) 'Ethnicities, Racism, Crime and Criminal Justice' in Maguire *et al*, above n 6, 451.
15. Greenwood, P and Abrahmse, A, (1982) *Selective Incapacitation* (Santa Barbara, RAND Corporation); and see generally Chapter 3 above.
16. Phillips and Bowling, above n 14, 447.
17. Hudson, above n 12, 232.
18. *R v Gladue* [1999] 1 SCR 688, 171 DLR (4th) 385, para 93.
19. Subsection 8(i) of the Sentencing Act states that a court 'must take into account the offender's personal, family, whanau, community, and cultural background in imposing a sentence': see Roberts, JV, (2003) 'An Analysis of the Statutory Statement of the Purposes and Principles of Sentencing in New Zealand' 36 *Australia and New Zealand Journal of Criminology* 249.
20. In the event, the provision has not been constitutionally challenged as a violation of s 15 of the Canadian Charter of Rights and Freedoms, which guarantees equality before the law.
21. Hood, R, (1992) *Race and Sentencing* (Oxford, Oxford University Press).
22. Tonry reaches a similar conclusion with respect to the United States; see Tonry, M, (1995) *Malign Neglect* (New York, Oxford University Press).
23. Hood, above n 21.
24. *Ibid*, 191. A similar trend emerges from research in the US: see Petersilia, J, (2003) 'Racial Disparities in the Criminal Justice System' in B Hancock and P Sharp (eds), *Public Policy, Crime, and Criminal Justice* (Englewood Cliffs, NJ, Prentice Hall).
25. See Heidensohn and Gelsthorpe, above n 6.
26. Walklate, above n 7.
27. Gender differences exist on a wide range of variables. For example, female offenders appearing for sentencing report much higher rates of physical and sexual abuse prior to sentencing. See Young, V and Reviere, R, (2006) *Women behind Bars* (Boulder, CO, Lynne Rienner Publishers).

Further Readings

Bowling, B and Phillips, C, (2002) *Racism, Crime and Justice* (Harlow, Longman).
Carlen, P, (1998) *Sledgehammer* (Basingstoke, MacMillan).
Carlen, P (ed), (2002) *Women and Punishment: the Struggle for Justice* (Cullompton, Willan).
Daly, K, (1994) *Gender, Crime, and Punishment* (New Haven, CT, Yale University Press).
Heidensohn, F and Gelsthorpe, L, (2007) 'Gender and Crime' in M Maguire, R Morgan and R Reiner (eds), *Oxford Handbook of Criminology*, 4th edn (Oxford, Oxford University Press) ch 13.
Phillips, C and Bowling, B, (2007) 'Ethnicities, Racism, Crime and Criminal Justice' in M Maguire, R Morgan and R Reiner (eds), *Oxford Handbook of Criminology*, 4th edn (Oxford, Oxford University Press) ch 14.

Tonry, M, (1995) *Malign Neglect: Race, Crime and Punishment in America* (New York, Oxford University Press).
—— (ed), (1997) *Crime and Justice, vol 21: Ethnicity, Crime and Immigration: Comparative and Cross-National Perspectives* (Chicago, IL, University of Chicago Press).
—— (2004) *Punishment and Politics: Evidence and Emulation in the Making of English Crime Control Policy* (Cullompton, Willan) ch 4.
Walklate, S, (2004) *Gender, Crime and Criminal Justice* (Cullompton, Willan).

8.1

Abandoning Sentence Discounts for Guilty Pleas

MICHAEL TONRY

Racial disparities in imprisonment should be viewed as a problem of crisis proportion that warrants emergency responses. Here are seven. First, most importantly,
reduce the prison population by one-third. Because blacks are heavily over-represented among prisoners, they would as a group disproportionately benefit from
down-sizing the prison population. Second, the Court of Appeal should announce a
one-third reduction in sentences specified in all existing guideline judgments.
Reduction in sentence lengths is a much more effective way to reduce population
than are reductions in prison admissions. Third, policies should be developed to
divert large numbers of minor cases from the courts and the prisons. This is not the
best way to reduce the size of the prison population, but it is the best way to reduce
the number of individuals whose lives are disrupted by imprisonment. Fourth, the
existing mandatory minimums for burglaries, violent crimes, drug offences and,
under the Criminal Justice Act 2003, firearms offences, should be repealed. Blacks
are heavily over-represented among persons in prison for many of these crimes.
Fifth, current guilty plea practices that award a substantial sentence reduction to
people who plead guilty should be changed. Black defendants less often plead guilty
and when they do, they do it later. The discount results in harsher sentences for
black offenders as a class. Sixth, racial disparity audits should be carried out
throughout the justice system in order to identify practices that disproportionately
adversely affect minority offenders; whenever possible those practices should be
changed. Pre-trial detention practices are particularly likely targets for improvement. Seventh, Parliament should require that every proposed change to laws
affecting sentencing or punishment be accompanied by a minority impact assessment that projects likely effects of proposed changes on all major ethnic groups. If
laws are going to be enacted that will worsen disparities, lawmakers should be
forced to acknowledge what they are doing and explain why it is justified.

Disparities in imprisonment occur mostly because proportionately more black
than white offenders are convicted of the kinds of drug and serious violent crimes
that typically result in prison sentences. Courts, of course, can sentence only those
offenders brought before them, but in relation to serious violent crimes there is no

From M Tonry, *Punishment and Politics: Evidence and Emulation in the Making of English Crime
Control Policy* (Cullompton, Willan Publishing, 2004), 73–87. References omitted.

substantial evidence that prosecutors and police treat whites favourably and blacks unfavourably when they decide whom to arrest or prosecute, or for what. Concerning drug crimes, the picture is a bit more complicated because police disproportionately target drug markets and trafficking in minority areas; however, there is no evidence of substantial racial differences in arresting and prosecuting people once they have been identified as playing major drug-trafficking roles (Bowling and Phillips 2001).

Once suspects have been arrested and prosecuted, however, a number of laws and procedures adversely affect black offenders, even though neither in principle nor by design are they meant to do so. The most prominent is the well-established doctrine that people who plead guilty promptly are entitled to a substantial reduction in sentence, with those who plead guilty later receiving progressively smaller reductions. This policy systematically disadvantages black defendants, as Hood (1992) showed in his ground-breaking research on ethnic differences in sentencing in Midlands courts. Black defendants are less likely than whites to plead guilty and when they do plead guilty, they do so at later stages. The racial difference in pleading guilty results in part from the greater alienation that blacks feel toward a criminal justice system that many believe treats them unfairly.

The circle that closes is a pretty grim one. Young black men are disproportionately stopped by the police and many feel – often no doubt rightly – that they are hassled and stopped under circumstances when young white men, or older black men, would not be. Not surprisingly, many distrust the police and the legal system and, when arrested or charged with a crime, act defiantly and uncooperatively. The criminal justice system lacks legitimacy in their eyes. As a result they do not plead guilty and, because of that, they are punished more severely. Put into a single sentence: young black men who believe themselves unfairly treated by the police understandably become angry and uncooperative, and are punished more severely as a result. Problems of this sort are significant causes of racial disparities .in imprisonment in England and Wales, and they must be solved if disparities are to be reduced.

The policy of giving a sentence discount for a guilty pleas, which may or may not exemplify 'institutional racism', produces longer sentences for black offenders than for whites because black offenders plead guilty less often and typically later in the process. Those longer sentences cannot be justified as a matter of social policy even though they have long been deemed justifiable as a matter of criminal justice policy.

Judges assume that the courts will grind to a halt if defendants are not offered substantial incentives to plead guilty, but there is little evidence that this is true. The limited amount of evidence from American plea-bargaining bans suggests that most defendants plead guilty even when they are not offered sentencing concessions (Blumstein *et al.* 1983, chap. 3). In any event, analysis of the subject would force officials to develop estimates of the cost savings associated with discount practices, and of the amount of increased imprisonment that blacks in England suffer as a result. Whether measurable cost savings that the discount achieves justify the increased racial imprisonment disparities they cause is a question to which reasonable people might offer different answers. It should be openly discussed and answered.

8.2

Individualizing Punishments

MICHAEL TONRY

Few informed people can any longer doubt that the "just-deserts" movement and the development of rigid sentencing policies based only on the offender's crime and criminal history were mistakes. They were well-intended mistakes, aimed at reducing sentencing disparities and race and class biases in sentencing. They may have been necessary mistakes that showed us how to protect against aberrantly severe penalties and exposed the injustices that result when sentencing shifts its focus from the offender to the offense. Mistakes they were, however, and we now know how to do better.

A just sentencing policy will simultaneously ensure that offenders receive penalties no harsher than they deserve and that judges are empowered to mitigate sentences for all defendants, irrespective of race, ethnicity, or sex, to take account of individual circumstances. Such a policy would have three elements. To protect against unjustly harsh penalties, guidelines scaled to the severity of the offender's crime would set presumptive maximum sentences. To protect against unnecessarily severe sentences, judges would be directed to impose the least restrictive appropriate alternative sentence. To protect against unduly destructive sentences, judges would be empowered in every case to mitigate sentences so as to take account of defendants' special circumstances.

Upper Limits

Before just deserts entered the penal lexicon and guidelines became part of sentencing, there were few protections against the possibility that defendants would receive aberrantly severe punishments. Under the rehabilitative ideology of indeterminate sentencing, there was no necessary link between the seriousness of the offender's crimes and the duration of his sentence. In the extreme forms of indeterminate sentencing in California and Washington, felons were sentenced to prison terms ranging from one year to the statutory maximum; the parole board would decide

From M Tonry, *Malign Neglect—Race, Crime, and Punishment in America* (New York, Oxford University Press, 1995), 190–195. References omitted.

when the prisoner could safely be released. It was possible and sometimes happened that offenders convicted of trifling crimes served lengthy prison terms.

Under the procedures of indeterminate sentencing, there was a chance but not an assurance that unduly harsh sentences would later be reduced. Until the 1980s, no American jurisdiction had a meaningful system of appellate sentence review (only two or three do now), so there was little possibility that an appellate judge would review the adequacy of the reasons for a sentence. The parole board could release a defendant at any time after he became eligible for release (usually after serving one-third of the maximum sentence), but often would not. Because unduly long sentences were often attributed to individual judges' idiosyncrasies or to racial or class animus, they were a major target of sentencing reformers.

One of the clear successes of sentencing guidelines has been a lower incidence of aberrantly harsh sentences. As the data presented in Chapter 6 demonstrated, "upward departures" from sentencing guidelines are rare in every jurisdiction for which data have been published. For a variety of reasons, including the legal presumption in favor of guidelines sentences, the one-way pressure of plea bargaining toward sentence reductions, and the availability of sentence appeals for departures, judges rarely impose sentences harsher than the applicable guidelines direct.

This is an accomplishment that adherents of every punishment theory can celebrate. Because maximum guideline sentences can be scaled to the offender's culpability or the severity of his crime, both just-deserts proponents like Andrew von Hirsch and limiting-retributivism proponents like Norval Morris should be pleased. Few offenders will receive penalties harsher than they deserve. Because the imposition of penalties harsher than public sentiment deems just will bring the law into disrepute, utilitarians like Nigel Walker and proponents of hybrid theories like H. L. A. Hart and C. L. Ten have reason to approve.

Proponents of different punishment theories disagree whether minimum penalties should also be scaled to the offender's culpability or the severity of his crime, but about maximum deserved penalties almost all agree. Thus, one un-controversial component of a punishment system that is both generally and racially just is that it contain sentencing guidelines that set presumptive maximum sentences scaled to the differing severities of offenders.

Least Restrictive Appropriate Alternative

A second element of a punishment system that is both generally and racially just is that it direct judges to impose the least restrictive or punitive appropriate alternative sentence. Most defendants in state felony courts, whatever their race, come from disadvantaged backgrounds. Forcing judges to impose harsher penalties than they believe appropriate is to make them do more damage to disadvantaged offenders than circumstances require, in effect gratuitously to impose unnecessary suffering.

A policy that directed judges to impose the least restrictive appropriate alternative would have the rare property that every legitimate consideration would be advanced. This is the policy opposite of the zero-sum game in which one person's gain is someone else's loss. Public safety interests would be advanced. The standard would direct the least restrictive *appropriate* alternative. When an offender's demonstrated dangerousness required that he be confined for the protection of others or when an especially heinous or notorious offense outraged public opinion, no sentence short of confinement would be appropriate. Such offenders and offenses are rare, however; a policy calling for the least restrictive appropriate alternative policy would save taxpayers billions of dollars a year. Tens of thousands of offenders are confined who need not be, and hundreds of thousands are held longer than serves any legitimate public purpose. Such offenders would not escape punishment but would instead be sentenced or released from prison to an appropriate community corrections program. It costs lots of money to operate good community corrections programs, but far less than it does to run prisons. Finally, not least, such a policy would do less damage to offenders and their families.

Preference for the least restrictive alternative is an aspect of indeterminate sentencing that was mistakenly jettisoned. Both the American Bar Association's first set of Criminal Justice Standards (1967) and the American Law Institute's *Model Penal Code* (1962) favored using the least restrictive alternative. The *Model Penal Code* created presumptions in favor of probation over imprisonment and in favor of releasing prisoners on parole when they first became eligible. The code also created a presumption in favor of relatively short sentences that could be overcome only by special findings that the offender was especially dangerous or a career offender. In each case the judge could reject the presumption but had to give reasons for doing so.

There is less consensus among proponents of different punishment theories concerning the appropriateness of the least restrictive alternative approach. Utilitarians and adherents of hybrid theories would support it on grounds of "parsimony": punishments by definition are painful; the infliction of pain, though sometimes necessary, is never a happy event; and a just punishment system would therefore never inflict more pain than is minimally required to achieve legitimate public objectives.

Some retributivists would disapprove. The most rigid retributivists would argue that for every crime there is a single appropriate punishment that in justice must be imposed. Some interpretations of Kant's writings on punishment attribute this position to him. Subtler retributivists like Andrew von Hirsch admit that in the abstract we can never agree on the single ideally appropriate punishment for any crime, but they argue that we can agree on the comparative severity of different crimes and can scale crimes to ensure that the penalties that offenders receive are proportionate to the severity of the crimes they have committed. For von Hirsch, a "principle of proportionality" means that both minimum and maximum penalties must be keyed to offense severity so that all offenders convicted of the same offense receive similar punishments and offenders convicted of different offenses receive proportionately different punishments.

That kind of analysis depends on an oversimplified view of offenders' culpability, in which the only meaningful differences among offenders concern their crimes and some consideration of their past criminal records. To the contrary, I believe that most people's intuitions about just punishment include more distinctions among offenders: between offenders who commit assaults in a moment of great emotion and those who commit assaults coolly and cruelly; between offenders without dependants and those with children who will be affected by the choice of punishment; between disadvantaged offenders who steal under pressure of want and affluent offenders who steal on a whim; between user-dealer sellers of drugs and nonuser distributors. No doubt there are countless other bases on which many people believe offenders should be distinguished.

The other argument for a rigid system of strictly proportionate sentences is that judges cannot be trusted to exercise their discretion ethically but will instead use their authority to mitigate only the sentences of affluent offenders. The principal problems with this argument are that most felons are sentenced in state felony courts and, as the data presented in Chapter 4 show, there are very few affluent offenders in state felony courts. Most of those who could conceivably benefit are disadvantaged, and many are members of minority groups.

Moreover, after twenty years of work with state and federal judges from many states, I have considerable confidence in the basic decency of most contemporary judges. This is not a Pollyannaish view. There are good and bad judges, smart and not-so-smart judges, cruel and compassionate judges. Nonetheless, with only a few exceptions who stand out because they are so rare, I have seldom encountered judges who are unaware of their immense powers over others' lives and who do not find sentencing the most difficult part of their jobs. In addition, today's judges include many more women and people from minority backgrounds. Given a choice between a system in which most offenders are treated unnecessarily harshly and one in which a few affluent offenders may be treated unduly leniently, I would opt for the latter every time.

There are two important policy implications of subscribing to a least restrictive alternative approach. First, all mandatory penalties should be repealed. For some especially serious crimes now subject to such provisions, guidelines should set presumptive minimum sentences. Most of the time, judges will impose at least the presumptive minimum sentence. In cases in which the offense or the offender's circumstances make such a penalty appear too harsh, judges would have the authority to order a lesser sentence if they give reasons for doing so. Should the prosecution wish it, the adequacy of those reasons could be examined on appeal.

Two centuries of experience with mandatory penalties demonstrate that judges and prosecutors often surreptitiously nullify mandatory penalties that they believe are too harsh. Whether that happens depends on the personalities of the officials involved and inevitably results in gross inequities among offenders. It is far better to authorize such mitigations and let them happen in the open where officials are accountable for their decisions.

Second, policies like those of the U.S. Sentencing Commission that forbid mitigation of sentences on grounds of the offenders' personal characteristics or special circumstances should also be repealed. There are only three arguments for such policies. The first, that justice requires strictly proportionate penalties based only on offenses and past criminality, was discussed a few paragraphs earlier and in Chapter 5. It lacks discernible merit and can be set aside. The second, that such policies make the application of guidelines more predictable and therefore are more effective deterrents, cannot be scientifically demonstrated and is probably wrong, as the evidence presented in Chapter 6 demonstrates. The third, that such a policy prevents preferment of middle-class offenders, is based on the fallacious belief that there are many middle-class offenders in felony courts. It too lacks merit. The result of such policies is to damage disadvantaged and minority offenders, especially those who have to some degree overcome dismal life chances. There is no ethical basis for a policy that produces such results.

8.3

Hanging Judges and Wayward Mechanics: Reply to Michael Tonry

IAN BROWNLEE

In his essay in this volume, 'Proportionality, parsimony, and inter-changeability of punishments', Michael Tonry gives us a succinct and closely argued synopsis of his opposition to theories of punishment and procedures for the distribution of punishments that are based on what he characterises as principles of strong proportionality. His opposition rests on two concerns for social justice. First, he expresses a conviction that a system based on strong proportionality constraints can (and in most places and times *will*) result in the imposition of unnecessarily severe punishments by pursuing formal equality at the expense of permissible leniency. Secondly, he cautions that those unnecessarily severe punishments will come to be borne disproportionately. Given the unjust circumstances of our social world, they will fall most often upon the economically marginal groups of society who currently contribute the overwhelming majority of persons at risk of punishment in the criminal justice systems of both the United States and, to a lesser but measurable extent, the United Kingdom.

Criminal Justice and Social Justice

The central contention of Tonry's paper is not that proportionality schemes cannot be made to work in practice. Certainly, given the elusiveness of the concept of 'harm', there are enormous practical difficulties in assessing the seriousness of offences and in ranking them on that measure. Problems, no less taxing, arise too from the attempt to devise graduated scales of punishments from which to choose appropriate responses. And, even if one succeeds in constructing two more-or-less generally acceptable tables on either side of the harm/response dichotomy, the relationship between the two is by no means obvious. But von Hirsch's general scheme, it is conceded, could eventually provide a comprehensive desert-based system of punishment. What is denied is that such a system would be wise and just, or possessed of more objective validity than a contending system that aimed to promote the principle of restraint or 'parsimony' above the application of equality before the

From A Duff, S Marshall, RE Dobash and RP Dobash (eds), *Penal Theory and Practice* (Manchester, Manchester University Press, 1996).

law. For Tonry, it is no justification, either, if aberrant severity is experienced universally; if punishments are 'wrong' because they are too severe, they are not 'right' merely because they are equally severe between different recipients.

The cornerstone of this argument is an attack upon the desirability of fixing objective measures of culpability in order to determine the level of 'penal deservedness'. This notion of objectively determinable culpability lies at the heart of retributive or blaming theories of punishment: punishment is a 'desert' because culpable harm has been done, and for the former to be quantifiable the latter must be measurable. In von Hirsch's scheme, as is well known, the seriousness of a crime, conceptually, has two elements: the degree of harmfulness of the conduct and the extent of the actor's culpability when committing the conduct (von Hirsch, 1986). The conceptual framework itself is not at issue in the present debate but, centrally, the desirability of measuring the level of culpability on 'standard case' criteria is.

Human Difference and Differing Culpability

Explicitly, the position advanced in Tonry's essay negates the existence of 'like-situated' offenders. That phrase, and the expression 'comparable crimes', are both 'artificial notions . . . Neither offenders nor punishments come in standard cases' (Tonry, ch. 3, p. 69). Remembering that the yardstick in this debate is the likelihood of an accretion in social justice arising from a particular mode of distributing punishment, we may ask not only whether this proposition is true, but also whether devising a system of punishment on the basis that it might be true, will actually result in a net gain in social justice.

Of course, on a purely anthropological level, the first part of that proposition is undoubtedly true. The issue for sentencers (and for those who seek to guide them) is to determine which of the myriad symbols of human diversity should properly influence the sentencing decision, and to what extent. Substantive criminal law principles supply some limited guidance on this by providing, for instance, that certain degrees of mental illness or varieties of automatism excuse from guilt altogether. However, as Tonry notes, substantive common law concepts like *mens rea* are not particularly attuned to the differing material conditions of life. Culpability is clearly a wider concept than intention (at least in the sense in which that latter term is employed by criminal lawyers in common law jurisdictions). As a consequence, a finding of guilt based upon a determination of criminal intention still leaves open most of the essential issues involved in determining culpability; it is this latter determination which, both sides of this particular debate would agree, should properly influence the choice of punishment.

To examine this issue further, it may be helpful to consider the hypothetical mechanic, Tonry's figure, not so much of straw, as of grease, oil and sweat. Certainly, there is much about his character which, in the absence of his most recent court appearance, would commend him. But the question remains: is the judge, who must now deal with him for his transgression of the criminal law, at fault if he or she does not mitigate his sentence to reward the defendant's struggles up to the point of that offence? In other words, is the level of his culpability (which, together with a measure of the harmfulness of his act, will determine his penal blame-worthiness) to be discounted *because of the sort of person he is*? The assertion that it should is, in essence, the core of Tonry's critique of desert theories, but in condemning schemes like the Minnesota guidelines for their refusal to consider the personal characteristics of the once wayward mechanic, Tonry, it may be argued, has opened the door to a labyrinth of personal preferences and judicial dislikes.

The mechanic in this story has been what might be called, perhaps patronisingly, a 'born loser'. For several years he has fulfilled society's low expectations of him but, of late, he has reformed, struggled, achieved. But let us suppose that six months ago he raped a woman at knife-point, after he had been called out to her broken-down vehicle. Despite a not-guilty plea, which necessitated a long and harrowing trial, he has been convicted of the offence.

The evidence has determined his responsibility, but what is to determine his culpability? Or to ask that question in a more practical way, how is the judge to 'see' him when she determines what sentence is appropriate? As an 'uppity nigger'? As a potential danger to women? As a person who has tried against all the odds, and temporarily failed? Or as a rapist, *simpliciter*? The first view offends any objective notion of justice, even if it does reflect a very visible symbol of human difference. The second would go against our hypotfietical rapist, presumably, on the questionable ground of predictability of dangerousness. The third, on the other hand, might resound to his favour, but *may* leave his victim feeling 'doubly victim-ised'. It is the fourth characterisation of the offender which, it may be argued, is the most appropriate, since it imparts the greatest level of neutrality to the assessment. Sentencing on the factual basis of proven offence leads, by definition, to the defendant being sentenced on the basis of what he has done, rather than who he is, has been, or might become. Such a claim, of course, is explicitly at odds with Tonry's own position.

If a further resort to hypothetical cases is permissible, let us imagine that the wayward mechanic took with him an assistant from the garage. This other young man is from the 'right side of the tracks', and is reasonably well educated. In short, he really has no social disadvantage to plead in mitigation. Despite an initial reluc-tance, he succumbed to his colleague's inducements and he also raped the stranded motorist.

The point is not to suggest that people from socially disadvantaged backgrounds make more willing rapists than those who come from homes higher up the social scale. The purpose in drawing the example in this way is to question the assertion, which one may deduce from Tonry's position, that the minority offender from a broken home and a devastated neighbourhood who has nonetheless managed a reasonably stable domestic life and so on, should be entitled to a mitigated sentence *on those grounds alone*. In the further hypothetical example he is the instigator of the second rape, and is responsible in a sense for more than half of the victim's suffering. Why he should carry anything less than half the total punishment awarded is by no means clear. If in this case the principles of proportionality and of parsimony are in conflict and if, as Tonry suggests, neither principle can claim anything more than a conditional objective validity, then can we say that reducing the severity of the punishment of one of the rapists below that of the other, merely on the grounds of prior disadvantage, is a demonstrably more just outcome?

Economic Crime and Social Disadvantage

Of course, it might be objected that rape has been chosen as the offence in these examples because it is an emotive crime for which few objective commentators can find much mitigation. A louder and, arguably, stronger case can usually be made on these grounds in respect of economic crimes. After all, common sense alone seems to suggest that the urge to steal is going to prove less resistible die more poverty-stricken one is. One does not have to adopt a full-blown determinism in order to draw links between certain conditions of relative economic deprivation and criminal behaviour.

Suppose for the sake of the present discussion that some such link, short of out-and-out determinism (which would, of course, undermine legal responsibility), can be demonstrated between social disadvantage and involvement in economic crime. Would such a circumstance demand that proportionality constraints be loosened so that the disadvantaged were inevitably to be treated more leniently than the better-off for equal amounts of dishonesty? Tonry argues this case strongly, asserting that a failure to adjust assessment of culpability to reflect social disadvantage merely serves to perpetuate the vast over-representation of the economically marginal in the custodial system. However, in both its moral and practical dimensions, this argument leaves some further avenues for the sceptic to explore.

Understanding and Blaming: The Victims' Perspective

To deal with the moral dimension first. By virtue of their office, judges are in the business of blaming. In other words, a judge in his or her public role has a duty to reflect the expectations of society and of offenders' victims, at least in as far as these do not stray over legitimate boundaries of revenge and vindictiveness. The legitimate interests of victims impose limits on the extent to which culpability may be reduced for the purposes of sentencing, and not only for pragmatic or utilitarian reasons. Indeed, as Tonry reminds us, Morris's parsimony principle calls for less severe punishments only in as much as they meet legitimate social purposes.

To take this argument further, if we are to believe the evidence of numerous victim surveys, it is not only the prison population that is disproportionately drawn from the economically marginal sections of society; the direct effects of much crime also fall disproportionately on the already disadvantaged. And if this is so, then the law's denunciatory function belongs as much to the poor and the disadvantaged as to the rich. On these grounds, therefore, the moral superiority of parsimony over proportionality in respect of socially disadvantaged offenders is not as clear-cut as Tonry's paper suggests. If the problem of "just deserts in an unjust world' is as much of a problem for strong proportionality theories as Tonry contends, then perhaps, in turn, the comparative absence of the victim's perspective from his paper permits the moral superiority of his own position to be overstated.

Challenging Social Justice: The 'Hanging Judge' as Social Reformer

This is not necessarily to argue that social disadvantage should be ignored altogether when culpability is in issue. Clearly, there must be room for some recognition of motive in general as well as exceptional cases, and proponents of strict proportionality will do well to address this thorny issue in their continuing work. However, as a generality, the question of how society is structured, and the possible consequences of the unequal distribution of opportunities within that structure, are essentially political issues. It may well be true that, within a capitalist division of labour, certain groups of people are more likely to engage in activity that is at odds with the prevailing criminal code; it may be equally true that within existing conditions certain, readily identifiable sections of the population are disproportionately susceptible to law enforcement and criminalisation. The combination of these two factors will undoubtedly lead to the sort of skewed distribution of classes and races within the prison population that now appears. It does not necessarily follow from this that it is for judges in their sentencing function to redress, on a piecemeal basis, the social inequities of the capitalist order.

In addition to these moral and political considerations, there are real practical difficulties in equipping judges with wide discretion to fix sentences on a subjective 'type of person' assessment. Tonry's paper seems to work on the premise that, in Minnesota's case for example, if the guidelines did not prohibit the practice, judges would invariably attribute the appropriate culpability discounts to the right sorts of personal characteristics. This may or may not be so, but the fact that Tonry sees the need to establish stringent standards to circumscribe the aggravation of sentences for 'the undeserving' suggests that he may have his own reservations about the progressiveness of some, at least, of the judges.

The image of the 'hanging judge' may be a crude stereotype, but the influence of hardline opinions among influential members of the judiciary would, surely, minimise the reductive effect of purely subjective sentencing. Clearly, as Tonry's 'sketched reconciliation' suggests, it is reasonable to expect that in order to make parsimony more certain, directions will have to be issued to the judges. Practical difficulties may then be envisaged in drafting such directions, particularly in juris-dictions with strict separation of powers notions in their constitutions. In addition, if the reported experience of reductionism in Germany is representative (Feest, 1988), in order to achieve any major reductions one would also have to regulate and change the behaviour of other agents within the criminal justice system, partic-ularly the prosecutors. The criminal justice process is multi-layered and interdependent, and interventions for change are more likely to succeed if they are also 'multi-faceted'.

So, it is contended that, when practicalities are considered, there is at least room to query whether the loosening of proportionality constraints on sentencers would necessarily bring about the increase in social justice that underpins the claims of opponents of desert theory to some sort of moral or ethical superiority.

Re-thinking the Tariff

Tonry's critique of strong proportionality contains a third concern, less central to the thesis but still of great importance to abolitionists and other penal reformers. This is the assertion that strong proportionality constraints limit and even exclude the use of non-custodial sentences, and it is predicated on the invariable linking of notions of proportionality with the seemingly inevitable use of 'carceral coin' as the standard unit by which to measure sentence severity. As many sentencing systems are presently constructed, the observation that 'alternatives' are invariably con-ceived of as alternatives to custody seems sustainable. And if proportionality inevitably means equal amounts of custody, at least at the 'heavy end' of the spec-trum of offences, then perhaps the criticism that strict proportionality constraints are inherently inimical to non-custodial sentences is made out. But one may query whether this is an a priori or merely an empirical criticism.

Proponents of desert theory have argued to the contrary that proportionate punishments can be exacted without increasing severity levels, provided that one observes the difference between ordinal and cardinal proportionality. While the demands of ordinal magnitude must be considered inviolable if the principle of treating unlike offenders differently is to have any meaning, the limits imposed by notions of cardinal magnitude may be treated largely as a matter of convention. As such, cardinal magnitude may be subject to revision downward provided only (it may be a large proviso) that conventional modes of judicial thought can be persuaded to change. On this rationale, what prevents the use of, say, intensive probation to punish house burglars is not the constraints of strong proportionality as such, so much as the existence of a 'tariff' that views probation as outside the range of punishments appropriate to that type of offence.

Tariffs like this evolve over many years, 'bolstered', to borrow Andrew Ashworth's phrase, by arguments from analogy and swayed by occasional moral panics (Ashworth, 1992, p. 91). Given this sort of origin, they are susceptible to change, although the mechanics of change may vary from jurisdiction to jurisdiction and rapid change cannot always be expected, judicial character being what it is. But once the tariff is revised, pro rata changes in all the available punishments are effected without offending principles of proportionality. After all, in Britain we still punish murderers more severely than sheep rustlers, although nowadays we hang very few of either.

Changes in judicial thinking of the kind required to effect a change in the ordering of punishments can be assisted by meaningful communication between those who sentence and those who provide disposals outside the custodial regime. The aim of this communication is not to persuade sentencers away from the view that offences of house burglary or of violence against the person are worthy of heavier punishment than, say, offences of minor damage. Rather, the reeducation is aimed at demonstrating that this or that particular form of non-custodial disposal is commensurate with serious offending.

In a sense, this kind of strategy for expanding the use of noncustodial sentencing reverses the order of logic employed in Tonry's scheme. Here, the method is to 'up-tariff' the severity of the punishment (at least in the perception of the sentencer), rather than to 'down-grade' the level of culpability of the offender and, as a consequence, the seriousness of the offence. This is clearly the approach implicit in the arguments offered in the British government's White Paper (Home Office, 1990) for increasing the use of community penalties, although that is hardly surprising given that government's conversion to desert theory (*ibid*., para. 2.9). Such an approach places the principle of proportionality at the heart of official justifications for punishment, while at the same time committing it to a reduction, rather than an expansion, in the use of custodial sentencing. Tonry's argument would suggest that these two aims are irreconcilable. The success or failure of the 1991 Act on the measure of percentage use of imprisonment will provide a good test of his critique.

References

Ashworth, A. (1995), *Sentencing and Criminal Justice* (2nd edn, London, Weidenfeld & Nicolson).
Home Office (1990), *Crime, Justice and Protecting the Public* (London, HMSO).
Tonry, M. (1995), *Malign Neglect* (New York, Oxford University Press).
Von Hirsch, A. (1986), *Past or Future Crimes* (Manchester, Manchester University Press).

8.4

Justice and Difference

BARBARA A HUDSON

From the standpoint of avoiding injustice to the socially disadvantaged, the most significant virtue of desert is its principle that punishment should be limited to punishment for crimes already committed, and any strategy which departs from that is bound to be discriminatory in its effects. Indeed, it is during the period in which desert theory has been influential that concern with discrimination has been to the fore. Whilst research and policy might have been directed at ensuring non-discrimination in process rather than equality of outcomes, it is only under a desert model that discrimination is problematic; indeed, it is only under a 'justice as fairness' model that the idea of discrimination has any meaning. If the goal of penal policy is to reduce reoffending, or to protect the public from the dangerous, then more severe punishment of those whose personalities and circumstances make them more liable to reoffend, is not just legitimate, it is desirable. This effect of the embrace of a future-oriented policy is illustrated by Norval Morris's consideration of the link between race and violent crime:

> Criminals X and Y had identical criminal records and had committed identical crimes, but X was not a school dropout, X had a job to which he could return if not sent to prison, and X had a supportive family who would take him back if allowed to do so, while the unfortunate Y was a school dropout, was unemployed, and lacked a supportive family. And let us suppose that past studies reveal that criminals with Y's criminal record and with his environmental circumstances have a base expectancy rate of 1 in 10 of being involved in a crime of personal violence. While no such calculations have been made for criminals like X, it is quite clear that they have a much lower base expectancy rate of future violent criminality. I suggest that Y should be held longer than X based on these predictions . . . As a matter of statistical likelihood, X is white and Y is black.[1]

Morris's theory of 'limited retributivism' argues for considerations of danger-ousness to be allowed to override equality of punishment, but within wide presumptive sentence bands, where the maximum term even for an offender assessed as posing danger of reoffending, must remain within the allowable limits

From BA Hudson, 'Doing Justice to Difference' in A Ashworth and M Wasik (eds), *Fundamentals of Sentencing Theory* (Oxford, Oxford University Press, 1998).

set by estimates of proportionality of penalty to current offence. He is urging a place for concerns of dangerousness and recidivisim in a basically desert-oriented system. The mass incarceration of black Americans[2] has accelerated as penal strategies have shifted from the desert ideal of 'doing justice' to a risk-oriented 'new penology'[3] concerned with prevention of risk of reoffending, and with managing a 'dangerous' underclass of people who are assumed to be likely to become more rather than less criminal as they develop. Morris's allowance of departures from equal distribution of punishment because of considerations of dangerousness takes on a new import if the idea of proportionality, of 'justice as fairness', is abandoned.

Both rehabilitation and desert are based on ideas of the essential similarity of criminals and non-criminals. For rehabilitationists, the offender is presumed to have the normal range of motivations, and through help, treatment, or counselling can reform; for adherents of desert, the criminal is like the non-criminal in being possessed of rationality and will, so that he/she can make prudential choices about the likely benefits and pains of crime, and can receive the moral communication conveyed in the pronouncement of sentences.[4] Contemporary penal strategies based on ideas of dangerousness and persistence incorporate much of the thinking of social theorists such as Charles Murray, who suggest that criminals really *are* different, that they have a crime-tolerant way of life and are quite content to live on welfare benefits topped up by the proceeds of crime.[5] This shift towards a criminology and penology of dangerousness and difference is signalled in James Q. Wilson's book, *Thinking About Crime*, which in the 1990s has become the work which most influences policy-makers, to a large extent displacing the political influence of Andrew von Hirsch's *Doing Justice* in the 1980s.[6]

If there are advantages of principle and practice in seeing offenders and non-offenders as having a fundamental equality in their possession of rights and of 'normal' motivational structures, a disadvantage of desert lies in the way in which it has conceptualized the 'equality' of penal treatment which it sees as a prime virtue of criminal justice. In particular, there are deficiencies in the way in which the idea of penal equality has been operationalized in proportionate sentencing policy and practice. The critique of sentencing disparity which desert theorists mounted against rehabilitation-oriented sentencing in the 1970s targeted dissimilar punishment of 'similar offences by similarly situated offenders'. Proportionality's weakness has been in its failure to specify criteria for similarity and dissimilarity of offenders' situations. Whilst desert theorists have been— rightly—concerned that over-emphasis on dissimilarity can produce enhanced punishment for disadvantaged offenders in future-oriented systems, they have been less preoccupied with the injustice that can occur because of disregard of dissimilarity of situation in past-oriented systems.[7]

Not only does strict proportionality make it difficult for sentencers to take into account discrimination—direct or indirect—at earlier criminal justice stages, it also makes it difficult to consider differences in opportunities to refrain from crime. In other words, desert in practice has not given as much attention to calculations of culpability as to rankings of offence seriousness; the desert principle that punishment should be proportionate to the blameworthiness of the offender has been overly focused on just one of the elements of blameworthiness.

This neglect of offenders' situations has been accomplished by substituting the idea of procedural equality for the phenomenological inequality of actual offenders acting in actual circumstances. Law takes to itself the right to specify what criteria of sameness and difference are relevant to its decision-making. If differences of gender, race, class, and so forth are ruled irrelevant, the criterion that is ruled relevant is agency: we are all presumed equally possessed of free will; we can all choose to commit crime or to refrain from crime.[8] The appeal to common-sense notions of 'justice' and 'fairness' that gave desert reformers so much credibility when they pointed to the differences in sentences being served by people convicted of the same crime, is, however, also readily enlisted if we ask whether someone committing a crime 'for kicks' deserves the same punishment as someone committing 'the same' offence because of economic desperation. Although the action might be the same, the culpability of the actors in the two situations is surely different.

Michael Tonry[9] has questioned the inflexibility of proportionate sentencing, raising the issue of whether someone confronted with adverse social circumstances should be given credit for past restraint from crime. He sketches an example of a minority group offender, raised in a single-parent, welfare-dependent household, who has cured himself of drug addiction, who works whenever work is available, and who supports his children and their mother, and argues that such a person should be treated leniently, at least for a first offence; he should be given credit for his efforts to 'overcome the odds'. The difficulty with Tonry's suggestion is that it incorporates notions of the 'deserving' and 'undeserving' poor:

what if he had not overcome his addiction; what if he had not managed to support his children? This selective, individual leniency is exactly the approach that the feminist research, quoted above, argues has disadvantaged those women who have not fulfilled conventional gender roles.

One possible solution might be to introduce some form of 'categorial leniency', such that offences which are characteristically associated with poverty are evaluated as being of lesser seriousness than more 'expressive' offences which are not correlated with economic circumstances. In effect, this would bring about a sentencing approach not unlike that envisaged in the Criminal Justice Act 1991, where offences of violence against the person were to be more severely punished than property offences. Property crimes are the most clearly statistically correlated with poverty, violent crimes the least, so this would not offend against a harm standard of seriousness; the difference would be that the definition of seriousness would incorporate a reference to culpability as well as to harm.

Such an approach would be consistent with the penal 'decrementalism' advocated by Braithwaite and Pettit,[10] who urge progressive lowering of penalties for the most common offences, to the point at which there are demonstrable, causally related increases in crime. It would, moreover, reverse the situation currently found in most Western jurisdictions, which is, Braithwaite has argued,[11] that where desert is least, punishment is greatest. In making this statement, he is referring to the discrepancies between the punishment of 'white-collar crime', such as tax fraud, insider dealing, computer fraud, and the crimes of the poor such as burglary, minor robberies, and social security fraud. Braithwaite's view, which I certainly share, and which would also be acknowledged by other writers on the differences between penalization of 'suite crime' and 'street crime', is that both criminalization and penalization are inescapably class-correlated, and future reform efforts should be in the direction of reversing the present bias towards excessive punishment of the crimes of the poor.

Another way of allowing for consideration of differences in situation would be to widen the concept of 'fair opportunity to resist', which is recognized in the defences of duress and mental incapacity, to include economic incapacity. This concept is mentioned by Hart,[12] who allowed that the ascription of responsibility might be less for people who were in circumstances such that conformity with the law was more difficult than for most people.

The idea that economic circumstances might influence blameworthiness is considered by desert theorists. Von Hirsch, for example, in spelling out his theory of proportionate penalties acknowledged that:

> the impoverished defendant poses a dilemma for our (retributive) theory. In principle, a case can be made that he is less culpable because his deprived status has left him with far fewer opportunities for an adequate livelihood within the law.[13]

Von Hirsch and other desert theorists decide against allowing for economic circumstances to have significant influence in sentencing decisions, however, partly because of the experience of the use of personal and social characteristics to enhance penalties for disadvantaged offenders in forward-looking, rehabilitative, and incapacitative systems, and partly because of the difficulty in operationalizing a 'hardship' defence.[14] There is concern that admission of a hardship defence or mitigation, especially along the lines outlined by Tonry, would bring back the discrimination and disparity seen in future-oriented sentencing practices, and also that reducing penalties because of economic constraints might mean that sentencing is sometimes inadequate to reflect the suffering of victims. This latter point is the principal reason given by Morris in arguing for desert setting the lower as well as the upper limit to punishments. Whilst this is undoubtedly a difficulty, my own view is that it is not possible always to 'do justice' to both offenders and to victims in the same part of the criminal justice system: the seriousness of the harm could be stated by the judge, who would then explain the reasons for assessing culpability as lower than in a standard case, and recognition of the victim's suffering should be made effective through adequate statutory compensation. Punishment is inflicted on offenders and it must therefore, as desert theory itself argues, be linked to the blameworthiness of offenders rather than to any other consideration.

Another formidable obstacle to the admission of a hardship defence is the conception of choice and freedom of will in law. In discussing Hart's consideration of choice, volition, and fault, von Hirsch states that proportionality:

> cannot be based on the idea of a fair opportunity to avoid the criminal law's impositions— since it concerns the quantum of punishment levied on persons who, in choosing to violate the law, have voluntarily exposed themselves to the consequences of criminal liability.[15]

It is this concept of choice that seems most crucial to the question of whether or not economic circumstances should be allowed to influence estimates of culpability. Are there circumstances or factors (poverty, gender, race, as well as addictions and physical duress) which deny or reduce freedom to choose one's actions?

Legal reasoning incorporates an either/or notion of choice and freedom of action: either one can choose or one cannot choose. It finds difficulty in accommodating the idea of choice as a matter of degree. In thinking about a mitigation or even a defence of restricted opportunity to conform, the question is whether one could first of all establish, and secondly operationalize, a concept of choice that envisaged degrees of freedom of action. Lack of income would not by itself signal lack of freedom of choice to comply with the demands of law. Someone might, for example, have a highly-paid job as a surgeon or company executive, but then give it up to pursue a career as an artist; a qualified computer analyst might take up an 'alternative' lifestyle. If the art career was unsuccessful, if the alternative lifestyle left the erstwhile computer analyst with his/her material wants unsatisfied, should this enable them to commit crimes without blame? Where poverty is a matter of choice, surely any resulting crime must also be a matter of choice?

Economic duress, if it is to be admissible at all as a 'relevant criterion' in establishing blameworthiness, must be allowable first and foremost in cases where the poverty which constrains choice to refrain from crime or not, is not itself out of choice. One attempt to defend an economic duress mitigation approaches the problem by considering life choices as structured. After arguing that although, in the sense used by existentialist philosophers, we are all free, Groves and Frank say that what matters is differences in life-chances: the millionaire and the ghetto-dweller might have the same number of choices available to them, but the millionaire's choices would be such as to enable them to achieve goods (money, shelter, social status, leisure activity) that are socially valued legitimately, whereas such opportunities would be severely restricted for the ghetto-dweller.[16] Freedom of socially meaningful choice, they conclude, is a matter of degree: only in law and existentialist philosophy is it an absolute.[17]

This absolutist conception of choice that is incorporated in law amounts to, as David Garland argues, a conflation of the ideas of *freedom* and *agency:*

> The idea of agency refers to the capacity of an agent for action, its possession of the 'power to act', which is the capacity to originate such actions on the basis of calculations and decisions. Agency is a universal attribute of (socialized) human beings . . .

Freedom, on the other hand, generally refers to a capacity to choose one's actions without external constraint. Freedom (unlike agency) is necessarily a matter of degree—it is the configured range of unconstrained choice in which agency can operate.[18]

Groves and Frank propose that freedom of choice should be reconceptualized as a continuum with four main divisions—compulsion; coercion; causation; and freedom. Compulsion would be something like having a gun pointed at one's head and being ordered to commit a crime, or it might be an extreme state of mental disorder; coercion would mean very strong persuasion either by persons, or by external or personal circumstances, and in these two cases responsibility would cither be absent (compulsion), or very much diminished (coercion). Causation— I would prefer the less determinist term motivation—could involve peer pressure, provocation, economic pressures, influence of drugs or alcohol, in situations where pressures were not so great as to amount to lack of choice, or where entering such states of economic or chemical influence had been voluntary. This 'caused' offence would be the 'standard case' where the desert penalty would be most clearly applicable. In such a case, the penalty would form part of the choice equation, tipping the balance of advantage and disadvantage against committing the crime, in situations where choices are clearly available, operating as a countervailing pressure to the pressures influencing the individual towards crime. This is the deterrent punishment scheme envisaged by adherents of rational choice theories of offending.[19] Complete freedom of choice would, say Groves and Frank, be relatively rare, and would be the situation of the anti-social actor who could gain socially valued goods as easily by legal as by criminal means. This person would be the most blameworthy, and culpability in such cases would be enhanced. In fact, rather than in the writings of Nietszche or Dostoevsky, such a criminal would be the suite criminal more often than the street criminal.

There is still the difficulty of how to measure economic pressure of the sort that produces compulsion or coercion rather than merely motivation. Groves and Frank (writing of the USA) suggest that the criterion would be a combination of an annual income of $6,000 or less; being unemployed at the time of arrest; and having less than a high school education. In England and Wales at the present time, one can readily think of groups of people who have no legitimate income at all sufficient to supply basic material needs, or who have no access to their supposed income. Young people who are not eligible for welfare benefits under the present regulations might come into this category: the young homeless and those with chaotic lifestyles who cannot accommodate themselves to the rules of the jobseekers' allowance; women whose men withhold money, or only give them money if they engage in prostitution or other criminal activity; people leaving penal, psychiatric, or residential care institutions who receive benefits in arrears but who need to pay for food and shelter immediately, would seem to be candidates for a defence or mitigation of economic duress.

These suggestions are attempts to combine what is, in my view, the prime) virtue of desert—that is, that people should only be punished for offences that they have already committed, not for crimes that they might (but might not) commit in the future—with the virtue of rehabilitative strategies—that is, sensitivity to offenders' situations. Such sensitivity, operationalized through social background enquiries, motivational interviewing, awareness of rates of unemployment, local climates of racism, etc., would not have the same deleterious impact if it is used in mitigating culpability rather than as a predictor of reoffending. This is the crucial point: knowledge about the offender should be used in assessments of culpability for crimes already committed, not for prognostications about crimes to come.

It could be argued that both these suggestions—defining crimes correlated with poverty as less serious than those with no such association, and establishing a defence or mitigation of economic duress—would introduce positive discrimination in favour of minority ethnic groups and women whose lives do not accord with standards of conventional femininity. If disproportionately more black than white offenders (male and female) are likely to be convicted of poverty-linked crimes and meet the conditions of economic duress, they would benefit disproportionately from such initiatives. On the other hand, the numbers of white offenders are so much greater than those of black offenders, that substantial numbers of the majority group would also benefit. More than anything, the penal system is the system which deals with the wrong-doing of the poor.[20] The penal system is 'voluntary' only for people whose actions are unconstrained by poverty, addictions or other compelling circumstances; the involuntarily impoverished, especially those with no legitimate income at all, cannot be said to 'choose' to violate the law. By far the greatest actual number of beneficiaries of such an innovation would be white, male, impoverished, offenders, because these are by far the greatest number of offenders. Although there might be a slight disproportion of benefit in favour of black offenders, such a result could not really be called positive 'discrimination', if the group which provides the largest number of beneficiaries is the majority group.

Another important critique of desert/proportionality's espousal of equal penal treatment is that 'equality' tends to mean 'like men'. If treating women differently has meant, on average, treating them more leniently, equality as gender-blindness must be disadvantageous for female offenders. Kathleen Daly has demonstrated how the desert and determinate sentencing reforms introduced throughout America in the 1980s have increased the imprisonment of women.[21] She points out that most states have sought to equalize the sentencing of men and women, either by making the presumptive sentences in punishment schedules and guidelines approximate the average terms passed on men, or by adopting a 'split the difference' tactic. This latter practice has had little or no ameliorating impact on the sentencing of men (because there are so many more male than female offenders), but has increased penal severity towards females. Whilst advocates for black offenders might reasonably posit parity with white offenders as a desirable goal, fit is suggested that parity with men would not seem so desirable for those advocating on behalf of women offenders.[22] This reasoning makes sense if 'parsimony' rather than 'equality' is seen as the most important penal aim, a position with which Tonry and Braithwaite are associated. Whilst parsimony as a general principle is something I would wholeheartedly support, special pleading on behalf of women seems uncomfortably close to the paternalism complained of by Edwards and some of the earlier critics of the treatment of women in the courts.[23]

This difficulty is resolved if 'equality' can be taken to mean punishment of equivalent severity or leniency, and of equivalent relevance to circumstances, for offences of *equal culpability given knowledge of circumstances,* rather than a simplified sameness, let alone a 'same as men' standard. To reject sameness is not fro reject equality, but is to ask for a more complex formulation of equality. The confusion of equality and sameness is built into much of the scholarship on discrimination in sentencing, as well as being embedded in law:

> to accept that 'justice' and 'equality' are to be achieved by parity of treatment is to collude in the acceptance of the inequalities which co-exist with such 'equal treatment'. To assume that justice for women means treating women like men is to ignore the very different existences which distinguish the lives of women from the lives of men of similar social status. Yet this attitude to 'justice' and 'equality' not only underlies legislative provision, it is also to be found in studies of the law and the criminal justice system.[24]

Many feminist legal theorists claim that the law 'is male', in that it incorporates an unreflexive male standpoint; it sees women only as men see them, and only in relation to men.[25] What is needed is that it should become 'gendered', not in the sense of reproducing and reinforcing stereotyped gender roles, but in being able to incorporate female as well as male world-views. Whilst progress is being made—recognition of the importance of domestic violence; some rethinking of the concept of 'provocation' to take into account the circumstances of abused wives—much is still to be accomplished.

This new thinking on provocation incorporates something like the notion of choice as structured by life circumstances, and as being a matter of degree, discussed above in relation to a defence or mitigation of economic duress. It also calls for recognition that choices are not structured just by economic circumstances, but also by race and gender. For example, from the male standpoint, the question usually asked about abused women is 'why didn't she leave?'; it has taken feminist psychologists and others to explain that although the choice to leave exists, battered women may lack perception of leaving as a real choice, because the abuse has shaken their confidence to such a degree that they no longer see themselves as active framers of their own destiny. Calculations of culpability should take into account the rich volume of research literature that is available showing the pressures which lead women towards crime in real-life situations.[26]

The call for different treatment then becomes not special pleading for leniency but for a 'woman-wise' penal strategy which does not increase female offenders' oppression *as women*. Such gendered criminal justice consciousness might very well lead to support for the abolition of imprisonment for women as a standard penalty. Abolition would not be because of special pleading, but because of the low numbers of women committing violent offences, and the even lower numbers of women who commit violent or serious offences because of consciously anti-social motives. Imprisonment would become an unusual response to an unusual crime, needing special justification.

In formulating her ideal of women-wise penology, Pat Carlen also demands that the punishment of men 'does not brutalize them and make them even more violently or ideologically oppressive towards women in the future'.[27] She suggests that because of the small numbers of women committing serious, violent offences, as well as being an appropriate response to the numbers and patterns of female crime, abolition of women's imprisonment could be used as an experiment in developing effective and constructive responses to crime, which could then be extended to the punishment of men. This once more demonstrates that feminist criminologists and legal theorists are not asking for special-case leniency, but that they are challenging the present assumption that the male penal norm is generalizable. Given the association between masculinity and crime, there is far more sense in demanding that the penal treatment of men take into account women's view of the world, than for the penal treatment of women to be the same as that of men! Experience of sentencing patterns of female offenders in the USA since 1980 and in England since the 1991 Criminal Justice Act, however, shows that 'parity of treatment' in practice has meant more imprisonment of women, rather than more rehabilitative, non-custodial sentences for men.

Conclusion

For sentencing to achieve equal appropriateness rather than equality of injustice, law needs to become open not just to a female standpoint, but also to the standpoints of different minority ethnic groups. Criminal justice should be reflexively 'racialized' in the same way that it has been suggested it should become gendered.[28] Again, some progress has been made, for example the recognition of racial motiviation as an aggravating factor in offences, but progress is slow and halting, and to an even greater extent than with the acknowledgement of a female standpoint, there remains much to be done.

In opening itself to multiple standpoints, law would be moving away from a simple rule-following logic towards the more relational '*ethic of care*' formulated by the feminist jurisprudence movement.[29] At the forefront of the proposals of these writers is that defendants should be considered in their relationships and circumstances, and that questions of blameworthiness and the choice of penalties should reflect such considerations. What this amounts to is appreciation that the subject being blamed is not the abstract 'reasonable person' of legal discourse, whose ascribed characteristics turn out to be those of the middle-aged, middle-class, white male; but a real, flesh and blood individual, an individual whose scope for action, whose perception of choices, whose life experiences, may be very different from those sitting in judgment.

These questions of desert, discrimination, and equality are difficult. It is too easy to shift from direct to indirect discrimination and thereby to make unfairness more difficult to challenge; it is too easy to become over-pessimistic when faced with evidence of the disadvantaging use of personal-social factors in the past; it is too easy to become confused about whether or not to advocate equal/the same treatment. What is beyond doubt is that responding to difference is the most challenging of tasks for criminal justice: the ideal of finding a response to difference which neither represses it, as in the future-oriented strategies of old-style rehabilitation and new-style incapacitation, nor denies it, as in oversimplified and unsophisticated proportionality schemes. Whilst proportionality of penalty to harm is an important element of penal justice, and whilst fairness and equality of treatment are vitally important values of law, 'justice' involves more than questions of distribution; it involves moving beyond the 'distributive paradigm',[30] towards acknowledging the demands of alterity, that is to say, of developing sensitivity to the needs of the 'Other',[31] someone who is like oneself in essential humanity and in the possession of rights, but unlike in biography and perspective. 'Justice' is about recognizing the Other in her/his individuality and ensuring that what is delivered by law is appropriate to that individual. 'Justice' cannot be done unless difference is acknowledged, and given its due.

I am suggesting here that the most fruitful approach to issues of equality and discrimination would be one that combined the desert principles of only punishing already committed crimes, and acknowledging the offender's right to desert upper limits on punishment, with a sensitivity to difference throughout the entire process of criminalizing harms, assessing culpability, and deciding appropriate penalties. Punishment theory needs to continue to explore problems of differences in culpability of offenders, and needs to recognize that 'equality' is not necessarily 'sameness'. Legal thinking about questions of blame and punishment must open itself to the understandings of feminist and post-modernist critiques of law in general, and of proportionality theory and practice, in particular, if justice is ever to be done to difference.

Notes

1. N. Morris, 'Dangerousness and Incapacitation', in R. A. Duff and D. Garland (eds.), *A Reader on Punishment* (1994), at p. 257.
2. Tonry (1995) n. 56 above, at p. 4, reports that in 1991 in Washington DC, and Baltimore, 42 and 56%, respectively of black males aged 18 to 35 were under justice system control.

3. M. Feeley and J. Simon, 'The new penology: notes on the emerging strategy of corrections and its implications', (1992) 30 *Criminology* 449–74, and 'Actuarial justice: the emerging new criminal law' in D. Nelken, (eds.) *The Futures of Criminology* (1994).

4. A. von Hirsch, *Censure and Sanctions* (1993).

5. C. Murray, *The Emerging British Underclass* (1990).

6. J. Q. Wilson, *Thinking About Crime* (1975), 2nd edn. (1983); A. von Hirsch, *Doing Justice: the Choice of Punishments* (1976).

7. B. Hudson, 'Beyond proportionate punishment: Difficult cases and the 1991 Criminal Justice Act', (1995) 22 *Crime, Law and Social Change* 59–78.

8. Hudson (1995), n. 66 above; Kerruish (1991), n. 41 above.

9. Tonry, M. 'Proportionality, parsimony, and interchangeability of punishments', in A. Duff, S. Marshall, R. E. Dobash, and R. P. Dobash (eds.), *Penal theory and practice: Tradition and innovation in criminal justice* (1994).

10. J. Braithwaite and P. Pettit, *Not Just Deserts* (1990); J. Braithwaite, 'Inequality and Republican Criminology', in J. Hagan and R. Peterson (eds.), *Crime and Inequality* (1995).

11. J. Braithwaite, 'Retributivism, Punishment and Privilege', in W. Byrom Groves and Graeme Newman (eds.), *Punishment and Privilege* (1986).

12. H. L. A. Hart, *Punishment and Responsibility: Essays in the Philosophy of Law* (1968), at pp.190–1.

13. A. von Hirsch (1976) n. 65 above, at p. 178. Von Hirsch's sustained commitment to a rational sentencing policy which respects the moral integrity and civil rights of offenders has produced a body of work which stands out as a powerful, principled challenge to the punitive politics of the harsh 'law and order' climate of the 1980s and 1990s. My differences from his position are very much those of a sociologist posing dilemmas of implementation and elaboration of his ideas in a class-, race- and gender-stratified society, rather than disagreements with the general principles of his approach, and I am happy to acknowledge his influence on my own work.

14. A. von Hirsch, *Censure and Sanctions* (1993), at pp. 106–8.

15. A. von Hirsch, 'Proportionality in the Philosophy of Punishment', in M. Tonry (ed.), *Crime and Justice: An Annual Review of Research,* 16 (1992), at p. 62.

16. W. B. Groves and N. Frank, "Punishment, Privilege and Structured Choice', in W. B. Groves and G. Newman (1986) n. 70 above, Ch. 5.

17. I have used a similar argument, in *Penal Policy and Social Justice* (1993), Ch. 6; and in 'Punishing the poor: a critique of the dominance of legal reasoning in penal theory and practice', in A. Duff *et al* (eds.) (1994) n. 68 above, pp. 292–305.

18. D. Garland, ' "Governmentality" and the problem of crime', (1997) 1, 2 *Theoretical Criminology* 173–214, at 196–7.

19. D. Cornish and R. Clarke, *The Reasoning Criminal: Rational Choice Perspectives in Offending* (1986).

20. B. D. Headley, 'Crime, Justice and Powerless Racial Groups', (1989) 16 *Social Justice* 1–9; B. Hudson (1993), n. 21 above.

21. K. Daly, (1994), n. 37 above.

22. K. Daly and M. Tonry (1997), n. 6 above.

23. S. Edwards (1984), n. 33 above.

24. M. Eaton, (1986) n. 33 above, at p. 11.

25. C. A. MacKinnon, *Toward a Feminist Theory of the State* (1989); C. Smart, 'The Woman of Legal Discourse', (1992) 1 *Social and Legal Studies* 29.

26. See, especially, the work of Pat Carlen, for example, (ed.) *Criminal Women,* (1985); *Women, Crime and Poverty* (1988); *Alternatives to Women's Imprisonment* (1990).

27. P. Carlen, (1990) n. 85 above, at p. 114.

28. K. Daly, 'Criminal Law and Justice System Practices as Racist, White, and Racialized', (1994) 51 *Washington and Lee Law Review* 431–64.

29. See K. T. Bartlett, 'Feminist Legal Methods', (1990) 103 *Harvard Law Review* 829–88; F. Heidensohn, 'Models of Justice: Portia or Persephone? Some Thoughts on Equality, Fairness and Gender in the Field of Criminal Justice', (1986) 14 *International Journal of the Sociology of Law* 287–98; B. Hudson, *Understanding Justice* (1996), pp. 145–9; C. Smart, *Law, Crime and Sexuality* (1995), Ch. 10.

30. I. M. Young, *Justice and the Quality of Difference* (1990), Ch. 1.

31. This perspective of 'justice-as-alterity' is being developed by post-structuralist writers on law and justice, such as Drucilla Cornell, *The Philosophy of the Limit* (1992). It draws on the philosophy of Levinas: E. Levinas, *Totality and Infinity* (1969), *Otherwise than Being or Bey ond Essence* (1981) and the critiques of his theories of justice offered by Derrida: J. Derrida, 'Violence and Metaphysics: An Essay on the Thought of Emmanuel Levinas', in *Writing and Difference* (1978); 'The Force of Law: the Mystical Foundation of Authority', (1990) 11,5–6 *Cardozo Law Review* 920–1045, and aims to develop a defence and elaboration of the ideal of justice whilst acknowledging deconstructionist and feminist critiques of law as an existing institution and set of practices.

Index

Aboriginals, 50, 170, 339, 342, 346
Abrahamse, A, 96, 97
access to justice, children, 314
adversarialism, 220–1
afflictive punishment, 65–8
Allen, Francis, 1, 7, 11–15
Alverstone, Lord Chief Justice, 229
American Bar Association, 356
American Friends Service Committee Report, 115
American Law Institute, 356
Andenaes, Johannes, 40
Andrews, DA, 19, 20, 23–4
apologies, 129–31, 179, 184–5, 190, 191, 212, 223, 224–5
appeals, sentencing consistency and, 243–4, 254, 276–8
Archard, D, 294–5
Ashworth, Andrew, 78, 85–8, 115, 123, 167, 195, 196, 199, 205, 211–17, 231, 243–55, 276, 364–5
Auld, Robin, 283
Australia:
  1918 police strike, 46
  Aboriginals, 50
  appeal decisions, 244
  mandatory sentences, 50, 252
  pro-social modelling, 23
  restorative justice, 170, 220, 222–3
  sentencing information system, 283, 286–7, 288
automatism, 360
autonomy, 42, 196
aversive conditioning, 12

Bala, Nicholas, 302, 338–41
Barton, Charles, 206
Bedeau, Hugo, 110–11
Beijing Rules:
  age of criminal responsibility, 296, 308
  choice of sanctions, 311–12
  discretion, 309
  diversion of cases, 310
  fundamental principles, 307
  human rights of offenders, 309–10
  minimum institutionalisation, 312
  proportionality, 308–9
  social inquiry reports, 310
  speedy procedures, 303, 312
  text, 307–12
Benaquisto, I, 72–3
Bentham, Jeremy, 39, 41, 43, 53–6
biological defects, 174

Bottoms, Anthony, 5, 7, 16–17, 78, 83–8, 115, 221–2, 224
Bowling, Ben, 344
Braithwaite, J, 170, 190, 200–1, 204, 214, 215, 368–9, 373
Brodeur, Jean-Pierre, 277
Brownlee, Ian, 347, 359–65
Brownsword, Roger, 78, 83–8
Bulger, James, 304

Canada:
  Aboriginals, 339, 342, 346
  Court of Appeal precedents, 244, 277
  deterrence, 72, 73
  equality principle, 343
  mandatory sentences, 252
  rehabilitation, 1, 19, 24
  sentencing circles, 170
  sentencing information system, 234, 283, 284–5, 287, 288
  tax evasion, 73
  youth justice, 302–3, 338–41, 339
capital punishment, 65, 66–7, 72, 311, 314
Carlen, Pat, 343, 374
Carlyle, Thomas, 208
Carter Report (2003), 25
causation, 371
causes of crime:
  economic duress, 369–72
  old and new criminology, 174
  rehabilitation and, 6, 30–1
  therapeutic theories, 12
Cavadino, Mick, 201
children
  see also young offenders
  definition, 313
  human rights, 297, 313–15
Christie, Nils, 36–7, 164, 165, 166, 168, 171, 173–7
civil law, 173
class conflicts, 174
cognitive-behavioural programmes, 3–4, 5, 6, 16–17, 24
Committee for the Study of Incarceration, 102
communication:
  community-based communicative sanctions, 207
  criminal justice and, 221
  mediation process, 187
  punishment as, 126–33
  restorative justice, 225
community:
  communicative sanctions, 207

communitarian approaches, 36–7
    restorative justice and, 167, 193, 201, 215
community sentences, 5, 167, 303
compromise theory of punishment, 201
conflict resolution:
    conflicts, as property, 173–7
    restorative justice, 164, 165
    specialization and, 174, 177
Consedine, Jim, 226
consent principle, 12
consumer offences, 168
contract, 102, 110, 113
convictions, popular perceptions, 59
core correctional practices, 23–4
corporal punishment, 67, 311
corporate offences, 168
Correctional Services Accreditation Panel (CSAP),
    20, 22
cost-benefit analysis, 64
Council of Europe, 254–5
counselling, 3, 190, 315, 367
Cretney, A, 224
crime prevention:
    deterrence and, 39–40, 43–6, 57–63
    mandatory sentences and, 50–1, 252
    methods, 53–4
    pain and, 208
    proportionality and, 119, 261
    punishment and, 197
    retribution and, 102–3, 119, 121–2
criminal justice:
    adversarialism, 220–1
    criminology and, 174
    deterrent effect, 46
    norm classification and, 175
    restorative justice and, 166–7
    social accounting, 196
    social justice and, 359–60
    stealing conflicts from victims, 173–5
    tort law and, 110, 113, 180
    transfer of conflict to state, 173
    victims' rights, 168–9, 173
criminal record *see* previous convictions
Cullen, Francis, 3, 28–32, 33, 34, 35
custody *see* prison

Daly, Kathleen, 167, 206, 209, 218–27
databases *see* sentencing information systems
Davis, G., 190, 197, 224
Davis, M, 102
death penalty, 65, 66–7, 72, 311, 314
decrementalism, 368–9
Denmark, 46
Derrida, Jacques, 218
desert *see* retribution
deterrence:
    active deterrence, 201
    afflictive punishment, 65–8
    attrition rate and, 46
    capital punishment, 66–7
    celerity, 40
    certainty, 40, 60
    complexities, 41–2

crime prevention strategy, 39–40, 43–6
    crime policy, 62–3
    marginal deterrence, 60–2
    state of research, 57–60
criminal justice system as, 46
development of theory, 40–1
discrimination and, 345
economic theory, 41–2, 45, 71
effectiveness, 43–6
    certainty effects, 60
    contingency, 62
    counterproductive effects, 63
    influence of penalties, 45–6, 71–4
    marginal deterrence, 60–2, 68
    new harsh sentencing regimes, 49–51
    research, 49–51, 57–63
    severity effects, 61–2
    threshold effects, 62
elements, 40
exemplary sentences, 43
general deterrence, 40
Hegel, 128
hybrid sentencing schemes, 107
intuitive appeal, 39, 44, 112
mandatory sentences, 50–1, 252
marginal deterrence, 60–2, 68
normative objections, 42–3
offenders' thought processes, 71–4
perceptions of risk, 45, 58–60, 71
popular perceptions, 59
prison, 68–9, 339
proportionality and, 43, 63
punishment of innocents, 42
rationality assumption, 64
research
    controlling for other influences, 57–8
    correlations, 57
    pooled time series, 49–50
    simultaneity, 58
sentencing objective, 39–40
severity, 39, 40, 61–2
    effects, 61–2
    proportionality, 43, 63
    upper limits, 64–9
special deterrence, 40
theory, 53–6
Dignan, Jim, 166, 193–4, 199–205, 215
disabled persons, 343
disadvantaged groups:
    criminal justice and, 359–60
    differential impact, 343
    disproportionate involvement, 342
    economic factors, 362, 369–72
    individualising sentencing, 354–8, 359–65
    reduced culpability, 347–8
    sentencing models and, 345–6
    stereotypes, 344
    victims, 362–3
discretion:
    appeal court regulation, 243–4, 254, 276–8
    codification of criteria, 239–40
    discrimination and, 347
    guidance *see* sentencing guidelines

guidelines *see* sentencing guidelines
hanging judges, 363–4
human difference, 360–2
individualising punishments, 347, 354–8,
   359–65
issues, 229–30
judicial independence, 230
lawlessness, 229, 237–42
least restrictive alternative, 355–8, 364–5
mandatory sentences and, 229, 252–3, 279–82
mistrust of judges, 357
reasons, 238
rehabilitationism and, 7
theoretical ideals, 240
uniformisation techniques, 243–55
young offenders, Beijing Rules, 309
discrimination:
  Blacks *see* ethnic minorities
  deterrence and, 345
  direct discrimination, 344
  disproportionate involvement of disadvantaged
     groups, 342
  equality principles, 343–4
  flexible sentencing and, 347
  gender, 347–8
  guilty pleas, 344, 347, 351–3
  indirect discrimination, 344–5
  individualising punishments, 361
  meaning of equality, 372–4
  positive discrimination, 372
  predictive sentencing, 345
  rehabilitation model, 345
  responses, 346–7
  restorative justice and, 345
  retribution, 107, 345–6, 366–72
  stereotypes, 344
diversion of cases:
  admissions of guilt, 301–2
  option, 234, 351
  restorative justice, 193
  young offenders, 301–2, 310
diversity:
  criminology of difference, 367
  individualising punishment, 347–8, 354–8,
    359–65, 366–75
  meaning of equality, 372–4
domestic violence, 105, 373
Doob, Anthony, 39, 45, 49–51, 71–4, 277, 284,
  286, 287
Dowden, C, 23–4
drinking and driving, 105
driving disqualification, 75
drug offences, 105, 279, 281, 282, 344–5,
  351–2
Duff, Anthony, 103, 115, 117, 126–33, 165,
  167, 178–88, 207–8
Dworkin, Ronald, 83, 85–8, 201

economic crime, 362, 369
economic duress, 370–1
economic theory, deterrence and, 41–2, 45, 71
England and Wales:
  community penalties, 365

consistency of sentencing, 229, 243, 276–8
Court of Appeal, 229, 243
  consistency, 276–8
  lack of coherent principles, 277–8
  weak impact of precedents, 276–7
death penalty, 67
deterrence, 40, 46, 57, 62–3
diversion of cases, 234
economic duress, 371
ethnic discrimination, 347, 352
female offenders, 343, 374
guilty pleas, 344, 347, 351–3
indeterminate sentences, 7
mandatory sentences, 252
prosecution rate, 4
recidivism, 4
rehabilitation, 5, 7, 17
  'What Works,' 16, 17, 21–5
restorative justice, 169, 218, 222
retribution, 102, 115
rising crime, 61
Sentencing Advisory Panel, 244, 245
Sentencing Commission Working Group, 246
sentencing guidelines, 230, 231, 232, 244–8,
  254
  magistrates' courts, 246–7
Sentencing Guidelines Council, 244–6
statutory sentencing purposes, 1
young offenders
  age of criminal responsibility, 296, 304
  borstal system, 40
  cautions, 301
  juvenile courts, 303
  proportionality, 300
  recidivism, 302
Engler, John, 282
Enhanced Community Punishment Scheme, 23
equality:
  justice and, 137
  meaning, 372–4
  principles, 343–4
  punishment, 137
  retribution and, 367–8, 372–4
  sentencing models and, 345–6
ethnic minorities:
  direct discrimination, 344
  guilty pleas, 344, 347, 351–3
  indirect discrimination, 344–5
  individualising sentencing, 354–8, 359–65
  Minnesota, 271
  responses to discrimination, 346–8
  stereotypes, 344
euphemisms, 13
European Convention on Human Rights, 343
European Court of Human Rights, Bulger case,
  304
exile, 75

fair hearings, young offenders, 304, 309–10, 315
fairness:
  legitimacy and, 140
  rehabilitation model, 35–7
  restorative justice, 194, 215, 222–3

retribution model, 104, 106, 368
rights, 85–7
family group conferences, 169–70, 220
Farrington, David, 57, 61, 80, 99
Feld, Barry, 303, 304, 331–7
feminism, 33, 37, 368, 373, 374, 375
Finland, 102, 115, 123, 248–9, 254
Finnis, JM, 102
first offenders:
　lapse perspective, 158–60
　leniency, 106, 148, 150–1
　US drug laws, 282
flogging, 67
Floud Report (1981), 77
Foucault, Michel, 12, 35
France, 191, 295
Frank, N, 370, 371
Frankel, Marvin, 229, 237–42
Frase, Richard, 79, 104, 105, 106, 119, 120,
　135–41, 231, 233, 270–5
fraud, 369
freedom of choice, 30–1, 370–2

Gardner, John, 103
Garland, David, 370–1
gemeinschaft, 222, 226
gender:
　differential impact of sentencing, 343
　discrimination, 347–8
　meaning of equality, 372–4
　stereotype roles, 344
Germany, 248, 295, 364
Gewirth, Alan, 201
Gilbert, Karen, 3, 28–32, 33, 34, 35
Glueck, Eleanor and Sheldon, 75
Green, TH, 206–7
Greenwood, Peter, 79–80, 96–9
group offending, 295, 319
Groves, W.B., 370, 371
guilty pleas, 141, 234, 252, 253, 344, 347,
　351–3

Halliday Report (2001), 5, 16–17
Hampton, Jean, 207, 208
hanging judges, 363–4
Hart, HLA, 103–4, 128, 355, 369, 370
Hayes, H, 225
health and safety, 168
Hegel, GWF, 102, 128, 206
Hood, Roger, 347, 352
Hough, M, 59
house arrest, 75
Hudson, Barbara, 218, 219, 346, 347–8, 366–75
human rights:
　children, 313–15
　competing rights, 83–4, 85–6, 87
　diversion of cases and, 301–2
　Dworkin, 83, 85–8
　equality of state concern, 83
　fairness, 85–7
　natural rights, 110
　restorative justice and, 201–3
　young offenders, 309–10

humaneness, 34–5, 137
Hutton, N, 277, 285–6, 289, 292
hybrid sentencing schemes, 106–7, 139–41

incapacitation *see* predictive sentencing
indeterminate sentences, 6, 7, 259, 354–5, 356
individualising punishment, 347, 354–8, 359–65
informal justice, 219
insider dealing, 369
Israel, sentencing information system, 283

Jareborg, Nils, 105, 115, 264–9
Johnstone, Gerry, 167, 206–10, 219
justice
　see also social justice
　core assumptions, 30
　Derrida, 218
　equality and, 137, 372–4
　individualising sentencing, 354–8
　informal justice, 219
　reform agenda, 29
　rehabilitation and, 30, 31
　retribution, 127
　retribution and, 110, 197
　social and criminal justice, 359–60
juvenile justice *see* young offenders

Kant, Immanuel, 42, 102, 112, 206, 356
Kazemian, Lila, 80, 95–100, 99
Kenyon, Judge David, 280
kinship, 222
Kleck, Gary, 45
Kleinig, John, 115
Kovandzic, T, 51

Langan, Patrick, 57
Langston, Bill, 280
law and order discourse, 30, 49, 197–8, 334
lawlessness in sentencing, 229, 237–42
lawyers, stealing conflicts from victims, 173–4
least restrictive appropriate alternative, 355–8,
　364–5
Lee, Youngjae, 150
Leeds Mediation and Reparation Project, 169
Levitt, Steven, 57, 58, 61
liberalism:
　consent principle, 12
　individual autonomy, 42
　rehabilitation and, 11–12, 28–32
Lipsey, M, 19, 20, 21
Liverpool, 46
living standards, retribution and, 143–5

McGuire, James, 5, 19–20, 22
McWilliams, Bill, 7
magistrates' courts, sentencing guidelines, 246–7
Maher, Lisa, 7, 33–7
mandatory sentences:
　circumventing, 253, 279–81, 357–8
　critique, 279–82
　deterrence and, 50–1, 252
　discretion and, 229, 252–3
　drug offences, 279

inflexibility, 279
repealing, 351, 357
safety valves, 281
severity, 279
shift of sentencing burden to prosecutors, 279
US experience, 251, 252–3, 279–82
Marcus, Michael, 283–4
Martinson, Robert, 14
Marvell, Thomas, 58
media, restorative justice and, 193–4
mediation:
   civil v criminal, 182–6
   communicative process, 187
   criminal mediation as punishment, 186–8, 192
   recognition of social wrongs and, 192–4
   restorative justice, 133, 164, 169, 182–8
Menninger, Karl, 113–14
mens rea, 360
mental health, 137, 360
Miller, Marc, 234, 283–93
Model Penal Code, 1, 135, 137
Moody, Carlisle, 58
Moore, Michael, 102, 103, 110–14
Morgan, N, 50–1
Morris, A, 222
Morris, Herbert, 111, 207, 208
Morris, Norval, 79, 90–4, 104, 105, 107, 119,
   120, 135–40, 203, 288, 292, 355,
   366–7, 369
motivation, 371
murder:
   compensation v punishment, 167
   prison murders, 66–7
   punishment, 66
Murphy, S, 71–2
Murray, Charles, 367

Nagin, D, 59, 60
National Academy of Sciences, 80, 97
National Association of US Attorneys, 281
National Rifle Association, 281
necessity defence, 65
negligence, 180
neighbourhood courts, 175–7
   lay-oriented courts, 176–7
   victim-oriented, 175–6
Netherlands, 283
New Zealand:
   Aboriginals, 342, 346
   appeal decisions, 244
   rehabilitation, 1
   restorative justice, 169–70, 218, 220, 222–3,
   226
   retribution model, 102
   sentencing guidelines, 230, 254
Northamptonshire Adult Reparation Scheme, 169

OASys, 5
objectivism, 113–14, 360

Palmer, Ted, 33
Park, NW, 286, 287
parking, 39

parsimony, penal parsimony, 105, 137–8, 205,
   356
Pataki, George, 282
paternalism, 7, 29, 297
Pavlich, G, 218
peer pressure, 295, 318–20
penal parsimony, 105, 137–8, 205, 356
penance, 103, 117, 131, 185–6
personality defects, 174
Pettit, P, 190, 368–9
Phillips, Coretta, 344
plagiarism, 159
plea-bargaining, 252, 275, 280, 352, 355
pollution, 106, 168
Portugal, 295
Posner, Richard, 41, 42, 46, 64–9
pre-modern societies, 222
pre-sentence reports, 25, 291, 310
predictive sentencing:
   accuracy, 76, 79, 91, 136
   clinical predictions, 94
   conviction of innocents, 91–4
   dangerousness argument, 78, 83–4, 90
      critiques, 85–6, 136
   discrimination, 345
   false positives, 76–7, 84, 91–4
   improving techniques, 97–8
   incapacitation methods, 75, 95
   indicia of dangerousness, 79, 80
   issues, 75–81
   likelihood of reoffending, 75
   limitations, 99–100
   proportionality, 78, 85, 86, 98–9, 120
   racial bias, 94
   restorative justice and, 201
   rights and, 83–4, 85–8
   selective incapacitation
      effectiveness, 80, 96–7
      ethics, 80–1
      improving predictive techniques, 97–8
      method, 95–6
      proportionality, 98–9
      United States, 79–80, 95–7
   tests, 84
   within desert limits, 79, 90–4, 136
   young offenders, 300
premeditation, 152–4, 156
previous convictions:
   discount approach, 158–62
   exclusionary school, 148
   premeditation and, 153–4, 161
   progressive loss of mitigation, 148
      discount approach, 158–62
      problems, 149–50
      proportionality, 156
   punishing character or conduct, 155–6
   recidivist premium, 148–57
      enhanced culpability model, 152–7
      problems, 161–2
   retribution model, 106, 135, 137
   rising prison population, 156
prison:
   alternatives, 282, 364–5

deterrence, 68–9, 339
differential impact, 343
disadvantaged groups, 342
discount rates, 69
justifications, 1
popular perceptions, 59
prison capacity constraints, 231, 274–5
prison conditions as punishment, 67–8
prison murders, 66–7
racial bias, 94, 351
reduction objective, 25, 351
rising prison population, 156, 282
Sweden, 268
women, 374
young offenders, 302, 311
   Canada, 338–41
pro-social modelling, 23
probation, 1, 7, 23, 25, 40, 121, 132–3, 136,
   140, 141, 146, 150, 161, 207, 238, 263,
   264–5, 269, 312, 340, 345, 358
progressive loss of mitigation, 148, 149–51,
   158–62
property:
   conflicts as, 173–5
   natural right, 110, 113
proportionality:
   crime prevention and, 119, 261
   deterrence and, 43, 63
   predictive sentencing, 78, 85, 86, 98–9, 120
   restorative justice, 215–16
   retribution model *see* retribution
   youth justice, 299–300, 308–9
prosecutions:
   discretion, 279
   diversion of cases, 234
   popular perceptions, 59
   rates, 4, 69
protective sentencing *see* predictive sentencing
provocation, 145, 371, 373
psychosurgery, 12
psychotherapy, 12, 22
public opinion, 59, 140, 152–3, 155
punishment:
   afflictive punishment, 65–8
   as communication, 126–33
   blame and, 104, 118–19
   compromise theory, 201
   consistency, 195
   crime prevention and, 197
   criminal mediation and, 186–8
   debates, 199
   decrementalism, 368–9
   equality, 137
   individualising, 347, 354–8, 359–65
   legitimacy and fairness, 140
   mixed theory, 128
   moral education, 207
   objectives, 53–4
   principles, 194–5
   quantum, 54–6
   reparative justice and, 167, 191–8
      fairness, 194
      punitive quality, 191–2

   recognition of social wrong, 192–4
   replacement discourse, 199, 205
   restorative justice as, 206–10
   revenge, 208
   state role, 103
   symbolic role, 103, 127, 129
   unjustified punishment, 56
   young offenders, 297–300
Pyle, David, 41–2

quarantine, 87–8

racism, 94
RAND, 96
Raynor, Peter, 5, 19–25
recidivism:
   age and, 80, 160
   likelihood, 75
   methods of prevention, 53–4
   patterns, 79
   prediction methods, 95
   predictive sentencing, 75–81
   premium, 148–62
   rehabilitation and, 34
   Sweden, 160–1
reconciliation, 184, 185
rehabilitation model:
   approaches, 2
   benefits, 2
   correctional approach, 3, 4, 5
   decline, 1, 11–15
   definition, 2–3
   discrimination, 345
   effectiveness, 4–5
      claims, 16–17
      measurement, 19–20
      uncertainty, 8
   fairness, 35–7
   future, 15
   heyday, 1
   humaneness and, 34–5
   hybrid sentencing schemes, 107
   ideology, 3, 30–2
   intuitive appeal, 112
   justification for imprisonment, 1
   liberalism and, 28–32
   methods, 3–4, 22–3
      extreme therapies, 12
      ignorance, 11, 14
      meaning of therapy, 13
      new orthodoxy, 14
      vagueness, 13–14
   objections, 6–8, 11–15
      authoritarianism, 7
      causes of crime, 6–7
      debasement, 11, 13
      discretion v accountability, 7
      disproportionate interventions, 7–8, 13, 36,
         354–5
      liberalism, 11–12
      Morris, 136
      positivism, 6
      uncertain effectiveness, 8

vagueness, 13–14
reaffirming, 28–32
recidivism prevention, 34
relational approach, 2, 4
research
  assessment, 19–25
  counter-productive attrition, 24
  difficulties, 4
  methods, 4, 8, 20–1
  negative findings, 1
  non-completers, 24
  systematic research reviews, 19–21
  'What Works,' 16, 17, 19–25
  widening scope, 24–5
reviving, 33–7
sentencing implications, 5–6
terminology, 2
US juvenile courts, 331, 333, 334, 336, 337
young offenders, 297–8, 300
Rehnquist, William, 282
Reilly, Barry, 58
reintegration, 2, 3, 4, 190, 192, 204, 207, 208, 210, 299, 300
reintegrative shaming, 170
remorse, 154–5, 182, 223
Reno, Janet, 282
reparative justice:
  apologies, 191
  benefits, 189
  civil v criminal, 185
  compensation, 190–1
  concerns, 165–6, 189–90
  consistency, 195
  fairness, 194, 215
  making amends model, 211–12
  nature, 190–1
  objective, 182
  paradigm, 163–4
  practice, 169
  punishment and, 167, 191–8
  punitive quality, 191–2
  recognition of social wrong, 192–4
  retribution and, 189–98
  supplementing conventional justice, 169
  symbolic reparations, 191, 207
replacement discourse, 199, 205
resocialisation, 2
responsibility:
  fair opportunity to resist, 369
  young offenders, 294–6, 308, 316–20
restorative justice:
  Aboriginal communities, 170
  achievements, 222
  alternative to treatment, 209–10
  apology, 179, 184–5, 190, 212, 223, 224–5
  assumptions, 218
  coherence and, 211, 217
  communities and, 165, 167
  conflict resolution model, 164, 165, 169
  conflicts as property, 173–7
  corporate victims or offenders, 168
  criminal justice and, 166–7
  critiques, 167–9, 211–12

discrimination and, 345
fairness, 194, 215, 222–3
family group conferences, 169–70
harm and wrongs, 178–81
justification, need, 200
limits, 218–27
  apologies, 224–5
  gaps, 222
  ideals v practice, 221–6
  no agreed definition, 218–20
  no fact-finding, 220–1
  penalty stage of criminal process, 220–1
  process, 226
  restorativeness, 222–4
  supporting structures, 221–2
making amends model, 212–17
  coherence, 217
  elements, 212
  guidance, 214–15
  imposition element, 213–14
  moral discourse, 213
  proportionality, 215–16
  retribution, 213
  scope of application, 215
  trade-offs, 217
mediation, 133, 164, 169, 182–8
  civil v criminal, 182–6
  criminal mediation and punishment, 186–8
  punitive quality, 192
  secular penance, 185–6
neighbourhood courts, 175–7
normative censure, 166
normative constraints, 199–205
  limits of just deserts, 203–5
  republican constraints, 200–1
  rights approach, 201–3
practice, 169–70
process centred, 182, 186, 204, 226
punishment
  alternative, 206–9
  compensation and, 167
  criminal mediation, 186–8
  fairness, 194
  punitive quality, 191–2
  recognition of social wrong, 192–4
  reparation model, 167, 191–8
reconciliation, 184, 185
reparation model *see* reparative justice
research, 170
resurgence, 163, 203
retribution and, 167, 178–88
  reconciability, 189–98
  reparation model, 189–98
scope, 218–21
sentencing circles, 170
specification of objectives, 211–17
theoretical foundations, 164–6
transitional justice, 163
victims' involvement, 163, 164, 165–6, 168
young offenders, 218, 222–6, 299
retribution:
  arguments for, 110–14, 372
  blame and, 104, 118–19

censoring function, 102, 105, 116–18, 127, 129, 182, 192, 203–4, 207, 212–13
communication
  apology, 129–31
  communicative sentencing, 132–3
  hard treatment, 128–32
  punishment as communication, 126–8
community support, 149
crime prevention and, 102–3, 119, 121–2
critique, 112–14
discrimination, 107, 345–6, 366–72
elements, 203, 206
equality, meaning, 372–4
evolution of tariffs, 364–5
fairness, 104, 106, 368
first offenders, 106, 148, 150–1, 158–60
guilty pleas and, 141
harshness, 34, 103, 204–5
  communication, 128–32
  critiques, 359, 369
  interest analysis, 146–7
  justification, 206–8
inflexibility, 368
intent, 104
intuition, 102, 112, 116, 120
just deserts, 28, 102, 110–14, 181–2
  limits, 203–5
  mistaken movement, 354
justice, 110, 127, 197
  meaning of equality, 372–4
  social justice and, 122–3, 359–60, 366–72
least restrictive alternative approach and, 356–7
legitimacy, 197
limited retributivism, 104, 135–41, 203
  guiding principles, 135, 136
  hybrid sentencing schemes, 106–7, 139–41
  limits, 135, 366–7, 369
  Morris, 135–40, 366–7, 369
  precision need, 138–9
  public perceptions, 140
living standards approach, 105–6, 143–5
mitigation, 122–3
objectivism, 113–14, 360
penal parsimony, 105, 137–8, 205
premeditation, 152–4
previous convictions see previous convictions
proportionality, 35–6, 102
  free will and, 370
  limits, 104, 119–20, 357
  ordinal proportionality, 104, 120
  primacy, 132, 140
  rating of crimes, 105, 143–5
  rationale, 118
  recidivist premiums, 155
  weak form, 141
  weakness, 367
protective sentencing and, 92–3
quantification, 104–6
rationalism, 297
recidivist premium
  enhanced culpability model, 106, 152–7
  premeditation, 152–4

premeditation and previous convictions, 153–4
  previous convictions, 152
  proportionality, 156
  punishing character or conduct, 155–6
  rising prison population, 156
reintegrative theory, 208
remorse, 154–5, 182
restorative justice and, 167, 178–98
revival, 115
secular penance, 103, 117, 131
social accounting, 196–7
strength, 107
theory, 102–7, 294
unfair advantage, 102
white collar crimes, 105, 369
young offenders and, 297
revenge, 208
right to liberty, children, 314
RISE project, 224–5
Roberts, Julian, 59, 106, 148–57, 161–2, 302, 338–41
Robinson, D, 24
Robinson, Paul, 140
Roman, E, 3
rule of law, 103, 229, 244, 246, 254

Scotland:
  appeal decisions, 243–4
  deterrence, 57
  sentencing information system, 234, 283, 285–6, 288, 289
  youth justice
    age limits, 303–4
    children's hearings, 298, 303–4
    determination of guilt, 303
secular penance, 103, 117, 131, 185–6
Sen, Amartya, 144
Sentencing Advisory Panel, 244, 245
sentencing circles, 170
Sentencing Commission Working Group, 246
sentencing guidelines:
  appeal courts, 243–4
  contents, 231–4
  databases see sentencing information systems
  effects, 355, 363
  England and Wales, 244–8
  magistrates' courts, 246–7
  Minnesota, 232–3, 249–51, 260
    Commission's early work, 273–5
    context, 270–1
    evolution, 271, 275
    mechanism, 272–3
    non-discrimination, 274
    prescriptive approach, 273
    prison capacity, 274–5
    scope, 272
  narrative guidelines, 244–8
  numerical guidelines, 249–52, 270–5
  personal characteristics, 360
  practices, 229–30
  statutory directions, 233–4, 248–9
  upper limits, 354–5

very serious crimes, 357
Sentencing Guidelines Council, 244–6
sentencing information systems:
    Australia, 283, 286–7, 288
    Canada, 283, 284–5, 287, 288
    consistency, 234
    experiments, 283–93
    geographic variations, 290
    Israel, 283
    judge involvement, 287
    language and grammar, 291
    law reform and, 288–93
    Netherlands, 283
    retrospective modelling, 291
    role of judges, 292
    Scotland, 234, 283, 285–6, 288, 289
    United States, 283–4, 291–2
Shearing, Clifford, 167, 211–17
Sherman, L, 170
Shover, N, 45
Simpson, Alan, 281
Singer, R, 155–6
social inquiry reports, 25, 291, 310
social justice:
    criminal justice and, 359–60
    hanging judges, 363–4
    retribution and, 122–3, 359–60, 366–72
solitary confinement, 13
South Africa, 252, 277, 343
Spain, 295
specialization, 174, 177
Spohn, Cassia, 232, 279–82
state, conflicts and, 165, 173
stereotypes, 344
stigmatisation, 194, 204, 301
STOP, 24
Strang, H, 170, 224
street crime, 369
Sweden:
    aggravation and mitigation, 263
    choice of sanctions, 262–3, 268–9
    culpability, 262
    deterrence, 57, 263
    graded sanctions, 264
    harm, 261–2
    imprisonment, reasons for, 264–5
    indeterminate sentences, 259
    neoclassicism, 258–61
    new law, 264–9
        enactment, 264
        final version, 265–6
        reform process, 258–60
        text, 266–9
    penal value, 261–2, 265, 266–8
    predicted risk, 265
    previous convictions, 262, 265, 267, 269
    proportionality, 260–1
    recidivism, 160–1
    rehabilitation, 258, 265–6
    retribution model, 102, 115, 123
    special circumstances, 263, 267
    statutory sentencing principles, 248–9, 254
symbolic punishments, 103, 127, 129

symbolic reparations, 191, 207

task-centred casework, 23
Tata, Cyrus, 232, 276–8, 285–6, 289, 292
Tavuchis, N, 224
tax evasion, 73, 215, 369
tax returns, 39
Ten, CL, 355
terminology, 2, 13
therapy:
    alternative to prison, 282
    meaning, 13
    psychotherapy, 12, 22
    restorative justice and, 190, 209–10
    socio-therapy, 210
tolerance:
    everyday life, 151
    first offenders, 150–1, 158–9
    young offenders, 328–9
Tonry, Michael, 105, 141, 252, 253, 281–2, 347,
        351–3, 354–8, 359–65, 368, 373
torts, criminal law and, 110, 113, 180
torture, 314
transitional justice, 163
treatment *see* therapy
trials, censuring function, 192
Trotter, C, 23
Tunnell, K, 72
Turmond, Strom, 281

UN Convention on the Rights of the Child:
    diversion from criminal proceedings, 301
    fair hearings, 315
    juvenile justice, 297, 314–15
    minimum use of custody, 302
    non-discrimination, 313
    proportionality, 299–300
    restorative justice, 299
    text, 313–15
    torture, 314
    welfare principle, 297, 313
unfair advantage, 102
United States:
    age of criminal responsibility, 295–6
    civil rights revolution, 332
    crime policy, 62
    criminology of dangerousness, 367
    deterrence, 49–50, 57, 60, 61
    drug laws, 281, 282
    due process, 332
    female offenders, 374
    Florida habitual offender law, 51
    horse thieves, 67
    images of youth, 334–5, 337
    indeterminate sentences, 354–5
    juvenile courts, 303, 331–7
        conceptual bankruptcy, 335–7
        creation, 331–2
        race, 332, 333, 337
        rehabilitative ideal, 331, 333, 334, 336,
            337
        transformation, 331–7
        triage strategy, 335

mandatory sentences, 251, 252–3, 279–82
Massachusetts recidivism, 75
mitigation of sentences, 358
Model Penal Code, 1, 135, 137, 356
plea-bargaining, 352
predictive sentencing, 76, 93–4
  selective incapacitation, 79–80, 95–7
prison population, 251, 271, 282, 367
racial bias, 94, 367
racial ghettos, 332
rehabilitation, 1, 19, 36
retribution models, 102, 115, 122
Sentencing Commission, 249, 251, 279–81,
  358
sentencing discretion, 229
sentencing guidelines, 139, 143, 229–30,
  231–2
  Minnesota, 232–3, 249–51, 260, 270–5
sentencing information systems, 283–4, 291–2
victim impact statements, 195
Victim Offender Reconciliation Programs, 169
young offenders, 304, 319
  separate courts, 303, 331–7
utilitarianism:
  corrective justice or, 110
  deterrence, 39, 41, 42, 43, 196
  penal parsimony, 137, 138, 356
  retribution and, 112

Varma, K, 73–4
victim impact statements, 164, 169, 195
victims:
  Anglo-American model, 165
  conflicts as property, 173–5
  disadvantaged groups, 362–3
  neighbourhood courts and, 175–6
  restorative justice
    benefits, 189
    interests, 224
    involvement, 163–4, 165–6
    perceptions, 209, 221, 225
    sentencing circles, 170
    unwillingness to participate, 168
  resurgence of concern, 163
  rights in criminal proceedings, 164, 168–9,
    173
vindication, 40
Von Hirsch, Andrew, 7, 33–7, 40, 57–63, 73,
  76, 77, 78, 80, 85–8, 95–100, 102–6,
  105, 115–23, 143–7, 158–62, 167,
  211–17, 233, 258–69, 276, 295, 300,
  355, 356–7, 359–60, 367, 369, 370

Waldorf, D, 71–2
Walgrave, Lode, 208–9
Walker, Nigel, 77–8, 147, 355
Warner, SB, 75
Wasik, Martin, 115
Wasserstrom, Richard, 116
weapons, 45
Webster, CM, 39, 45, 49–51, 71–4
'What Works,' 16, 17, 21–5
white collar crimes, 105, 369

Wichaya, T, 49–50
Wikström, Per-Olof, 6, 57
Wilson, D, 20
Wilson, James Q, 79–80, 367
Witt, Robert, 58
women:
  conventional images, 347, 372
  discrimination, 347–8
  impact of sentencing on, 343
  meaning of equality, 372–4
  prison, 374
  stereotype roles, 344
Worrall, A, 343
wrongs:
  crimes as public wrongs, 180
  restorative justice and, 178–81
    recognition, 192–4

Young, DeJonna, 282
young offenders:
  age of criminal responsibility, 295–6, 308
  Beijing Rules, 296, 303, 307–12
  blame and, 36
  capacity for self-esteem, 328
  capital punishment, 311
  child poverty, 298
  choice of sanctions, Beijing Rules, 311–12
  cognitive abilities, 317, 323, 324–6
  community-based measures, 303
  competent authorities, 310
  concept, 294
  corporal punishment, 311
  culpability, 323–7
  delayed proceedings, 303, 312
  deterrence, 40
  developmental approach, 298–9, 320–1
  differences, 294
  differential impact of punishment, 327–8, 343
  diminished responsibility, 294–6, 316–20,
    323–7
  discretion, 309
  diversion of cases, 301–2, 310
  fair hearings, 304, 315
  group offending, 295, 319
  human rights, 309–10, 313–15
  juvenile courts, 303–4, 331–7
  minimum institutionalisation, 312
  minimum use of custody, 302, 311, 338–41
  peer pressure, 295, 318–20
  penal parsimony, 137
  predictive sentencing, 300
  proportionality, 299–300, 308–9
  reasons for punishing, 297–300
  reduced sanctions
    punitive bite, 327–8, 343
    rationale, 300, 323–9
    reduced culpability, 323–7
    special tolerance, 328–9
    youth discounts, 326–7
  rehabilitation model, 297–8, 300
  restorative justice, 218, 222–6, 299
  risk management, 321
  room-to-reform policies, 320–1

self-control, 295, 317–18, 323, 326
separate policies, rationale, 316–22
separate sanctions, 301–3
social conditions, 298
social inquiry reports, 310
torture, 314

transitional behaviour, 320–1
UNCRC, 297, 299–300, 301, 302, 314–15

Zedner, Lucia, 164, 166, 167, 169, 189–98
Zehr, Howard, 206
Zimring, Franklin, 294–5, 298–9, 316–22, 329